A Biography of Melvil Dewey

IRREPRESSIBLE REFORMER

Melvil Dewey (1851–1931). Water color portrait (1924) by Elizabeth Goudy Baker.

A Biography of Melvil Dewey

IRREPRESSIBLE REFORMER

Wayne A. Wiegand

American Library Association
Chicago and London, 1996

Acquisition Editor: Arthur Plotnik
Project Editor: Louise D. Howe
Picture Editor: Arthur Plotnik
Text Design: Dianne M. Rooney
Cover: Richmond Jones

Composition: the dotted i in ITC Caslon 224 and ITC Fenice
on Xyvision.

Printed on 50-pound Arbor Smooth paper, insert on 60-pound
Sterling Litho Gloss, pH-neutral stocks; bound in 10-point C1S
cover stock by Edwards Brothers, Inc.

The paper used in this publication meets the minimum
requirements of American National Standard for Information
Sciences—Permanence of Paper for Printed Library Materials,
ANSI Z39.48-1992.∞

Library of Congress Cataloging-in-Publication Data
Wiegand, Wayne A., 1946–
    Irrepressible reformer : a biography of Melvil Dewey / Wayne A.
    Wiegand.
        p.   cm.
    Includes index.
    ISBN 0-8389-0680-X
    1. Dewey, Melvil, 1851–1931.   2. Librarians—United States—
Biography.   3. Educators—United States—Biography.   4. Social
reformers—United States—Biography.   I. Title.
Z720.D5W54   1996
020′.92–dc20   96-1732
[B]

Printed in the United States of America.

00 99 98 97 96   5 4 3 2 1

To Gene Trani,
who helped me find
my field of dreams

Contents

Epilogue

Abbreviations

Illustrations

Frontispiece
Portrait by Elizabeth Goudy Baker

Figures

Plates

Following page 76

Following page 260

Preface

If you ask some of the 100,000,000 Americans who used public libraries last year to identify Melvil Dewey, many are likely to say: "inventor of the Dewey Decimal Classification" (DDC). Of course they're right. If you ask potential readers of a Dewey biography what they expect to find featured in its pages they'll probably give the same answer. For this biography, they'll be wrong; *Irrepressible Reformer* devotes only 12 of its 378 pages to the DDC because Dewey's interests, accomplishments, and legacy span a much wider spectrum of activities. But because previous scholarship on Dewey concentrates almost entirely on his library activities, published perspective on the role he played in American society during his lifetime (1851–1931) is one-dimensional, and the broader record of his legacy has thus been overlooked by historians. This book represents an attempt to correct that perspective, and seeks to locate Dewey's role and influence in the wider context of the times in which he lived.

At the same time, however, let the reader be forewarned. There is much to like and admire about Melvil Dewey, but there is equally as much (and perhaps even more) to dislike about his character. Perhaps the latter in part explains why over the decades this important figure in American history has been under- or poorly studied by social historians in general, and education and library historians in particular. But there has been no lack of interest among nonhistorians. In 1983 I decided to do a biography of Dewey while finishing another book.[1] As word spread that I had begun research, scores of people asked me questions in

---

1. Wayne A. Wiegand, *Politics of an Emerging Profession: The American Library Association, 1876–1917* (Westport, Conn., 1986).

subsequent years that usually began: "Is it true that Dewey . . .", then continued by recounting scandalous behavior they had heard about somewhere. Sometimes I answered "Yes," more often, however, "Not that I have been able to discover." Myths surrounding Dewey are myriad. Divorcing them from the historical reality I see has been a challenging, yet fascinating, research assignment. The portrait of Melvil Dewey that emerges from these pages shows a hero and a villain. I hope I have fairly captured the life and times of the colorful and irrepressible character who revealed himself to me in the manuscript materials I have been perusing for the past fifteen years. I hope I have done Melvil Dewey the historical justice he deserves by resurrecting him from relative obscurity and identifying his broader legacy—for good and ill—to contemporary generations.

Researching and writing this biography provided several unique challenges. First among them was Dewey's regular use of Lindsley's Tachigraphy, a form of shorthand no longer in practice. While on the one hand Dewey's decision to use this shorthand greatly expanded the record he left for scholarly perusal, on the other it created nightmares for biographers. Some help came in 1932 when Robert Hood, Dewey's secretary during the last two years of his life, transcribed many shorthand diary entries into simplified spelling for Grosvenor Dawe's authorized biography.[2] Where relevant, I have used these transcriptions in the simplified spelling forms Dewey practiced in the final years of his life. Sometimes Dewey used his shorthand in drafts of letters to vent anger and frustration. Generally I have found it unnecessary to transcribe these drafts because his prose in letters he did send is already lively. Previously untranscribed shorthand material that I have quoted or cited is labelled "tr" in the footnotes.

A second challenge to biographers is Dewey's use of simplified spelling. Because it significantly changed over time, one looks in vain for consistency. I generally refrain from use of "[sic]" when quoting Dewey for two reasons: first, I wanted to avoid unnecessarily cluttering the text and interrupting the narrative; second, I wanted to preserve the flavor of Dewey's correspondence and create for readers some sense of how people felt when they read his missives.

---

2. Grosvenor Dawe, *Melvil Dewey, Seer: Doer: Inspirer, 1851–1931* (Lake Placid, N.Y.: 1932).

A word about footnotes. In order to condense them as much as possible, I have abbreviated extensively. "Dewey to Godfrey Dewey, 11/25/31, Box 23, Dewey Mss" means "Letter, Melvil Dewey to Godfrey Dewey, November 25, 1931, Box 23, Melvil Dewey Papers, Rare Books and Manuscripts Reading Room, Butler Library, Columbia University, New York, New York." The last two digits in the date sequence refer to years between 1851 and 1932. Dates beyond 1932 give the full year. Hyphens inserted between slashes in the date sequence mean the exact month, day, or year was not given on the original document. Readers will find a listing of all abbreviations used for manuscript collections and newspaper, periodical, and document titles cited in the footnotes on pages 379–86. Finally, because all of Dewey's diaries are located in one box I opted for "Dewey Diary [date]" rather than "Dewey Diary [date], Box 35A, Dewey Mss" in the footnotes.

Except for manuscript collections consulted and for newspaper, periodical, document titles frequently checked, the reader will find no bibliography at the end of this book. Instead, I have tried to identify relevant secondary literature in footnotes, especially those works that have informed my interpretation of Dewey and the times in which he lived. Readers interested in exploring issues raised here should consult the bibliographies in these works. As for works by and about Dewey, I recommend the bibliography in Sarah Vann's biographical sketch, and the contents of two extensive bibliographies of published and unpublished secondary literature compiled by Arthur Young, Don Davis, and Mark Tucker.[3]

One does not undertake a study of this size without incurring many debts. Because the study in part grew out of earlier work, for research support between 1975 and 1985 I owe thanks to the University of Kentucky Graduate School and Research Foundation, to the American Library Association for the 1975 Herbert Putnam Award, and to the Newberry Library in Chicago for a Research Fellowship in the Humanities in January 1976. A Council on Library Resources–sponsored project on prominent

3. Sarah Vann, ed., *Melvil Dewey: His Enduring Presence in Librarianship* (Littleton, Colo., 1978), pp. 234–72; Arthur P. Young, *American Library History: A Bibliography of Dissertations and Theses* (Metuchen, N.J., 1988); Donald G. Davis, Jr., and John Mark Tucker comps., *American Library History: A Comprehensive Guide to the Literature* (Santa Barbara, Calif.: 1988).

American academic librarians between 1925 and 1975[4] made visits to archives in the Far West possible, and the American Library Association's practice of locating annual and midwinter conferences around the country frequently enabled me to combine professional service with professional research.

To Forest Press (and especially John Humphry and Peter Paulson) I express my thanks for a research grant that allowed me to spend the summers of 1983, 1984, and 1985 researching Dewey's papers at Columbia; to the National Endowment for the Humanities I extend my thanks for "Travel to Special Collections" assistance, and to the Graduate School and Research Foundation of the University of Wisconsin-Madison, I owe much for the summer research support and a sabbatical leave that enabled me to complete the study. To Tim Sineath, former Dean of the College of Library Science at the University of Kentucky, and Jane Robbins, former Director of the School of Library and Information Studies at the University of Wisconsin-Madison, I extend my thanks for their support and encouragement over the years, and to Donna Sykes and Diana Bobb, both of whom transcribed a lot of Dewey notes and ran off numerous copies of Dewey drafts, my thanks for their exceptional patience and many kindnesses.

To the librarians and archivists who have served my research needs at the institutions cited in my footnotes (and especially those at Columbia University and Jim Corsaro at the New York State Library) and to the librarians who have spent decades accumulating extensive collections I have mined at the University of Kentucky, the University of Wisconsin-Madison, the State Historical Society of Wisconsin, Columbia University, and the Library of Congress, my highest compliments for a job well done. To Corinne H. Rieder of Columbia University I owe thanks for permission to read the Columbia College Trustees Minutes for the years 1883–1889. To John Lansing of Lake Geneva, New York, I owe thanks for permission to peruse the early archives of the Lake Placid Education Foundation that at the time were under his care. And to Marisa Finkey and Judith Jablonski I owe thanks for their work on the index.

---

4. Wayne A. Wiegand, ed., *Leaders in American Academic Librarianship, 1925–1975* (Pittsburgh, Pa., 1983).

Four people read all or parts of the manuscript in various stages of development: Phyllis Dain, Edward G. Holley, Carl Kaestle, and Dee Garrison. To each I say thanks for valuable comments; to each I apologize in advance for my own shortsightedness in not accepting the wisdom of all their suggestions. Although these accomplished scholars should share in whatever praise may come to this biography, none should in any way be held responsible for its shortcomings. That responsibility belongs to me alone. I would also like to thank Editorial Director Art Plotnik and the staff at ALA Editions; working with them has been a pleasure.

Of course, researching and writing history does not occur in a vacuum. I started this project when all my children were still at home, still in grade school or high school. I finished it after all were out of college and after welcoming my first grandchild into the world. To Andy, Scott, and Cori I wish to extend my thanks for not laughing too loudly when their friends asked what their dad was doing on all those trips to New York. To Shirl, my fellow traveler in life, I wish to extend my thanks for her unintentional yet undying efforts to make my life interesting and challenging. Finally, I dedicate this book to someone who put a lot more time into my development as a scholar than ought to be expected of any dissertation advisor. I hope this book will in part serve to justify his efforts.

Acknowledgments

Grateful acknowledgment is given for permission to reprint excerpts from the following items:

"Catalog of 'A.L.A.' Library (1893): Origins of a Genre," in Delmas Williams et al. (eds.), *For the Good of the Order: Essays in Honor of Edward G. Holley* (Greenwich, Connecticut and London, England: JAI Press Inc., 1994), pp. 237–54.

"'Jew Attack': The Story behind Melvil Dewey's Resignation as New York State Librarian in 1905," *American Jewish History* 83 (September 1995): 359–79. Reprinted by permission of the Johns Hopkins University Press.

"Melvil Dewey and the Origins of the New York Library Association," *Bookmark* 48 (Winter 1990): 81–84.

"Wresting Money from the Wily Scot: Melvil Dewey's Designs on Carnegie's Million," from *Libraries & Culture,* vol. 31:2; by permission of the University of Texas Press.

Grateful acknowledgment is also given to Mr. Jonathan Marshall for permission to quote from the manuscript collection of his grandfather, Mr. Louis Marshall, which is located at the American Jewish Archives at Hebrew Union College in Cincinnati, Ohio.

Permission to reproduce the following pictorial items from the Melvil Dewey Papers, Rare Book and Manuscript Library, Columbia University, has been kindly granted by the owners, Columbia

University Libraries: Figures on pages 9, 129, and 310; Plates 6, 8, 10, 12, 17, 18, 19, 20, 21, and 24.

The following pictorial items are reproduced courtesy of the American Library Association Archives at University Archives, University of Illinois at Urbana-Champaign University Library, with special thanks to ALA Graduate Assistant Ellen Swain: Figures on pages 26, 31, 35, and 366; Plates 11, 14, 15, and 23.

Plate 27 is used by permission of OCLC Online Computer Library Center, Inc. Copyright OCLC Online Computer Library Center, Incorporated. 1922–96. All Rights Reserved. DDC; Dewey Decimal Classification; Dewey Decimal Classification, Additions, Notes and Decisions; Forest Press, and OCLC are registered trademarks of OCLC Online Computer Library Center, Inc. Mr. Dewey and his Dot is a trademark of OCLC Online Computer Library Center, Inc.

PART ONE

Launching a "World Work"

1851–1888

1

Child of the Burned-Over District

1851–1876

On the night of November 1, 1860, members of an all-male Republican club called the "Wide-Awakes" embarked from Adams Center for the nearby village of Lorraine in New York's Jefferson County to attend a rally for Abraham Lincoln. All rode in open carriages, and as they formed a line extending more than a mile that snaked over hill and dale, the procession gave off an eerie glow because one man in each carriage held a torch. At Lorraine the rally went off smoothly. A band played patriotic music, a glee club sang patriotic songs, and several men spoke of their patriotic duty to vote for Lincoln. Then, after the audience gave three hearty cheers for the candidate, Wide-Awakes re-formed for the trip back home, complete with torches. Joel Dewey drove one of the carriages. Sitting next to him, holding the torch and sporting the red cap and cape worn by all Wide-Awakes, was his youngest son, Melville.[1]

---

1. *Jefferson County News*, 10/18/60; 10/26/60; and 11/8/60. Dewey recalled this incident in a speech he delivered later in life. See *Lake Placid News*, 11/1/12.

"R" on a Cufflink: Early Years
1851–1870

People took their politics and their religion very seriously in Jefferson County. Oftentimes the two became inseparable as wave after wave of evangelism and reform swept this northwestern edge of the state of New York between 1800 and 1850, leading historian Whitney Cross to label it the "Burned-Over District" a century later. In the first half of the nineteenth century this region witnessed the greatest revivals of Charles Grandison Finney and gave birth to Mormonism and Millerism. It had welcomed and fostered the growth of the Shakers, the Oneida perfectionists and Fourierists; it harbored abolitionists, temperance advocates, and educational reformers. It even spawned a midcentury women's rights movement. Over time causes changed, but intensity did not.[2]

At midcentury Adams Center was a cozy little village of five hundred located in the middle of rich farmland ten miles south of Watertown, three miles west of Adams. Joel and Eliza Greene Dewey moved there from Adams shortly after they married on July 16, 1832. Over time the Deweys acquired six small pieces of property (including three stores), but Joel and Eliza's primary income came from a store which mostly manufactured and sold boots and shoes. Their family grew slowly. Marion ("Mate") was born in 1833, Manfred in 1839, Marietta (who died in infancy) in 1842, and Marissa ("Mit") in 1844. Then, on December 10, 1851, Eliza gave birth to her second son, Melville Louis Kossuth Dewey. It was not uncommon for residents of the Burned-Over District to name children after perceived freedom fighters.[3]

---

2. For background information on religion in early 19th-century upstate New York, see Whitney Cross, *The Burned-Over District: The Social and Intellectual History of Enthusiastic Religion in Western New York, 1800–1850* (Ithaca, 1950). Other works that add detail include Lawrence Foster, *Religion and Sexuality: The Shakers, the Mormons, and the Oneida Community* (N.Y., 1981); David Rowe, *Thunder and Trumpets: Millerites and Dissenting Religion in Upstate New York, 1800–1850* (Chico, Calif., 1985); Michael Barkun, *Crucible of the Millennium: The Burned-Over District of New York in the 1840s* (Syracuse, 1986); and Paul E. Johnson, *A Shopkeeper's Millennium: Society and Revivals in Rochester, New York, 1815–1837* (N.Y., 1978).

3. Dewey never used his middle names. For background information on Adams Center, see Samuel Durant and Henry B. Pierce, *History of Jefferson County, New York* (Philadelphia, 1877), pp. 250–51; John A. Haddock,

By this time, society in the small community was going through a religious transformation forced by local evangelists. Before midcentury, Protestant evangelists had generally been preoccupied with salvation from personal guilt and getting into heaven. After midcentury, however, they began applying their moral and material resources to social problems. Evangelicals generally opposed frivolity and fashion, card playing, dancing, profanity, slavery, and the use of tobacco; were ardent temperance advocates, very patriotic, and believed a white Christian America had a manifest destiny to expand across the continent. They were also well practiced in setting up and interlinking benevolent societies, and from them publishing tracts, newsletters, and periodicals. They held the sanctity of property dear, but manifested a confused attitude toward money—"despising it," yet "embracing it, and putting it to use," historian Charles Cole writes. "Of the three, the importance of stewardship became a recurrent theme." In his study of evangelical abolitionist Joshua Leavitt, Hugh Davis discovered three characteristics linking Leavitt's evangelicalism to his reform activity: a drive to eliminate self-worship; a compulsion to bear witness against immorality; and an aggressive self-righteousness pushed by an overbearing personality. Generally, these evangelists did not make good businessmen; priorities forced by their reforming zeal were inconsistent with conservative business practices. Within membership of the churches these evangelists created, women greatly outnumbered men; they were also highly visible, regularly conducted weekly holiness meetings, authored articles and poetry for the religious press, and spearheaded missionary endeavors.[4]

Most Baptists were driven by a passionate desire to reform the world morally, but they often overdebated fine points of

---

The Growth of a Century: As Illustrated in the History of Jefferson County, New York, from 1793 to 1894 (Albany, 1895), pp. 388–89; and Edgar C. Emerson, *Our County and Its People: A Descriptive Work on Jefferson County, New York* (Boston, 1898). Census records for 1850 identify Joel Dewey as a "Shoemaker" owning real estate worth "$3,500."

4. Charles Cole, *The Social Ideals of Northern Evangelists* (N.Y., 1954), pp. 103–4, 168 (quotation taken from here), 175, 190, 228–31; Hugh Davis, *Joshua Leavitt: Evangelical Abolitionist* (Baton Rouge, 1990); Timothy L. Smith, *Revivalism and Social Reform: American Protestantism on the Eve of the Civil War* (N.Y., 1957), pp. 144–45; 148–62. See also Nancy A. Hewitt, *Women's Activism and Social Change: Rochester, New York, 1822–1872* (Ithaca, 1984), p. 19.

dogma. In March 1852, when some Adams Seventh Day Baptist Church fathers began disagreeing with dogma preached by the presiding clergyman, the latter formed the Independent Seventh Day Baptist Church of Adams. Inevitably the controversy ripped through Adams Center. In December, fifty members of the Adams Seventh Day Baptist Church (with women leading the way) started their own church in Adams Center. Eliza Dewey became a charter member. Four months later, thirty-two Adams Center residents who disagreed with Seventh Day Baptist dogma formed the Adams Center Baptist Church. Joel Dewey became a charter member. Within a year, then, Adams Center had three small Baptist churches, two of which were represented in the Dewey family. There is no indication Joel or Eliza forced any of their children to choose between churches. All except Melville, however, chose their mother's church. Melville attended both, but was baptized into his father's church at the age of twelve.[5]

The Deweys were part of a rising native-born middle class in upstate New York whose profile has been detailed by Mary Ryan. Families of small shop owners established homes in which sexual constraint, a sense of social responsibility, and temperate habits were inculcated from childhood. They stressed hard work and deferred gratification, and urged a conformity to a set of genteel social standards they regarded as appropriate vehicles to status and success. They favored education—especially self education—as a necessary tool for young men on the rise. The goal was to build "character," a blend of morality and will necessary to meet the moral challenges and at the same time ensure the material success required to meet the coming industrial world. The building of character, they believed, was a lifelong process, and those possessing it had dual responsibilities—to promote the welfare of society and improve oneself morally, culturally, and educationally. That the ideals upon which this

---

5. The breakup of the congregations is described in Durant and Pierce, *Jefferson County,* pp. 250–51; and Emerson, *Our County,* pp. 417–18. Dewey later recorded his feelings about the fractionalized Adams Center Baptist community in an undated memorandum, Box 24A, Dewey Mss. See also Curtis D. Johnson, *Islands of Holiness: Rural Religion in Upstate New York, 1790–1860* (Ithaca, 1989), chapters 4–10; Cross, *Burned-Over District,* pp. 177 and 237; and Daniel Walker Howe, "The Evangelical Movement and Political Culture in the North during the Second Party System," *Journal of American History,* 77 (3/1991): 12.

process was based carried the patriarchal stamp of the class and race of the group espousing them was little noticed.[6]

Most of this was communicated to the next generation by example. Dewey's parents, he later recalled, were "famous . . . for being the hardest working in town." A contemporary remembered that Eliza Dewey was "very firm" and "of strong religious conviction"; Dewey thought she "never feared anything." She did all the housework and handbound many of the shoes custommade in her husband's shop, but she was so busy "she had no time to fuss with babies"; Mate took care of young Melville. His father "was a great worker" especially interested in local politics who "always put his whole soul in anything in which he engaged." Together, Eliza and Joel Dewey created a highly active home environment with an extended family. "Our house resembled a small country hotel in the number of visitors," Dewey later recalled. "Relatives were as thick as blackberries." Morality practiced in the house aimed at group needs rather than self-development. Both parents were against liquor and tobacco; both advocated moral reform in church and at home; both taught stoicism as a code of conduct; and both preached humility. "Praise to the face is an open disgrace," Eliza often told her son; "don't waste," Joel preached. While these messages stuck with the Dewey children, they were delivered without warmth. "I often regret exceedingly," Melville later wrote his brother, "that there was never much affection manifested in our immediate family."[7]

---

6. Mary P. Ryan, *The Cradle of the Middle Class: The Family in Oneida County, New York, 1780–1865* (Cambridge, 1981), pp. 238–39. See also Johnson, *A Shopkeeper's Millennium* (1978). The concept of "character" in 19th-century America is discussed in more depth in Warren I. Susman, "'Personality' and the Making of Twentieth-Century Culture," in John Higham and Paul Conkin, eds., *New Directions in American Intellectual History* (Baltimore, 1979), pp. 212–16; and Paul Mattingly, *A Classless Profession: American Schoolmen in the Nineteenth Century* (N.Y., 1975).

7. *Jefferson County News*, 4/3/56; 9/9/58; 12/16/58; 9/1/59; 8/23/60. Dewey reflects on his relationship with his parents and siblings in Dewey Diary, 8/30/72; and Dewey to Manfred J. Dewey, 11/1/74, Box 38, Dewey Mss. See also Dewey, "3/4 of a Century," -/2/26, Box 23; Dewey to Dorothy Canfield Fisher, 12/20/26, Box 31; and Dewey to Godfrey Dewey, 11/25/31, Box 23, Dewey Mss, for his recollections of his parents' maxims. See Ryan, *Cradle of the Middle Class,* pp. 141, 152–53, 238–39; and Karen Halttunen, *Confidence Men and Painted Women: A Study of Middle-Class Culture in America, 1830–1870* (New Haven, 1983), pp. 12–13, for discussions of the rising middle class family at midcentury.

The boy showed early signs of willingness and courage to act on his convictions. Days were spent in school (weather permitting), evenings divided between working at his father's store, studying on his own, and prayer meetings at the two Baptist churches. On weekends he did household chores and often attended services at his mother's church on Saturday, his father's church on Sunday. At thirteen he walked ten miles to Watertown to buy an unabridged dictionary. At fourteen he joined the Templars. At fifteen he began a diary, and on his birthday noted he was five feet five "and a fourth" inches tall, weighed 120 pounds, and was worth $125.00.

Like many male teenagers in midcentury upstate New York, Dewey skated in the winter, played ball, hiked, hunted and fished in the summer, and spent "much time lying face down on the carpet & reading" year-round. Unlike others, however, he was obsessed with thoughts about his future. Sometimes after he locked his father's store at night, he stretched out on the hides to contemplate his "destiny." He was much concerned about "foolish wastefulness and a desire to leave the world better than I found it." After one particularly restive night, he settled on "reform" as a "life's work"; next day he bought a pair of cufflinks inscribed with the letter "R" as "a constant reminder . . . that I was to give my life to reforming certain mistakes and abuses." "Reform" was a big arena, however, even for a child of the Burned-Over District where scores of social problems were discussed daily. At sixteen Dewey was anxious to identify his "life's work."[8]

On April 15, 1867, Dewey attended an orientation for teacher certification in the State of New York—not because he wanted to teach, he admitted, but mostly to explore the possibility of taking classes "to learn what I could." That Dewey valued education highly was not unusual. For many evangelicals religion and education were synonymous; sometimes they approached both with an overpowering zeal. One of the commis-

---

8. Dewey Diary, 12/10/66. The incident concerning the dictionary is taken from an interview with Dewey that appeared in the *Albany Times,* undated clipping found in Box 37, Dewey Mss. Templars membership is described in Durant and Pierce, *Jefferson County,* p. 256. See also Dewey Diary, 4/3/67; 4/10/67; 5/6/67; 5/26/67. Information on his adolescent reading habits is taken from an undated, untitled document Dewey penned later found in Box 24A, Dewey Mss.

Beginning at age fifteen, Dewey kept this table of accounts. In ten years he went from 5'5¼", 120 pounds, and $125 in assets, to 5'11½", 174 pounds, and a zero financial balance.

sioners present said that if Dewey agreed to teach at a nearby school that summer, he would give Dewey a temporary certificate. Dewey made no commitment, but his interest was piqued. Education, he began to think, might be an appropriate vehicle for reforming spirit. In June he visited Hungerford Collegiate Institute, one of hundreds of New York academies functioning as the state's secondary school system in the nineteenth century.

Dewey was impressed. "I think I shall go to school there in the fall," he confided to his diary.[9]

Instead of teaching that summer, however, he focused on gaps in his own education. He began attending a new local school for adolescents, and through a boyhood friend gained access to a family library. In early September he helped organize a "Young People's Lyceum," became editor of its journal, and two months later was elected president. On December 16 he began classes at Hungerford. Each institution provided him with opportunities to hone his oral and writing skills on topics that caught his reform zeal. On October 9, for example, he advocated in a Lyceum composition that the U.S. adopt the metric system of weights and measures. On November 18 he criticized the consumption of alcohol in an address entitled "Our Future" at his local school. On December 23 he made an oral presentation on the same subject at Hungerford.[10]

The winter of 1868 witnessed an interruption in Dewey's studies which indirectly forced a watershed in his life. On January 29 Dewey was in class at the Institute when fire broke out in the building. He reacted by carrying as many books out as time permitted, but in the process inhaled a lot of smoke, and when the fire got out of control he stood and without adequate clothing watched the building burn to the ground in the January cold. Within a week Dewey contracted a deep cough that persisted well into the spring. A local physician predicted he would not live beyond two years.

Death was an immediate reality for mid-nineteenth-century Americans. This was especially true for Dewey because he helped

9. Dewey Diary, 5/26/67; 6/1/67; 6/28/67, Dewey Mss. The Collegiate Institute in Adams is discussed in Haddoch, *Growth of a Century,* pp. 392ff. See also Wilson F. Rusho, "A History of the Hungerford Collegiate Institute at Adams, Jefferson County, New York, with a Biographical Sketch of Solon D. Hungerford," undated term paper, Jefferson Community College Local History Collection, Melvil Dewey Library, Watertown, N.Y. See also Cole, *Social Ideas of Northern Evangelists,* pp. 5–6; and George F. Miller, *The Academy System of the State of New York* (Albany, 1922).

10. Dewey Diary, 5/8/67; 5/22/67; 6/30/67; 7/21/67; 8/11/67; 9/2/67; 9/6/67; 9/23/67; 11/1/67; 12/27/67, Dewey Mss. Prospectus for the lyceum journal can be found in Box 36, Dewey Mss. Copies of "The Metric System of Measurement" and "Our Future" can be found in Box 36, Dewey Mss. Copy of speech in which Dewey later recalled the chronology of his conversion to metric in Box 67, Dewey Mss.

his father maintain the local "Union Cemetery." Diary entries for 1867 are filled with news of death and burials, especially for children and relatives.[11] That Dewey was repeatedly forced to confront his own mortality at such a young age, and that he himself was told he probably would not live to see his nineteenth birthday, appeared to have had a profound effect on his view of time and the future. Thenceforth he showed an excessive preoccupation with efficient use of time; he also worked at honing a fatalistic optimism about life.

These he combined with characteristics developed in his evangelical Adams Center upbringing—a strong sense of self-discipline targeted at moral responsibility, a desire for reform, and an attachment to institutions like the church and school that posed little threat to the prevailing domestic order.[12] Cumulatively, they appeared to have created in Dewey an obsessive desire for doing what he perceived to be as much good for humanity as possible in the limited time God granted him on earth. What he had not yet figured out, however, was a way to do it. The youngster was caught up in an exaggerated desire to reform, characteristic of several children of the Burned-Over District; he anguished over identifying the channels most suited to his interests in order to effect necessary reforms.

Eventually the severity of the cough diminished so that Dewey was able to resume a normal life. Sometime in early 1869 he moved with his parents to live with his older brother and family in Oneida. There Dewey looked over the Oneida Institute, which at that time was sponsored by Free Will Baptists. Dewey liked what he saw. Since 1843 the Institute had been coeducational and biracial. Late winter found him enrolled in the "academy," where he finished the spring term at the head of his class.

August proved a busy but exciting month. Dewey took a summer job canvassing northwest New York for William Smith and Samuel Barnum's *Bible Dict*, Zachary Eddy's *Immanuel, or*

---

11. Dewey Diary, 1/30/68; 8/21/68, Dewey Mss. For examples of Dewey's entries on the deaths of friends and relatives, see 12/23/66; 12/26/66; 6/5/67; and 8/17/67. For an account of a contemporary's preoccupation with death, see Rodney D. Olsen, *Dancing in Chains: The Youth of William Dean Howells* (N.Y., 1991): pp. 58–59; 69–70.

12. Howe, "The Evangelical Movement," 18–19. See also Colleen McDannell, *The Christian Home in Victorian America, 1840–1900* (Bloomington, Ind., 1986), pp. 17, 143.

Life of Christ, and a periodical entitled *Home,* put out by the American Baptist Publication Society.[13] He saw firsthand the limited access rural New Yorkers had to reading materials; he also witnessed the American Baptist Publication Society's efforts to develop a vast distribution network and national constituency for its missionary products, including books, tracts, and periodicals. Much of the distribution was being done by temporary colporteurs like himself.

When he returned to Oneida at the end of August, he talked to Charlie Phalen—an old friend from boyhood days—about future college plans. Dewey took Charlie to the Seminary, and thereafter they visited the nearby Oneida Community. Dewey's diary descriptions of the visit suggest he was particularly interested in the community's silk and trap factories, its assembly hall and carefully manicured grounds, and especially its headquarters with a reading room and library of 3,200 volumes. Nothing in the entry, however, indicates an interest in the community's lifestyle or its Perfectionist beliefs. On October 30 Dewey confided to his diary he intended to enroll at Alfred University, a Seventh Day Baptist institution, at the beginning of the next term.[14]

Fall gave him time to reflect and jot a few more thoughts into his diary. His health continued to improve, and he commented on the imminence of death less frequently. On November 15 he recorded another watershed decision: "I have now about fully decided to devote my life to Education. I wish to inaugurate a higher education for the masses." He judged New York's district and academic school system "1/2 failures" because the system itself compelled students "to waste so much time in acquiring so little knowledge." Dewey was convinced that making

---

13. Sir William Smith, *A Comprehensive Dictionary of the Bible. Mainly Abridged from Dr. Wm. Smith's Dictionary of the Bible, but Comprising Important Additions and Improvements from the Works of Robinson, Gesenius, Furst [and others].* Edited by Rev. Samuel W. Barnum (N.Y., 1869); Zachary Eddy, *Immanuel; or, The Life of Jesus Christ Our Lord* (Springfield, 1868); *Home,* Philadelphia, American Baptist Publication Society.

14. Dewey Diary, 8/9/69; 8/11/69; 8/13/69; 8/17/69; 8/27/69; 8/28/69; 9/6/69; 9/10/69; 10/30/69, Dewey Mss. See also Thomas B. Stillman to Dewey, 10/13/84, Box 33A, Dewey Mss, for a friend's recollection of "tramping through the hills of Allegheny &c in 1869." The American Baptist Publication Society is described in Albert Henry Neuman, *A History of the Baptist Churches in the United States* (N.Y., 1893), pp. 475, 487.

the system more efficient would allow the masses to learn twice as fast, and he perceived an urgent need for the right kind of people committed to improve it. "Such a one I would be," he wrote, "It seems to me that my life work is here. It is congenial to my tastes in all respects. . . . It has justice on its side and must prevail." Dewey considered the "cause" so important it became for him "the companion of religion." The reforming spirit born in Adams Center and nurtured in evangelical surroundings had taken one step closer to finding its most effective vehicle for expression and application. Three days later he noted: "I am anxiously waiting for the day when I shall take my destined place, for it seems that destiny impels me to undertake this as a life work."[15] At just under eighteen Melville Dewey was talking about his destiny.

While Dewey's faith in God remained unshaken and his own Protestant Christianity continued to fuel his humanitarian reform goals, his faith in Baptist dogma diminished. He continued to question the advisability of disputing minor points of scriptural interpretation, and in a mild gesture of defiance began attending other Protestant churches. Just as he perceived formal education wasted a lot of student time, so he came to believe organized religion wasted its parishioners' time by concentrating on meaningless differences rather than doing greater good for humanity at large.

After spending Thanksgiving in Adams Center, Dewey returned to Oneida to prepare for Alfred. But there he learned his Oneida teachers, who assumed Dewey would begin study for the ministry at the Seminary, had arranged for him to teach a ten-week session for primary grades at Bernhard's Bay, a little village on the north shore of Oneida Lake. Under the circumstances, Dewey felt obliged to accept, even though "it will cost me a term on college preparation."

The session passed rapidly, in part because Dewey had developed a close rapport with the children. On his final day, he reported in his diary, he conducted a short general exercise. "I then gave them a short account of myself, my intentions and the circumstances which sent me to them. After urging them all to be chieftains and giving them my reasons, we all kneeled and closed school with a heartfelt prayer." Suddenly, "I was unable to

---

15. Dewey Diary, 11/15/69; 11/18/69; 12/9/69, Dewey Mss.

control my feelings and so I was child with them and we devoted a half hour to a good cry. I haven't been so much affected at parting before in all my life." He especially remembered one little girl who kept near him until he dismissed them at the end of the day. "I saw she wanted to kiss me good bye so I stooped down and kissed her. This was what the rest were waiting for & we had a time of kissing." For Dewey, the experience appears to have been the first time he allowed himself to show the kind of outward affection his family had suppressed at Adams Center. The tenor of his diary entry for that day suggests he liked the feeling of closeness and intimacy, but worried it showed lack of self-discipline. When he left Bernhard's Bay the next day, twenty school children met him at the train station, each bearing a farewell note. Dewey read the notes on the way to Oneida, then reread them regularly for several weeks thereafter.[16]

Although Dewey spent the spring term at Alfred, he ultimately decided against returning in the fall. His travels through northwestern New York in 1869 had whetted his appetite for the best in higher education, and shortly after arriving at Alfred he had begun inquiring about admission to established New England schools. In part he was also emboldened to explore other possibilities because his father offered to advance some money realized by the sale of his Adams Center shoe store towards Dewey's education. Dewey's efforts proved successful. In October 1870, Dewey became one of seventy-four members of the Amherst College Class of '74. At the time, he was six feet tall, 160 pounds, and by his own calculations worth $225.[17]

"Filling the Vessel": Amherst College 1870–1874

In 1870 Amherst College was a small, comfortable, almost family-like school nestled in the scenic Connecticut River Valley. Founded in 1821, it was strongly tied to orthodox Christianity,

---

16. Dewey Diary, 12/3/69; 12/9/69; 2/4/70; 3/12/72, Dewey Mss.
17. Dewey Diary, 4/14/70; 6/18/70; 7/8/70; 12/10/70. See also 4/11/68 for record of disposition of his father's store. Dewey once calculated his parents spent as much on his education as they did on all of their other children combined.

and much more interested in discipline than research and intellectual inquiry. Student coursework was typical for a classical curriculum. Freshmen took Latin and Greek prose composition, geometry, algebra, and trigonometry, and read Cicero, Homer, Livy, and Horace. Sophomores continued reading the Latin and Greek classics, began learning French and German, and took some chemistry. Juniors expanded coverage of Greek and Latin classics and supplemented these with courses in philosophy, botany, chemistry, and astronomy. Seniors were introduced to psychology, geology, biblical history, logic, constitutional law, political science, and history. All students were required to do "exercises in physical culture" half an hour per day four days a week under the watchful eye of Edward Hitchcock. Amherst faculty who taught the curriculum were a dedicated, albeit conservative and traditional group; most were Amherst alumni. Among them, Elijah Harris taught chemistry, Edward P. Crowell Latin, William S. Tyler classics, Julius H. Seelye philosophy, and beginning in 1873 John W. Burgess history and political science.[18]

One of the jobs of any nineteenth-century institution of higher education was to build moral character, and at Amherst—like most other New England colleges—the building blocks used to construct character came from a combination of Protestant orthodoxy and Western culture and classics. The curriculum was designed to communicate universal truths already known and unquestioned, not to expose students to contemporary political issues or contemporary literature. It influenced students toward a particular world view, inculcated a definition of the role of education, and identified the rules to which and the authorities to whom they should look in later life for guidance in making sense of their world. The curriculum also reinforced the concept of

---

18. Amherst College. *Catalogue of the Officers and Students of Amherst College for the Academical Year, 1870–71; 1871–72; 1872–73; 1873–74* (Amherst, 1871–74). Hitchcock believed exercise would increase human stature and channel the "animal spirits" of undergraduate males away from masturbation and the town saloon. See Helen F. Horowitz, *Campus Life: Undergraduate Cultures from the End of the Eighteenth Century to the Present* (N.Y., 1984), p. 53; J. Edmund Welch, *Edward Hitchcock, M.D.: Founder of Physical Education in the College Curriculum* (Greenville, 1966), and James C. Whorton, *Crusaders for Fitness: The History of American Health Reformers* (Princeton, 1982), Chap. 9. See also Dewey to Prof. A. S. Bickmore, 12/16/98, Box 31, Dewey Mss, in which Dewey reminisced, "It was only the gymnasium at Amherst that carried me there."

"mind as vessel"; education was a process by which the student would passively "fill" the "vessel" with the best that white Western (and, of course, Christian) civilization had to offer. That Dewey agreed wholeheartedly with the concept is obvious from his subsequent activities; it formed the foundation for all his educational reform schemes.

Throughout his years at Amherst, Dewey worried about finances. In August 1872 he confided to his diary two methods of keeping costs down: (1) "I . . . have gone without many books I wanted very much, making most of the library;" and (2) "My social expenses are less than other boys because I keep clear of nearly all of them & am satisfied." For most of his first two years Dewey boarded at Phoenix Hall, where he became a member of the Delta Kappa Epsilon fraternity, one of four at Amherst. In the 1870s Amherst's Greek societies discouraged idleness and extravagance, fostered educational activities, and publicly frowned on drinking, card playing, and idle conversation. Dewey fit right in. At the end of his sophomore year, he moved to a private home with fourteen of his classmates.[19]

By that time Dewey had already found four causes which would occupy his reforming passions for the rest of his life. In April 1871, he visited the office of Boston's Sealer of Weights and Measures. The length of his diary entry shows Dewey was fascinated by what he saw. "My visit strongly confirmed my dislike for our present complicated sistem and my faith that it is soon to give way to a better."[20] Another cause found an audience at the Amherst Reading Circle on December 8, 1870, when Dewey delivered a talk on "regularity" in language. He argued that the English language—although beautiful—was so rife with spelling irregularities it was difficult for non-Anglo-Saxons to learn.

---

19. Dewey's personal account books, starting in 1869, are in Box 97, Dewey Mss. A preparatory note for the 1872 account book addresses the issue of settling personal accounts in case of death. See also Dewey Diary, 8/1/72; 12/10/72; 3/23/73; 8/1/72; 9/29/72; 12/11/72. See also Dewey to Biscoe, 12/-/29, Box 30, Dewey Mss.; William S. Tyler, *A History of Amherst College during the Administrations of Its First Five Presidents from 1821 to 1891* (N.Y., 1895), pp. 262–65; and Claude Moore Fuess, *Amherst: The Story of a New England College* (Boston, 1935), p. 193. On Amherst's Greek letter societies, see John W. Burgess, *Reminiscences of an American Scholar* (N.Y., 1931), p. 167; and Thomas Le Duc, *Piety and Intellect at Amherst College, 1865–1912* (N.Y., 1969), pp. 121–39.

20. Dewey Diary, 4/11/71.

"Great minds have tried with carefully developed plans to reduce the many irregularities to order," he told his audience and made specific reference to Benjamin Franklin and Noah Webster's advocacy of spelling reform. Unlike many others, however, Dewey advocated "gradual" reform. When "we meet cases where there is good authority for two spellings," he said, the simpler should be adopted; that way English would evolve naturally out of its complications.[21] Resistance to this evolution was counterproductive to the goal of educating the masses in the shortest time possible, and by extension, to assimilating non-English-speaking immigrants into the dominant culture. A third lifelong interest was use of shorthand. During the fall of 1873 Dewey read a lot of pamphlets on shorthand and notetaking in order to find the best system. By his twenty-second birthday, he had decided on Lindsley's Tachigraphy, and began using it regularly in his diary (subject to his own modifications and simplification over time) and in drafting correspondence or penning notes to himself.[22]

Metric and spelling reform and use of shorthand fed Dewey's obsession for simplicity and efficient use of time, and the first two especially could benefit the masses if an entrenched educational establishment could be convinced to adopt them. But Dewey's fourth cause fell into an area of education at the time lacking fortified bureaucracies ready to defend age-old conventions. Eventually this cause became the arena in which he had his greatest influence of lasting duration. On October 20, 1872, in order to reduce the debt he was accumulating at Amherst, he began keeping account books for the college library. At the time the library—although open five hours a day for reference, one hour a day for loans—was little used, largely because

---

21. Copy of the speech in Box 10, Dewey Mss. See also Eliza Burns to Dewey, 1/19/74, Box 83, Dewey Mss. For general discussions of spelling reform movements in post-Revolutionary America see Dennis E. Baron, *Grammar and Good Taste: Reforming the American Language* (New Haven, 1982), Chap. 4; Kenneth Cmiel, *Democratic Eloquence: The Fight Over Popular Speech in Nineteenth Century America* (N.Y., 1990), pp. 83–85; 158–61; and Cynthia S. Jordan, "'Old Words' in 'New Circumstances': Language and Leadership in Post-Revolutionary America," *American Quarterly* 40 (12/1988): 493.

22. See David Phillip Lindsley, *The Compendium of Tachygraphy; or Lindsley's Phonetic Shorthand* (Hartford, 1864). See also Dewey Diary, 12/10/73; and entries in his reading notebooks for 11/73 and 1/28/74, Box 99, Dewey Mss.

Amherst instructors assigned textbooks for each course and relied heavily on class recitations as a standard form of pedagogy.
Dewey looked beyond this, however, and foresaw its potential for
educating the masses. He began to read systematically the limited amount of literature on libraries that was available and to
keep notes on his reading.

His reading notebooks during the fall and winter terms
reveal a mind structuring a lifetime of work in libraries. He read
the annual reports of several public libraries, but the note he
penned after reading Edward Edwards's *Memoirs of Libraries* is
particularly revealing: "The free school and the free library I con-
ceive to be the great engines," he wrote on December 10, 1872.
"I feel thankful for the strong interest in the work that has come
to me during the last year. . . . My World Work—Free Schools &
Free Libraries for *every soul.*"[23]

". . . for *every soul.*" Dewey's use of these words characterized a mind nurtured in a small town on the edge of the Burned-
Over District. To it he harnessed an intense desire to reform
indicative of some of its greatest evangelists, and a commitment
to humanity dressed in altruism and assuming the moral imperative of a crusade.

To understand the dimensions of what Dewey envisioned,
however, it is also necessary to look at the state of American education in 1872, especially in New York. At the time it consisted
of thousands of inefficiently run one-room elementary schools
designed to teach basic reading and mathematics skills, and
some writing skills. The common school constituted the only formal education most Americans received. Supplementing this
loosely structured system of elementary education was an equally
loose but much smaller system of secondary schools, usually
called "academies," that helped prepare students for teaching
in primary schools or entering colleges. In Dewey's eyes, access
to education and self-improvement for most Americans largely
ceased once they achieved basic literacy and mathematics skills
in elementary schools. What especially concerned him was lack

---

23. See entry for 10/20/72 in Dewey's account books, Box 97, Dewey
Mss. See reading notebook entries for 12/10/72 (quoting Edwards); 1/24/73;
and 1/25/73, Box 99. Account book entry for 3/28/73, Box 97, shows Dewey
earned $18 for working in the college library. On 12/8/73 he earned $50.
The text Dewey read was Edward Edwards, *Memoirs of Libraries: Including
a Handbook of Library Economy* (London, 1859).

of access to "good reading." Nineteenth-century evangelists took the act of reading very seriously, and agencies like the American Tract Society and the American Sunday-School Union constantly pushed it as a vital component in the process of moral development and personal growth that so preoccupied them.

For Dewey, the ability to read—"to get the meaning from the printed page," he said—constituted "the ultimate cornerstone of education." People's lives would improve immeasurably, he argued, if they could build upon their elementary education in an informal self-paced way that accommodated demands capitalism placed upon them, and the best vehicle for this informal education was a free public library stocked with shelves of "good reading" that, with the church and school, constituted one of the three "great engines" of education.[24] But Dewey felt he needed to learn more, much more than the library literature he read over his Christmas vacation in 1872. By this time he had even greater motivation. Since he had shown so much interest in library matters, Amherst College gladly allowed him to assume more responsibility for its library.

Dewey tackled his new responsibilities with the intensity of a crusader. In January 1873 he read Charles C. Jewett's "A Plan for Stereotyping Titles." Dewey very much liked Jewett's recommendation for building a common catalog. "This wd secure accuracy & uniformity . . . , save expense after e first few libraries were catalogued," and because some central institution could print from its plates "a full & perfectly accurate catalog of all books in e lib's of America . . . a Universal Catalog wd be feasible." In February 1873, he returned to Boston to visit and study the Boston Public Library, the Boston Athenaeum, and the Harvard College Library. He especially enjoyed meeting Athenaeum Director Charles Cutter, who at the time was "in the throes of cat. printing." Dewey peppered him with questions, especially

---

24. Dewey's words are quoted from a reminiscence in Dewey to LPEF Trustees, 7/28/30, LPEF Mss. For a discussion of reading at that time see Louise L. Stevenson, "Prescription and Reality: Reading Advisers and Reading Practice, 1860–1880," *Book Research Quarterly* 6 (Winter/1990–91): 43–61. See also Richard T. Altick, *The English Common Reader: A Social History of the Mass Reading Public, 1800–1900* (Chicago, 1957), pp. 132–40; David Vincent, *Literacy and Popular Culture: England, 1750–1914* (Cambridge, 1989); and Carl F. Kaestle et. al., *Literacy in the United States: Readers and Reading since 1880* (New Haven, 1991), especially Chap. 3.

about his classification scheme. "He puts the books on the horse under 'horse' & not under 'zoology.'"[25]

When Dewey returned to Amherst, he reviewed its operation and arrangement more carefully. He also continued to pore over library literature. On February 22 he read St. Louis Public School Superintendent William Torrey Harris's article, "Book Classification," which had appeared in an 1870 issue of the *Journal of Speculative Philosophy*. Dewey noted that Harris's idea that books ought to be arranged alphabetically under each subject forced a relative rather than fixed location of books, "& of this I am inclined to be a friend."[26] On March 7 he read a pamphlet he had "blundered on" in the library that was privately printed in 1856 by Nathaniel Shurtleff and entitled *A Decimal System for the Arrangement and Administration of Libraries*, and "of course took it home. My heart is open to anything that's either decimal or about libraries." He admitted liking Shurtleff's concept of marrying the decimal system to library administration and arrangement, but criticized the details because the author laid "altogether too much stress" on the decimal system at the expense of efficiency and saving time. A second reading on April 29 did not change his mind.[27]

Dewey also read the Cincinnati Public Library's fifth annual report by director William F. Poole, who "heartily" defended the fiction reading which accounted for 75 percent of the library's

25. Dewey Diary, 2/11/73, Dewey Mss. See also "extracts from MD's comments on books he had read," Box 27, Dewey Mss. See also Charles C. Jewett, *A Plan for Stereotyping by Separate Titles, and for Forming a General Stereotyped Catalogue of Public Libraries in the United States* (Washington, 1851).

26. Reading notebook entry, 2/22/73, Box 99, Dewey Mss; William T. Harris, "Book Classification," *Journal of Speculative Philosophy* 4 (1870): 114–29.

27. Reading notebook entries, 3/7/73; 4/29/73, Box 99, Dewey Mss; Nathaniel B. Shurtleff, *A Decimal System for the Arrangement and Administration of Libraries* (Boston, 1856). Although his reading notebooks do not reflect it, Dewey may also have read publications of the U.S. Centennial Commission sent to Amherst in early 1873, one of which was a 42-page pamphlet outlining a system probably of decimal classification and notation. That he commented on Shurtleff twice but not the Centennial Commission report suggests that the latter had no impact on him even if he had read it. For a discussion built on speculation that concludes the latter, see John Maass, "Who Invented Dewey's Classification?" *Wilson Library Bulletin* 47 (12/1972): 335–41.

circulation. "These novels educate taste to better books," Dewey noted, "& cause those to read & get good who cannot read heavier bks." Several days later he read the American Social Science Association's *Free Public Libraries* and liked it. "The sugtons . . . are not the visionary schemes of some Prof. of Metaphysics but are deduced fr the experience of the best libraries."[28] He disliked the New York State Library's system of organizing its collections— "They arrange the books alfabetically paying no attention to subjects"—but liked the system of recording the library's holdings on cards (one card per title) that Jacob Schwartz used at the New York Mercantile Library. On February 20 he asked Schwartz about the location symbol in the upper left-hand corner of the card. "The use of the number is not essential to the system," Schwartz replied, "& may be omitted or used, at the discretion of the librarian."[29]

Cutter, Harris, Shurtleff, Jewett, and Schwartz—all had developed firm ideas about classification schemes or cataloging practices which Dewey thought showed strengths and weaknesses. But classification schemes especially intrigued him, and their weaknesses especially troubled him.[30] "For months I dreamed night and day that there must be somewhere a satisfactory solution." Then, "one Sunday during a long sermon by Pres. Stearns," he recalled fifty years later, "the solution flasht over me so that I jumpt in my seat and came very near shouting 'Eureka!' Use

28. Reading notebook entries, 3/11/73; 3/22/73, Box 99, Dewey Mss; American Social Science Association, *Free Public Libraries. Suggestions on Their Foundation and Administration, with a Selected History of Books* (Boston, 1871).

29. Dewey Diary, 4/1/73; Schwartz to Dewey, 2/20/73, Box 33A, Dewey Mss.

30. A comprehensive discussion of the origins and early years of the decimal classification scheme is John Phillip Comaromi, *The Eighteen Editions of the Dewey Decimal Classification* (Albany, 1976), Chap. 1. That none of the historians of library classification makes mention of Shurtleff in connection with Dewey's system suggests they may not have looked at the former. Dewey does not acknowledge Shurtleff in the Preface of his original edition, although he does mention Shurtleff in an 1879 *LJ* article (see *LJ* 4 [2/79]: 61). Comaromi quotes this article, but fails to pursue the clue (see Comaromi, p. 630). Ainsworth Rand Spofford, who was Librarian of Congress when Dewey copyrighted his scheme in 1876, notes: "What is known as the decimal or Dewey system of classification was originally suggested by Mr. N. B. Shurtleff." See Ainsworth Rand Spofford, *A Book for All Readers* (N.Y., 1900), p. 269.

decimals to number a classification of all human knowledge in print."[31] Dewey's approach was characteristic. Adopt from existing practice only those features that promised to make the new system easy to use, and centralize the system to avoid duplication of effort. At this point the scheme he conceived joined strong points from Cutter, Harris, and Shurtleff. Dewey's contribution to classification was joining them together, not creating anything new.

He submitted his decimal scheme to the Amherst College Library Committee on May 8, 1873. Conceptually, it was constructed on the premise that knowledge could be divided into nine main classes (e.g., the main class "4" might represent "Science"). Each of the main classes could be divided into nine more subclasses by adding a decimal to separate the subclass from the main class signifier (e.g., "4.7" might represent "Chemistry"). Further subdivisions of subclasses could be added by assigning a second digit after the first subclass signifier (e.g., "4.75" might represent "Organic Chemistry"). "Thus the sub-classes may be increased in any part of the library without limit; each additional decimal place increasing the minuteness of classification tenfold."

Within each of these classes, Dewey then proposed a sub-arrangement alphabetically by author under that class (e.g., "4.75" with "Bain" immediately beneath it might represent a book on organic chemistry written by Bain). If the library owned more than one book on the subject by that author, however, books would "stand in the same order on the shelves as the titles of the same in the catalogue" (i.e., all books on organic chemistry by Bain would be shelved in the order they were listed in the catalog, probably their order of acquisition by the library).

Thus, the call number for any item in the scheme as Dewey originally conceived it would consist of a single-digit class number to the left of a decimal point, followed by one or more digits to the right of the decimal point, under which catalogers would add the author's surname. "Readers will call for books thus located by their 'class number' (instead of 'shelf')," he explained, "and author's name as printed in the catalogue (instead of 'number on shelf.')" Books of a general character on more than one topic, like a dictionary of science, would receive no subclas-

---

31. Dewey recalls these events in "Decimal Classification Beginning," *LJ* 45 (2/15/20): 151–52.

sification, but sit on the shelf with only the main class number (e.g., "4").[32]

Although Dewey had settled on a basic outline for his scheme, he still sought outside advice, especially for identification of appropriate classes. On May 9 he wrote William T. Harris for more information on his classification scheme. The "general plan" concerned Dewey most at this point, because it identified an acceptable way to divide knowledge into nine major classes. Dewey later acknowledged his debt to Harris. "In filling the nine classes of the scheme the inverted Baconian arrangement of the St. Louis Library has been followed."[33] Harris had built his system on two sources: (1) ideas of Sir Francis Bacon, who had argued that the three faculties of the human mind—memory, imagination, and reason—produced three categories of learning— history, poetry, and philosophy, each of which could be further subdivided; and (2) the ideas of F. W. Hegel, who inverted Bacon's order to give a more prominent role to philosophy, from which the rest of the structure follows. From philosophy, Harris saw a natural structure of knowledge progressing to theology, government, philology, nature, the useful and the fine arts, and finally, geography, biography and history. Dewey largely superimposed Harris's structure on his own decimal scheme, but was willing and ready to modify the former if it conflicted with his priorities. "The most rigid economy must rule," he wrote in his diary; "our free libraries will all need to exercise their strait economy & any sistem that does not allow such saving must be defeated for users."[34]

---

32. Dewey had originally proposed ten, but abandoned that because use of ten added another digit to one of the numbers and reduced the scheme's simplicity. The original document is in an envelope marked "Special Historical Material about Melvil Dewey," unmarked box, LPEF Mss.

33. Dewey to Harris, 5/9/73, as found in Kurt F. Leidecker, "The Debt of Melvil Dewey to William Torrey Harris," *LQ*, 15 (4/1945): 139. See also Harris to Dewey, 5/13/73, Box 13, Dewey Mss; [Melvil Dewey], *Classification and Subject Index for Cataloging and Arranging the Books and Pamphlets of a Library* (Amherst, 1876), p. 10.

34. Dewey Diary, 4/21/74, Dewey Mss. Comaromi discusses the influence of Hegel on Harris's scheme on pp. 25–27. For a fuller account of Bacon's influence on classification schemes, see Leo La Montagne, *American Library Classification, with Special Reference to the Library of Congress* (Hamden, 1961).

On July 9, 1874, Melville Dewey graduated near the middle of a class of sixty-six, all of whom were white male Protestants of Anglo-Saxon heritage, two-thirds of whom were from New England. No Jews, no Roman Catholics, no women, no African Americans, and no ethnic minorities at the time seasoned the social stew in America's melting pot. Nothing Dewey encountered at Amherst induced him to question the dominant culture of late-nineteenth-century American life; his college experience constituted an immersion in Anglo-Saxonism. In some respects Dewey was much like generations of Amherst graduates who preceded him, in others much different. On the one hand, his continued adherence to rigid rules of piety directed him away from worldly pleasures. Dewey's primary goal as an undergraduate was to "fill the vessel" with the right elements necessary to build character and reinforce the basic values of his sociocultural origins. On the other hand, he was part of a new group of serious students who looked to college as preparation for careers in newly emerging social professions that promised energetic young men with little capital opportunities to address significant social problems. Dewey felt closely connected to this group, and especially to the educators, whose motives seemed most altruistic of all.[35]

Dewey's graduation from Amherst College was a major accomplishment for an upstate New Yorker of limited means, but his four years there give little indication he was destined for leadership. He had not participated much in college social life, nor had he distinguished himself as a scholar; he certainly showed little inclination for deep thinking. His reading notebooks show minimal interest in philosophy, history, the arts, or the sciences. They do, however, reflect a crusading interest in the education of the masses, and especially in a commitment to minimize waste in that education by focusing on pet interests—the metric system, simplified spelling, use of shorthand, and, especially since December 1872, free libraries. By July 1874 he had already developed a framework for a classification scheme he was convinced would make free libraries more efficient, increase their usefulness, and thus help them assume their rightful place in educating the masses. Although his Amherst undergraduate years

---

35. Helen Lefkowitz Horowitz calls this group "outsiders." See her *Campus Life,* p. 62. It is from this base that Dewey later recruited his original Lake Placid Club membership.

allowed him to define his niche in a future of education reforms, he nonetheless accepted a temporary appointment as Assistant Librarian at Amherst after graduation to run its library and implement his ideas. The appointment also gave him a chance to repay some of his student loans.[36]

"In Proper Order": Assistant Librarian, Amherst College 1874–1876

In the summer of 1874 Dewey was clean shaven except for sideburns carefully trimmed to below his ears. His most prominent facial feature was a strong chin which jutted out, giving the impression of determination and seriousness. For exercise he bought a horse and rode her twice a day, six days a week. He also began to socialize more, in large part because his circle of acquaintances expanded when he joined the local Congregational Church. Congregationalists differed from evangelical Baptists; they adhered to similar standards of piety, but tended towards the quieter channels of reform characteristic of a more reserved society. Dewey admitted to his sister-in-law that he picked a Congregational church mostly for its society, which included a pool of unmarried women "of respect and virtue." He began dating several and with one became especially serious. By February he was even talking about matrimony; a month later, the romance cooled.[37]

Dewey also developed a close friendship with Mrs. S. F. Pratt, widow of an Amherst alumnus. An unfortunate set of circumstances brought them together. After graduation Dewey took a room in the home of William W. Hunt. In March 1875, however, Hunt arranged to exchange houses with Pratt so she could be closer to her church and the school her three children attended. Dewey assumed he would be moving out with Hunt, but Pratt offered him a room with a bath if he would stay and help her with her business affairs. Dewey agreed. On March 29—before

---

36. Trustee Minutes, Amherst College, Vol. IV, pp. 814, 815, 825, ACA. See also miscellaneous Amherst materials, Box P-1, Dewey Mss; Dewey to Biscoe, 1/19/75, Wyer Mss; and Dewey Diary, 12/4/75.

37. Dewey Diary, 12/10/74; 1/29/75; 2/1/75; 3/3/75; Dewey to Lottie Dewey, 12/27/74, Box 36, Dewey Mss.

the deeds had been signed and the property legally changed hands—Dewey helped Hunt move out and Pratt move in. Three days later he began reviewing Pratt's accounts, but when he looked at the figures on the exchange of houses he discovered Hunt unfairly made $1,500 on the exchange. At first he did not tell Pratt what he found, but instead asked Hunt about the figures. Hunt indignantly accused Dewey of meddling in affairs of no concern to him. Dewey returned home, unsure of his next step.

But Amherst was a small town, and because many people had been involved in the transaction, rumors began to circulate that something was amiss in the exchange. Somehow Pratt sensed the problem, wrote Hunt a letter, and asked questions Hunt could not satisfactorily answer. Ultimately the issue was submitted to a committee of local businessmen, who recommended that Hunt and Pratt move back to their original houses to avoid a lawsuit. Both parties agreed. The move took place April 29. Pratt asked Dewey to return with her to her original house, and by May 1 everyone had resettled. Eventually Dewey told Pratt he had discovered the problem, and what he had done about it. She

In a May 1, 1875, letter to a friend—on borrowed library stationery—Dewey notes, "I have behaved pretty wel this year—havnt girld it at all but only a little necessary gallantry. I am getting stronger physically (thanks to the black mare) & I humbly hope stronger mentally & morally."

indicated she was sure his actions played a large part in Hunt's decision to follow the committee's recommendation.[38]

But the Pratt episode was only a temporary diversion from educational initiatives which so preoccupied his interests. In the fall of 1874, Dewey convinced the college to let him teach a "takigrafy" class to Amherst freshmen in the winter term; sixty-nine enrolled. Dewey met his first few classes before learning that the faculty refused to sanction the class for credit. Students protested. For a while it appeared students and faculty were headed for confrontation, but on January 27 Dewey told Burgess he would teach the course for nothing if the faculty would sanction the course for credit. Burgess's colleagues quickly approved. "I hav to saw wood to earn my board," he wrote a friend, but Dewey was willing to make personal sacrifices so others would become converts to shorthand.[39]

A second interest that surfaced regularly was spelling reform. Shortly after graduating he dropped the "le" from his first name and forever after signed it "Melvil." He began to use simplified spelling more frequently in his private correspondence, and took advantage of opportunities to sell its benefits to anyone who would listen. On January 9, 1875, he tried to convince the principal of a local academy to use it in his curriculum. He argued it eventually would save students time by not forcing them to memorize irregularities in the English language. On the 18th he lectured Amherst College freshmen on the same subject, noting especially that it would speed the assimilation of non-English-speaking immigrants into the dominant American culture.[40]

---

38. Dewey Diary, 3/29/75; 4/7/75; 4/12/75; 4/21/75; 4/29/75, Dewey Mss. See also Dewey "To My Dear Fellows" (circular to DKE classmates), 5/1/75, Wyer Mss. Dewey began recording Pratt's accounts in his own notebook June 10. See 1875 account book, Box 97, Dewey Mss.

39. Dewey Diary, 1/14/75; 1/18/75; 1/23/75; 1/25/75; 1/27/75; 3/17/75, Dewey Mss; Dewey to Biscoe, 1/19 and 29/75, Wyer Mss. See also *Amherst Student* 8 (1/30/75): 14.

40. Dewey Diary, 1/9/75; 1/22/75, Dewey Mss; Dewey to "My Dear Fellows," 5/1/75, Wyer Mss; Dewey, "3/4 of a Century," 2/26, Box 23, Dewey Mss. For notes on Dewey's speech to Amherst College freshmen, see entry 1/18/75 in his 1875 notebook, Box 99, Dewey Mss. The *Amherst Student* teased Dewey: "As that gentleman's proclivities in regard to our present system of orthography are well known, we would remark that it is to be hoped that these freshmen will not be compelled to stand an exam in spelling during their college course." See *Amherst Student* 8 (1/30/75): 14.

Dewey also paid attention to metric reform. On December 29 he was appointed to the American Metrological Society's Committee on Mural Standards, and began attending AMS meetings. At a May 19, 1875, meeting, he learned that representatives of most of the world's powers had recently met in Paris to form a permanent Metric Bureau to perpetuate "forever without change" the basic units of the metric system. The Bureau's establishment reinforced Dewey's belief that U.S. adoption of the system was only a matter of time. Dewey voted in favor of an AMS resolution urging Congress to ratify the Paris convention and appropriate money to support the new Bureau.[41]

Diary entries for most of 1875 indicate Dewey was enjoying his work at the library, busying himself with selecting books for rebinding, clearing out and selling duplicates, paying bills, and working on a book catalog. By mid-May he had arranged the entire collection "in proper order," the first time "it has been so straightened up since I have been there."[42] Two months later he got the offer he had been hoping for; President Stearns called him into his office and asked him to take charge of the library with "at least a tutor's salary" of $900 and the rank of assistant librarian in charge. "I of course accepted."

Stearns may have been partially motivated to find money for Dewey's salary because he knew that both of the college literary societies—the Athenian and the Alexandrian—were about to donate their libraries (about 4,000 volumes each) to the college. Someone had to go through them, identify and weed duplicates, dispense with unnecessary materials beyond repair, and recatalog and classify the rest into the college library's regular collection. As part of the arrangement, Dewey promised to accession society collections during his free time if he could sell books duplicated in the college collection and pocket the money. Stearns agreed. Dewey started immediately.[43]

---

41. *MB*, no. 7 (1/77): 102, 104–7. See also American Metrological Society, *The Metric System: Detailed Information as to Laws, Practices, Etc.* (N.Y., 1896), p. 8, for a copy of the articles presented at the Metric Convention on 5/20/75.

42. The *Amherst Student* kept track of Dewey's progress. See 7 (9/16/76): 116–17; 8 (1/16/75): 4–5.

43. Dewey Diary, 1/2/75; 1/4/75; 1/5/75; 1/22/75; 5/13/75; 7/12/75; 1/3/76, Dewey Mss; Dewey to Biscoe, 1/15/75, Wyer Mss.

Much of his 1875 in-library time was also spent on developing his classification system. He sent drafts to people like Jacob Schwartz, W. T. Harris, Frederic Beecher Perkins of the Boston Public Library, William Isaac Fletcher of the Watkinson Library in Hartford, Connecticut, and Annie Godfrey of the Wellesley College Library. This action had the collateral effect of advertising the scheme in advance of publication. Although the general hierarchical system he had adopted from Harris's scheme worked reasonably well, he looked to certain Amherst faculty members to identify the appropriate headings for subclasses. Crowell assisted with the literature section, and Hitchcock helped with medicine, but Seelye and Burgess regularly came to the library to work on the scheme. Dewey once complimented Seelye for "giving me quite a lift." In his diary, Dewey gives no indication he ever questioned or disagreed with their advice. As a result, the hierarchical arrangement Dewey cemented into the DDC had the effect of framing and solidifying a worldview and knowledge structure taught on the Amherst College campus between 1870 and 1875. By the end of November Dewey had completed his scheme and was ready to have it printed.[44]

On December 7, 1875, Dewey left Amherst for Boston to sell literary society duplicates. While there he was contacted at his hotel by Edwin Ginn, who had established the educational publishing house of Ginn and Company with his brother Fred in 1869 and who had heard Dewey might be looking for a "new situation." Dewey went to Ginn's office, where he spent the afternoon discussing "quite a little biznes." Dewey told Ginn about his commitment to popular education, his hopes for spelling and metric reform, and the role he predicted public libraries would play in educating the masses beyond formal schooling. All these reforms, he argued, would create a substantial market for "educational" tools and standard forms and appliances. Ginn listened attentively and was impressed enough to invite Dewey back the next day to resume their conversation with his business associates. Dewey accepted.

44. Dewey Diary, 2/5/75; 5/22/75; 6/2/75; 6/7/75; 6/8/75; 11/29/75, Dewey Mss. See also Comaromi, Chap. 2; Burgess, *Reminiscences,* p. 218; and *Amherst Student,* 7 (9/19/74): 116–17. A lengthier discussion appears in my "'The Amherst Method': The Origins of the Dewey Decimal Classification Scheme" (unpublished).

When Dewey returned, Ginn showed him the company's manufacturing department and let him peruse its stock of educational materials. Hours later he outlined a business arrangement. He offered to buy all extra copies of Dewey's decimal scheme and serve as publisher for future editions. He also agreed to establish a "metric department" in the company which would "have everything needed for the teaching, introduction, or actual use of the system furnished at reasonable prices," and put Dewey in charge. Finally, he asked Dewey to become part of his sales staff. Other salesmen, Ginn promised, would be asked to promote devices Dewey developed in his metric department. Ginn was also mildly interested in Dewey's plans for public libraries, but uninterested in spelling reform. Dewey was not disappointed; spelling reform, he was convinced, could still be addressed by other means.

When he returned home, Dewey discussed Ginn's proposal with Pratt. Four days later Ginn sent him over $100 worth of sample stock from the company's storeroom. The tactic worked; Dewey decided to accept his offer, and on the 21st Dewey returned to Boston. Next morning Ginn took Dewey to three banks, sold some bonds to raise capital, and had a note for the capital endorsed over to Dewey to which Dewey added his own endorsement for $7,000. From these amounts Dewey received a balance of $6,600 against which he could encumber funds to pay for the manufacture of metric devices. Proceeds from sales would be divided between Dewey and Ginn Brothers. Dewey would depend on sales for his livelihood; Ginn would stand to recover his original investment and make a handsome profit if Dewey's predictions about the future of the metric system and public libraries proved true. And Dewey was happy because he felt in control of his own destiny.[45]

Amherst tried to convince Dewey to stay, but Dewey declined. He recommended former classmate Walter S. Biscoe to

45. Dewey Diary, 12/6/75; 12/9/75; 12/10/75; 12/11/75; 12/13/75; 12/16/75; 12/19/75; 12/21/75; 12/22/75; 12/23/75; 4/17/75. See also "Chronicles of '74," *Amherst College, 1873–74,* pp. 15–18 (a pamphlet found in Box 10, Dewey Mss), where Dewey gives his motives for entering the agreement with Ginn in an open letter to his classmates. See also *MB,* nos. 3&4 (9/76): 26–27, for more background information on arrangement between Ginn and Dewey, and Dawe to H. E. Davidson, 7/27/32, Box 27, Dewey Mss, for Dawe's summary of financial arrangements with Ginn.

Dewey's ingenuous request for copyright of the Decimal classification scheme, March 22, 1876. He enclosed one dollar "for copyright, which I believe costs that amount. Having had no experience in these matters I am not at all sure that I hav made applicasn [application] in proper form," he wrote.

succeed him, and after Stearns and the library committee agreed, they authorized Dewey to offer Biscoe exactly what Dewey was getting—$900, plus "the chances of a windfall on extra sale of duplicates." In mid-March Dewey supervised sales of duplicates, from which he and Biscoe realized over $300. He also wrote the Register of Copyrights in Washington, D.C., asking permission to copyright "a little work just passing thru" the press entitled "A classification & Subject index with direction for their use." He enclosed one dollar to cover the cost of copyright, and later forwarded two published copies of the scheme to guarantee copyright protection. By this time the scheme had evolved to its more familiar ten divisions with an ill-defined initial section (000) for bibliographies, periodicals and encyclopedias preceding Philosophy (100), Theology (200), Sociology (300), Philology (400), Natural Sciences (500), Useful Arts (600), Fine Arts (700), Literature (800), and History (900). Each division accommodated subdivisions within subdivisions by utilizing both of the remaining digits, and expanded the capacity of the system even more by allowing classifiers to add numbers after placing a decimal to follow the third digit. In 1876 it was hard for Dewey to believe library collections would ever outgrow the decimal classification's ability to organize them bibliographically.

By the end of March Dewey was anxious to get to Boston to begin his new venture. On the 26th he and Biscoe spent "a couple of hours . . . going thru my plan for keeping students' books." On March 31, he stopped at the library to pick up his things "for the last time." He spent the next several days running errands, closing accounts, packing his belongings, making social calls, horseback riding, hunting with friends, and saying goodbye to close associates. He wanted to be in Boston in early April; because of his affinity for decimals he preferred the 10th. Dewey did not sleep peacefully that night; he was up the next morning at 5:00, and on the train for Boston at 6:15, ready to start fulfilling his destiny.[46]

Dewey left Amherst in a hurry; he arrived in Boston in a hurry. His six years at Amherst had given him the opportunity to build upon the moral certainties inculcated in him as a child of the Burned-Over District, to find direction for a commitment to reform he had made as a teenager, and to fill his mind with the

---

46. Dewey Diary, 3/26/76; Dewey to Biscoe, 1/5/76, Wyer Mss.

right ingredients for building character. In order to undertake his "world work," in order to achieve his goal of educating the masses toward improvement, he had identified three "causes" which would receive his crusading zeal—adoption of the metric system, acceptance of simplified spelling, and the efficient operation of free public libraries properly stocked with "good reading." Adoption of the first two, he calculated, promised to reduce the amount of time needed to complete elementary and secondary education by at least two years, thus releasing more time for productive, meaningful educational work. Accomplishing the latter, he believed, would give the masses an opportunity to build on their formal education at their own level, at their own pace, and—within limits fixed by printed texts the dominant culture prescribed—according to their own direction. For Dewey, as we have seen, the free public library constituted the third "great engine" of education. If uniform systems, appliances, and organizational schemes suitable for the efficient operation of all free libraries could be invented and implemented, all Americans would benefit. Dewey had already taken a major step by creating the decimal classification scheme which harnessed a mid-nineteenth century male white Western (and largely Christian) view of the world.

His goals were noble, he believed, and his causes just, but when he left Amherst he assumed metric reform would be easier to promote than simplified spelling or public libraries. For the previous two years Dewey had watched the former make rapid progress. He attributed that progress in large part to the existence of the American Metrological Society, to its able leadership, and to its organ of communication. Edwin Ginn had been especially attracted to Dewey's vision of the market potential for metric reform because an organization and journal already existed which could lobby for its adoption. Spelling reform and public libraries, however, did not have organizations or journals to act as national voices for their interests. Dewey planned to change that as soon as possible; he was in a hurry to get started when he stepped off the train in Boston on April 10, 1876.

2

Creating Bureaus
and Organizations

1876–1879

Although the Boston to which Dewey moved in April 1876 had not yet worked its way back from the Panic of 1873, Dewey seemed unconcerned. Boston had one of the best education systems in the country, and its array of high profile libraries assured him of the kinds of audiences he needed for his "world work." For Melvil Dewey, Boston was indeed "The Hub," and he began work immediately. He moved into offices at 13 Tremont Place (paid for by Ginn), and had business cards printed identifying him as "Manager" of their "Metric Bureau."[1]

Several times he traveled to Harvard, and on April 18 delivered a lecture to the library staff on the decimal scheme. On the 19th he talked to Cutter about "starting a library bureau and publishing a library monthly." Both piqued Dewey's reform spirit; both he considered necessary to shift the other great engine of education into a higher gear. He decided to discuss them with his employers, and by May 5 negotiated an agreement whereby they offered $2,000 to help Dewey set up an all-purpose bureau with interests in spelling reform, shorthand, wider adop-

---

1. Dewey Diary, 4/11/76; 4/13/76; 4/14/76. Copies of the business cards can be found in Box 66, Dewey Mss. See also Dewey's account book entry for 4/14/76, Box 97, which shows the first entry for Ginn Brothers.

> # MELVIL DEWEY
>
> ### 13 TREMONT PLACE
>
> Manager
> ## AMERICAN METRIC BUREAU
>
> BOSTON

Dewey sets up in the "Hub."

tion of metric, and enlarging a free public library system. In return they asked 10 percent of the profits from sales of the bureau's metric and shorthand materials. Dewey would have to come up with money for advertising and manufacturing costs and office rental.[2]

His approach to raising capital, however, was unorthodox. Since he had little money or collateral himself, he began constructing a system of business connections whose financial interests became interlinked through "bureaus." For example, at the end of April he arranged for Ginn to publish J. P. Putnam's "Metric School Chart." He also negotiated agreements with the G. M. Eddy Tape Works, the Keffel and Esser Drawing Materials Company, and the Fairbanks Scale Works to supply him with metric scales and measuring devices at cost, promising that subsequent sales would justify their investment once metric conversion swept the country. All of the companies believed they were working with Ginn and were unaware they were actually making arrangements with a separate "bureau" using Ginn's sales network to market its products. Sometimes Dewey sold their products at 100 percent markup; at other times he gave them away if he thought he could win converts to metric reform.[3]

At the same time Dewey worked on his library interests. In mid-April he discussed a library journal with Harvard librarian John Fiske, who thought Harvard might contribute "$100 or $200" to save employees the "labor" of answering requests from hun-

---

2. Dewey Diary, 4/20/76; 5/2/76.

3. Dewey Diary, 4/25/76; 4/27/76; copy of contract between Ginn and Putnam can be found in Box 68, Dewey Mss. Dewey was also negotiating with Putnam to publish Putnam's forthcoming book on the metric system with Ginn. See Dewey Diary, 5/3/76 and 5/4/76; and Dewey to H. Richards (AMS Secretary), 9/4/24 and 2/9/25, Box 66, Dewey Mss.

dreds of librarians across the country seeking advice. Dewey also approached Cutter about the journal, and in their conversation found out Cutter had written U.S. Commissioner of Education John Eaton about Dewey's new classification scheme. Cutter knew Eaton was planning a major report on U.S. public libraries as part of the 1876 centennial celebration, and because Dewey's scheme was "one of the most important contributions to library economy that has been made for many years," he told Eaton, the report "would be very incomplete without some account of it." Several days later the Bureau asked Dewey for "a list of my library sistem." Before replying, however, Dewey pushed Cutter on the subject of a library journal. Together they agreed to "try for a place for our journal in the library volume." Dewey then wrote Eaton directly, asking for "simpathy in the library project."[4] Eaton did not respond immediately.

On May 16 Dewey left for New York on the overnight boat from Boston for an American Metrological Society (AMS) meeting. He arrived at 7:00 A.M., had breakfast, and since he was not obligated until that afternoon decided to visit the offices of *Publishers Weekly (PW)*. There he found editor Frederick Leypoldt and Associate Editor Richard R. Bowker. His intentions were clear. He wanted to alert *PW* to plans for a library journal and for a bureau which would deal in library supplies. Leypoldt "sed at once" he was interested in the journal. He also told Dewey about a forthcoming *PW* editorial suggesting librarians, as other scientific and educational groups were doing, meet in Philadelphia during the nation's centennial. Dewey loved the idea and together the three men quickly drafted a "preliminary call" for a conference of librarians on August 15. Leypoldt forwarded copies to several Boston librarians along with a cover letter signed by him and Dewey asking them to endorse the call. Bowker drafted another circular signed by Leypoldt, Dewey, L. E. Jones (manager of the *American Catalogue*), and William Isaac Fletcher to be sent with the preliminary call the next morning to prominent librarians all over the country.[5]

---

4. Dewey Diary, 4/18/76; 4/19/76; 4/20/76; 4/21/76; 4/22/76; 4/27/76 (quoting 4/20/76 letter from Cutter to Bureau of Education); 4/28/76; 4/29/76.

5. Dewey Diary 5/11/76; 5/12/76; 5/13/76; 5/16/76; 5/17/76. See also undated "Prospectus" for *LJ* in Box 29, Dewey Mss. Dewey describes his

At 4:00 P.M., Dewey went to Columbia College to attend the AMS meeting and was promptly elected to its Council. Toward the end of the meeting Dewey spoke convincingly about his plans to develop a bureau that would facilitate manufacture of metric appliances needed to introduce the system into America's educational establishment. In response, AMS President F. A. P. Barnard empowered a committee to compose a circular to elementary and secondary school officials expressing the Society's opinion "of the importance of having illustrations of the metric system placed in all schools."

Next morning Dewey returned to the *PW* offices. Leypoldt indicated he was not interested in a "bureau" for library supplies, but he did want to publish a library journal. Dewey said he could make no deal without first consulting Ginn, but he, Leypoldt, and Bowker did discuss terms if Ginn made no objection. Leypoldt said he wanted to own, print, and distribute the journal from New York, but that Dewey could become its Managing Editor in Boston. Except for rent, Leypoldt would cover all Dewey's office expenses connected with running the journal and pay Dewey $500 a year for his work, plus 20 percent of the journal's gross receipts.[6]

On May 19 Dewey met Eaton in Philadelphia. Eaton endorsed the idea of a library conference and offered to mail a conference call to librarians all over the country through Bureau offices. He also offered to include a prospectus on the library journal in the public libraries volume the Bureau planned to publish later that year. "I was greatly pleased at the interest he manifested," Dewey noted in his diary.[7] By May 22 Dewey was

changing business relationship with Ginn in *MB,* nos. 3&4 (9/76): 27. When William F. Poole, now director of the Chicago Public Library, received his call, he wrote Boston Public Library Director Justin Winsor that because it was "from a party in New York I did not know," he would withhold use of his name until he knew more about the matter. Most of the correspondence preceding the librarians' conference is reprinted in Edward G. Holley (ed.), *Raking the Historic Coals: The A.L.A. Scrapbook of 1876* (Pittsburgh, 1967), pp. 24–29. Holley carefully details the sometimes complicated chronology leading up to the conference. See also R. R. Bowker, "Library Journal and Library Organization: A Twenty Years' Retrospect," *LJ* 21 (1/96): 7–8.

6. Dewey Diary, 5/17/76; 5/18/76; *MB,* no. 7 (1/77): 107–9. A copy of the contract Leypoldt proposed to Dewey, dated 5/18/76, can be found in Box 64, Dewey Mss.

7. Holley, *Raking,* pp. 31, 34, 36; Dewey Diary, 5/19/76.

back in Boston, successfully persuading librarians at Harvard and the Boston Public to endorse the conference call. Several also agreed to join the new library journal's editorial board. But progress did not always go smoothly. On May 31 Poole, who still had not signed the conference call, told Winsor about a conversation Librarian of Congress A. R. Spofford had with Julius Seelye, who called Dewey "a tremendous talker and a little of an old maid."[8]

On June 3, after Ginn released Dewey from any obligation to publish a library journal under a Ginn imprint, Dewey formally accepted Leypoldt's offer and prepared the library journal prospectus for Eaton's report. He also asked Cutter to write Poole, who had still not signed the conference call. Two days later Cutter reassured Poole Dewey was "no imposter, humbug, speculator, dead beat, or anything of the sort." The ploy worked. Poole consented to use of his name, and the first printed call for a conference went out June 9, 1876. Other signers included Winsor, Cutter, Dewey, Eaton, John Langdon Sibley of Harvard, Reuben A. Guild of Brown, Lloyd P. Smith of the Library Company, and Henry A. Homes of the New York State Library.[9]

Dewey continued to work on his metric and library interests simultaneously. On June 8 he showed a friend a revised copy of an AMS circular about the metric bureau he was planning, then joined Putnam to discuss publication of his charts. Dewey also checked copyright and patent laws his bureau would have to follow for its publishing and manufacturing ventures, and convinced W. F. Bradbury and Putnam to join him in organizing it. All agreed to a meeting on June 17 to incorporate the bureau under Massachusetts laws.[10]

An active May and June were only prelude to an even more hectic July, when Dewey's specific plans for his educational reform interests took shape. Before discussing them, however, it is necessary to identify the three financial sources Dewey interlinked to launch and sustain his schemes. First, his family. Dewey had not been born to wealth, but because he was the last-born male child, he benefited more than his brother and sisters. By

---

8. Dewey Diary, 5/20/76; Holley, *Raking*, pp. 37–38; 41–44, 48–49.
9. Dewey Diary, 6/3/76; 6/5/76; Holley, *Raking*, p. 52. Poole quotes from Cutter's 6/5/76 letter in Poole to Dewey, 12/28/83, Box 1, Dewey Mss.
10. Dewey Diary, 6/5/76; 6/8/76; 6/10/76.

the summer of 1876 Manfred had successfully established himself in a profitable music store in Oneida. Thus, Dewey had two sources of collateral—his parents' money and his brother's business. Second, his friends. Because he had won Pratt's confidence in 1875, she offered investments worth $22,000 as collateral for Dewey's ventures. On June 10 she signed a note giving Dewey "entire control of all my money on bonds belonging to me." Third, his business associates. Because the money he could raise from collateral against investments made by family and friends still did not cumulate to significant sums, Dewey also had to rely on partners with capital, whom he invariably involved in contracts with complicated contingencies. For example, when he was initially hired by Ginn, the company provided him with office rent and expenses at 13 Tremont Place. After renegotiating his contract in late April, however, Ginn moved money allocated for Dewey's office rent to venture capital for Dewey's Metric Department. Dewey then shifted his obligation for office expenses to Leypoldt. As a result, by the end of June Dewey was ready to launch a Metric Bureau and journal out of an office being paid by Leypoldt for a library journal. Profits from sales of metric supplies to schools would be shared with Ginn. Leypoldt would reap no benefit from Dewey's metric interests.

But Dewey's plans were even broader than that. He also intended to establish "bureaus" for the manufacture and sale of library and spelling reform supplies, and to begin a journal for the latter. He planned to manage all his interests from his Boston office, and to link the accounts for each into a single set of books, thus allowing him to extend his limited financial base by shifting funds from one account to another as he deemed necessary. Most business contemporaries would have judged Dewey's methods irresponsible and reckless, but to an irrepressible reformer shunning personal gain who was intensely committed to education of the masses, their use seemed warranted. For Dewey, the ends— so noble, so altruistic—justified the means. And to gain those ends Dewey worked long hours, lived very frugally, and rolled back into his ventures almost all the money he earned. He was also convinced that his causes were so just anyone who scrutinized his activities would understand his motives, see his altruism, recognize his lack of desire for personal gain, and thus excuse or overlook unconventional business practices. In June of 1876 patterns generated by this blind spot were not yet evident to business associates.[11]

As the summer of 1876 progressed, Dewey turned his reform interests into more concrete shape. First came metric. On July 4 he incorporated the American Metric Bureau (AMB) and announced the forthcoming *Metric Bulletin.* The former would make available simple metric weights and measures like barometers, thermometers, and densimeters and instructional devices like conversion charts, the demand for which would inevitably accelerate in the wake of AMS "agitation" of legislative bodies and educational institutions to adopt the system. The *Bulletin* would bring together all news pertinent to the adoption of the metric system, including legislation and AMS and AMB transactions and announcements. He then appealed to every "friend" of the movement to join the AMB, subscribe to its *Bulletin,* and use its services.[12]

Dewey immediately pressed the cause. On July 8 he told the editor of a local magazine that the AMB was ready to supply "linear measures in the metric system." He also told Commissioner Eaton about the Bureau and expressed hope he would lend his name to an agency which sought no profits. To President Barnard he suggested the AMS plan a meeting on centennial grounds in Philadelphia about August 15, and offered to pay costs for a circular announcing the conference. Although he did not mention the librarians' conference, he did note spelling reformers planned to meet on the 15th, and he was sure they would be interested in metric reform. But Barnard balked; he preferred that the Society schedule its regular December meeting for Philadelphia instead.[13]

---

11. Evidence of Dewey's practice of using investments of family and friends as collateral for his ventures can be found in B. H. Williams to Dewey, 12/24/77, Box 34; Dewey Diary, 4/25/76; and in document dated 11/13/76 beginning, "I, Melvil Dewey, hereby acknowledge to have received from Mrs. S. F. Pratt . . ." Box 38, Dewey Mss. The 6/10/76 memo in which Pratt signed control of her financial matters over to Dewey can be found in Box 33. Dewey later commented in a 10/31/11 letter to his brother about the $20,000 he had "loaned" Edwin Ginn in 1877, Box 52.

12. *MB,* no. 1 (7/76): 3–9. See also circulars promoting the Metric Bureau in Box 66, Dewey Mss; and *MB,* no. 3&4 (9/76): 27.

13. Dewey to Editor, *Club* 7/8/76; Dewey to Eaton, 7/8/76; Dewey to Conkin, 7/8/76; Dewey to Barnard, 7/8/76, Box 29, Dewey Mss.

Second came spelling reform. Dewey was among delegates to an "International Convention for the Amendment of English Orthografy" in Philadelphia August 14–17 that was sponsored by the American Philological Association (APA). American spelling reformers, like spelling reformers in the English-speaking world in general, were a diverse lot. At one end of the spectrum were radicals convinced English would be much easier to learn if words were spelled phonetically. Often referred to as "cranks," they were attractive targets for nineteenth-century English-language purists who wanted no changes. At the other end were reformers looking for gradual change. They favored modifications like dropping the silent "e," using the "u" in any word with a long "u" sound (e.g., "thru" for "through"), and substituting "f" for "ph" (e.g., "orthografi" for "orthography"). Gradual reformers felt as intensely as radical reformers, but they believed a slower pace promised greater success.

At the conference, delegates predictably divided into several groups along a wide spectrum. Although Dewey identified with gradual reformers, he actively worked the conference to persuade attendees to support a bureau that would function as an information clearinghouse, issue a journal, and facilitate the manufacture of supplies, teaching devices, and books and pamphlets. He found a sympathetic audience; at the end of the conference several delegates agreed to form a Spelling Reform Association (SRA). Frederic March of Lafayette College was elected president, W. T. Harris, S. S. Haldeman, and W. L. Whitney vice presidents, and Dewey secretary. "Our spelling reform convention was a great success," Dewey wrote a friend later, "more than double what the most sanguine hoped." By mid-August, Dewey was handling SRA accounts.[14]

Third came libraries. The prospectus for a library journal Dewey drafted for the Bureau of Education report is illuminating for what Dewey hoped to accomplish through journal pages.

---

14. See Abraham Tauber, "Spelling Reform in the United States," (Ph.D. diss., Columbia University, 1958), pp. 34–35, 90–91; Frederic A. March, *The Spelling Reform* (Washington, 1893), pp. 16–17; Dewey to Wilson, 7/8/76; Dewey to W. N. Parker, 7/8/76; and Dewey to Leypoldt, 7/8/76, Box 29, Dewey Mss. See also entry for SRA for 8/21/76 in Dewey's account book, Box 97; copy of speech Dewey delivered to Efficiency Society in New York, 5/27/13, Box 40, Dewey Mss; and E. B. Burns, "Progress of Speling Reform," undated document found in the Library of Congress.

"The science of library management, and particularly that part of it which relates to the elevation of the tastes of readers, is yet but in its infancy," he said. The journal would accelerate the growth of that science in special ways. First, the journal would become a "medium of communication" so librarians could learn from each other's experiences. Second, emphasis would be not so much on identifying quality books as on methods for getting those books read. Third, the journal would also facilitate "early completion" of a new edition of *Poole's Index to Periodical Literature* (compiled by Poole as a Yale student in the 1840s) and effect "a national organization" dedicated to "bringing the libraries into intimate relations." Finally, Dewey forecast a library "bureau" that would "serve as a guide in selecting the best forms of the various library supplies." The "bureau" would also explore printing titles of new books "in such a way that they can be used for the catalogues of all libraries." Although these could be distributed to subscribing libraries at "slight expense," they would inevitably lead to "an immense saving of time" because each title would be cataloged only once. In effect, Dewey had turned a prospectus for a library journal into an outline for a library association and a library bureau, all three of which he believed would facilitate the development of uniform systems and increase efficiency. That, according to Dewey, was the function of a library science.[15]

By July 6 Smith, Winsor, and Poole had settled on October 4 through 6 for conference dates, and Smith had reserved rooms at the Pennsylvania Historical Society. Dewey forwarded one copy of the completed call to the Bureau of Education and sent a second copy to Leypoldt for the next issue of *PW.* He complained to Leypoldt that Winsor "gets me stuck for the dog's work," but vowed to see the conference through in order to boost the journal. Leypoldt worried about Dewey's single mailing address for all his reform interests, but Dewey told him he liked the setup because "it saves time often." Two days later he noted in his account book receipt of his $125 salary from Leypoldt for three months' work. It was the same book in which he recorded

---

15. Dewey to Winsor, 6/27/76, as found in Holley, *Raking,* pp. 75–76. Dewey's undated draft of a prospectus for a library journal is in Box 29, Dewey Mss. Points he raises in the draft suggest it was written 6/27 or 6/28/76.

accounts for business dealings with Ginn, the Spelling Reform Association, and the American Metric Bureau.[16]

On July 28 Dewey hosted the first AMB members' meeting at his Boston office. The six "directors" (including Cutter) who attended approved an organizational structure and adopted the constitution and bylaws Dewey had written. In mid-August Dewey sent out the first number of *Metric Bulletin,* which consisted of the AMB constitution and bylaws and a pitch for new members. Anyone was eligible, as long as he or she paid annual dues of $5.00. For that sum members would receive copies of all AMB publications, including its *Metric Bulletin.* For $25 individuals could become "honorary members"; for $50, life members. Money brought in by life memberships would be pooled into a "sinking fund" and used as collateral for funding the manufacture of articles needed to teach use of metric. Dewey wrote his altruism into bylaw nine: "No officer of this Bureau shall receive from its funds any compensation for his official services." As AMB corresponding secretary and treasurer, Dewey would draw no salary.[17]

Dewey then broadened his campaign for metric and spelling reform. In late August he handpicked two committees of twenty educators (consisting largely of state normal school principals and teachers who specialized in elementary teaching) because they were "most familiar with the problem." One studied metric, the other spelling reform. After a month, he later recalled, "they reported unanimusli" that if "we had scientific spelling and abolisht the absurdities of 'compound numbers' and used only international weits and mesures," the average child would save three to four years time between first grade and graduation from college.[18] Their reports became reference points for Dewey the rest of his life.

He also began contacting presidents of colleges and universities. To Daniel Coit Gilman of Johns Hopkins he wrote that the Bureau wanted to add Hopkins to its list of colleges endorsing metric adoption. Gilman replied that Hopkins would conform to

---

16. Correspondence dated 7/7/76 in Box 29, Dewey Mss. See also Holley, *Raking,* pp. 81–84; Dewey to Leypoldt, 7/8/76, Box 29; and entries for 7/10/76 and 11/7/76 in Dewey's account book, Box 97, Dewey Mss.

17. *MB,* no. 1&2 (8/76): 11–15; no. 3&4 (10/76): 27–28.

18. See Dewey to "Foundation Trustees," 9/3/28; copy of Dewey's opening statement to annual LPEF meeting, 7/28/30, LPEF Mss; copy of speech to Efficiency Society, 5/27/13, Box 10; Melvil Dewey, "What 80 years experience has taut me to believ," 12/-/31, Box 23, Dewey Mss.

the system of weights and measures then in use. Dewey pressed, ignoring the fact he was a little-known secretary of an organization only a month old. "We . . . wish you to do more." Several Amherst faculty were incorporating use of metric into their lectures, he said, and Amherst itself required knowledge of metric for admission. "We should like to announce . . . that the J. H. University required a knowledge of the metric system as a condition of admission."[19] It is not known if Gilman replied.

Much of September was spent preparing for the library conference. The first issue of the *American Library Journal* went out at the end of September and carried with it advance proofs of the conference program. Dewey predicted the conference would have several outcomes, "not the least" of which "should be the proposed national organization." The issue also carried an article by Dewey entitled "The Profession," which summarized his view of librarianship's potential. He noted the best librarians were "positive, aggressive characters" who stood "in the front rank of the educators of their community, side by side with the preachers and the teachers." Because people increasingly obtained their ideas and motivation from reading, and because "this influence may be wielded most surely and strongly through our libraries," librarians had a responsibility to make it easy for readers to elevate their reading tastes, and in the process teach them about prudent self-selection. "Children of the lower classes" who had to leave school for work at an early age often subsequently developed "bad reading" habits—a taste for dime novels and story papers. The library had to counter this by supplying reading "which shall serve to educate." Since the librarian was now "in the highest sense a teacher," Dewey concluded, "can any man deny to the high calling of such a librarianship the title Profession?"[20] The article reads much like a mid-nineteenth-century Protestant sermon.

---

19. Dewey to Gilman, 8/24/76; 8/30/76, Gilman Mss. See also Dewey to Fairbanks, n.d. (tr.), in which Dewey boasts how he "got 6 of Amherst faculty to join Bureau"; and Dewey to Prof. Coon of Alfred University, n.d. (tr.), Box 29, Dewey Mss.

20. *ALJ* 1 (9/76): 5–6. For a good summary of Dewey's ideology of reading, upon which his argument that librarianship is a profession was grounded, see Melvil Dewey, *Librarianship as a Profession for College-Bred Women: An Address before the Association of Collegiate Alumnae on March 13, 1886* (Boston, 1886). Dewey's design for the library profession easily fits the model Michael Denning outlines to link the dominant culture's desire to control working-class reading. See Denning's *Mechanic Accents: Dime Novels and Working Class Culture in America* (N.Y., 1989),

At 10:15 A.M. on October 4, in the center of the city the federal government had authorized to celebrate the nation's centennial, Boston Public Library Director Justin Winsor called the librarians' conference to order at the Historical Society of Pennsylvania. After preliminary courtesies, he invited a committee on organization to nominate officers for the conference. Results were not surprising. For the duration of the conference Winsor became president, Poole, Smith, Spofford, and James Yates (public librarian from Leeds, England) shared the office of vice president, and Dewey, Guild, and Charles Evans (librarian at the Indianapolis Public Library and one of Poole's protégés) shared the office of secretary. After the conference unanimously approved the nominations, Winsor took the chair and deferred to Smith's motion for the appointment of three committees—one on business, one on resolutions, and one on permanent organization. After the motion carried, Dewey announced that a representative from the Bureau of Education was en route from Washington with copies of the *Special Report on Libraries.* Smith then moved a conference recess until 3:00 P.M.[21] It had been a successful morning; Dewey's efforts were beginning to pay dividends.

When Winsor reconvened the meeting at 3:20, he introduced the scheduled section of the program. First up was Poole. Next to Winsor, Poole was the most prominent American librarian, in part because of the periodical index he had completed while a Yale student. Poole's demeanor was "bluff, hearty, breezy"; he also regularly chafed at New England dominance of the nation's developing library community, and he did not follow easily. He thought it more important to foster "the spirit" of library work than to emphasize its mechanics and techniques. Characteristics like these made clashes with an equally strong but reform-minded technocrat like Dewey probable. The fact that Poole also chewed tobacco, and on occasion smoked, made clashes predictable.[22]

---

pp. 47–50. See also Dee Garrison, *Apostles of Culture: The Public Librarian and American Society, 1876–1920* (N.Y., 1979), Chap. 4.

21. *ALJ* 1 (11/76): 90, 140; Poole to Dewey, 6/17/76, quoted in Holley, *Raking,* p. 61.

22. The portrait of Poole is drawn from William E. Foster, "Five Men of '76," *BALA* 20 (10/26): 314–16; James I. Wyer to Carl B. Roden, n.d., Roden Mss; and an unpublished "Autobiography" by John V. Cheney in Cheney Mss. See also *Proceedings, 1894,* 168; *1916,* 383; and William L. Williamson, *William Frederick Poole and the Modern Library Movement* (N.Y., 1963), pp. 48–49.

Poole's paper on fiction in libraries generated the "most earnest discussion" of the conference. He did not believe reading fiction would lead to immorality, irresponsibility, or reckless living. Once people made reading a habit, he argued, they would "elevate" their own reading tastes. Not everyone in the audience agreed. Most acknowledged that reading fiction influenced social behavior. Good fiction led to good behavior; bad fiction to bad behavior. No one argued about what good fiction was; they had come to know it (and the standards by which recently published works ought to be judged) through their classical college curricula. Defining and identifying bad fiction, however, presented a problem.[23] Conference attendees did not resolve the fiction question at Philadelphia, but the positions they took reflected the thinking of leading professionals at the time. Most agreed that the mass reading public was generally incapable of choosing its own reading judiciously. Public libraries had a responsibility to intervene for the benefit of society by acquiring and prescribing the best reading materials. This approach represented a significant break with the past when the librarian's societal role was merely to acquire and preserve. By adding a new dimension—advocating the efficient use of the carefully acquired quality collections under their care—librarians attending the conference placed themselves in the vanguard of their profession. Dewey, who had been uncharacteristically quiet during the discussion, wholeheartedly agreed with the premise on good reading and with the librarians' proactive attitude toward promoting it. All of it appealed to his reforming instincts and zealous nature.

From the touchy fiction question, conference speakers then passed to more practical issues. Discussions on cooperative indexing and especially Poole's *Index* led Dewey to move the appointment of a committee on the subject, and after that motion carried to move that the committee report a plan for cooperative cataloging. The rough outlines of a "library bureau" were surely on his mind. Success in both areas, he argued, would enhance general library efficiency, save time, and reduce costs. His motion passed unanimously. Later in the conference a committee on sizes of books issued a report to which Poole took exception. "I am not aware that we adopted all the points in the report . . . just read." Dewey quickly interjected that the missing points prob-

---

23. *Proceedings, 1876,* pp. 45–51, 98, 99.

LIBRARIANS' CONVENTION.

The Librarians of the City of Philadelphia request the pleasure of your company, on Friday Evening, Oct. 6, 1876, between the hours of 8 and 11, at the rooms of the Historical Society, No. 820 Spruce St.

PLEASE PRESENT THIS CARD AT THE DOOR.

After Dewey had played his part in founding the American Library Association in Philadelphia, conference guests spent an evening in "informal social intercourse, during which an elegant collation was served" (*American Library Journal*, Nov. 30, 1876).

ably had been agreed to when Poole "felt constrained to retire— shall I say it?—to smoke." The report was adopted, but the self-righteous and public way in which Dewey used his glib tongue and sharp wit to needle Poole left bad feelings.

The committee on permanent organization then reported a preamble to a still unwritten constitution. "For the purpose of promoting the library interests of the country, and of increasing reciprocity of intelligence and goodwill among librarians and all interested in library economy and bibliographic studies," the preamble stated, "the undersigned form themselves into a body to be known as the AMERICAN LIBRARY ASSOCIATION." Dewey signed first. Because conferees could not reach consensus on the constitution itself, however, Dewey moved that they "elect a board of Officers, and entrust the preparation of the Constitution and By-laws to them, in order that there may be full opportunity for discussion and comparison of views." A nominating committee reported Winsor as president, Poole, Spofford, and Homes as vice presidents, and Dewey as secretary and treasurer. Dewey would handle ALA accounts. Smith's motion to make the *American Library Journal* the new association's official journal was also adopted. Most of the remainder of the conference focused on

Dewey's decimal scheme, about which Dewey was reluctant to talk because of "the prominent part which I have had in calling this Conference." After a brief discussion of the system, he asked conferees to sign requests for copies of the *Special Report on Public Libraries,* which had arrived on October 5.[24]

The 1876 conference set the tone and direction of the American Library Association for the next fifteen years. The new breed of librarians, represented by Winsor, Poole, and Dewey, looked to create a missionary spirit among fellow professionals who believed that public exposure to good reading (as the dominant culture defined it) would inevitably lead to a better informed, more orderly society. While they marched forward with conviction, however, they failed to recognize they were also products of a socioeconomic and cultural value system in which they had been raised and educated. All ALA officers were white, Anglo-Saxon Protestant males born in the Northeast. Most were educated in northeastern schools; most were reared in middle- or upper-class families. The conference itself reveals several characteristics about leading members of the profession. Like Dewey, librarians were more concerned with practical and technical matters than with debating substantive philosophical questions. Except for Dewey they were hardly zealous reformers. For them, ALA served as a focus for a professional *esprit de corps* and a center for information exchange.[25]

At 25 Melvil Dewey was the baby of the group; significant differences with other ALA leaders can be found in his complex reform interests. While he certainly shared their belief in the power of reading and the educational mission of the library, he was convinced the best way to maximize the library's potential was to create relatively uniform collections of quality materials and increase service efficiency by standardizing internal library procedures with common forms, appliances, and rules and sys-

---

24. *Proceedings, 1876,* 106, 134, 140, 141. See also Melvil Dewey, "A Decimal Classification and Subject Index," in U.S. Bureau of Education, *Public Libraries in the United States of America: Their History, Condition and Management, Special Report, Part 1* (Washington, 1876), pp. 623–48.

25. The best discussion of the social ideals of early library leaders remains Garrison, *Apostles of Culture.* See especially Chap. 3. A more detailed demographic profile of ALA leaders is in my "American Library Association Executive Board Members, 1876–1917," *Libri* 31 (1981): 22–35.

tems of arrangement. Throughout the conference Dewey was the only prominent participant to focus on the needs of small public libraries which, he realized, stood to gain most from standardization and systematization. His Adams Center origins were obvious here. Small public libraries, he believed, had the greatest potential to meet the educational needs of "children of the lower classes" beyond the elementary school.

After the conference Dewey stayed in Philadelphia several days to tour Centennial grounds. He collected scores of metric samples, all of which he took back to Boston for an AMB directors meeting on the 9th, then returned to Philadelphia for an October 19 SRA meeting. By this time Dewey had manipulated the SRA to reflect his point of view. Although it accepted some connection with radical spelling reformers, gradual reformers controlled it. At the meeting, members voted to establish a "Committee on New Spellings" to monitor all changes in SRA publications. "Only such new spellings as could be changed once for all" would be approved, the motion stated. "The dead-weight of mere passive resistance is so enormous that a sudden complete overturning of the present orthography is simply hopeless." Other actions also demonstrated control by moderates. Members agreed to write newspaper, magazine, and professional journal editors to encourage adoption of simplified spelling, and to create SRA "branches" in order to permit organized groups of local reformers to pressure local print media.[26] The SRA was rapidly taking the shape of a "bureau."

By the middle of October 1876, after the last of the conferences he had organized adjourned, Dewey moved his offices to more spacious quarters at 1 Tremont Place where he continued to make every effort to tie all his reform interests together. Metric reform promised the most immediate success, in large part because it attracted influential members among scientific professions and educators adjusting to a rapidly industrializing capitalist economy. By mid-October Dewey had issued another number of the *Metric Bulletin* in which he reported the AMB board had invited 150 individuals to membership; sixty accepted. Thirteen took out life memberships, a number sufficient to warrant elec-

---

26. *MB*, no. 6 (12/76): 74; *BSRA*, No. 1 (4/77): 10–13. Changes recommended by the Committee on New Spellings were ultimately sanctioned at the SRA's first annual meeting in Baltimore in 1877.

tion of a board of trustees to take charge of the funds.[27] By the beginning of 1877 the AMB boasted a membership of 140, a metric collection of 323 items, and arrangements with several American manufacturers to produce necessary metric instructional devices. Dewey's plans for the future included creation of a series of metric sample depositories throughout the United States under the supervision of "persons having an intelligent interest in the matter." Here educators would find metric educational devices at reduced costs, in large part because the sinking fund would permit savings on volume purchases of materials.[28]

Dewey's efforts for metric reform assumed consistent patterns. He solicited new members, pushed periodicals and newspapers to publish information on metric, and encouraged college and universities to ease it into appropriate courses. By the end of 1877, he boasted, his office had sent out more than 500,000 circulars and placards to "nearly every township" in the United States and had set up depositories of sample collections in Ginn's New York, Philadelphia, and Chicago offices; he also bragged he had convinced the U.S. Post Office to commit to a standard-size 7.5 × 12.5-centimeter postcard. But Dewey was especially proud of the efficient way he managed AMB offices. "Every practical labor or money-saving device has been employed to make the most of our limited efforts and means," he told Bureau members in March, 1879. Office equipment included duplicating machines, an electric pen, and a typewriter. Office material included forty-five different circulars, thirty bulletins, and hundreds of pre-printed postcards used to respond to common inquiries. Dewey did not mention this equipment was also being used for the American Library and Spelling Reform Associations, and for both their journals.[29]

---

27. *MB,* no. 3&4 (9/76): 30, 35–38. See also Dewey to Barnard, n.d. (probably early in October); and Dewey to Brooks, n.d., Box 29, Dewey Mss. Because of subjects discussed, it is obvious the latter was sent between the conclusion of the SRA Conference in Philadelphia and the AMB meeting of 10/28/76.

28. *Supplement to the Metric Bulletin, November, 1876,* pp. 61–63; *MB,* no. 5 (11/76): 43, 47, 48, 53; no. 6 (12/76): 77–78; no. 7 (1/77): 111. For evidence of Dewey's plans for a depository in Chicago, see Dewey to Hazen, n.d. (tr.), Box 29, Dewey Mss.

29. *Proceedings,* AMB, I, p. 71; postcard dated 1877 soliciting new AMB members found in Box 66, Dewey Mss (Dewey probably sent this to

Despite successes, however, lack of capital continued to hamper progress on metric reform; for spelling reform the situation was even worse. SRA directors met in Dewey's office January 13, 1877; twenty-five new members were elected, then appealed to for money. Most of the meeting covered the proposed constitution, which looked very much like the AMB's. The constitution provided for a *Bulletin* to be issued by a Publications Committee. Dues were $1.00 per year; life membership $25.00. A bylaw provided that no change in orthography would be recommended for SRA publications without approval of the Committee on New Spellings. Dewey had made sure moderates would retain control. When the first number of the *Bulletin of the Spelling Reform Association* came out in April, Dewey invoked his exaggerated sense of timing. "Never before in the history of the language has there been so much promise of a reform in our orthography as at the present time," he said, and called upon *Bulletin* readers to capitalize on the momentum. "But there is one very serious obstacle to further progress—lack of means to pay the absolutely necessary expenses." Dewey's language and direction echoed the approach he took in the *Metric Bulletin,* but with spellers he added a touch of chauvinism— "to the English race" the "value" of spelling reform "cannot be over-estimated." All the SRA needed was money.[30]

He was more successful in his library efforts. Before conferees left Philadelphia in October 1876, they had authorized the executive board to draw up a constitution. Winsor, Poole, Spofford, Homes, and Dewey submitted the document on March 31, 1877. It was simple and straightforward—the way Dewey liked it. Article II stated ALA's object "shall be to promote the library interests of the country by exchanging views, researching conclusions, and inducing cooperation in all departments of bibliothecal science and economy; by disposing the public mind to the founding and improving of libraries; and by cultivating goodwill among its own members." ALA activities would thus be directed

---

anyone he was told might be interested in metric reform). See also Dewey circular to AMB membership, 11/15/77; A. E. Haynes (of *Hillsdale* [Mich.] *Standard*) to Dewey, 11/29/77; newspaper clipping from *Winstead* [Conn.] *Press* dated 12/13/77; *Boston Globe,* 12/28/77; and circular entitled "Our First Thousand Days," 3/27/79, Box 66, Dewey Mss.

30. *BSRA,* no. 1 (4/77): 1–2; 14–15. See also March, *The Spelling Reform,* (1893), p. 29.

toward improving library practice, not theory.[31] Article IV, Section 6, determined that a "Co-operation Committee shall consider and report upon plans designed to secure uniformity and economize in methods of administration." Dewey's footprints were all over this section.

An executive board of five would control ALA.[32] The president would appoint a nominating committee at the beginning of each conference; the committee would report a slate of five names for membership approval at the end of the conference. As a result of this practice, ALA leadership largely became a self-perpetuating body. Winsor and Poole seemed quite satisfied with this. Poole retained suspicions about "Eastern librarians," but found it easy to work with Winsor since both agreed ALA's mere existence manifested professional progress. Dewey, on the other hand, wanted to initiate cooperative schemes to systematize and make practical library routines more efficient. He also championed small libraries. While these differences occasionally surfaced at conferences, most ALA members seemed blissfully unaware of—or perhaps more accurately, indifferent to—opposing views. They probably recognized ALA needed Dewey's drive, energy, and free labor to survive an uncertain embryonic period; but they also probably believed ALA needed the stable leadership of scholar-librarians like Winsor and Poole who commanded respect both inside and outside the profession.

Undaunted, however, Dewey pushed his agenda from three positions he held—*ALJ* managing editor, ALA secretary, and secretary of an ALA Cooperation Committee he formed in the spring of 1877. Membership on the latter also included Cutter, Frederic Perkins, and Frederick Jackson of the Newton (Mass.) Public Library. Dewey hosted monthly meetings at his office. Initially,

---

31. The ramifications of this decision upon library graduate education and upon subsequent claims for a place for librarianship in the community of professions would not be felt seriously until the twentieth century. For a provocative analysis of the role that a theoretical body of knowledge plays in the historical development of a profession, see Magali Sarfatti Larson, *The Rise of Professionalism: A Sociological Analysis* (Berkeley, 1977), especially Chap. 4. For a more persuasive analysis, see Andrew Abbott, *The System of Professions: An Essay on the Division of Expert Labor* (Chicago, 1988).

32. "American Library Association," *ALJ* 1 (3/77): 253–54.

members were asked to "confine themselves to recommending good library appliances," leaving the role of supplying these appliances to others. And Dewey was ready to take advantage of any opportunity. For example, he reported in the April issue of *ALJ* that the committee had selected 5 × 12.5 cm as the catalog card's standard size. *ALJ* carried an advertisement for the stock, which could be ordered from Dewey's AMB offices; prices charged, the ad indicated, covered cost of production and shipping plus "a slight advance as a contingent fund belonging entirely to the Association and subject to its disposal."[33]

Then, on June 30, 1877, Dewey unilaterally turned the library portion of the supplies business he was running through Ginn over to ALA to create an ALA Cooperation Committee "Supply Department." So eager was he to accelerate his reform agenda he promised all profits to ALA and accepted all liabilities. Because of his willingness to sacrifice, he argued, the committee could now act as agent for ordering standard supplies from manufacturers, and he promised volume buying could effect significant savings. In late winter of 1878, Dewey persuaded ALA to remake the committee's supply department into an "ALA Supply Department" located at 32 Hawley Street in Boston, where he had recently moved his other reform interests. In effect, Dewey created another bureau, and like metric and spelling reform controlled it from a central office. But unbeknown to ALA, Supply Department accounts were entered into the same books as the AMB and SRA, and its funds combined into a single account solely controlled by Dewey.[34]

The ALA's first annual meeting was held in New York on September 4 and 5, 1877; sixty-six people attended. Because Dewey organized it, Winsor opened a conference that reflected the ALA secretary's overriding concern for practical matters. Topics arousing interest led conferees to establish committees to explore publishers' discounts to libraries, to exchange duplicate books between libraries, and to improve the distribution of pub-

33. *LJ* 1 (4/30/77): 284, 285; (5/77): 323–24, 433; (6/30/77): 365; (7/31/77): 396; (8/31/77): 432–33; 3 (7&8/79): 52, 286–87.

34. See entry for 6/30/77 in Dewey's account book, Box 97, Dewey Mss. See also Fremont Rider, *Melvil Dewey* (Chicago, 1944), pp. 63–64; *LJ* 3 (3/78): 2, 35; (4/78): 59–60; (5/78): 102, 113; (8/78): 222–23.

lished documents issued by the federal government. As chair of the standards committee, Dewey successfully established two sizes for indexing. One was called the "Harvard College" size— 5 × 12.25 cm, adopted from a system Ezra Abbott devised; the other the "P" or postal card size—7.5 × 12.5 cm. The latter was adopted as the standard size for a catalog card and became a fixture in librarianship. The *Journal* summarized the conference as "no less successful" than its immediate predecessor.[35] After the conference, many ALA members sailed to London for a meeting of British librarians that led to establishing the Library Association of the United Kingdom. En route Winsor took delight in writing his wife that Dewey was "playing his first game of cards," and that he had been "entrusted" to look after Wellesley College Librarian Annie Godfrey by her mother. But because he did not want others to know, Winsor said Dewey "pays little attention to her."[36]

Annie Godfrey, however, did pay particular attention to Dewey. She was born on February 11, 1850, in Milford, Massachusetts, where her father, Benjamin Davenport Godfrey, had established a shoe factory known for innovative use of laborsaving machinery. Her mother, Annie Roberts, who, like her husband, was very religious, was from a "respected" Philadelphia family. After graduation from Milford High School Annie Godfrey went to the Gannett Institute in Boston, then to Vassar. She left Vassar after her junior year to become Wellesley College's first librarian in 1875. Wellesley had been established in West Needham, Massachusetts, by Pauline and Henry Fowler Durant, who ten years earlier had converted to evangelical Christianity. Like other women's colleges established in the late nineteenth century, Wellesley was intended for "the serious, hardworking daughter of the middle class." Almost all of these daughters were white Protestants of Anglo-Saxon heritage. Annie Godfrey considered herself lucky. She was present at the creation of a unique insti-

---

35. *Proceedings, 1877*, 29, 35–49. The ALA Supply Department began selling stock in the latter size, but as it grew in popularity Boston stationers stole its market by buying up large quantities of uncut Harvard stock (20 × 25 cm) at half price, and then underselling the Supply Department by 10 to 20% after cutting it to "P" size. See Dewey to William Alcott, 1/16/31, Box 39, Dewey Mss. See also *ALJ*, 2 (9/77): 4.

36. *LJ* 2 (10/77): 221; Winsor to Mrs. Winsor, 9/9/77, Winsor Mss.

tution, and she became imbued with the evangelical sense of
mission permeating its corridors.[37]

Annie Godfrey had been interested in Dewey's new decimal
scheme since assuming her position, and on several occasions
wrote him about it. She also had attended the 1876 conference,
where they probably discussed professional matters of mutual
concern. Thereafter the two struck up a correspondence and, on
occasion, Dewey would ride out to Wellesley for visits. Annie
later recalled "that summer day when we thought it would help
us to be friends" and how Dewey's "purpose and devotion to your
life work was firm and strong. It called forth more of admiration
and respect from me than I had felt for any man." Like Dewey,
Godfrey was a child of the WASP evangelical middle class which
regarded activism as a responsibility; like Dewey, she found in
education and libraries appropriate vehicles for that activism. By
August 1877, Godfrey was addressing Dewey as "Melvil" in her
letters.

In Annie Godfrey, Dewey sensed a willing partner for educational reform. Their courtship centered around long but infrequent conversations during which Melvil waxed eloquent about
his causes. He lamented waste and inefficiency and noted how
spelling reform and metric adoption would reduce by three years
the time required for an elementary education. He praised the
potential of the public library to build upon this elementary education and become the chief informal educational institution for
the masses if only the library community could agree on basic
collections of the best reading, common cataloging rules, and a
single classification scheme. He also talked of plans for establishing a library school. To all this Godfrey listened with rapt attention. She recognized his leadership, thought him charismatic,
and was very attracted to his intensity and his irrepressible spirit
of reform. His reform goals became her reform goals. Both advocated Christian love, humility, self-control, the Golden Rule, and

---

37. See Florence Morse Kingsley, *The Life of Henry Fowler Durant*
(N.Y., 1924), p. 328, as quoted in Helen Lefkowitz Horowitz, *Alma Mater:
Design and Experience in the Women's Colleges from Their 19th Century
Beginnings to the 1930s* (N.Y., 1984), pp. 85, 147, 155. See especially Chap.
3 for brief background of the origins of Wellesley. The best biographical
sketch of Annie Dewey is Emma H. Gunther, "Annie Godfrey Dewey,
February 11, 1850–August 3, 1920," *Journal of Home Economics* 15 (7/23):
357–69.

a sense of duty wrapped tightly in a concept of lifelong service to humankind. Both were more concerned with Christian ethics than dogma, and both were more interested in improving the lot of humankind upon earth than in preparing for the hereafter. Both had intense faith in the work ethic, and both were convinced that the proper and efficient utilization of existing resources would effect longer lasting and more beneficial reform for the masses than class struggle or the adoption of socialism. Progress for all would come through reform, not revolution.

Both shared another reform vision. In late nineteenth-century America, members of the middle class worried that problems brought by immigration and industrialization might tear the social fabric and usher in the breakdown of order. In response, scores of new professions (such as librarian) were established, and the mostly middle-class WASPs rushing to fill their ranks worked long hours at low pay, often under significant stress. Melvil and Annie worried that these professionals (and especially educators) needed opportunities to rest, recreate, and rejuvenate in a carefully run community located in rural (and preferably sylvan) surroundings that not only reflected but also exemplified values they held so dear. They planned eventually to establish a model community that would function as a laboratory where underpaid middle-class reformers like themselves could observe the benefits of efficiency and order and enjoy the positive effects of healthy activity in a clean environment, and they committed themselves to vacation a part of each summer in resorts around the country that offered some promise for permanently locating the model community they intended to establish.[38] When Dewey

---

38. It is tempting to view the Deweys' plans as envisioning a utopian community, and there is much about them that would suggest close parallels. For three good discussions of the ideological frames in which many late-19th-century utopian schemes were launched, see Edward K. Spann, *Brotherly Tomorrows: Movements for a Cooperative Society in America, 1820–1920* (N.Y., 1989); Robert S. Fogarty, *All Things New: American Communes and Utopian Movements, 1860–1914* (Chicago, 1990), and Howard Segal, *Technological Utopianism in American Culture* (Chicago, 1985). Their views, however, do not accommodate the purpose for which Melvil and Annie were planning their community. They wanted to establish a vacation "home," a place to which low-paid middle-class professional reformers could come only temporarily and at low expense for rest and idea exchange. These professionals were fully expected to return to their work, better prepared to effect their social reforms. Over the years Dewey made

finally asked Annie to marry him, she realized he was also asking her to become partner in a crusade for causes to which he had dedicated his life.

Annie Godfrey and Melvil Dewey were married on October 19, 1878. For Dewey it meant he "married up" on the social scale. The Godfrey family had more education and money than his; and Annie's connections to her parents' money allowed Dewey to expand the collateral against which he could borrow for his reform schemes. After a brief honeymoon, they moved in with Annie's parents. Annie took a position at the Harvard College Library, but spent much time indexing periodicals for the forthcoming edition of *Poole's Index*. Shortly after they were married Dewey's mother urged Annie to check Melvil's propensity to "tax himself." To Melvil she wrote, "I suppose you sleep alone. You always told me if you had a wife you should sleep alone."[39]

Dewey continued his duties as managing editor of *American Library Journal* (renamed *Library Journal [LJ]* after the London conference), but things were not going well; *LJ* lost $1,100 its first year of operation. By late 1878 Bowker felt compelled to cut expenses by insisting *LJ*'s business management be returned to New York. Dewey reacted sharply. On January 8, 1879, he threatened to start an "opposition journal" with the help of "leading men of ALA" from Boston unless *Journal* publishers gave him a more favorable contract. Bowker bristled. *LJ* could not continue to duplicate expenses at Dewey's Boston

---

repeated references to the plans he and Annie made in 1878 to someday establish the Lake Placid Club community, which will be discussed in subsequent chapters. See, for example, "Lake Placid Education Foundation," undated address given before the Lake Placid Club, LPEF Mss; *Club Notes*, no. 161 (4/25): 1275; Dewey to "Foundation Trustees," 9/3/28, LPEF Mss; Dewey to "5 town commissioners, clerk and attorney," 5/22/31, Box 44, Dewey Mss; "80th Birthday letr," 12/10/31, copy found in Wyer Mss. For another point of view on the origins of the Deweys' ideas for Lake Placid, see Dierdre C. Stam, "Melvil and Annie Dewey and the Communitarian Ideal," *Libraries & Culture* 24 (1989): 123–45.

39. The Deweys' rent receipts for 1878 and 1879 are in Box 31; their marriage certificate in Box 19, Dewey Mss. See also Eliza Dewey to Annie and Melvil, 11/29/78, Box 29, Dewey Mss. Although it may be impossible to determine if they slept together during the early years of their marriage, records show that by 1889 they were sleeping in separate bedrooms. See account books, FPA.

office for services which could just as easily be covered at Bowker's New York office, he said, and if Dewey persisted, he would show Cutter and Winsor Dewey's January 8 letter. Bowker fully recognized that Dewey was using his ties with ALA to press *LJ* into keeping its business management in Boston. What he did not realize, however, was how closely Dewey had tied all of his reform interests to his Boston office, how tenuously the whole structure balanced on money Dewey had interlinked into a single account, and how threatened that structure became when any one component was removed.[40]

The incident demonstrates a set of circumstances that would have a significant impact on ALA for years. Since October 1876, Dewey had served as the link between ALA and *LJ*. On the one hand, he used *LJ* columns as a forum to keep his ideas of expanded library cooperation and efficiency before the eyes of the nation's library community. He also used its advertising sections for marketing AMB and SRA products, but instead of paying for that space, Dewey "traded" it with advertising space in the *Metric* and SRA *Bulletins*. No money exchanged hands; the value of the trades occurred entirely in the columns of Dewey's account books. That spelling reformers and metric reform advocates might not be the most promising market for *LJ* subscriptions did not seem to bother Dewey; in his mind all these activities were part of a large game plan he ran from his "bureaus" in Boston. And since he was not after material gain he could not understand that some people might consider his motives suspect. Still, Dewey had no reservations about harnessing his ALA ties to evoke a better financial deal with *LJ,* and using that money to shore up the educational reform empire he was trying to piece together in Boston. By mid-January 1879, as both the ALA executive board and *LJ* publishers saw more and more evidence of Dewey's involved machinations, their willingness to trust him began to diminish. If Dewey recognized this changing situation, he did little to regain lost ground.[41]

ALA limped along for most of 1877 and 1878 with mixed success. Dewey had three particular pet schemes he was push-

---

40. Bowker to Dewey, 1/9/79, Bowker Mss. See also Bowker to Cutter, 1/13/79; Bowker to Winsor, 1/15/79, Bowker Mss.

41. See, for example, Bowker to Winsor, 6/16/79, Winsor Letters, *LJ*/RC; and Leypoldt to Bowker, 7/1/79, Bowker Mss.

ing. First, he encouraged ALA's committee on uniform entries to develop a plan for issuing preprinted slips which publishers could use to advertise their books and which Dewey hoped librarians could use to attach to catalog cards. Second, he suggested that ALA develop a collection guide of 10,000 annotated titles recommended for any type of library. In response, the ALA cooperation committee began work on an annotated guide, but decided to narrow its scope to 5,000 titles, arrange entries in a subject classification, and ask for a guarantee against loss by soliciting advance subscriptions of $2.50. Third, Dewey pressed the ALA "Supply Department" to expand its vision, but met lethargy at every turn. In its first year the department generated less than $300 in sales. Some ALA members came to refer to its products as "Dewey's gimcracks."[42] Ultimately, Dewey could not wait for ALA to catch up with his vision. In March 1879, he decided to pull the Supply Department out of ALA and start a whole new organization—the Readers and Writers Economy Company.

By that time, however, Dewey could look back two and a half years to an impressive series of accomplishments. He had helped start three associations and four journals, and continued to play a central role in each. He had also published a classification scheme libraries across the country were seriously considering for adoption. Finally, he had married a soulmate who promised to be a productive partner in all his reform causes. Things looked bright for the immediate future.

---

42. Dewey comments on references to his "gimcracks" in a speech dated 5/17/13, copy of which is in Box 40, Dewey Mss.

3

"Dui" in Business for Himself

1879–1883

The Readers and Writers Economy Company
1879–1881

To provide a financial foundation for the Readers and Writers Economy Company (RWEC), Dewey raised the money by borrowing against Mrs. Pratt's estate and investments Annie's parents had made for her. He also convinced F. B. Perkins and Cutter to invest, suggesting to the latter they might unite their classification ideas and market the results through RWEC offices. Finally, he convinced Frederick Jackson to invest $10,000 for an equal share of RWEC stock and made him treasurer. The move reunited in RWEC all members of the original ALA Cooperation Committee. Dewey served as manager of the company and owned $10,000 of the $25,000 worth of stock.

The agreement that Dewey drafted with Jackson called upon both parties to "loan" all dividends and salary back to the company at 8 percent interest, and specified that all receipts from the ALA, AMB, SRA, and *LJ* "be shared equally with Jackson by direct payment" into the RWEC treasury. Dewey would, "if necessary," be permitted to withdraw up to $300 from *LJ* and Metric Bureau accounts "to meet living expenses." Jackson was guaranteed a salary of at least $1,500 per year as treasurer, and Dewey agreed to take no more "than $3,500 per year including all commissions on subscriptions and advertising for the *Library Journal.*" Jackson also agreed to loan the RWEC another $2,350; in return Dewey pledged thirty-five original and twelve preferred AMB life memberships as collateral.[1] So far as is known, neither Dewey nor Jackson ever informed other affected parties about these arrangements.

Business grew rapidly. By late May Dewey had moved to larger quarters at 32 Hawley Street and by early June removed partitions between rooms 6, 7, and 8 to create one big Economy Company office to accommodate all his reform interests. On June 10, he presided over the first meeting of the RWEC Board of Directors. Those present included Dewey, Perkins, and Herbert E. Davidson, a Ginn employee who had been attracted to Dewey's spelling and metric reform schemes.[2]

While setting up the RWEC, Dewey did not neglect other interests. In fact, he continued to mix them together. He insisted, for example, that ALA report his comments and speeches in its official proceedings in simplified spelling; he did the same with AMB circulars sent out over his name. Many complained, but Dewey persisted. In spring, he conceived the ALA motto—"The best reading for the largest number at the least expense"—and planned to submit it for approval at the summer conference. He forewarned Winsor in mid-June, however, that except for the cooperation committee, others "are not doing anything."[3]

He was right. When Winsor opened ALA's second annual conference on June 30, 1879, most committees reported little or no progress. Cutter reported the cooperation committee's decision to transfer the "stock and goodwill" of the ALA Supply Department to the Readers and Writers Economy Company, but the subject that received most attention was a symposium on

1. "Readers and Writers Economy Co.," Dun Collection, MA 80/p. 358. Dewey's contract with Jackson, dated 5/8/79, Box 81; "Promissory Note," 5/7/79, Box 61; "Agreement Made at Boston," 5/8/79, Box 81; Dewey to K. A. Eichorn, 1/23/25, Box 29, Dewey Mss. See also Dawe to W. P. Cutter, 7/7/32, Box 27, for Dawe's summary of Cutter's involvement with the RWEC; and *Library Bureau Catalog* for 1882 and 1883.

2. "A New Century Notion: - And a Good One," *The Paper World* (7/80): n.p.; from clipping found in Box 64; "Minutes," 6/10/79, RWEC, Box 61, Dewey Mss.

3. *LJ* 3 (4/78): 43–44; (7/78): 186; *PL* 11 (3/06): 55; Dewey to Winsor, 6/14/79, Winsor Letters, *LJ*/RC. For AMB spelling reform practices and complaints, see Dewey to Charles H. Swan, 10/31/79, Box 69, Dewey Mss.

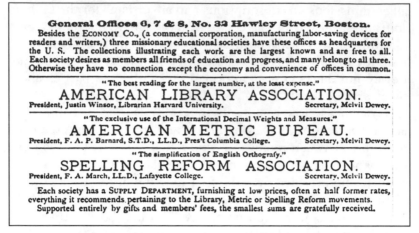

Dewey lumped his three enterprises on one business card, just as he lumped together their accounts.

fiction and children's reading. As in 1876, conferees could not agree on a consistent policy concerning fiction in public libraries. Cutter summed up the problem accurately in his report to the *Nation.* "There is, in fact, no single remedy."[4]

The conference adjourned on July 2, and except for *Poole's Index* and the adoption of Dewey's motto, ALA was not much closer to goals Dewey had set for it in 1876 and 1877. In fact, he had taken the "bureau" out of the ALA, and the *ALA Catalog* was making no progress. On October 15, the executive board announced $1,207 had been pledged to develop the *Catalog.* At Dewey's prompting the board appointed Frederic Perkins editor. What Dewey did not tell the board, however, was that he deposited *Catalog* money in RWEC accounts, and from that source advanced Perkins $350 for his work. By that time Perkins was a full-time RWEC employee. On January 24, 1880, Perkins announced a provisional list of 5,000 books would be subdivided by subject and soon sent "to the best authorities for revision and annotation." On February 23 he issued a circular inviting special-

---

4. *Proceedings, 1879,* 282, 286–87, 289, 300, 303. Cutter's report to *The Nation* is reprinted in full in *LJ* 4 (7–8/79): 311–12. The transfer of the ALA Supply Department stock to Dewey's Readers and Writers Economy Company is explained more fully in Francis L. Miksa, "Melvil Dewey and the Corporate Ideal," in *Melvil Dewey: The Man and the Classification,* ed. Gordon Stevenson and Judith Kramer-Greene (Albany, 1983), pp. 80–91.

ists to participate. That summer, however, he became director of the San Francisco Public Library and work on the *Catalog* ceased.[5]

Metric and spelling reform fared slightly better. In the spring of 1878, J. P. Putnam and Edward Wigglesworth agreed to loan AMB's sinking fund $7,000 in return for a mortgage on the entire stock of AMB's Supply Department. Dewey used the money to accelerate Bureau promotional activities, which he subsequently reported in a memo entitled "Our First Thousand Days" sent to AMB members March 27, 1879. (He did not mention RWEC in the memo, even though the AMB and RWEC shared an office address.)[6] The SRA welcomed formation of the RWEC, in large part because Dewey offered "to furnish, free ov al charges, ofis accomodashuns for the S.R.A. at least for the yer 1879." In return, Dewey asked that Jackson be made SRA treasurer in order to coordinate all SRA work and accounts in one office. The SRA board agreed.[7] In the fall of 1879, Dewey convinced others to invest in RWEC, including Wigglesworth, Herbert Coolidge, William Nichols, and Thomas Bicknell; Dewey was particularly pleased to recruit Bicknell because of his connections to four education journals in which the RWEC could cross-advertise.

December 10, 1879, was a significant day in Dewey's life. On his twenty-eighth birthday he officially changed the spelling of his last name to "Dui" and incorporated the SRA in Connecticut and the ALA in Massachusetts.[8] He also incorporated the

---

5. *LJ* 4 (11/79): 404; 5 (1/80): 77. Dewey's disposition of ALA funds will be discussed later, but for evidence of his arrangement with Perkins, see the latter's note to Dewey, 3/19/81, Box 1, Dewey Mss.

6. See mortgage agreements between Putnam, Wigglesworth, and the AMB in Box 66; copy of Wigglesworth "To My Executor," 5/27/78, Box 68; and document entitled "Our First Thousand Days," Box 66, Dewey Mss. See also *Proceedings, AMS, II,* pp. 14–15, 47.

7. See Dewey "To board of Officers of the S.R.A.," n.d., Box 87, Dewey Mss. See also E. B. Burns, "Progress of Speling Reform"; and *BSRA* no. 14 (9/79): 1–9.

8. Incorporation, Dewey said, would (1) give the association a "permanence and dignity not to be secured under our present organization"; (2) allow ALA to "hold property legally and without taxation . . ."; (3) permit ALA to become an individual under the laws, thereby eliminating the liability of members reluctant to undertake cooperative schemes like the ALA Catalog without legal protection; and (4) encourage contributions from "the wealthy quarter" of society. *LJ* 4 (12/79): 443. See also newsclipping

RWEC as a joint stock company, assumed the position of president, and capitalized it at $100,000 by dividing 4,000 shares at $25.00 each. Stockholders included Dui (800), Jackson (800), Cutter (20), W. J. Watson (200), Coolidge (100), and Nichols (100). Bicknell was also credited for 40 shares, but payment would come in the form of advertising in the four journals he controlled.

Dui claimed RWEC as sole manufacturers of four hundred "improved devices for desk, study and library" designed "to save time, money and labor." He included among his stock the Economy Book Support, the Economy Study Table, the Economy Eye Shade, and the Economy Sloping Book Case, the Harvard Book Rack, the Reader's Readyrest Perfect Vacuum Inkstand, the Reader's Cot Chair; the Noyes Dictionary Holder, metric rubber bands, and "all supplies recommended by the American Library Association." RWEC also acted as sole agents for the A. T. Cross Stylographic Pen, Russell's Common-Sense Revolving Book Cases, and Clark's Book Rests, and claimed status as special agents for student lamps, hand stamps, and ventilating stoves. The RWEC showroom was located at 27 Franklin Street in Boston, but the company also had distribution offices in New York and Chicago. By February 1880 RWEC opened a second salesroom in New York; in late April it had a payroll of 120 and major manufacturing contracts with factories in Albany and Boston, and in late May it opened a third salesroom in Chicago.

Because the company was growing and changing so rapidly, its financial status became confused. Dui was not sure how much he ought to be compensated for services rendered as RWEC president since December 10, 1879. To clarify the situation, on April 14 he asked the board to fix his salary as president and determine the value of his RWEC investments. On May 5 he told the board he wanted to resign as RWEC treasurer, in part because he was overburdened with work, in part because the RWEC looked too much like "a one-man operation." The board accepted his resignation at a subsequent meeting, and to clarify Dui's compensation and RWEC investments on May 12 appointed a "Committee on Past Salary" consisting of Coolidge, Nichols, and Bicknell.

---

dated 1/10/80 (noting SRA incorporation) in Box 87; Dewey, "A Personal Note about Spelling," Box 88, Dewey Mss; and Dawe, *Dewey;* pp. 177–78. I will use "Dui" in the text until he changed back to its original spelling in 1883.

When Bicknell took an extended trip later that summer Wigglesworth replaced him on the committee.[9]

RWEC successes affected metric and spelling reform. On the one hand, Dui convinced the AMB to let the RWEC assume control of the sales and distribution of the entire stock of the Bureau's Supply Department. He then convinced Putnam and Wigglesworth, who held the mortgage against those supplies, to trade it for RWEC stock of equal value. After striking these agreements, Dui then took control of AMB supplies, listed Putnam and Wigglesworth as RWEC stockholders, recorded the sale of stock in RWEC books, and deposited AMB supplies income in RWEC bank accounts. On the other hand, Dui was too busy to attend the summer 1880 joint APA-SRA meeting. March later wrote that "we mist you . . . a good deal," and told Dui that because he was preoccupied elsewhere, the SRA had decided to transfer responsibility for dues collection from Dui to Thomas Vickroy in St. Louis. "When you ar a millionaire and cease to worry day and night about the [RWEC] machinery, you can giv spelling reform a great lift," he closed cheerfully.[10]

His RWEC responsibilities did not seem to affect his library interests, however. In fact, his connection to ALA grew stronger. When Frederick Jackson became ill in 1879, Dui agreed to temporarily replace him as ALA treasurer; as a result he assumed responsibility for ALA funds. Dui then made a note to himself: "A.L.A. *money.* This money has been paid in directly . . . and deposited to the credit of the Economy Company. It may be some time before the Society will require it and in the meantime I am willing to let it remain in the treasury to help out the bank account."[11] His relationship with *LJ,* however, continued to deteriorate. Before Bowker left for England to become a London correspondent for *Harper's* in June 1880, he got Leypoldt to agree to suspend publication of *LJ* and consolidate it with *PW.* When

---

9. For listing of RWEC products, see RWEC letterhead stationery, Box 61, Dewey Mss. See also RWEC minutes for 1/28/80; 2/11/80; 3/10/80; 5/5/80; and 5/12/80, Box 61, Dewey Mss; and Eaton to Dui, 1/9/80, LCE-NA. The *New York Independent* described the RWEC in a 5/-/80 issue. See also Amherst College, "Chronicles of '74," p. 16–17.

10. March to Dui, 9/25/80, Box 83, Dewey Mss. Copy of renegotiated "Agreement with Putnam and Wigglesworth about Metric Mortgage" in Box 66.

11. Note is undated, but found in Box 61, Dewey Mss.

Leypoldt made the announcement, however, the library community deluged him with protests and forced him to recant. Bowker was angry and suspected Dui had been instrumental in the campaign. Not so, Leypoldt wrote later. "Dui had no hand in this." Leypoldt's wife was less charitable. "I never believed in the *Library Journal,* because I knew it would not pay and I thought Dewey about as miserable a specimen of a gabbling idiot as I had ever beheld."[12]

Fall brought more problems for Dui. As the RWEC's Committee on Past Salary began to go over the books in September, members discovered what Dui had been doing to its accounts. Cash from the SRA, ALA, and AMB memberships ran in and out of a central RWEC account. So did the AMB sinking fund, which Wigglesworth knew was heavily collateralized. Money taken in from AMB Supply Department sales also came through the RWEC account, and for a period of time so did *LJ* subscriptions. Some things were confusing. Dui was editor of *LJ, MB,* and *BSRA;* he advertised in each, but instead of paying advertising costs directly he recorded paper transfers between journals. For example, he often located advertisements for AMB supplies in *LJ* pages, then advertised *LJ* in *MB* pages. No cash passed hands, but Dui still recorded it as income for each journal. Finally, the matter of office supplies, personnel, space, postage, distribution, and inventory was a mess. The committee could not determine who owned what, who was paying for what services, or which personnel had responsibilities for which of the organizations connected to Dui through his interlocking secretaryships. Because RWEC books were so complicated, committee members decided to hire an outside accountant to figure them out. They did not, however, tell Dui.

When the accountant submitted findings that confirmed the committee's suspicions in early October, the committee quickly reported their investigation to RWEC directors, and the directors decided to take immediate action to protect their interests. On the morning of October 11, 1880, Wigglesworth, Coolidge, and Cutter visited a local judge to ask for an injunction against Dui. In their complaint, they noted Dui credited himself with 2,684 shares of RWEC stock but did not have the capital to back it up.

---

12. *LJ* 5 (7–8/80): 207–8; (9–10/80): 248–49; Leypoldt to Bowker, 8/11/80; and Augusta Leypoldt to Bowker, 9/18/80, Bowker Mss.

They said they were forced to ask for an injunction because Dui's majority control would allow him to block any move against his control of the corporation, and they needed an independent audit to figure out RWEC books. Until that audit was complete, they argued, Dui ought to be denied access to RWEC accounts and prevented from incurring any debts. The judge agreed, and granted the injunction.

That afternoon, at a regularly scheduled RWEC directors meeting, the committee surprised Dui by presenting him with the accountant's report and serving him with the injunction. Dui was caught off guard, and insulted at finding that his motives were suspect. He felt he had no choice but to resign as president and director of RWEC, both of which were unanimously and immediately accepted. Wigglesworth and Coolidge were then elected president and treasurer, and a motion approved to hire an attorney to submit the RWEC case against Dui to arbitration. The directors also told their lawyer to open any mail addressed to Dui "through our box." The accountant's report had shown that orders and correspondence concerning Economy Company products were just as likely to be addressed to Dui personally or to Dui as secretary of the ALA, AMB, or SRA.[13] Again the board approved unanimously.

Dui was hurt by their action. For the next two months he put on a public front of resilience and combativeness, but in private manifested strains of emotional instability. On the evening of his resignation he drafted a circular "To my business and educational friends." In it he announced he had severed ties with RWEC, and asked his readers from henceforth to send all non-RWEC communications to another Boston address. His intention was clear. If RWEC directors were going to dismiss him, he would take all business generated by his reform interests with him. He especially mentioned his secretaryships of ALA, AMB, and SRA, his editorship of *LJ,* and concluded "It is with intense pleasure that I shall resume my old activities in pushing forward the interests which . . . for the past year, have gone on simply by their own momentum."[14]

---

13. The "complaint" of the committee, the injunction of the judge, and the minutes of the 10/11/80 RWEC meeting are in Box 61, Dewey Mss. See also Nichols to Winsor, 12/27/80, copy found in Box 81, Dewey Mss.

14. Copy of the circular found in Wyer Mss.

Understandably, however, Dui's "interests" resisted. The injunction against him froze their accounts. On October 14 Barnard wrote Dui (through Davidson) that the AMB board would meet on the weekend to discuss "the financial status and management of the Bureau." On October 19 Putnam asked Dui to stop by his office for information on the AMB sinking fund. Samuel Green, chairman of the ALA finance committee, was more forthright. "I shall await the results of the investigations with great interest." Frederick Leypoldt, who had been subjected to Dui's "clogging business complications" for four years, had already decided. ". . . your peculiar way of doing business has cost this office more in time than all that you claim could amount to." At the end of the contract year, he said, Dui would be dropped as *LJ* editor.[15]

For the remainder of October Dui tried to control the damage. He portrayed (and probably believed) himself an advocate for educational reforms against profit-driven RWEC directors who had forced his resignation. He could not understand how anyone associated with these organizations could question the purity of his motives. After all, had he not committed his time, energy, and talents—indeed his very life—to unselfishly improving education for the masses? Had he not demonstrated his altruism in the publications, constitutions, and bylaws of all affected organizations? That was the logic he used with Cutter in an October 15 letter. When the facts were all known, Dui wrote, he would be vindicated and Cutter would apologize for acting in concert with RWEC directors on the injunction.[16]

Despite the public bravado, however, privately Dui was stymied and harried. His freedom to move was blocked by his inability to access RWEC accounts. At first he looked for alternatives. On October 21 he asked Nichols for AMB membership lists. Nichols refused, so Dui asked Barnard to transfer certificates of AMB memberships to his control. When Barnard agreed, Dui immediately borrowed against the certificates to pay AMB Supply Department bills. Sometimes his actions were silly. On November 11 he asked Biscoe about a $12.00 debt. "The 2 yrs. interest

15. Postcard, Barnard per Davidson to Dui, 10/14/80, Box 66; Putnam to Dui, 10/19/80, Box 66; Green to Dui, 10/25/80, Box 7; Leypoldt to Dui, 10/4/80; 10/7/80, Box 1, Dewey Mss.

16. Dui to Cutter, 10/15/80, Box 81, Dewey Mss.

1.44 you may disregard if you can send me the 12.00 . . . this week." He also tried to charge Perkins interest on the $350 advance for work on the *ALA Catalog,* but Perkins refused.[17] In late October, Dui seemed near a breaking point. "I can't stand this," he wrote Wigglesworth on the 22nd. "My wife joins me in throwing ourselves entirely in your hands."

By that time Dui's reform organizations were beginning to respond to his situation. On November 20 the AMB authorized Vice President Bradbury to re-execute the $5,000 mortgage extended to the sinking fund by Putnam and Wigglesworth. Dui was not consulted, just informed. ALA also moved quickly. When Dui did not appear at an ALA executive board meeting December 5, the board accepted a resignation he had not tendered and empowered Green to take control of ALA funds and books. On the 11th Winsor also ordered finance committee member James L. Whitney to retrieve all ALA supplies, books, and funds from Dui's possession, and on the 21st told postal authorities that all correspondence to ALA or its secretary should be delivered to Whitney instead of Dui. Dui protested, but to no avail. "We argue to no purpose," Winsor replied.[18]

The arbitration process itself was contentious, in large part because Dui wavered between bravado and begging while attempting to represent himself in negotiations. After he retained legal counsel, progress finally accelerated, and Dui and the RWEC settled on January 10, 1881. For his part, Dui agreed to clear all claims against RWEC from business associates and professional organizations he represented. For its part the RWEC agreed to

---

17. Dui to Barnard, 10/25/80, Box 61; Barnard to Dui, 10/26/80, Box 66; Dui to Jackson, 10/19/80, Box 61; Jackson to Dui, 10/23/80, Box 31A, Dewey Mss; Dui to Biscoe, 11/21/80, Wyer Mss. Biscoe returned a check for $13.44, and asked curtly if he owed Dui any other money. Dui expressed surprise at "the tone of yr letter." See Dui to Biscoe, 11/15/80, Wyer Mss. See also Perkins to Dui, 3/19/81, Box 1, Dewey Mss, where Perkins wrote: "I do not acknowledge this $27.66 [interest] as a just charge against me."

18. A copy of the AMB renegotiated mortgage is in Box 66. See also Dui to Winsor, 12/13/80; Winsor to Dui, 12/14, 20, 23, and 31/80; 1/14 and 25/81, Box 7, Dewey Mss. Dui was obviously feeling pressure. Box 29 contains an undated postcard in his hand with the following: "When the board or its members choose to listen to an interested adventurer rather than me its high time I got out of it. You may consider this please as my resignation of all connection with the ALA." The postcard bears no cancellation mark, and was probably never sent.

return all personal property to Dui and "the three societies in
Dui's charge," to transfer "all its rights & title to any good will,
patronage, or influence" of the SRA, AMB and ALA "or the supply
departments pertaining to each," and to sell Dui at cost any articles owned by RWEC connected with these organizations and
departments. The settlement showed no clear winners or losers.
The RWEC's major goal was to rid the company of Dui and "his
clogging business complications." Dui realized assets totaling
$19,000, but he received nothing for the business nor any com-
pensation for the work he had put into it. Many people he recruited into the company lost their entire investments. "The
toughest thing," Dui later wrote Bowker, "is that [the RWEC] wil
swindle poor Cutter. . . . They got him to pay in $1250. more . . .
& I fear wil make it a dead loss to him."[19]

The Library Bureau
1881–1883

Dui lost no time founding a new business. He used most of the
cash realized from the settlement to pay debts to the ALA, SRA,
and AMB treasury and to creditors with claims against him as
RWEC president, and with money realized from paid-up stock
that he pledged as security against the AMB sinking fund, he was
back in business at 32 Hawley Street. It was from that address he
sent out a four-page circular on March 20 announcing his new arrangement. On the first page he recounted (and exaggerated) his
role in organizing the ALA, the AMB, and the SRA, and in co-
ordinating "supply departments" for all three. He also complimented himself for pioneering work in founding *LJ* in 1876, and
organizing the RWEC in 1879. On the second page he said that
because he had been "overwhelmed with over-work" he had severed his relation with RWEC, resigned "all connections" with *LJ*,
and relinquished his SRA responsibilities as treasurer and corresponding secretary to Vickroy. On page three he announced he

---

19. Copy of the agreement in Box 61, Dewey Mss. See also Nichols
and Coolidge "To President and Life Members of the American Metric
Bureau," 1/11/81; and Dui to Perkins, 1/15/81, Box 81, Dewey Mss. Dui
details the financial ramifications of his settlement in Dui to Bowker,
6/6/81, Bowker Mss.

had retained positions as secretary of ALA and AMB, and that he was now reassuming responsibility for the Supply Department of SRA, ALA, and AMB. On page four he informed readers of the significant personal sacrifice he was making on behalf of each of these societies, and he called upon members of each to increase orders to his supply departments. "All Metric articles will be sold as before under the name METRIC BUREAU." The "Library Supply Department," on the other hand, "will go under the name LIBRARY BUREAU." He told readers he had secured four regular and three special assistants, and invited everyone to visit him at his "old offices."[20]

While the agreement Dui struck with RWEC did not show him as a clear loser, the March 20 circular reflected a different picture. He was out of *LJ* altogether, no longer had control of the treasuries of SRA and ALA, and had also lost the confidence of leaders in all three organizations. There is no evidence that ALA, SRA, or AMB members considered Dui dishonest, but it is obvious most worried his irrepressible reform spirit needed proper guidance, especially in his business practices. On March 21 his brother Manfred wrote from Oneida, "I have often found fault with you for this style of doing biz," he said. "You can hardly afford to play the philanthropist until you get more chink."[21]

Between his negotiated settlement with RWEC and reopening business the beginning of March, Dui paid some attention to ALA matters. ALA opened its fourth conference on February 9, 1881. Committee reports indicated that the new edition of *Poole's Index* was making satisfactory progress (in large part because Annie Dui was doing so much of the work), but progress on the *ALA Catalog* had ceased since Perkins moved to San Francisco. Dui remarked that the cooperation committee had not met since the Boston conference in June 1879. The membership also formally ratified the executive board's December 10, 1879, incorporation of ALA, and Dui unsuccessfully moved that the executive board be requested to "establish (if they find it practicable,

20. Dui's 3/20/81 circular in Box P-36, Dewey Mss. See also Dui to "Metric Friends," 3/20/81, *MA*, no. 37 (4/81): 486. A fuller account of the origins and early years of the Library Bureau is contained in Gerri Lynn Flanzraich, "The Role of the Library Bureau and Gaylord Brothers in the Development of Library Technology, 1876–1930" (Ph.D. diss , Columbia University, 1990).

21. M. J. Dewey to "Bro Mel," 3/21/81, Box 38, Dewey Mss.

without pecuniary liability to officers or members of the A.L.A.) a library bureau as a center for library interests" to facilitate the collection and dissemination of products generated by ALA co-operative activities. The finance committee then issued a report on ALA funds which said nothing about Dui's resignation. Just before the conference adjourned a nominating committee replicated the usual slate of executive committee members. All were unanimously reelected.[22]

The executive board met in Boston February 28, elected the usual slate of officers, and then discussed the *ALA Catalog*. Dui was very anxious to get it for the Library Bureau. He had some reason for concern. In 1880 Lyman Abbott had published *Hints for Home Reading*, a series of separately authored essays addressing "books and their use." Perkins wrote one chapter entitled "What to Read," while the book's publisher, George Palmer Putnam, had included another chapter entitled "Suggestions for Libraries" consisting of lists of "500, 1,000 and 2,000 volumes of the most desirable and important books."[23] Dui worried that librarians would begin taking advice on "best reading" from profit-driven publishers instead of professional librarians with more altruistic motives who looked to growing numbers of outside experts for guidance. Responsibility for compiling this "bibliography of the highest sort" he considered librarians' professional turf, and he wanted to move forward on the *ALA Catalog* project to check Abbott's direction. Rather than giving Dui any financial control of the project, however, Winsor moved that the executive board allow Dui to "receive . . . the unfinished mss," but to hold its disposition "subject to the decision of the Board as to its continuance."[24]

In the period between his resignation as RWEC president and the opening of Library Bureau offices in March 1881, Dui received several job offers. Houghton Publishing made inquiries, but Dui turned them away. He was not interested in a position

22. *Proceedings, 1881,* 122, 131, 133, 135, 140; *LJ* 6 (6/81): 181; Dewey to Bowker, 6/6/81, Bowker Mss.

23. Lyman Abbott (ed.), *Hints for Home Reading: A Series of Chapters on Books and Their Use* (N.Y., 1880). The anthology went through several editions.

24. *LJ* 6 (2/81): 181, 314; Dewey to Bowker, 6/6/81, Bowker Mss; Perkins to Dui, 10/21/80, Box 9; Dui to Perkins, 1/15/81, Box 61; Perkins to Dui, 1/26/81, Box 9; Green to Dui, 3/1/81; and Perkins to Dui, 3/19/81, Box 1, Dewey Mss.

reason Dui read anything outside practical studies between 1879 and 1882. He wrote long critical annotations on books dealing with practical matters, short and vague comments on cultural, literary, and intellectual books that may have challenged his values.[29]

For Melvil Dui, the years between 1876 and 1883 had been highly productive and highly tumultuous; they were also gratifying and painful. He started and lost one business, and started another like it within weeks. He developed credibility for his reform goal, then lost it, then began to rebuild it all over again. Throughout he retained his boundless energy, intense commitment, self-righteous arrogance, and irrepressible reform spirit. He made many friends and many enemies. Most who came in contact with him, however—whether superior, peer, or subordinate—quickly recognized him as a forceful personality not easily swayed from goals he had set for himself as a child of the Burned-Over District.

But in 1883, Dui was also "open to some engagement where I think I can do good work." On May 7, he found it. On that day decided to return to New York by accepting an offer to become Librarian of Columbia College. He saw it as a good opportunity to develop, implement, and ultimately demonstrate the of most of the library reforms (and some of the metric and ing reforms) he had been pushing for nearly ten years.

---

9. See also daily comportment notebooks in Box 19; reading note-Box 99, and especially entries for 3/-/80; 4/7/81; and 7/15/81.

that did not match his "world work." Commissioner Eaton asked Dui to head up a Library Division of the Bureau of Education, but Dui considered the $1,800 annual salary too low. The Census Bureau also offered him a position as chief of a division on library statistics, but Dui turned that offer down for the same reason. Instead he stayed in Boston. "I am getting metric matters in good shape & organizing the Library Bureau," he wrote Bowker June 6. "Both these after a time I can turn over to someone else. . . . Then I shal be open to some engagement where I think I can do good work."[25]

Until that time, however, Dui busied himself with business interests, and in the wake of the RWEC debacle, maintained a low profile in the organizations he helped found. Although he was still SRA secretary, he was no longer treasurer nor editor of its new journal, *The Fonetic Techer*. Both responsibilities had been transferred to Vickroy the previous year. The SRA met for a fifth time in 1881, but Dui did not attend. After 1882, the SRA and APA met concurrently, but Dui did not attend those meetings either. Although he did submit secretarial reports, they lacked his usual enthusiasm. Dui was equally quiet on metric matters. In April he announced he was changing the title of *Metric Bulletin* to *Metric Advocate,* and registering it with the Postmaster General as a periodical to qualify for lower postal rates. Page 502 of the *Advocate* carried an advertisement for *Fonetio Techer;* page 503 carried one for *Library Journal.* Even on ALA matters Dui maintained a low profile. He met other executive board members on January 1, 1882, to plan the forthcoming Cincinnati conference, but did not attend the conference itself. Without Dui's energy and prodding, ALA activities between conferences inevitably slowed. Board meetings occurred infrequently, usually only to elect officers or fill committee assignments.[26]

Instead, Dui paid most attention to the Library Bureau. R. G. Dun & Company, which compiled credit reports on American

---

25. Dui to Bowker, 6/6/81, Bowker Mss. See also Henry Waite (Special Agent, Census Office, Department of the Interior) to Dui, 3/18/81, Box 72, Dewey Mss.

26. March, *The Spelling Reform* (1893), pp. 31–32; and Dui's "Annual Report of the Secretary of the Spelling Reform Association," 7/13/82, Box 87, Dewey Mss. See also Tauber, "Spelling Reform," pp. 108–9; *MA,* no. 37 (4/81): 487; *LJ* 7 (1/82): 4; *Proceedings, 1882,* 192, 195, 197, 201, and 205; *LJ* 7 (9/82): 226–28; (12/82): 290.

businesses between the 1840s and 1880s, described Dui in 1881 as "a sanguine well-meaning man, full of little schemes for economizing the time and labor of librarians & literary men" who had "no capacity for bus. affairs and no means worth mentioning." Dun's assessment of Dui's worth, however, predated a slightly improved situation. Annie Dui received an inheritance upon her father's death in 1880, and because her mother sold property in the fall of 1881 had larger investments against which her husband could borrow. On May 31 Dui incorporated the "Library and Metric Bureau" in the State of Massachusetts.[27]

The seven stockholders (Melvil and Annie Dui owned a majority) agreed not to draw over 6 percent interest on money invested, and when earnings exceeded that amount the Bureau promised to reduce prices or increase quality. "This makes the enterprise really 'cooperativ,'" Dui told readers in a circular letter, "We hav . . . agreed to take the risk of getting less than 6 per cent, and if the business is supported as it should be and it erns more, to giv the excess to the library interest." Dui continued to advertise his altruism, blissfully unaware the practice reflected an exaggerated ego he concealed even from himself by masking it in an obsessive devotion to select causes. Dui also sought to assure interested parties that the Bureau's "future has been carefully planned on a safe and conservative basis." No officer "has any authority to giv any note or contract any debt in its name." Officers he mentioned included himself as president, John S. Lockwood as vice president, W. E. Parker as treasurer in charge of the office, bookkeeping and shipping, and H. E. Davidson (who left RWEC in May) as secretary. Davidson, Dui said, devoted his entire time to selling and manufacturing.

Dui had not been silent or idle on the subject of classification after the publication of his decimal scheme in 1876. In 1882

27. Dui handled his mother-in-law's property transfers. See his correspondence with James T. Eldridge, 10/5/81; 10/6/81; 10/8/81; and 10/24/81, Box 31, Dewey Mss. Without Dui's energy, RWEC could not sustain itself. On January 20, 1882, Dui purchased all remaining supplies from RWEC and rights to complete contracts on all RWEC goods ordered out of its 1879 and 1880 catalogs. By July 14, 1882, the RWEC had gone out of business. See flyer entitled "Specialties of the Former Readers and Writers Economy Company," 2/1/82, Box 64, Dewey Mss. See also "Readers and Writers Economy Co.," MA 80/p. 426; and "Library Bureau," MA 88/p. 184, Dun Collection.

Wellesley hired him as a Library Bureau consultant to reclassify its collections. Dui used the opportunity to expand his original decimal scheme, and he trained several Wellesley Class of 1883 members to implement the changes. By the time he had completed his consultation, he had already determined the substantive changes and new headings for a second edition. His experienc at Wellesley was beneficial in other ways. The Wellesley Colleg to which Annie Dui returned in 1882 was somewhat differe from the one she left in 1877. Henry Durant, who had envision a university "with stately buildings," had died in 1881; that sa year Pauline Durant, who thought students had a greater r for quiet and isolation, gave Wellesley its first cottage. A se was built the following year, and there were plans for mor were designed to look like informal summer homes; all had ing and eating quarters; all were intended to nurture the tian faith and facilitate the social and moral goals of education; all had more applicants than space available t the need.[28]

Dui so concentrated on his causes between 1879 that he had little time for social or personal matters. sure they used their time and energies wisely, he and veloped a regimen. At the beginning of each month draw up a list of assignments for personal improvem categories included: "Exercise 1 hr; Self-Culture, min; Don't waste a minute." Melvil's categories inc back 3 a week; Dress *well*; Short, organized lett eat slowly; Make no promises; Breathe deeply, cash daily." At the end of the month they r mance in each of these categories, and discus time they dropped some categories, added o 1879 they joined the "Saturday Club," an i met to discuss literature. Each member ma discussions on that selection for one s reading notebooks show membership in

28. See Comaromi, Chap. 3, for more ment of the second edition; and Horowitz, discussion of the cottage system at Wellesl Wellesley can be found on one of Dewey's tion, in which he marked the changes Wellesley. This copy, which is in Forest LJ 7 (9/82): 237. See also Comaromi,

that did not match his "world work." Commissioner Eaton asked Dui to head up a Library Division of the Bureau of Education, but Dui considered the $1,800 annual salary too low. The Census Bureau also offered him a position as chief of a division on library statistics, but Dui turned that offer down for the same reason. Instead he stayed in Boston. "I am getting metric matters in good shape & organizing the Library Bureau," he wrote Bowker June 6. "Both these after a time I can turn over to someone else. . . . Then I shal be open to some engagement where I think I can do good work."[25]

Until that time, however, Dui busied himself with business interests, and in the wake of the RWEC debacle, maintained a low profile in the organizations he helped found. Although he was still SRA secretary, he was no longer treasurer nor editor of its new journal, *The Fonetic Techer.* Both responsibilities had been transferred to Vickroy the previous year. The SRA met for a fifth time in 1881, but Dui did not attend. After 1882, the SRA and APA met concurrently, but Dui did not attend those meetings either. Although he did submit secretarial reports, they lacked his usual enthusiasm. Dui was equally quiet on metric matters. In April he announced he was changing the title of *Metric Bulletin* to *Metric Advocate,* and registering it with the Postmaster General as a periodical to qualify for lower postal rates. Page 502 of the *Advocate* carried an advertisement for *Fonetic Techer;* page 503 carried one for *Library Journal.* Even on ALA matters Dui maintained a low profile. He met other executive board members on January 1, 1882, to plan the forthcoming Cincinnati conference, but did not attend the conference itself. Without Dui's energy and prodding, ALA activities between conferences inevitably slowed. Board meetings occurred infrequently, usually only to elect officers or fill committee assignments.[26]

Instead, Dui paid most attention to the Library Bureau. R. G. Dun & Company, which compiled credit reports on American

25. Dui to Bowker, 6/6/81, Bowker Mss. See also Henry Waite (Special Agent, Census Office, Department of the Interior) to Dui, 3/18/81, Box 72, Dewey Mss.

26. March, *The Spelling Reform* (1893), pp. 31–32; and Dui's "Annual Report of the Secretary of the Spelling Reform Association," 7/13/82, Box 87, Dewey Mss. See also Tauber, "Spelling Reform," pp. 108–9; *MA,* no. 37 (4/81): 487; *LJ* 7 (1/82): 4; *Proceedings, 1882,* 192, 195, 197, 201, and 205; *LJ* 7 (9/82): 226–28; (12/82): 290.

businesses between the 1840s and 1880s, described Dui in 1881 as "a sanguine well-meaning man, full of little schemes for economizing the time and labor of librarians & literary men" who had "no capacity for bus. affairs and no means worth mentioning." Dun's assessment of Dui's worth, however, predated a slightly improved situation. Annie Dui received an inheritance upon her father's death in 1880, and because her mother sold property in the fall of 1881 had larger investments against which her husband could borrow. On May 31 Dui incorporated the "Library and Metric Bureau" in the State of Massachusetts.[27]

The seven stockholders (Melvil and Annie Dui owned a majority) agreed not to draw over 6 percent interest on money invested, and when earnings exceeded that amount the Bureau promised to reduce prices or increase quality. "This makes the enterprise really 'cooperativ,'" Dui told readers in a circular letter, "We hav . . . agreed to take the risk of getting less than 6 per cent, and if the business is supported as it should be and it erns more, to giv the excess to the library interest." Dui continued to advertise his altruism, blissfully unaware the practice reflected an exaggerated ego he concealed even from himself by masking it in an obsessive devotion to select causes. Dui also sought to assure interested parties that the Bureau's "future has been carefully planned on a safe and conservative basis." No officer "has any authority to giv any note or contract any debt in its name." Officers he mentioned included himself as president, John S. Lockwood as vice president, W. E. Parker as treasurer in charge of the office, bookkeeping and shipping, and H. E. Davidson (who left RWEC in May) as secretary. Davidson, Dui said, devoted his entire time to selling and manufacturing.

Dui had not been silent or idle on the subject of classification after the publication of his decimal scheme in 1876. In 1882

---

27. Dui handled his mother-in-law's property transfers. See his correspondence with James T. Eldridge, 10/5/81; 10/6/81; 10/8/81; and 10/24/81, Box 31, Dewey Mss. Without Dui's energy, RWEC could not sustain itself. On January 20, 1882, Dui purchased all remaining supplies from RWEC and rights to complete contracts on all RWEC goods ordered out of its 1879 and 1880 catalogs. By July 14, 1882, the RWEC had gone out of business. See flyer entitled "Specialties of the Former Readers and Writers Economy Company," 2/1/82, Box 64, Dewey Mss. See also "Readers and Writers Economy Co.," MA 80/p. 426; and "Library Bureau," MA 88/p. 184, Dun Collection.

Wellesley hired him as a Library Bureau consultant to reclassify its collections. Dui used the opportunity to expand his original decimal scheme, and he trained several Wellesley Class of 1883 members to implement the changes. By the time he had completed his consultation, he had already determined the substantive changes and new headings for a second edition. His experience at Wellesley was beneficial in other ways. The Wellesley College to which Annie Dui returned in 1882 was somewhat different from the one she left in 1877. Henry Durant, who had envisioned a university "with stately buildings," had died in 1881; that same year Pauline Durant, who thought students had a greater need for quiet and isolation, gave Wellesley its first cottage. A second was built the following year, and there were plans for more. All were designed to look like informal summer homes; all had sleeping and eating quarters; all were intended to nurture the Christian faith and facilitate the social and moral goals of women's education; all had more applicants than space available to satisfy the need.[28]

Dui so concentrated on his causes between 1879 and 1883 that he had little time for social or personal matters. To make sure they used their time and energies wisely, he and Annie developed a regimen. At the beginning of each month they would draw up a list of assignments for personal improvement. Annie's categories included: "Exercise 1 hr; Self-Culture, 1 hr; Sing 15 min; Don't waste a minute." Melvil's categories included "Horseback 3 a week; Dress *well;* Short, organized letters; Rise early, eat slowly; Make no promises; Breathe deeply, sing, and settle cash daily." At the end of the month they rated their performance in each of these categories, and discussed progress. Over time they dropped some categories, added others. Sometime in 1879 they joined the "Saturday Club," an informal group which met to discuss literature. Each member made a selection and led discussions on that selection for one session. Entries in his reading notebooks show membership in the Club was the only

---

28. See Comaromi, Chap. 3, for more information on the development of the second edition; and Horowitz, *Alma Mater,* pp. 86–90, for a discussion of the cottage system at Wellesley. Evidence of Dewey's work at Wellesley can be found on one of Dewey's personal copies of the first edition, in which he marked the changes influenced by his experiences at Wellesley. This copy, which is in Forest Press Archives, is also discussed in *LJ* 7 (9/82): 237. See also Comaromi, pp. 117–18.

reason Dui read anything outside practical studies between 1879 and 1882. He wrote long critical annotations on books dealing with practical matters, short and vague comments on cultural, literary, and intellectual books that may have challenged his values.[29]

For Melvil Dui, the years between 1876 and 1883 had been highly productive and highly tumultuous; they were also gratifying and painful. He started and lost one business, and started another like it within weeks. He developed credibility for his reform zeal, then lost it, then began to rebuild it all over again. Throughout he retained his boundless energy, intense commitment, self-righteous arrogance, and irrepressible reform spirit. He made many friends and many enemies. Most who came in contact with him, however—whether superior, peer, or subordinate— quickly recognized him as a forceful personality not easily swayed from goals he had set for himself as a child of the Burned-Over District.

But in 1883, Dui was also "open to some engagement where I think I can do good work." On May 7, he found it. On that day he decided to return to New York by accepting an offer to become Chief Librarian of Columbia College. He saw it as a good opportunity to develop, implement, and ultimately demonstrate the value of most of the library reforms (and some of the metric and spelling reforms) he had been pushing for nearly ten years.

---

29. See also daily comportment notebooks in Box 19; reading notebooks in Box 99, and especially entries for 3/-/80; 4/7/81; and 7/15/81.

Plate 1. Melvil Dewey's mother, Eliza Green Dewey (1808–1885), was a firm-minded woman of strong religious conviction. She preached humility to her children, telling them, "Praise to the face is an open disgrace." Melvil said she never feared anything.

Plate 2. Joel Dewey (1810–1889), Melvil's father, ran a shop in upstate New York that manufactured and sold boots and shoes. A hard worker interested in politics and moral reform, he told his children, "Don't waste." The Dewey house, however, often flowed with guests.

CALL FOR A LIBRARY CONFERENCE.

THE undersigned, connected with the library interest of this country, believing that efficiency and economy in library work would be promoted by a conference of librarians, which should afford opportunity for mutual consultation and practical co-operation, issue this preliminary call, inviting librarians and all interested in library and bibliographical work, to meet at Philadelphia, on the 15th of August next, or otherwise as may be found more generally acceptable.

Lack of time forbidding more general consultation by direct correspondence, the present method is used as the most available for soliciting further signatures and suggestions for the preparation of the formal and general call to be issued at a later date. Those approving of the plan and willing to indorse such a call, whether they may be able to be present or not, are requested to send their names, with suggestions as to topics to be presented, etc., to MELVIL DEWEY, care of the PUBLISHERS' WEEKLY, 37 Park Row, New-York.

Plates 3–5. At 25, two years after graduating from Amherst in 1874, Dewey (below, left) helped organize the conference that would establish the American Library Association. There he needled the formidable William F. Poole (below, right), director of the Chicago Public Library, for missing a point of business when, as Dewey announced, "he felt constrained to retire—shall I say it?—to smoke."

Plate 6.   Involved in numerous endeavors including spelling reform, Dui—as he now spelled his name—found little time for such diversions as this 1882 "Misses Ball" in Lancaster, N.H. Nevertheless he posed with gusto on the rear coach wheel. His wife, Annie, is fifth from left. Together they had a rigid program for "self-improvement," evaluating themselves monthly.

Plate 7 (right). Dewey in 1885. His wife, Annie, whom he married in 1878, treasured this photo. On the back she wrote, "My only picture of my husband for which I have waited light years. <u>NOT</u> to be given away to <u>anyone</u>."

Plate 8 (below). The Deweys' only child, Godfrey, was born in early September 1887 and named the "ALA Baby" at the American Library Association Conference that same time. In 1888, when this photo was taken, Dewey was in troubled times as librarian of Columbia College.

Plate 9. Dewey's groundbreaking School of Library Economy at Columbia College, 1888, into its second year and still opposed by factions at the college. May Seymour (fifth from left) and Florence Woodworth (center, with pen) were among Dewey's lifelong admirers. Annie is fifth from right.

Plate 10 (left). Dewey took his library school with him in 1889 when he moved from Columbia College to Albany, N.Y., to serve as State Librarian and Secretary to the Board of Regents of the University of the State of New York. In this detail of the Class of '89, the woman at left is Katharine Sharp, who, along with faithful supporters Woodworth and Seymour, became known as one of "Dewey's girls."

Plate 11 (below). Mary Salome Cutler, vice-director of the library school, stands by Dewey in this detail from an 1893–94 faculty portrait. Cutler believed the school should be strong on reading theory for book selection; Dewey opposed her, favoring practical skills.

Plate 12 (above). Dewey's office in the Capitol. Here, between 1889 and 1899, he "worked in a quiet fury" for reforms in New York's education system—and still managed to sign 279,444 Regents' high school certificates. Many of the pigeon holes were used for daily communications with staff.

Plate 13 (right). The Deweys' spacious home at 315 Madison Avenue, Albany, where extended hospitality to library school students and others sometimes raised charges of impropriety—adamantly denied.

Plate 14 (right). This unidentified outing might have been at the 1894 ALA Conference at Lake Placid, N.Y. Dewey (foreground) was hoping to attract interest in the resort that he and his wife were developing nearby. In the background (with white beard) is Justin Winsor, ALA's first and thirteenth president, who died in 1897.

Plate 15 (below). This undated photo shows Dewey with (from left) Frederick Crunden, fourth ALA president; Mary Ahern, longtime editor of *Public Libraries;* Katharine Sharp, who died tragically at Lake Placid in 1914; and "Miss M. McIlvaine." Of Dewey, a note on the back says, "see the Placid look on his face."

4

"To Ride a Fast or Frisky Horse": Columbia College

1883-1888

On March 29, 1883, Columbia College President F. A. P. Barnard wrote Dui, "There is to be a librarian appointed to take charge of the Library of our College. Please let me know if I may put your name in nomination."[1] But Barnard's general inquiry masked a specific goal. Since its establishment in 1754 as Kings College, Columbia had supported a classical curriculum. When Barnard arrived in 1864, however, he determined to turn the institution into a university. On the one hand that meant implementing a system of elective courses, establishing graduate education, and creating and improving technical and scientific schools. On the other it meant struggling against a board of trustees strongly influenced by the clergy, a relatively conservative faculty that viewed new ideas generated by research as a threat to established truths they taught in their classrooms, and a loyal and vocal alumni ready to support both when rallied. Barnard also hoped to provide opportunities for higher education for women, to improve teacher training, and to spread college and university services to a larger population through

---

1. Barnard to Dewey, 3/29/83, Box 18, Dewey Mss.

home study and university extension. Finally, he also wanted to build a library worthy of a great university.[2]

In 1883 Columbia's library was undistinguished. It could boast no separate building, and as of 1876 ranked sixth in size among collections in New York City. At the time the library was managed by Reverend Beverly Robinson Betts, who represented the stereotypical early-nineteenth-century academic librarian. He looked upon himself as a custodian of books and did not believe the library all that important to the institution's educational program. At the end of each fiscal year, in fact, Betts regularly returned book appropriations he had not expended. Barnard soon became irritated with Betts's apathy. In his 1880 annual report he called for the geographic consolidation of all Columbia's schools and libraries into one campus, and got trustees to agree. On January 3, 1881, they appointed a building committee to develop plans. One month later, committee members recommended locating a new library that combined the College Library with the libraries of the Schools of Mines and Law on 49th Street between Madison and Fourth Avenue.[3] Trustees approved.

As the time neared to move into new quarters two years later, trustees asked their library committee to analyze what a united library system with uniform cataloging would do to existing rules and regulations. The committee solicited Betts for ideas, but trustee F. Augustus Schermerhorn did more. On his own, he visited several prominent Boston librarians. When the library committee met on February 12, 1883, Betts submitted an unimpressive plan that merely adapted the existing system to the new building. Schermerhorn submitted a second plan much more comprehensive and elaborate in scope.

In his report Schermerhorn addressed library governance, funding, organization, circulation rules, hours of opening, and

---

2. See Nicholas Murray Butler, "Introduction," in William F. Russell (ed.), *The Rise of a University, vol. 1: The Later Days of Old Columbia College* (N.Y., 1937). pp. x–xi. See also Gerald Graff, *Professing Literature: An Institutional History* (Chicago, 1987), Chap. 1; and Frank Rozwadowski, "From Recitation Room to Research Seminar; Political Economy at Columbia University," in William J. Barber, ed., *Breaking the Academic Mold: Economists and American Higher Learning in the Nineteenth Century* (Middletown, Conn., 1988), p. 189.

3. *President's Report, 1880*, p. 41; Burgess, *Reminiscences*, p. 216; CCTM, 2/7/81; "College Notes," *Acta Columbiana*, 14 (10/1/81): 12.

the arrangement and cataloging of collections. In addition, he relayed a conversation he had had with Cutter about the Athenaeum's classification system and catalog rules; "the relative position of the classes and divisions and subdivisions . . . never changed," he said. Schermerhorn concluded with a series of recommendations: (1) increase appropriations; (2) create separate departments within a single system covered by "one general catalog minutely classified"; (3) extend library hours; (4) combine the stack and alcove systems; (5) adopt a new system of allocating book purchases by department; (6) create a card catalog; and (7) reorganize the staff under a competent director. Here Schermerhorn became very specific: "The chief librarian should be a very efficient man" who knew cataloging systems and shelf arrangement, had the ability to supervise and select qualified subordinates, and possessed management skills sufficient to implement the library rules and practice approved by the Library Committee. The committee approved the report and voted to forward Schermerhorn's recommendations to the board as a series of resolutions. Betts immediately recognized what had happened. On March 17 he wrote Board Chairman Hamilton Fish that "if the resolutions be presented, respect both for the office and myself would require that my resignation be presented with them."[4] Twelve days later Barnard asked Dui about coming to Columbia.

The "old boy" network made Dui's candidacy seem natural. First, Barnard had known Dui personally since 1874 from their metric reform efforts. Second, Boston librarians had probably mentioned Dui's name in conversations with Schermerhorn. Third and perhaps more important, however, was John Burgess, whom Barnard had recruited to Columbia from Amherst in 1880. On March 31 Burgess wrote Barnard about Dui's "fine genius for minute classification and convenient arrangement," his "faculty of accomplishing a great deal of work in a brief period of time," and his ability to get "an extraordinary amount of work out of his subordinates." Despite the encomiums, however, Dui seemed a reluctant candidate; he worried that tying himself to a single

---

4. CCTM, 1/3/83; TLCM, 1/11/83; 1/12/83. See also Barnard to Low, 12/15/88, Box 18, Dewey Mss. The Schermerhorn report is bound into "Papers on the Arrangement of Shelving in the New Library Building," Columbiana. See also Betts to Fish, 3/17/83, Fish Mss.

institution would limit his usefulness on "a larger scale." He also thought the $3,500 salary too low.[5]

On April 2 the Library Committee presented its recommendations to the trustees: (1) consolidate Columbia's libraries in one building and under one administration; and (2) reorganize the staff. The committee also advised the board to notify present library staff members that their services would not be needed after August 15, and to appoint as soon as possible a librarian-in-chief at a salary of $3,500. (The standard salary for senior faculty members at that time was $5,000.) The trustees accepted the report, approved its recommendations, and resolved to elect a librarian-in-chief at their next meeting. After the board also accepted Betts's resignation, Barnard pressed Dui. "Certainly [for] whatever plans you have for being useful on a large scale," he wrote, "New York is a better standpoint than any other in the country," and asked Dui to come to New York April 18 to meet the library committee. "Don't fail to be there. . . . I shall be content with no librarian but yourself." But Barnard worried about one matter. He reported that Schermerhorn had recently criticized Dui for an "eccentricity" evident in "the spelling of his name." He forewarned Dui, "I should not like to have a matter of that secondary interest interfere with our plans for the more important work."[6]

The April 18 meeting took place as planned. Minutes show that Melvil "Dewey" attended,[7] recommended a substantial financial commitment to consolidate, recatalog, and reclassify Colum-

---

5. Barnard describes some of the chronology of Dui's appointment in Barnard to Low, 12/15/83, copy found in Box 18, Dewey Mss. See also Burgess to Dui, 4/4/83; and Burgess to Barnard, 3/31/83, Box 18. Barnard sent a copy of the latter to Dui, who subsequently penciled in a few corrections to Burgess's biography and sent it back to Barnard. See also Burgess, *Reminiscences,* p. 218.

6. CCTM, 4/2/83; TLCM, 4/18/83; 5/22/83; Barnard to Dui, 4/3/83; 4/11 and 13/83; Burgess to Dui, 4/4/83; Schermerhorn to Barnard, 4/14/83; Barnard to Dui, 4/15/83, Box 18, Dewey Mss. See also Columbia College Library. School of Library Economy, *Circular of Information* (N.Y., 1884), pp. 21–23.

7. He must have changed the spelling of his name sometime between April 15 and 18. Poole wrote on April 23, "I am very glad to see that you write your name *Dewey.* Now pray lay aside some, at least, of your orthographical peculiarities, and spell like common folk." Poole to Dewey, 4/23/83, Box 76, Dewey Mss.

bia's library collections, indicated his desire to establish a School of Library Economy if he came to Columbia, and asked for a salary of $5,000. The committee could not promise the latter, but they did offer "hearty support" for everything else. After the meeting Dewey urged a number of friends to write Columbia about his qualifications. Among others Smith, Poole, and Cutter sent endorsements, which Dewey promptly forwarded to Barnard. When Barnard circulated them to board members, however, two expressed reservations about the hyperactive young man. Seth Low worried about Dewey's business reputation; Joseph W. Harper, Jr., worried about the cost of implementing Dewey's proposals.[8] At their May 7 meeting, trustees agreed to hire Dewey as "Librarian-in-Chief" at $3,500 per year. They also patiently listened without comment as Barnard detailed Dewey's plan for "A School of Library Economy," then approved a $10,000 appropriation for the library's reorganization.[9] Barnard quickly communicated the terms of Columbia's offer to Dewey, who just as quickly accepted.

On June 4 Dewey outlined his ambitious plans for the future to the Library Committee. He recommended that Columbia consolidate its collections into a single library, create a shelf list, print a complete table of classification for reader consultation, construct a complete catalog in one alphabet, and build a subject catalog that included periodical articles, society transactions, and book chapters. He advocated that hours of opening be increased from fifteen per week to fourteen per day "throughout the year, vacations and holidays included." All of this, Dewey said, could be accomplished in three years with careful planning, adequate appropriations, and judicious staff appointments and supervision. Consolidation of libraries would eliminate two positions; recataloging and extended hours, however, would force the hiring of other personnel, including two women for the circulation

---

8. TLCM, 4/18/83; Barnard to Dui, 4/19/83; Barnard to Dewey, 5/4/83, Box 18, Dewey Mss. See also Barnard to Low, 12/15/83, Box 18, for additional details on 4/18/83 meeting. Low quoted in Barnard to Dewey, 5/2/83, Box 18, Dewey Mss. See also Harper to Barnard, 5/4/83; Barnard to Dewey, 5/4/83, copies found in Box 18. Throughout his tenure at Columbia Dewey was careful to use conventional spelling in all correspondence he considered "official."

9. CCTM, 5/7/83; Gerard Beckman (Clerk, Columbia College Board of Trustees) to Dewey, 5/10/83, Box 18, Dewey Mss.

department, two men for the classification department, four women for the catalog department, and one woman each in the accessions department, the binding and repair department and the secretary's office. Annual cost of the additional personnel would be between $9,700 and $15,100. Although it was a stiff request, the committee recommended Dewey's plan to the board but suggested that half the $10,000 appropriation be granted through November 1, at which time the board could reassess its investment. The board approved, but also asked for another report on "the expediency of instituting a school for training librarians."[10]

Dewey had his mandate. Many, like Barnard and Burgess, sympathized with his goals; others, who preferred that Columbia remain a traditional college, did not. Most Columbia officials did not fully understand Dewey's vision and the impact that vision might have for library service to Columbia. They wanted a librarian whose highest priority was Columbia, whose primary goal was to serve the college community. Dewey certainly did not disagree with these goals, but his priorities extended far beyond the campus. He had "larger interests." He looked upon his appointment as an opportunity to demonstrate to the rest of the world how educationally valuable an efficiently run library with a properly arranged and judiciously selected collection could be. Most of his energies, most of his innovations and plans, and indeed most of the controversy which surrounded him for the next five years can be traced to Columbia's fundamental misunderstanding of Dewey's priorities. Columbia officials wanted a librarian to take responsibility for the college library; they got that, but they also got much more. In 1883 they had hired a librarian who took responsibility for all of American librarianship and was prepared to roll over any obstacles standing in the way of his "larger" responsibilities.

Librarian-in-Chief
1883–1887

On June 1, 1883, Dewey started work in a new and attractive English Gothic building, which, in addition to the library, housed

---

10. *Report of the Committee on the Library, as to the Organization of the Staff of Service. Presented to the Trustees, June 4, 1883* (N.Y., 1883). See also TLCM, 5/9/83; and CCTM, 5/7/83.

The new Columbia College Library in New York, where Dewey spent five and a half years (1883–1888) as Librarian-in-Chief.

classrooms, the School of Law, and the astronomical observatory. Library users entered through a stack room that opened up into a larger main reading room with a 58-foot ceiling. Because the book stacks were so high, Dewey had brass steps installed along their base and attached handles to the stacks so readers could balance themselves while reaching the top shelf. "Courtesies" offered included a separate coat- and checkroom, stamps, postcards, and stationery for sale at the loan desk, and hourly mail pickup. The library also provided "running ice water with a tray of glasses on the wall" in a lobby equipped with benches. All patrons had access to the regular stacks, and alumni were given the same borrowing privileges as undergraduates. Dewey had a mail slot cut into his office door so patrons could slip him "suggestions or criticisms . . . signed or anonymous."

Dewey was especially concerned with noise. He had rubber tips placed on chairs and tables, rubber wheels on book trucks, and issued slippers for all pages. All new readers were handed cards requesting them to step lightly across the room and not talk away from the loan desk, even in low tones. They were told not to use tobacco, wear hats, put their feet on chairs or tables, or litter the premises. Dewey even had a card printed which read "I picked up these pieces in the hall and infer that you threw them on the floor. My time and that of my assistants is too valuable for this work. Still we prefer to do it rather than have the building so disfigured." Principle above diplomacy. That he thought these rules worthy of adoption by others is obvious; he had the Library Bureau print them up for distribution to peers across the country.[11]

Except for William G. Baker, the School of Mines librarian he had inherited from his predecessor, Dewey had the luxury of hiring all members of his own staff. He assigned William Baker to reference and bibliographic responsibilities for the sciences, arts, and serials, then hired George H. Baker, one of his Amherst classmates, to consolidate the Political Science Library into the main library. Eventually Dewey gave the latter reference and bibliographic responsibilities for law, political science, and history. For the major project of reclassifying and recataloging the collections, Dewey turned to his old friend, Walter S. Biscoe who, next to Dewey himself, best understood the decimal classification scheme.

---

11. See M. G. Van Rensselaer, "Recent Architecture in America," *Century Magazine,* 28 (5/84): 65–66; and *Views of Columbia College* (Boston, 1886). See also Columbia College, *Handbooks of Information as to the Course of Instruction . . . in Columbia College and Its Several Schools* (N.Y., 1884), p. 253; Columbia College Library, *Rules* [of Columbia College], November 10, 1883, copy found in Box 18, Dewey Mss; Columbia College Library. *First Annual Report of the Chief Librarian, May 31, 1884* (N.Y., 1884), p. 25; circular entitled "Information for Readers," Box 18, Dewey Mss; Columbia College Library. School of Library Economy, *Circular of Information* (N.Y., 1884), p. 11; and Henry Tedder, "Mr. Melvil Dewey's Work at Columbia College," *Library Chronicle* 1 (11–12/84): 186–91. Card entitled "Library Rules" printed by Library Bureau and card concerning trash in the Library both in Box 18. For another account of Dewey's tenure as Columbia College Librarian-in-Chief, see Winifred B. Linderman, "History of the Columbia University Library, 1876–1926" (Ph.D. diss., Columbia University, 1959), pp. 87–183.

To assist Biscoe, Dewey took risks he thought promised high gain for low cost; he hired seven women on a campus described in 1883 as "almost as hermetically sealed to women as is a monastery." Six were dubbed "the Wellesley Half Dozen" because of former connections to that institution. There they had been relatively free to define their own standards of success, to experience their own concept of power, to be aggressive, strong, and direct. There they bonded and developed a sense of mission. Because he was a child of the Burned-Over District where women played active—albeit subordinate—roles, Dewey had no reservations about importing women into the library profession and onto an all-male campus. He and Annie looked forward to entertaining them in their New York apartment.

Hiring college-educated women fit Dewey's concept of librarianship's professional boundaries. Their credentials indicated they possessed the right "character" for librarianship, and thus would come to Columbia knowing the "best reading" and understanding the rules by which it was determined. Because they were grateful for new professional opportunities, they would also come for less money (George Baker was hired at $1,000 salary, the Wellesley Half Dozen for $500 each). Everything fit together nicely. Although he did not say it, Dewey was, he believed, setting an example for the rest of librarianship; he was recruiting a work force with high character for low cost.[12] Dewey also knew Barnard would not object. For years Barnard had wanted to open Columbia to women, but trustees and faculty resisted. In June 1883, Barnard won a partial victory. Trustees grudgingly approved a separate course of study; women admitted were not allowed to attend lectures, but they could request two conferences per term with course instructors and take final exams.[13]

12. For personnel appointments, see Biscoe to Dewey, 6/5/83, Box 18; "Librarians—William G. Baker," *LJ* 27 (2/02): 105; TLCM, 6/14/83; *First Annual Report of the Chief Librarian,* p. 6; Alice Freeman (President, Wellesley College) to Dewey, 5/16/83; 5/23/83; and 7/6/83, Box 18, Dewey Mss. See also letter from Mary Tyler Buckham (one of the Wellesley Half Dozen), quoted in Rider, *Dewey* (Chicago, 1944), p. 79. Other members of the group included Alice Ayers, Mary M. Deveny, L. Adelaide Eaton, Louise Langford, and Nellie Page.

13. For trustee consideration of admitting women, see CCTM, 3/15/83 and 6/4/83. Dewey's clearest statement on the role he saw for women in

In October Dewey supervised the move into the new library, which united the 50,000 volumes scattered in six different libraries in nine different locations. Even more important, however, was reclassifying and cataloging collections, and here Dewey was determined to make Columbia an example for all of librarianship. He compiled an author and a title catalog on small cards, but placed his subject catalog on large cards. The latter was deliberate; Dewey hoped that over time he could induce faculty members to add annotations. "The cards will contain the best advice the librarians and professors can give," he wrote several years later. He also had blue cards with bibliographical notes like "The best scholarly treatise is _____," and "The best popular treatise is _____" interfiled with the larger subject cards, and asked faculty members to fill in the blanks and add any other notes they thought beneficial to the library user. Cards were arranged under 20,000 subject headings. Within five years the size of the subject catalog more than doubled. Dewey made use of this activity in other ways; the Columbia experience led to a second edition of the decimal classification scheme in 1885 and publication of *Rules for Author and Classed Catalogue* in 1888.[14]

To correct inequities in the collection Dewey showed creative energy and considerable vision. First, he relied heavily upon faculty assistance. He assigned boxes in the library to each faculty member, and had library staff put notices of potential acquisitions or possible unnecessary duplications in those boxes. Second, he envisioned a shared acquisitions practice with other

librarianship is *Librarianship as a Profession for College-Bred Women.* See also Susan Coultrap-McQuinn, *Doing Literary Business: American Women Writers in the Nineteenth Century* (Chapel Hill, 1990), pp. 8–10, for a good summary of what she calls the late 19th-century "Vision of New Womanhood," which justified women's participation in certain segments of professional society while not violating the doctrine of "separate spheres." Dewey's speech clearly identifies him with this "Vision."

14. *Second and Third Annual Reports of the Chief Librarian, June 30, 1886* (N.Y., 1886), p. 31. See also Columbia College Library. School of Library Economy, *Circular of Information* (N.Y., 1884), p. 7; *Rules for Author and Classed Catalogue as Used in the Columbia College Library* (Boston, 1888); Melvil Dewey, *Decimal Classification and Relativ Index for Arranging, Cataloging, and Indexing Public and Private Libraries and for Pamphlets, Clippings, Notes, Scrap Book, Index Rerums, etc.* 2d ed., rev. and greatly enl. (Boston, 1885). A more complete discussion of publication of the second edition can be found on pages 113–14.

New York libraries to which the Columbia College community could have access, thus making it unnecessary for his library to purchase titles in areas in which other metropolitan libraries had special strengths. To create an organizational structure in which this could take place he invited seventy-two New York City librarians to meet in his office on June 18, 1885, and after some discussion they voted to form a New York Library Club whose "object shall be by consultation and cooperation to increase the usefulness and promote the interests of the libraries of New York and vicinity." The Club agreed to meet quarterly at Columbia and, at its first official meeting on November 12, appointed a committee to propose a union list of serials for New York City libraries. It was published in 1887.[15]

To meet collection goals Dewey developed a system of five grades. Columbia would attempt to acquire everything (whether by gift or purchase) in higher education, law, political science, mining, engineering, library economy, and Columbiana, all of which, Dewey argued, were areas the institution declared as teaching and research specialties. In areas taught but not researched, the library would acquire by gift or purchase "all important works" needed by the undergraduate population. A third category included works on subjects not directly taught in the curriculum, but which were considered part of general knowledge. For this category Dewey especially wanted to rely on gifts, and looked to Columbia alumni for contributions. The fourth category included specialties not in the curriculum; here Dewey would buy "only exceptional items," and relied heavily on other metropolitan libraries. Finally, the fifth category included rare books and popular fiction, all of which would come by gift.

15. *LJ* 11 (1/86): 14–17; 12 (4/87): 164–65; 12 (12/87): 556–58; 13 (3–4/88): 99; Dewey to John Shaw Billings, 5/2/87, Billings Mss. See also New York Library Club, *Union List of Periodicals Currently Received by the New York and Brooklyn Libraries* (N.Y., 1887). Dewey was also present at the creation of the National Sunday School Library Union and the Children's Library Association, both of which had their origins in his office. The latter formed in 1885 "to provide children with wholesome reading and counter the influence of the injurious literature so freely offered them in New York." After 1887, several of Dewey's library-school students volunteered their "activ assistance." A pamphlet describing the Children's Library Association from which the quotations are taken can be found in Box 12, Dewey Mss. See also *LJ* 12 (5/8): 183, 185–86; and *LN* 1 (3/87): 261–63.

Dewey encouraged Columbia to push for endowed funds for regular library acquisitions, but the college did not have much success while he was librarian-in-chief.[16]

Among his "larger interests," Dewey also considered library reference service an area of professional practice demarcating his generation from the previous one. "The Library offers students the best bibliographies, cyclopaedias, dictionaries, and other works of reference," he wrote in Columbia's 1884 *Handbook of Information,* "and aims to induce them . . . to know these books, to use them intelligently, and to acquire the habit of hunting down a needed fact or verifying a mooted point." Dewey wanted his staff to teach users how to find things for themselves. Once taught, they would need only limited assistance in the future.[17]

Dewey also set up a series of bibliographical lectures delivered by Columbia faculty at the college's regular Saturday morning series for the public. Lectures aimed at four general areas: (1) those on "practical bibliography" would teach students "what author and treatise is wanted"; (2) those on "books" would teach "what edition to buy or borrow whenever there is a choice of editions"; (3) those on "reading" would teach students "how to get from the book what is wanted, and no more, most quickly and most easily"; and (4) those on "literary methods" would teach students "how to remember, record, classify, arrange, index, and in every way make most available for future use what has been gained from the books."[18]

One result Dewey hoped would come out of this initiative was a catalog of best reading suitable for all libraries. Not only did he want to make Columbia a model for standardizing library practice, he also wanted to identify a basic collection of "best

---

16. See *Annual Report of the Chief Librarian, 1884,* pp. 15–18; *1887,* pp. 3–4. See also Biscoe's handwritten notes for an unpublished *LJ* article, Box 18, Dewey Mss; "Notices," *LN* 1 (10/86): 144; and Dewey to Banyor Clarkson (Secretary, Huguenot Society), -/-/88, Jay Family Mss.

17. Columbia College, *Handbook of Information as to the Course of Instruction . . .*(N.Y., 1884), p. 257; Columbia College Library, *Paid Help Department and Facilities for Non-Resident Readers* (N.Y., n.d.); Columbia College, *Handbook of Information, 1886–1887* (N.Y., 1886), pp. 247–48; and *Annual Report of the Chief Librarian, 1887,* p. 6.

18. See *Columbia College Library. School of Library Economy, Circular of Information* (N.Y., 1884), pp. 17, 19.

reading." Herein, he was convinced, lay the greatest potential for libraries, no matter the type. At a May 3, 1884, meeting of the library committee Dewey outlined his ideas. He recounted the history of the "forthcoming" *ALA Catalog,* and explained that ALA had recently given him "responsibility" for its compilation. The Bureau of Education seemed willing to publish it, he said, but the work being done at Columbia would hasten its completion. Here Dewey was referring to the annotations being compiled in his subject catalog, the bibliographical lectures being delivered by faculty at Columbia's Saturday morning lecture series, and the results of his reclassification of Columbia's collections. From this activity, he reported, would evolve a new catalog of 5,000 titles recommended for most libraries that were suitably annotated by Columbia faculty and properly arranged in the Decimal Classification used at the Columbia library.[19]

Because Dewey pushed so hard so relentlessly, it was only a matter of time before dissatisfaction with his administration began to appear. Initially, Dewey's "larger interests" and the size of library expenditures represented his most vulnerable points. At first trustees had been supportive. Dewey passed a six-month review when trustees approved his request for the remaining $5,000 in November. And in May 1884 they raised his annual salary to $5,000 and added "Professor of Library Economy" to his title. As time passed, however, they were less forgiving. Hamilton Fish indicated his displeasure at Dewey's "tendency to the Free Library idea." Seth Low complained to Dewey: "We do not want a public library either in range or extent." The costs of cataloging and reclassification were particularly troublesome, especially because trustees saw no immediate end to the process. "We have to expend $19,000 per annum *before we can buy any books,*" trustee Charles Silliman wrote Fish on February 27, 1886. "If the Dewey system of cataloging is 'Automatic', or

---

19. See TLCM, 5/3/84. Dewey may also have been thinking of the benefits of locating this activity on a campus planning to launch *Political Science Quarterly,* a new scholarly periodical which would include thirty articles and a hundred reviews in a volume year. He undoubtedly saw the potential for connecting the reviews and his catalog, and capitalizing on the authority of the former to enhance the quality of the latter. The emerging system promised the kind of efficiency which appealed to Dewey, and fit his developing sense of the role of librarianship in the system of emerging professions.

labor-saving, it should save us something by dispensing with employees."[20]

Dewey was aware of growing criticism, and to cut expenses he decided to fire William Baker; he badly miscalculated. The faculty of the School of Mines quickly protested the dismissal of "their" librarian, and Barnard asked Dewey to rehire Baker for the immediate future. Dewey refused; it was much more important to keep pace on cataloging and reclassification, he argued. He forced the library committee to vote on the issue, and won endorsement by a bare majority. The School of Mines faculty protested again, and convinced the library committee to reverse itself. As a result, Baker was back on the payroll and Dewey was forced to acquiesce.[21] Library committee action represented a major defeat for Dewey, who continued to give Columbia plenty of reason to be cautious of his ambitions. The next significant test in a tug-of-war between Dewey's "larger interests" and Columbia's narrower needs came when Dewey opened the School of Library Economy on January 5, 1887.

A Bootleg Operation: The School of Library Economy 1884–1887

Dewey had been toying with the idea of formal library-school education since 1876, and had even discussed it with ALA members on the 1877 boat trip to England. The concept eventually found a niche in his grand plan of reform and soon became another "cause" worthy of sacrifice that masked his exaggerated ego. A number of prominent librarians endorsed the idea, but Dewey had some problem convincing ALA. At its 1883 conference discussion of the subject was animated. Several "librarians of weight" considered it another of Dewey's "foolish fads." Ultimately, ALA agreed to a compromise resolution: "That this asso-

---

20. CCTM, 5/5/84; Silliman to Fish, 2/27/86, Fish Mss.

21. See Columbia University, "[Letters from President Barnard, the Faculty, and others, with Resolutions, etc. Relating to the Retention of William G. Baker as Assistant Librarian in Columbia University Library, Dated May 5, 1885 to June 17, 1887]", Columbiana; TLCM, 12/24/85; 1/4/86; 12/11/86; 5/6/87; 5/27/87; and 6/17/87; CCTM, 1/4/86.

ciation desires to express its gratification that the trustees of Columbia College are considering the propriety of giving instruction in library work, and hopes that the experiment may be tried."[22] Hardly the ringing endorsement Dewey hoped for, but, characteristically, he was undeterred.

On May 5, 1884, Barnard presented Dewey's plans—endorsed by the library committee—to the trustees. He mentioned three key points: (1) "its novelty" would draw favorable public and press attention; (2) it "would be recognized as meeting and supplying a public want"; and (3) it "will be self-sustaining so far as any outlay for its maintenance is involved." Columbia already had the necessary library building and operational system "as a basis for study." A "reasonable" fee charged to all students "will more than cover all expenses," he noted. The library school would be placed under the control of the library committee, but the librarian-in-chief would have direct administrative responsibility for its operation, and for this he would receive the title "Professor of Library Economy." Without dissent, trustees approved a resolution to establish the school, but only if it would "involve no charge upon the treasury but on the other hand may prove an actual source of income." The message was clear; Dewey would not be allowed to tax the college treasury with his library school as he had with his reclassification project.[23]

Initially Dewey tested his concept in a reconfigured apprenticeship program. In 1884 and 1885 he hired nine "pupil assistants", all were expected to attend Saturday morning bibliography lectures. In the spring of 1886 he started mailing a *Circular of Information* about the school to prospective students. The aim of the curriculum "is entirely practical," he said. Tuition

22. In an 1879 *LJ* article entitled "Apprenticeship Librarian," Dewey suggested the creation of a "librarians normal school" which he argued "must be attached to some considerable library." *LJ* 4 (5/31/78): 147–48. See also *LJ,* 8 (9–10/83): 285–94; and *Proceedings, 1905,* p. 169, for one man's recollection of the 1884 discussion in Buffalo.

23. Barnard's report for the Library Committee can be found in Russell, *Rise of a University,* pp. 331–35; his letter of 5/14/84 to Dewey is in Box 18, Dewey Mss. See also CCTM, 5/5/84, for the official resolution concerning the school. By giving Dewey the title of "Professor of Library Economy" trustees automatically increased his annual salary to Columbia's professor level of $5,000.

was set at $50.[24] In the summer Dewey also began publishing *Library Notes,* projected to be a quarterly issued by his Library Bureau and written in a conservative form of simplified spelling. In part, he hoped *Notes* would fill a gap left by the *Library Journal,* which many librarians considered too esoteric and expensive. In part, Dewey wanted a journal he could control. The first issue contained notices encouraging college women to apply to the new School of Library Economy, now scheduled to open in January 1887.[25] The announcement made no mention of the fact that Columbia was still a male enclave; Dewey had not been given permission to advertise the school outside college publications, and certainly not to women.

The opening of the library school, which was very closely tied to Dewey's campus identity, occurred at the same time he was meeting increased resistance to his management of the library. Dewey did not flinch at any opposition, however. So committed was he to those "larger interests" he felt morally justified in circumventing anyone who got in his way. They would eventually understand his good intentions, he thought, once the ends he won began to bear fruit. But Columbia was also to blame for sending him mixed signals. Just as it had authorized a separate collegiate course for women several months before Dewey hired the Wellesley Half Dozen, in the fall of 1886 it was considering whether to issue degrees to women who successfully completed the course. This may in part explain Dewey's willingness to openly advertise for female students in *Library Notes* in 1886.[26]

By fall word passed among trustees that Dewey was going to admit women to his library school. In late November Dewey heard that Trustee Charles Silliman was going to present a resolution against the library school at the December 11 meeting. Dewey asked Barnard to protect the school. At the meeting Silliman "took the ground . . . that the admission of *women* to the School of Library Economy would be contrary to the expressed will of the Board." After considerable debate, trustees decided to table

---

24. See TLCM, 11/1/84. Copies of the application form, dated "1884," are in Box 18, Dewey Mss. See also Columbia College Library. School of Library Economy, *Circular of Information, 1886–87,* pp. 26–33.

25. *LN* 1 (6/86): 4–28.

26. In February 1887, the trustees in fact approved it and enrolled 25 women. See CCTM, 2/7/87. This separate program was canceled in 1889, when Barnard College was established.

the motion pending further discussion. After the meeting Barnard advised Dewey to be patient. "There seems to be no general interest [for it] among the Trustees," he said, "and some, I think, disapprove it. Let them have their way for the time being."[27]

But Dewey was determined. He had already admitted twenty students to the first class, and was committed to open January 5, 1887. Silliman was equally determined. Although he could not cite a board vote denying Dewey authority to open the library school if it included women, he could, as chair of the board's committee on buildings, deny Dewey permission to use Columbia classrooms. He so informed Dewey on January 4. But Dewey would not give up. He told Columbia janitors to clean out the unused storeroom above the chapel across the street (which was not technically a College classroom) and furnish it with salvaged furniture. Then, "without giving a hint of the volcano on which we all stood," Dewey later recalled, he opened the library school on schedule to twenty students, seventeen of whom were women. Dewey had honored the letter of the board's law, but clearly violated its spirit. His "larger interests" had dictated this brazen move, and he was willing to risk the consequences—even if he had to run a bootleg library school—confident that in the end the school's successes would prove him right, trustees wrong.[28]

And he was determined that the school would work. He led a group of "regular" faculty for the first term, which also included Biscoe, George Baker, and library assistant William E. Parker. Library employees Mary Salome Cutler, Carrie Frances Pierce, and Annie E. Hutchins also delivered lectures. All were on Dewey's staff; none could have been considered faculty at the all-male Columbia College. To "regular" faculty Dewey added two groups of lecturers. The first consisted of members of the library community like Bowker, Spofford, S. S. Green, Caroline Hewins, and

---

27. Barnard to Dewey, 11/20/86 and 12/12/86, Box 18, Dewey Mss.

28. Dewey described these early January 1887 events much later. See Rider, *Dewey*, p. 44; and Dawe, *Dewey*, p. 189. Nicholas Murray Butler also later recalled that shortly after the school opened several trustees asked why Dewey should not be dismissed for admitting women, for which there had been no provision. But when Barnard pointed out that "there had been none against these" either, trustees were forced to allow the school to continue on "that very legalistic technicality." See Butler, "Address," *Library Service News*, 6 (2/1937): 10. See also Dewey's recollection in Dewey to Wyer, 12/18/16, Box 23, Dewey Mss.

Hannah P. James. Annie Dewey sometimes spoke on indexing. All offered their services free; most stayed with the Deweys while visiting New York to minimize expenses. The second consisted of Columbia faculty members, including Nicholas Murray Butler, H. T. Peck, and Charles Sprague Smith, all of whom lectured on bibliography and the literature in their areas of expertise. Many appeared as part of the Saturday morning public lecture program.[29]

The skeletal framework of this curricular structure is important to understand for its impact on the development of formal library education. Three components combined to give the framework its shape. The first enveloped the late-nineteenth-century concept of "character," and was most evident in the type of information requested in the school's application form (e.g., health, education, foreign languages, personal reading profile, library experience, church affiliation and frequency of attendance).[30] The second addressed the emphasis on training in library practice, and is most evident in lectures delivered by library school faculty and visitors. Their job was to build upon the "character" base of the students, inculcate the "library spirit" (for Dewey, that meant a commitment to service), and pull students through a curriculum that above all focused on two practical areas Dewey considered unique to librarianship—managing the library and developing the expertise necessary to efficiently link library patrons with the information they wanted. The third component spoke to the locus of "authority" to determine what the library's public should read, and is most evident in faculty bibliography lectures. In subject bibliography lectures Dewey asked Columbia faculty to discuss the best authors, translations, and treatises and the leading learned societies, associations, and their publications (especially the periodicals). In literature bib-

---

29. I am indebted to Professor Francis Miksa for allowing me to read his transcriptions of shorthand notes of lectures written by George Watson Cole, member of that first class. The notes are in the Cole Mss. Copies of the transcriptions are in possession of Professor Miksa. See also Francis L. Miksa, "Melvil Dewey: The Professional Educator and His Heirs," *Library Trends* 34 (1986): 359–81; and "Columbia Library School," *LN* 1 (3/87): 255. Dewey lists the schedule of Saturday morning lectures for January through April 1887, in *LN* 1 (12/86): 202–3.

30. A copy of this application form can be found in Box 62, Dewey Mss. See also *School of Library Economy of Columbia College, 1887–1889: Documents for a History* (N.Y., 1937), pp. 247–50.

liography lectures, he asked for "a comprehensive and comparative view of the leading literatures of the world, thus giving an excellent basis for the work which every successful librarian must do in general literature."[31]

This curricular structure clearly reflected Dewey's perception of the library profession's appropriate jurisdictional boundaries. The authority to decide the "best reading" would be left to experts outside librarianship who would exercise their authority in classrooms (where future library school students would acquire the right "character") and in reviews published in a growing number of new disciplinary journals and literary periodicals like *Political Science Quarterly,* the *New England Magazine,* the *Book Buyer,* the *Literary World,* and the *New Princeton Review.*[32] Dewey built his practical curriculum—always aimed at the library institution and the expertise needed to run it—upon that base, confident that authorities outside the profession would ultimately develop a dependency on and a gratefulness for librarians and library institutions. As he carved out this niche for librarianship, however, Dewey did not realize that this structure effectively robbed librarianship of a direct claim to the "authority" to determine "best reading," thus significantly limiting its potential power in the world of professions. His optimism for librarianship and his ideology of reading blinded him to this shortcoming.[33]

---

31. Dewey identified these intentions in a report that appeared in *Regents AR, 1888,* p. 402.

32. Dewey, in fact, advertised the *Book Buyer* (which reviewed recently published books of American and foreign literature) in *Library Notes.* He noted in another issue that the *New Princeton Review* was intended to acquaint readers with the "best work" in "philosophy, politics, science, religion & morality, fiction, art history and education." See *LN* 1 (10/86): n.p.; and 2 (12/87): 188.

33. For evidence of the curriculum as Dewey structured it, see *Circular of Information, 1886–7,* especially p. 31, where Dewey outlines a "Course in Bibliography"; *LN* 1 (3/87): 269–70, where he discusses "Changes in the Library School for the Second Year"; and *LN* 2 (12/87): 236, where he outlines C. S. Smith's role on the library school faculty. The conclusions presented here largely grow out of readings on the concept of professional authority presented in Paul Starr, *The Social Transformation of American Medicine* (New York, 1984); and of professional jurisdictions presented in Abbott, *The System of Professions* (1988). They are developed more fully and applied to librarianship more specifically in my "Perspectives on Library Education in the Context of Recently Published Literature on the History of Professions," *Journal of Education for Library and Information*

Toward spring Dewey tried to strengthen the library school's position on campus by asking trustees to approve several changes. First, he wanted to change its name to the "School of Library Science" and list among its faculty the president, library director (who would also be library school dean), and all instructors, including faculty members who delivered lectures on subject and literature bibliography. He also wanted to limit admission to "graduates of literary colleges" and anyone else who qualified by means of a special examination, and asked that the trustees authorize degrees of B.L.S., M.L.S., and D.L.S. Barnard submitted this proposal to the trustees on May 2, 1887, and supplemented it with an appeal for "convenient" classroom space. But the trustees referred the library school proposal to the committee on courses and statutes, passed control of library funds to the president, then voted an addition to their statutes: "No woman shall be admitted as a student in any department of the College, other than the Collegiate Course for Women, except by special order of the Trustees."[34] Dewey's School of Library Economy would remain a bootleg operation.

An Opposition Forms
1887–1888

The library committee met May 6. In addition to routine matters, the committee also took up the cost of printing Dewey's lengthy annual reports. Many people on campus objected to the way he described the Columbia library experience; others disliked the way he represented himself to the outside world. His *Circulars of Information,* his articles in *Library Journal* and *Library Notes,* all were regarded by some campus officials as unjustifiably "long and boastful statements . . . not in accordance with academic propriety and the dignity of the College." By resolution the library committee ordered Dewey to limit the narrative part of

---

Science 25 (1986): 267–80; and "The Socialization of Library and Information Science Students: Reflections on a Century of Formal Education for Librarianship," *Library Trends* 34 (1986): 363–89. See also Samuel Haber, *The Quest for Authority and Honor in the American Professions, 1750–1900* (Chicago, 1991), p. 292.

34. "Outline of Policy and Plan of Classes and Degrees for Library School," 5/2/87, Columbiana.

his annual report to six pages; although he followed the order, Dewey was piqued at the committee's attitude.

Dewey had also irritated several powerful faculty members. In December 1886, for example, Mathematics Professor I. H. Van Amringe complained that Dewey's method of bookkeeping had shorted the math department on book purchases. Dewey responded to his complaints, then concluded: "You don't seem to 'Take to' my scheme of raising an alumni fund of $10,000 for math books . . . I suppose you wd like the money but not the bother of getting it?" Dewey could ill afford to provoke Van Amringe, who, as secretary of the board, had responsibility for monitoring the printing of all college publications authorized by the trustees. Van Amringe was understandably angry with Dewey's cavalier treatment. He wrote specific objections to Dewey's points across Dewey's letter, then filed it.[35] He also began objecting to Dewey's practice of using Library Bureau offices to print material about Columbia without having it approved by college officers. Dewey frequently used this avenue when Columbia blocked his printing requests, and since as time passed he was meeting increased opposition on campus, more and more he turned to the Bureau for printing needs which he then charged back to the College.[36]

The board's executive committee met May 29, and among other issues resolved to retain Baker at $1,200. Barnard objected, arguing that such action would damage library service, but the committee refused to reconsider. "What should I do?" he wrote Dewey in frustration. Dewey had two suggestions: fire someone else on campus to compensate for Baker's salary; contact alumni, librarians, perhaps even newspapers, to mobilize against the trustees. Barnard opposed both. "To use more force now would be like *teasing* the board and would do more harm than good."[37] Also, on May 29 the trustees rejected Dewey's request for new furnishings in the library school and on June 6

---

35. Copy of this letter from Dewey to Van Amringe, dated 12/18/86, over which the latter penciled in red, is in Box 18, Dewey Mss. An explanation of the chronology concerning college printing is summarized in the resolution on Dewey's dismissal, dated 12/3/88, and found in Box 19.

36. See Barnard to Dewey, 6/30/87; Barnard to G. P. Putnam's Sons, 8/5/87; and Dewey to G. P. Putnam's Sons, 8/5/87, Box 18, Dewey Mss.

37. Barnard to Dewey, 5/30/87; 6/3/87, Box 18, Dewey Mss. See also TLCM, 5/6/88, and Dewey to Seth Low, 11/10/88, Box 18, Dewey Mss.

voted against granting degrees or changing the name of the library school. "Library Economy is an intelligible term," they said. "It is an art, . . . not a Science in the proper sense of that term," and thus did not merit parity with Columbia's other schools.[38]

By early fall, campus resentment with Dewey seeped into the press. On October 4, the *New York Tribune* quoted a Columbia alumni association report that noted "general dissatisfaction . . . by the Trustees and Faculty with the administration of the library." Barnard reacted to this public disclosure quickly; he asked faculty reasons for their discontent. "In so far as it related to the Trustees," he wrote, "I am very confident it is a mistake." Responses crossed Barnard's desk throughout October and November. Many were laudatory. John Quackenbos complimented the library staff on its service and courtesy; B. F. O'Connor said he always found the library willing to meet his demands as far as funds permitted; Charles Sprague Smith pointed out that "the library, hitherto a comparatively useless appendage, has been brought into organic connection with the university and is doing in its sphere a most valuable work." Nicholas Murray Butler later observed that the younger and more recently appointed faculty members "wholeheartedly supported every proposal for the expansion and improvement of the library."

Others were critical. "If I . . . have any cause of dissatisfaction with the library administration," William Carpenter wrote, "it arises from the fact that there's too much rather than too little." He disliked the "complicated classification" and detested the constant shifting of books. Thomas Price cited two problems: (1) the library "suffered terribly" from an inadequate book budget; (2) its use "is made difficult by the false system of arranging books." H. H. Boyeson complimented Dewey's management of the library, but noted flaws in his personality. "The chief librarian seems to delight in writing absurd and often impertinent circulars to the members of the faculty." Ogden Rood complained that the library spent nearly $17,000 per year on salaries for staff, but only $50 on physics books. And Dewey's "official

---

38. In May 1887, Dewey wrote in his comportment journal, "Avoid dif. faculty, trustees. Stop *thinking*." Box 19, Dewey Mss. Proposal for changing the name of the library school in a manuscript cited by Carl M. White, *A Historical Introduction to Library Education: Problems and Progress to 1951* (Metuchen, N.J., 1976), pp. 80–81. See also CCTM, 5/7/87 and 6/17/87; and correspondence relating to Baker in Columbiana.

communications" he said, were "flavored with arrogance, and this circumstance has led me as far as possible to avoid the gentleman in question." Dewey's strongest critic, however, was Van Amringe, who pulled his December correspondence with Dewey out of his file, red penciled over Dewey's inaccuracies and misstatements, and sent them all to Barnard. Van Amringe also cited an "objectionable spirit" in treating faculty concerns evident in Dewey's "persistent attempt to dismiss Baker" and his "offensive display" of boastfulness in the 1886 report.

Barnard collected all of this correspondence together, and passed it back to Dewey. "The animus of some of these letters is so obvious that I doubt the feasibility of removing prejudice by explanation. I incline to think it is best to be silent."[39] But Dewey retreated only slightly. He remained silent on faculty complaints, yet pushed as hard as ever for his library reforms. He continued to press for more funding for the library and for acceptance of the library school which began its second year, and foolishly persevered in efforts to dismiss William Baker. Although he knew about the opposition building against him, he seemed oblivious to its cumulative effect and took no measures to reduce it. And over subsequent months trustees and the faculty continued to block his initiatives. The former controlled the purse strings, and scrutinized Dewey's expenditures very carefully. The latter looked for opportunities to criticize Dewey, and in his zeal, he left them plenty of openings.

Dewey was most vulnerable on reclassification costs. When awarded extra appropriations for reclassification in May 1883, he had promised to reduce expenses for library administration within three years. Five years later it appeared he still had not reduced expenses. Although he could not say so, the problem was not reclassification; that work was winding down. The problem was the library school. To win approval of the school, Dewey had promised that it would not increase Columbia's costs. He badly miscalculated. He had not anticipated the large amounts of time

---

39. *NYTr,* 10/4/87; Barnard to "Columbia Faculty," 10/5/87; copy in Box 18, Dewey Mss. Correspondence with faculty, dated between 10/5/87 and 10/22/87, can be found in Box 18, Dewey Mss. See also Van Amringe to Dewey, 12/18/86 and 3/16/87; and Dewey to Van Amringe, 12/18/86, all in Box 18. See also Barnard to Dewey, 9/22/87, Box 18; and Nicholas Murray Butler, *Across the Busy Years: Recollections and Reflections,* vol. 1 (N.Y., 1935), p. 95.

library school faculty had to devote to student needs, and to compensate, in January 1887 he began switching staff time from the reclassification project to the library school. At least one staff member complained. In August George Baker asked for a salary increase. Dewey denied it, claiming insufficient funds. Baker protested. "Money enough was voted," he wrote, but the "Library School and other enterprises consume the administration fund while I and perhaps others suffer financially for it. . . . the establishment of the school &c is a good thing, but ought not to be done at others' expense."

Dewey's budget request to the library committee for 1888–89 showed his dilemma. He wanted the library's salary appropriations divided between the library administration and library school and asked for a "modest" appropriations increase of $5,000 "for salaries of instructors, and for some compensation to the lecturers, who have thus far given their services." When the committee refused, Dewey looked for alternatives. Two that he thought showed promise were a correspondence school for library work and a summer school for librarians. Each promised less demand on faculty time; both promised additional revenue. Dewey wanted the former to focus on cataloging and classification, the latter to function either as a joint endeavor with an existing summer school (like Chautauqua), or as an independent school in some attractive natural setting, or as a joint venture with several large libraries on a rotating basis.[40]

Despite the obstacles, despite the opposition, Dewey forged on. Publicly he reported that except for lack of funds and furniture, the library school's second year was highly successful. One hundred people had applied, twenty-two were admitted, sixteen of them women; eleven (nine of them women) had stayed on from the previous year for additional work. He extended the term from three to seven months, and announced efforts to match "other schools of the university" by expanding school offerings to the full college year beginning October 1, 1888. As in

---

40. See TLCM, 3/16/88; "Summer School for Librarians," *LN* 2 (3/88): 289–96; and Baker to Dewey, 8/8/88, Box 18, Dewey Mss. See also *Acting President's Report, 1889* (N.Y., 1889), p. 17, for evidence that Columbia's officers understood Dewey's efforts to move administrative expenses of reclassification and cataloging into covering for unanticipated expenses in running the library school. See also Barnard to Dewey, 9/18/88, Box 18; and *Second Annual Report*, p. 30.

the previous year, lectures (sixty-seven in 1888) were delivered by library school faculty, by visiting authorities like Cutter and Bowker, and by resident Columbia faculty.[41] Privately, he began looking for options. In 1887 he encouraged Annie Nathan Meyer to "start a college yourself" when she complained of Columbia's treatment of women. He also watched Butler open a two-year College for the Training of Teachers under the auspices of the Industrial Education Association in September 1887. Butler hoped the college would develop into a professional school he could someday attach to Columbia. If either Meyer's or Butler's efforts were successful, Dewey would have a convenient place to park his School of Library Economy should problems with Columbia persist. Through Meyer, he might get his students degrees; through Butler, he might find a more convenient way to attach his library school to Columbia's regular curriculum.[42]

On May 7, 1888, however, his prospects for the future changed dramatically; Barnard resigned as president of Columbia because of poor health. This single action removed Dewey's strongest ally on campus and left him even more vulnerable to concerted efforts against his agenda. By that time he had alienated most trustees, including his own library committee, won the umbrage of many faculty members for his haughty treatment of their library needs, and was looked upon with suspicion by many members of the alumni who were privy to faculty conversation. And since Henry Drisler (Columbia's senior professor who had feuded with Dewey on several occasions in the recent past) had been appointed to replace Barnard as acting president, it was only a matter of time before forces ranged against Dewey coalesced into an organized opposition.

---

41. *Fifth Annual Report*, pp. 22–31. See also *Circular of Information, 1888–89*, p. 35.

42. Butler's College for the Training of Teachers later became Teachers College of Columbia University. See Butler, *Across the Busy Years, Vol. 1*, pp. 176–82, and Richard Whittemore, *Nicholas Murray Butler and Public Education, 1862–1911* (N.Y., 1971), pp. 39–46. Dewey ran a full-page ad for the "Educational Monographs and Leaflets" put out by Butler's school in the December 1887 issue of *LN*. See *LN* 2 (12/87): n.p. See also Horace Coon, *Columbia: Colossus on the Hudson* (N.Y., 1947), pp. 189–94; Annie Nathan Meyer, *Barnard's Beginnings* (N.Y., 1935), p. 32; and Lynn Gordon, "Annie Nathan Meyer and Barnard College: Mission and Identity in Women's Higher Education, 1889–1950," *History of Education Quarterly* 26 (1986): 505.

But in the summer of 1888, the campus was preoccupied with a larger issue. Barnard's resignation had reignited a power struggle dating back to 1880 between conservatives like Drisler and Van Amringe, who wanted Columbia to remain a traditional institution with a classical curriculum, and activists like Burgess and Butler, who wanted to transform it into a university. In 1888 Burgess counted only ten of twenty-four trustees who favored the university plan. The faculty was also split. When Barnard resigned, trustee Charles Da Costa decided to force the issue by getting the board to solicit votes from the faculties of the various schools on whether Columbia should be reorganized into a university. Minority, and even individual, opinions were encouraged.

The vote, however, gave mixed signals to the trustees—two faculties (Political Science and Law) were unanimously for the university plan; two were against, one of which (Mines) gave it a bare majority. In the other (Arts), a strong minority voted for the university plan. It became evident that the selection of Barnard's successor would be crucial to resolving the issue. Trustees Morgan Dix and Joseph Harper, both of whom were against the university plan, pushed for Drisler. Trustees Da Costa and Fish, both of whom were for the university plan, argued that no member of the existing faculty should fill the vacant slot.[43] In the next few months the struggle intensified, and it was inside this larger arena with much higher stakes for Columbia that Dewey's sideshow was played out. Unlike Burgess and Butler, however, Dewey could not count on solid support from strong segments among the faculty, trustees, or alumni.

Moves against Dewey began in late October 1888, when Acting President Drisler ordered Dewey to encumber no more funds against the library's annual appropriations. Since the board was scheduled to meet November 5, Dewey must have sensed his tenure at Columbia would be a subject for discussion. What he did not know, however, was that Drisler and Van Amringe had been discussing Dewey's printing bills. "Fifty pages on the Library

---

43. Burgess, *Reminiscences,* p. 224; 231–34; Butler, *Across the Busy Years,* vol. 1, Chap. 7; Munroe Smith, "The University and the Non-Professional Graduate Schools," *A History of Columbia University, 1754–1904* (N.Y., 1904), pp. 231–34; Coon, *Columbia,* pp. 84–87; and R. Gordon Hoxie, *A History of the Faculty of Political Science, Columbia University* (N.Y., 1955), pp. 20–44.

and School of Library Economy besides the regular *Report*,"
Drisler wrote trustee Hamilton Fish on October 25; the law
school had taken only twenty-six. He told Fish he had asked Van
Amringe to submit a report on college printing connected with
the library and library school for the forthcoming meeting. Fish
agreed; the library administration, he said, had been "running
wholly beyond its bounds."[44]

At the meeting, trustees took action against Dewey which
seemed well rehearsed. First, Edward Mitchell resolved that "it is
the pleasure of the Trustees to dismiss Mr. Dewey." Instead of
acting directly on the resolution, however, the board approved a
special investigative committee consisting of Mitchell, Da Costa,
and Seth Low (chair), who then presented a second resolution:
"That Melvil Dewey be suspended from the office of Chief Librarian pending the report of the Special Committee appointed
this day to consider the dismissal of Mr. Dewey." A third motion
directed Drisler to designate someone from the library staff as
Acting Chief Librarian, and a fourth aimed at the library school:
"That it be referred to the Committee on the Course and the
Statutes to consider whether the School of Library Economy is a
desirable adjunct to the Library, and if so, whether the instruction to be given in it shall not be committed to others than the
librarians of the College." In another, seemingly unrelated, move
trustees authorized the appointment of a "Special Committee on
Printing" to "consider and report a scheme to secure a proper
oversight of all the printing for which appropriations are made in
the Board."[45] Drisler told Dewey of the board's action the next
day; a short time later Low told him the special committee would
meet November 9, and asked him to be present. Dewey said he
welcomed the investigation, expressed confidence he would be
exonerated, but implored the committee and trustees to avoid
open discussion of his situation and to guard against leaks to the
press.

The investigating committee met as scheduled, and although
no record of the session exists, analysis of documents considered by the committee and the many letters that passed between Dewey and Low over subsequent weeks makes it possible

44. See Drisler to Fish, 10/25/88; Fish to Drisler, 10/27/88, Fish Mss.
See also Burgess, *Reminiscences,* p. 231.
45. See CCTM, 11/5/88.

to piece together issues addressed and charges made.[46] Low's committee wanted to find out whether Dewey surreptitiously avoided college offices in order to free himself from college controls. His critics accused him of creating an "employment registry" for library school graduates, advertising correspondence courses and a summer school, and printing a form that required applicants to describe their physical features. All of this had been done without college approval through the Library Bureau and *Library Notes,* and as evidence his critics cited an issue of *Notes* in which Dewey predicted that "sum degree, corresponding to Bachelor of Library Science (B.L.S.) wil we think hereafter be establisht to be conferd on those who complete the full course." Dewey had no authority to make this statement, his critics charged, and because he had identified his Columbia affiliation, he clearly implied he was officially speaking for the college.

Dewey responded to these charges in two lengthy letters to Low dated November 10. The first was intended for all members of the committee. In it he acknowledged that regular reference to his position and Columbia faculty in Bureau publications and *Notes* might give the wrong "impression." As for application forms, these he had synthesized from state normal school applications solicited from across the country. In each, he noted, the form used by principals of these normal schools requested descriptions of personal appearance. On many occasions he had sent trustees publicity items about the employment registry, "but I have yet to learn that they were read. . . . I was simply *snubbed* into keeping my own counsel except to the President." Dewey then cited several articles praising the Columbia College Library system and its library school, and directed the committee's attention to an accompanying package of letters "which Barnard handed me five years ago" (Dewey did not mention he himself had solicited these letters) "to show you that you had warning that enthusiasm & energy were my strong points & *anti*-conservatism." He then slipped into a revealing metaphor. "A man who thinks it undignified or dangerous to ride a fast or frisky horse" ought not to expect it to become "a good reliable beast for the plow," and rather than "shoot or cripple" the horse

---

46. These documents, which shall be discussed in subsequent paragraphs, were collected by the committee and later placed in the Columbiana collection.

to slow it down "had best let [it] go to some one that wants that peculiar type." It was the first time Dewey alluded to taking another position.

In the second letter, marked "Private" and intended only for Low, Dewey elaborated his allusion. He reminded Low that for more than a year he had been discussing the New York State librarian's position with Regents of the University of the State of New York (USNY) and said that these interviews had become more serious in previous weeks. "I told you last winter . . . I shd not hesitate a moment to go as soon as I could honorably leave CC *except* for the School. You said you doubted the willingness of the trustees to have it abandoned or moved." But, Dewey wrote, a question about "giving up the school" put to him by Da Costa at the investigating committee meeting "almost betrayed me in my sudden recognition of a solution agreeable to the trustees." Dewey recommended that trustees authorize a committee to close the school at the end of the academic year and allow him to transfer it to Albany if he could convince the Regents to accept it.[47]

Before trustees met to deliberate Dewey's fate on December 3, they received three committee reports. The report from the special committee on printing complimented Van Amringe, who, as the person responsible for monitoring college printing, had performed his duties "with fidelity, discretion and good taste, and—considering the unbusinesslike methods of the Librarian in furnishing copy—with commendable patience." It criticized Dewey by noting that circulars had been issued by "a Library Bureau" in Boston which looked as though they had come from the college and which "in orthography and general appearance were not creditable," that Dewey's annual reports represented "long and boastful statements," and that the reports themselves promised scholarships to library school applicants that trustees had not authorized. The report from the committee on the course and statutes expressed "great doubt as to the expediency of continuing" the library school, and recommended that it be placed under the direction of the acting president for

47. If Dewey had entertained plans for moving the library school to Barnard when it opened or merging it with Columbia through Butler's College for the Training of Teachers, he quickly abandoned them when he realized he might be able to move the school with him to Albany. Dewey to Low, 11/10/88, Box 18, Dewey Mss.

the rest of the term, after which its future ought to be reconsidered. The third report, which came from Low's committee, concluded that because Dewey and Barnard had agreed on the library school application form "more than a year ago," Dewey had not acted unilaterally and without authority. Based on its findings, the committee recommended the resolution calling for Dewey's dismissal be tabled and the suspension lifted.[48]

By this time Low was probably aware Dewey had been offered a joint position as State Librarian and Secretary to the USNY Board of Regents, and when trustees met December 3 to consider the committee's recommendations, they probably knew Dewey would accept the offer. They had nothing to lose by following Low's advice. He had tightly controlled the boundaries of the investigation, and since Dewey was going to leave anyway, had convinced others that opening the investigation beyond those narrow confines would be counterproductive. Low also convinced the board that its November 5 action against Dewey should "not appear in the printed minutes." As a result, he managed to choreograph a situation that allowed Dewey to submit a seemingly untainted resignation after receiving a public offer from the Regents, and walk away from Columbia with dignity and reputation intact.

Evidence gathered from unpublished sources, however, demonstrates the real reasons Dewey left are much more complex, and must be analyzed within the larger context of Columbia's painful shift from college to university. Under the circumstances, any library director would have had difficulty managing the transition. Despite that context, Dewey had done little to help himself. Nicholas Murray Butler later observed that Dewey "went so far and so fast . . . he sawed off the limb upon which he was sitting." Many trustees, faculty, and alumni disliked women on cam-

---

48. Reports of the Special Committee on Printing and the Committee on the Course and Statutes can be found in CCTM, 12/3/88, and in Box 19, Dewey Mss. The "scholarships" Dewey offered had strings attached: "Those winning these honors being required to discharge certain duties in the college library as part of their training." See "Changes in the Library School for the Second Year," *LN* 1 (5/87): 269. Dewey may have intended to use library personnel appropriations to cover these "stipends," and to justify it because of the work stipend holders had to perform. Copy of Low's report, dated 12/3/88, can be found in Columbiana. Dewey's recollections of these events can be found in Dewey to Wyer, 12/18/16, Box 23, Dewey Mss.

pus, for which they thought Dewey was to blame (and for which he subsequently took most of the credit); many disliked him as a person and as a library administrator; many loathed his abrupt and haughty manner and his exaggerated self-righteousness; several subordinates were displeased with his willingness to compromise their careers for his agendas.

All this combined to encourage his detractors to seize upon several issues for which Dewey could easily be criticized: advertising for library employees without prior approval; admitting women to library school without explicitly seeking permission; supporting the library school with funds most trustees thought had been targeted for a reclassification project; enforcing new library rules tactlessly; issuing reports which seemed highly self-serving; mailing circulars and dispensing information about Columbia in simplified spelling from noncollege sources. And throughout it all, Dewey seemed so focused on his "larger interests" he made little attempt to secure his base of operations. This neglect eventually cost him his job. While the record shows he was not dismissed and that his suspension had been revoked, the outcome would undoubtedly have been considerably different had he chosen to stay and fight. The disposition of the library school appears to have tipped him towards Albany, and Columbia was not unhappy to see him and his library school go. Dewey submitted his resignation on December 20, the day after receiving an offer from the Regents; trustees accepted his resignation January 7, 1889.[49]

Despite the ugliness of his parting, Dewey left the Columbia campus with a significant legacy. In May 1883 he had inherited a collection of 50,000 poorly cataloged and indifferently classified volumes scattered over nine departments; in December

---

49. CCTM, 1/7/89. Trustee Morgan Dix penned into his diary that day: "The most important thing was the reception of the resignation of Mr. Dewey whereat there was great exultation, with pity for the Regents of the University." See Morgan Dix, "Diary," 1/7/89, typewritten transcript in Columbia Libraries. Dewey was succeeded at Columbia by George H. Baker, who assumed the position of "Librarian" ("Chief" was dropped from the title) at $3,500 per year. At their January 7 meeting trustees also set in motion a series of moves to release the library school to Albany, which took place officially April 1. At that time Columbia also shipped all the curricular materials and said goodbye to four employees who followed Dewey to Albany.

1888 he left a collection of 100,000 uniformly cataloged and classified volumes and 500 serial subscriptions located in a central library where a public catalog pointed readers to other locations. He had also doubled the acquisitions budget and quadrupled the personnel budget and significantly expanded services and hours of opening. During his first year alone he increased circulation 500 percent. He had also established a collection development policy and encouraged other metropolitan New York libraries to cooperative ventures. His initiatives were being copied by other academic (and public) libraries across the country and around the world. He recruited a devoted, hard-working staff, and helped to introduce Columbia to women on its campus. He used his experience at Columbia to monitor two more editions of the *Decimal Classification,* and opened the world's first library school. Nicholas Murray Butler, who referred to Columbia in the 1880s as the "Barnard-Burgess-Dewey revolution," traced the origins of Columbia University's modern library system directly to Dewey's administration.[50] For a period of five tumultuous years during which Columbia chose to "ride a fast or frisky horse," its library traveled a much longer distance than any of its peers.

---

50. Butler to Dewey, 12/7/31, Butler Mss. See also Butler, *Across the Busy Years,* vol. 1, pp. 94–95.

5

Other Interests

1883-1888

Dewey was so preoccupied with efforts at Columbia that for five years he let metric and spelling reform interests slide. He was still Secretary of the American Metric Bureau, which remained solvent throughout the 1880s in part because Dewey had little time to play with its Sinking Fund, but he attended AMS conferences infrequently. In 1888 metric reform was no farther along than 1883. Spelling reform experienced more activity, but no more success. The SRA continued to meet coterminously with the American Philological Association, but its annual meetings were lightly attended. Toward the end of 1886 the SRA showed some movement. The *Bulletin* had never been financially successful, and SRA's association with *Fonetic Techer* had proved a serious liability. At its December 30, 1886, meeting, the Executive Committee voted to start a new quarterly entitled *Spelling* that would be published by the Library Bureau at no profit. But the first issue looked anemic. Most of its contents consisted of two- and three-paragraph quotes from notables who had endorsed spelling reform. By December 1887, the SRA was already projecting a deficit of $300 for the first volume year. *Spelling* did not appear again until April 1892.[1]

---

1. See March to Dewey, 12/28/86, Box 83; SRA Executive Committee Minutes, 12/30/86, Box 87, Dewey Mss; and *Spelling,* 1 (May 1887): 36–38.

The Library Bureau, on the other hand, was much more active during Dewey's Columbia years. On May 9 he "sold" the Bureau's inventory to Herbert Davidson in the form of a $9,000 loan and, except for retaining "certain articles & rights," allowed Davidson to manage the business as he saw fit. Always, however, he made sure to retain "veto power against any changes that would diminish [its] usefulness to libraries." From the start, the Bureau struggled, in part because Dewey ran up his Columbia College Library bills on supplies needed for reclassification and recataloging. Davidson repeatedly begged him to stop, but without success. Only the Library Committee's willingness to release the second half of the $10,000 Columbia promised Dewey in May eased the burden.[2]

Davidson was a congenial fellow, a loyal subordinate, and an excellent salesman, but he had difficulty managing the Library Bureau within constraints Dewey placed upon him, and especially suffered from Dewey's control of prices on Bureau products. On October 17, 1885, a Bureau employee informed Dewey that Davidson had no more credit at local banks, and because by extension that meant the Library Bureau had no credit either, she reported Davidson was avoiding the office because he did not want to confront creditors. To correct matters Dewey made another employee, Arthur N. Brown, responsible for bookkeeping, but allowed Davidson to retain sole authority to sign checks and pay bills. On February 5, 1886, Brown told Dewey that Davidson had written several checks against the business without telling him, "and I knew nothing about them until they came back from the bank." Brown suggested the business ought to incorporate. Dewey refused. Instead, he courted Columbia trustee F. A. Schermerhorn to give Davidson a $5,000 loan to settle his personal finances, and convinced William E. Parker to leave Columbia for Boston to take care of the business. Parker quickly teamed with Miss E. W. Sherman, a very competent bookkeeper Davidson had hired earlier in the year. Together Parker and Sherman implemented a new accounting system. With Bureau finances in more competent hands, Dewey decided to send Davidson on the road

---

2. See "Library Bureau," Dun Collection, MA88/p. 184; Davidson to Dewey, 9/17/83; 10/9/83; 10/25/83; 10/27/83; 11/3/83; 11/8/83; and 11/12/83, Box 61, Dewey Mss; *LJ* 8 (9–10/83): 256; and "Brief History of the Library Bureau," *LB Monthly News,* Supplement, 1916, no. 24, pp. 4–5.

as a salesman. He thought these actions would settle the Bureau's financial problems, and at the same time capitalize on Davidson's strengths.[3]

For a while he proved right. Davidson performed well and the Bureau was beginning to show signs of growth. Davidson was especially successful at building a substantial trade in index card systems among banks, railroads, government departments, and corporations. But after a short time he again began using his Bureau stock as collateral for personal loans, and because he was regularly delinquent on payments, he continually got the Bureau in trouble. By January the situation had deteriorated so much Dewey had to step in for a second time. He forced an agreement to have all financial transactions countersigned by Parker. "The business must go on for its usefulness to libraries," he advised his lawyer, but told him to "be *very cautious* not to take any step that wil get out & cause comment." Dewey did not give all the reasons he wanted to keep matters quiet. If the Bureau failed, he would be subject to further suspicions at Columbia, and educational reform groups whose fortunes Dewey had tied to the Bureau through binding agreements would suffer financially. In January 1888, for example, *Spelling* was particularly vulnerable.[4]

But Davidson proved unable to meet his obligations, and in early April his creditors forced the issue. Dewey's lawyer advised him to surrender the business, but Dewey refused. "My life work involves having a successful LB . . . & I must make sum sacrifices." Davidson's creditors judged his assets at $23,000 and his liabilities at $27,000, including $20,000 he owed Dewey. A committee of creditors then decided that if the Library Bureau was going to survive, either Davidson or Dewey would have to buy it by paying off Davidson's creditors.[5] Davidson could not come up

---

3. See Mattie Parker to Dewey, 10/17/85; A. N. Brown to Dewey, 2/5/86, all in Box 61, Dewey Mss. Copies of the $5,000 note from Schermerhorn to Davidson can be found in Box 33A, Dewey Mss. See also Schermerhorn to Dewey, 4/21/87, Box 33. Dewey's personnel moves at the Bureau are evident from numerous letters dated April and May 1887 in Box 62.

4. Dewey to Samuel J. Elder, 1/21/88, Box 61, Dewey Mss. See also C. P. G. Scott to Dewey, 2/7/88, Box 83, for evidence of the links between *Spelling*'s future and Library Bureau fortunes.

5. Dewey to Elder, 4/11/88, Box 61, Dewey Mss; Walter Raymond (chairman of the special committee for the creditors) to Elder, 4/12/88, Box 61; Boston *Herald*, 4/13/88.

with the money, but on April 21 the committee convinced Dewey to offer 40 cents on the dollar payable in ten days. In effect, the agreement required him to raise an additional $3,000 (part of which he borrowed from his brother) to satisfy Davidson's creditors. It allowed him to save the Bureau, retain control of its future, and rid himself of Davidson's troubles.[6]

Because creditors had to issue a public report, however, Dewey could not keep the agreement out of the press. R. R. Bowker, still editing *Library Journal,* felt it his duty to report the news because so many Bureau customers were also *Journal* readers. He also drafted an editorial charging that "the Bureau has really undertaken to do more good than it could afford to do on a business basis," and sent proof sheets to Dewey for comment. Dewey suggested several modifications, and requested that Bowker print an unsigned story arguing that until Dewey went to New York in 1883 all organizations under his management had prospered. Bowker refused. He argued that the complicated contract which gave Dewey control of prices undercut Davidson's chances of turning the Bureau into a financial success. Bowker also rejected Dewey's modifications on page proofs, which, he said, made Davidson "by inference the scapegoat." The story and the editorial ran without modification.[7]

To counter, Dewey wrote *LJ* a letter. The Bureau was one of four important agencies advancing library work, he argued; the other three were the ALA, the *Journal,* and the School of Library Economy. Dewey then recounted the Bureau's history, always being careful to put distance between himself and its operation since 1883. "Since selling," he wrote, "I hav been in no sense partner, having no interest whatever but a creditor's, in the profits." The recent crisis, however, forced him to rescue the great agency, but now, after much personal financial sacrifice, he was ready to incorporate and was looking for investors willing to accept 6 percent interest on the capital invested. He then scolded library peers for patronizing other library suppliers who either charged higher prices for the same goods as the Bureau or charged the same prices for goods of lesser quality. "Experiences of this

6. Elder to Dewey, 4/17/88, Box 61; Dewey to Mr. Fairfield, 4/18/88, Box 29; M. J. Dewey to Dewey, 4/29/88, Box 38, Dewey Mss.

7. See "Editorial," *LJ* 13 (4–5/88): 68; "The Library Bureau Failure," *LJ* 13 (4–5/88): 96; proof sheets of "Library Bureau Failure" article in Box 64; Bowker to Dewey, 5/8/88, Box 64, Dewey Mss.

kind dull one's enthusiasm greatly in trying to improve and cheapen library fittings and supplies." Dewey promised to push ahead anyway, secure in the belief that enough librarians would patronize the Bureau to make it successful. Characteristically, throughout his letter Dewey claimed altruism, not capitalism, as his motive. Characteristically, the letter was self-serving, vainglorious, absent of any hint of guilt or blame, and distorted the truth even as Dewey knew it.[8]

On May 26, the reorganized and soon-to-be-incorporated Library Bureau held its first meeting, at which Dewey announced the company had a declared capital of $15,000. Stockholders included Melvil Dewey (130 shares), Annie Dewey (7), Annie Brown Jackson (10), and Walter S. Biscoe, W. E. Parker, and E. W. Sherman (one each). Dewey was elected president, Parker treasurer. Although Davidson was named secretary, his duties were defined more specifically as "manufacturing and selling." On September 20, the Bureau moved into new offices at 146 Franklin Street, Boston, and was back in business. Once again Dewey had weathered a storm and survived.[9]

The second edition of the *Decimal Classification,* which appeared in a print run of 500 copies late 1885, was published by the Library Bureau. It totaled 314 pages (270 more than the original), and in an enlarged introduction Dewey vigorously defended close classification, decimalism, and a "Relativ Subject Index" he had expanded from 2,000 to 14,000 entries.[10] The second edition was significantly different from the first. Dewey continued to place a higher value on practical than theoretical consistency, but he made radical changes in Law (340) and Religion (200) and greatly expanded Natural Science (500) and Literature (800). By including an additional subdivision for American literature (810), he forced reclassification for libraries that had already adopted

---

8. *LJ* 13 (5/88): 145–46. Some librarians agreed with Dewey's complaint that the profession did not patronize the Bureau sufficiently. See Henry Utley (Director of the Detroit Public Library) to Dewey, 5/24/88, Box 34, Dewey Mss.

9. Minutes of first meeting of newly organized Library Bureau, dated 5/26/88, can be found in Box 100, Dewey Mss. See also "Reorganization of the Library Bureau," *LJ* 13 (6/88): 183; "New Library Headquarters," *LJ* 13 (8/88): 236; and Annie B. Jackson to Dewey, 7/30/88, Box 31A, Dewey Mss.

10. Melvil Dewey, *Decimal Classification and Relativ Index,* 2d ed. rev. and greatly enlarged (Boston, 1885).

his system. He also introduced the use of three digits in the first division (renamed "General Works") by placing a "0" before the first number. He abandoned the practice of using book numbers beyond the third digit to designate accession number, substituting instead the letters of the author's surname behind the initial. He added a decimal after the third digit to accommodate expansion of subdivisions, and refined the "divide-like" principle that permitted one class to adopt the patterns of another. This was especially beneficial for subdividing major sections geographically and topically like "Bibliography of" (e.g., English history = 942; Bibliography of English history = 016.942).

Like its predecessor (and successors) the second edition also perpetuated Anglo-Saxonism. Christianity continued to be heavily favored. "Education of Females" (370) in the first edition was changed to "Education of Women" in the second, but was also expanded into subdivisions like "Physical Capacity of Women" (376.1) and "Mental Capacity of Women" (376.2). In the area of literature, Dewey relied on the advice of authorities to identify the best writers by country, period, and literary form, and then assigned a number to each. "Dewey seems not to have realized that scholarly tastes are relative," DDC historian John Comaromi explains, "and that it was an academic exercise at best to assign numbers to virtually every individual who had ever written a poem or play."[11] Work on a third edition began immediately, but for the most part Dewey left it (and all future editions during his lifetime) to others. Some work on the third edition undoubtedly took place on Columbia time; most, however, was probably done on personal time in order to advance "the great work to which some of us hav given our lives." Dewey continued to consult experts for their opinions of particular parts of the classification, but most of this was done by form letter and handled through the Bureau. The basic structure of the system remains unchanged to the present day.[12]

---

11. Comaromi, Chap. 4. Quote taken from p. 150.

12. An example of the form letter is reprinted in Comaromi, p. 197. See also pp. 193–204 for discussion of the third edition, which appeared in 1888 in the midst of the Library Bureau's bankruptcy and like its predecessor came out in a print run of 500 copies. Many of the second edition's typographical errors were removed, and the size of the index doubled. Medicine (610) was also considerably expanded.

Dewey began reasserting himself in ALA shortly after moving to Columbia. At the 1883 conference, for example, he used his secretary's report to summarize the Library Bureau's progress. When he reported lack of progress on the *ALA Catalog* Poole argued Dewey should take "direct responsibility for completing the *Catalog*." Dewey quickly reminded "our Nestor of librarians" that work on the *Catalog* had a four-year history; the second edition of *Poole's Index* took thirty. Poole also challenged Dewey's library school. "There is no training-school for educating librarians like a well-managed library," he argued, although "I do not wish to throw cold water upon the scheme." One audience member could not resist a rejoinder. "It seems to me that the gentleman has thrown a whole pool." Conferees laughed. Dewey said he welcomed the "cold water" as a "tonic," then with characteristic immodesty inaccurately reminded his audience while Poole was out of the room that "when I proposed in 1876 to organize this Association, and to found the *Library Journal,* I was assured, by the same element that questions the school idea today, that there was no room for either." Dewey predicted the "chief hydraulic factor in this discussion" would probably have to admit error again.[13]

Poole did not know what Dewey said until he read the conference proceedings much later. On December 17 he asked Dewey who he meant as "the chief hydraulic factor." Dewey thought it "perfectly clear" he meant Poole, then quickly added he "depended upon your taking it . . . in as good part as I always take the hits you enjoy giving me." But Poole was not appeased. He called Dewey's claims to have organized ALA and founded *LJ* "absurd and impossible," and reminded Dewey that Leypoldt "comes in for a strong claim as the originator of the idea" of a national library conference. He concluded: "You have done me a great wrong, and owe me an apology, and a retraction in the *Library Journal*."

Dewey's response shows why peers often found him so difficult. First, he delayed answering for nine weeks because "I have

---

13. *Proceedings, 1883,* 225, 261, 263, 267, 288, 289, 293, 294, 295. Dewey had some indication of Poole's opposition to a formal library training school before the conference. See Poole to Dewey, 7/14/83, Box 1, Dewey Mss.

been simply driven to death with work and could not get at any personal matters." Then he said Poole was magnifying "the importance of the matter about which everyone else has long since forgotten." He stressed a desire to write with "utmost frankness" because he had no "time for circumlocution," and then proceeded to circumlocute freely. Dewey refused to admit error or apologize. He skirted details surrounding his impolitic comments and resorted to generalities about circumstances in which they took place. He promised not to repeat the incident again, and offered to disclaim "anything that reflects on your loyalty to the ALA" at next conference. "I hope you will be able to send me word that you accept my friendly assurance," he concluded, "and that the little hatchet you have whetted for my scalp is safely buried." Nowhere did Dewey suggest he had done Poole "a great wrong," nor did he offer to apologize publicly in *LJ*. Eventually Poole decided to let the matter pass. He responded by saying he had "no hard feelings" and was "willing to let it go unsettled. I will allude to the late unpleasantness only to say that you were mistaken."[14]

Between conferences ALA matters proceeded at a snail's pace. For a short time it appeared the Bureau of Education might publish separately issued sections of the *ALA Catalog* free of charge. Dewey wanted to push for it for several reasons. First, annotated book lists of recommended titles remained popular. Caroline Hewins's *Books for the Young: A Guide for Parents and Children* (1882) and Frederic Perkins's *Best Reading* had become standard guides for building library collections. Second, he had plans to organize the *Catalog* in DDC (at the time being revised for a second edition) and assign each entry a decimal number, thereby expanding adoption of his classification scheme. Third, as Columbia's chief librarian he could tap a small army of volunteers in the New York City area to work on the manuscript. For example, he had no trouble convincing Astor Public Library Director C. Alex Nelson to help because of "the *boom* and *position* in the library world" that "getting the *ALA Catalog* out" would give him. Fourth, Dewey wanted closer ties with the Bureau. If cultivated properly, the relationship promised advan-

---

14. Poole to Dewey, 12/17/83; Dewey to Poole, 12/19/83, Box 1; Poole to Dewey, 12/28/83, Box 3; Dewey to Poole, 3/6/84, Box 1; Poole to Dewey, 3/13/84, Box 7, Dewey Mss.

tages to the nation's libraries, ALA, and the School of Library Economy.[15]

Because of scheduling complications, ALA decided to cancel its 1884 conference. At the 1885 conference Poole delivered opening remarks for an absent ALA President Winsor. Poole's speech was controversial. He stressed differences in librarianship between East and West, pointed with pride to the West's willingness to support public libraries with tax dollars, and wondered why states like New York, New Jersey, and Pennsylvania had enacted no similar enabling legislation. Dewey followed with a secretary's report that was a rallying cry for increased energy. He called for more activity in cooperative cataloging, increased membership, a campaign to divorce all library appointments (and especially state library appointments) from the political spoils system, and a permanent paid ALA officer (perhaps funded by the federal government). He also announced a cooperative agreement between ALA and the Bureau of Education to publish the *ALA Catalog*. Much of the remainder of the conference concentrated on topics Dewey had scheduled into the program. Conferees discussed such practical matters as book supports, book sizes, typewriters, handwriting, cataloging costs, small library buildings, galleries, stacks, and shelves. Before adjourning, conferees voted an executive board which subsequently chose Poole as ALA president for 1885–1886 (Dewey continued to serve as secretary), and Milwaukee as its next conference site. By selecting Milwaukee, ALA was attempting to accommodate librarians in the West who were increasingly complaining about East Coast control of the association.[16]

After Poole delivered a presidential address in Milwaukee on July 7, Dewey followed with his secretary's report.[17] He used

---

15. *LJ* 9 (4/84): 69; Nelson to J. L. Koopman, 7/25/84, Koopman Mss; Eaton to Dewey, 7/7/85, LCE-NA. For comments on the works by Hewins and Perkins, see *LJ* 7 (10/82): 249; and 10 (4/85): 91. See also Dewey to Rutherford P. Hayes, 1/19/83 and 12/12/84, Hayes Mss.

16. Quotes taken from *Proceedings, 1885,* 296, 309, 310, 311, 333, and 342. See also Ernest C. Richardson, "Bibliothecal Science and Economy—Article II of the A.L.A. Constitution," *LJ* 10 (9/85): 244–45.

17. Although delivered in the same oral English used by everyone else at the conference, Dewey insisted that the written version of his remarks that appeared in the *Proceedings* be in simplified spelling. ALA leaders disliked this intensely; it made the association look foolish to outside

it to digress on several of his own schemes. He noted that the cooperation committee had developed a plan for a new ALA "Publishing Section," and announced publication of *Library Notes*. He said he wanted *Notes* to "build up" the proposed ALA publishing section, expedite publication of the *ALA Catalog,* and facilitate dissemination of preprinted catalog cards to reduce duplicate cataloging of widely used titles. Dewey also acknowledged the Library Bureau had a pecuniary interest in all of these initiatives.

Most conference discussion, however, centered on practical library matters, although ALA did at Dewey's urging vote to establish a publishing section "to secure the preparation and publication of such catalogs, indexes, and other bibliographical helps as may best be produced by cooperation." After approving a constitution for the section, members elected Whitney chair, Harvard's William Coolidge Lane treasurer, and an executive committee consisting of William I. Fletcher, Dewey, Bowker, Cutter, and Green. Before the conference ended, the ALA executive committee announced it had elected Poole to a second term as president. Dewey had anticipated their action. During the last moments of the conference, he moved two constitutional amendments: (1) "that no officer be reelected more than once"; (2) that "the A.L.A. shall annually elect, by written ballot, a President and an Executive Board, four members beside the President, who shall choose from the Association a Vice-President, a Secretary, a Treasurer . . . and any other needed officers or standing committees." Both motions were direct challenges to what had become ALA's standard operating procedure. Both failed, however. In 1886 Dewey still lacked enough support to challenge the old guard's hold on ALA.[18]

The 1887 conference met at Thousand Islands, New York. For the first time over half the conferees were women. Dewey took partial credit for that milestone; "for the past three years the largest single delegation has come from Columbia College Library," he announced proudly. S. S. Green delivered a glowing report on Columbia's library school; it "fully justified the opinion

---

parties, they argued, but they had to agree with Dewey "that neither side had any right to dictate how the other shoud spell." See *Proceedings, 1886,* p. 381.

18. *Proceedings, 1886,* p. 203, 303, 341–42, 351, 376, 381.

of those persons who favored its establishment."[19] Nonetheless, he warned against "certain dangers," such as provincialism and "the exaggerations of the importance of instrumentalities by its pupils." One lecture that especially caught Dewey's attention was delivered by Johns Hopkins University Professor Herbert Baxter Adams, who described the university extension movement in England and suggested that American libraries function as sites for extension lectures. William I. Fletcher reported progress on all Publishing Section undertakings, and indicated the Bureau of Education had agreed to issue the *ALA Catalog* in sections. The executive board decided to alter the method for electing an ALA president: no person would be nominated two years in a row; and "an informal ballot [would] be taken and put in the hands of the committee without announcement, as a guide to the preferences for president." Dewey was among the majority openly supporting both moves. Before convening the executive board selected Cutter as president.[20]

But once again activities stagnated between conferences, and, in fact, because of a public dispute involving St. Louis Public Library director F. M. Crunden the ALA executive board decided to cancel the 1888 conference scheduled for that city. In its place Cutter called an informal meeting for September at Kaaterskill Falls, New York. There several committees issued reports, and although ALA elected no new officers, those present committed to meeting in St. Louis the following year.[21]

One other issue somewhat related to ALA occupied large amounts of Dewey's attention between 1883 and 1888. Dewey always felt Bowker and Leypoldt had not fairly recompensed him as *LJ* managing editor between 1876 and 1880 and persistently pressed his case after Leypoldt fired him. Because Leypoldt died in March 1884, however, Dewey was forced to switch to Bowker to win "restitution." In January 1885 he decided to press for

---

19. Not all ALA members agreed. Charles Evans snidely referred to Columbia's library school students as "cheap help." See Evans to Poole, 4/8/88, Poole Mss.

20. *Proceedings, 1887*, pp. 423, 427, 438, 457. See also *LJ* 12 (11/87): 512, where *LJ* quotes a letter H. B. Adams sent the *Springfield* [MA] *Republican* arguing that "every good public library should become, in its own field, a people's university, the highest of the school in the community."

21. *LJ* 13 (1/88): 3; Cutter to Dewey, 10/17/87, Box 2, Dewey Mss; *Proceedings, 1888*, 301, 302.

"vindication." But Bowker knew Dewey too well by this time, and refused to accommodate his tactics. He castigated Dewey for writing "one of those letters which purports to be friendly and really is most unfriendly," urged him to "put your claim in such simple written shape as to be evident to the ordinary business-man," and mail it rather than hand-carry it because he did not want to see Dewey at *LJ* offices for fear of "reopening" a "painful" experience for Leypoldt's widow. Dewey mailed the claim, but Bowker quickly judged it without merit. When Dewey persisted, Bowker advised him to sue. Bowker also refused to carry any more Library Bureau advertising in *LJ;* he would, he said, have no more "double back action patent elliptical business compli-cations of the old sort!" But Dewey would not cooperate; he refused to bring suit. Instead he wanted to settle his claim face-to-face, or submit to a neutral referee. If Bowker refused both options, Dewey argued, "I am *forced* to believe you are conscious of your unfairness and taking this course to avoid justice." Bow-ker gave no ground. "I cannot but distrust a 'friendship' which can descend to such abuse." He said he was glad Annie Dewey was "not cognizant of this attack upon me, for I regard her good opinion highly."

But Annie was cognizant. "I chanced to pick up your note . . . as his letters and papers have always been so free to me," she wrote Bowker on April 2, 1886. She expressed sadness that the two fought so bitterly. "I am not blind to Mr. Dewey's faults," she admitted, but the situation "requires a little putting aside of pride" for both men. She urged Bowker to select a referee. Bow-ker agreed. Five days later, Dewey wrote Bowker that "I don't care a show what the decision is—it is only to get it and bury all memory of the thing forever." Bowker probably was uncon-vinced; if experience was any teacher, he had reason to be cau-tious. Dewey further promised "never to let a thing get so snarled again" and pledged to "scrub away for *LJ* and put through a scheme for increasing its and the ALA list." Another year passed, however, before Dewey and Bowker submitted their dispute to an arbitrator, who eventually determined instead of the $1,300 Dewey claimed he was owed, the sum ought to be $204.19. Bow-ker paid him December 21, 1889.[22]

---

22. See Bowker to Dewey, 1/19 and 24/85; 4/27/85; 5/18/85; 12/18; 23/85; 3/4/86; Dewey to Bowker, 3/23/86; and Bowker to Dewey, 3/30/86;

While professionally Dewey's life was tumultuous between 1883 and 1888, domestically he enjoyed the few leisure moments he allowed himself. In 1885 he and Annie joined the Episcopal Church and remained with it for the rest of their lives. For most of their Columbia years, they lived in a seventh-floor apartment at 48 West 59th Street. There they hosted most of the out-of-town speakers he brought through the library school; there they entertained library school students and faculty on alternate Friday evenings. The Deweys worked hard to develop a feeling of extended family among subordinates and students who shared their "world work." This sense of "family" was most evident in pictures taken of the staff and student bodies, all of whom closely gathered around Dewey; many of the photos included Annie.

Melvil and Annie also continued their practice of vacationing a part of each summer at various resorts around the country, always in search of the perfect place to locate the club to which they had committed themselves when they married. By this time Annie was experiencing severe allergies, and the vacation offered an annual relief. Melvil's problems with hay fever had also increased. Then, on September 3, 1887, Godfrey Dewey was born while his father was attending the Thousands Islands Conference. The association officially took note of the birth and declared Godfrey the "A.L.A. baby."[23]

But by mid-December 1888, Dewey was ready and eager to pack up his family and move his reform interests to a larger and more public arena. At that time he was still directing the Library Bureau, although from a distance and by means of majority stock ownership. Between 1883 and 1888 he had kept the Bureau bound tightly to his other reform causes and launched two new periodicals—*Spelling,* a new quarterly issued by the Spelling

---

Box 64, Dewey Mss; Annie Dewey to Bowker, 4/2 and 10/86; and Dewey to Bowker, 4/15/86, Bowker Mss. The large file containing all the correspondence relating to this dispute can be found in Box 64, Dewey Mss. See also Dewey to Bowker, 12/21/89, Box 91, Dewey Mss.

23. Dewey comments on his affiliation with the Episcopal Church in a letter to *NYTr,* 2/12/05, Box P-16. Haber, *Quest for Authority,* p. 240, notes upper-class Americans tended toward the Episcopal Church in late-19th-century America. For an example of the sense of family Dewey was cultivating, see recollections of student Mary Loomis, 2/17/27, Box 19, Dewey Mss. Indications are that the Deweys had wanted a child for some time. "To our great regret, we have as yet no child," he wrote to his Amherst classmates in 1885. See Amherst College, *Chronicles of '74,* p. 17.

Reform Association, and *Library Notes,* a small quarterly aimed at delivering practical information to beginning librarians. The Bureau also continued to serve the publishing and manufacturing interests of the American Metric Bureau. But all had not gone smoothly. In 1888 he had had to intervene directly to reorganize the company when Herbert Davidson nearly bankrupted it.

Back in New York City Dewey had helped form the New York Library Club, the Children's Library Association, and had fostered a cooperative spirit among all metropolitan librarians that manifested itself in a shared acquisitions program and a union list of periodicals. He had also worked his DDC through two more editions, although he had largely relinquished the work for the third to his subordinates. And his family had grown; he now had responsibility for providing for an additional life. By this time he was developing a receding hairline and had begun to sport a full albeit shaggy beard. The prominent jaw was still evident, perhaps even exaggerated, under the beard. He was over six feet tall, weighed nearly 200 pounds, and continued to manifest an active, nervous temperament. He was rapid in movement, rapid in speech, and rapid in dispatching his business. One library peer once commented he wished "my tongue [were] as glib as yours."[24] As he packed for Albany, Dewey's spirit for reform was as irrepressible as ever; he looked to his new position as an opportunity to magnify the impact of the goals he had set out for himself early in life. He could hardly wait to get there.

---

24. See picture dated 1885 in Box 78, Dewey Mss (Plate 7). See also R. A. Guild to Dewey, 5/8/85, Box 2; and sketch of Dewey in *Albany Times,* undated, but done shortly after he arrived in Albany, in Box 74.

PART TWO

The Albany Years

1889–1906

6

"Jockeying for Position": Regents' Secretary

1889–1892

Dewey began his work as Regents' Secretary boldly and aggressively. The day after he took office in early January, he attended a dinner for several new state officials. Chance placed him next to Governor David B. Hill, who had just delivered his third call for abolition of the Regents in his annual message to the legislature. During the course of the meal, Dewey leaned over to the governor and said he had wagered a friend the price of a dinner that Hill would soon become "my strongest helper in the big job I am undertaking." The governor chuckled. He reminded Dewey he had opposed the Regents since 1887, and saw no reason to change his mind. Dewey smiled; he was not worried, he said. Once the governor recognized the value of reforms Dewey would institute over the coming months he would change his mind.[1] Dewey's experience at Columbia had not tempered his irrepressibility.

Although the Regents had courted Dewey for nearly a year to become their State Librarian, their decision to make him Regents' Secretary as well had been much more recent. Chapters 6, 7, and 8 will detail Dewey's tenure as Regents' Secretary; Chap-

---

1. Dewey recalled (and probably embellished) this incident much later in a letter to New York Governor Al Smith, 2/7/28, Box 33A; and made reference to it in a letter to Hill, n.d., Box 31A, Dewey Mss.

ters 9, 10, and 11 will cover his activities as State Librarian and his continuing role in other reform efforts. Despite the fact that these activities are separated out here for clarity, however, in Dewey's mind they always remained part of a grand scheme constituting his "world work." What he accomplished as Secretary significantly impacted his other interests, especially his library interests.

Entering a Glass House with a Plan
1889

In 1889 the State of New York was characterized by growth and expansion. Its population was not only increasing rapidly (from 5,000,000 to 9,000,000 between 1880 and 1910), but also substantially diversifying culturally and ethnically. These changes inevitably influenced the dynamics of New York politics. Activities in the legislature, for example, were marked by animosity between urban (especially New York City) and rural communities. Periodic investigations revealed what Theodore Roosevelt called a "corrupt alliance" between big business and local, state, and national politics. Groups also separated by economic interests, social customs, and philosophies of life. In 1889, Democrats controlled the executive branch. Governor Hill had recently weathered an investigation and started his second term coming off battles with the legislature over issues of ballot reform and the excise question. And for a third time Hill had called for the abolition of the Board of Regents (an "idle and useless body," he said) and the reassignment of its powers to the Department of Public Instruction.[2]

This was the political milieu Dewey inherited when he took office. As he looked around the Capitol, he saw plenty to dislike, plenty to ignite his self-righteousness. He was contemptuous of American politics in general, and New York politics in particular, especially where they intersected with his educational interests. He realized, however, that as a public servant he would live in a glass house where his activities would be open to public scrutiny

---

2. Herbert J. Bass, *"I Am a Democrat": The Political Career of David Bennett Hill* (Syracuse, 1961), Chaps. 5–7. Hill's words are quoted in *Regents AR, 1888,* p. 23. See also Harlan Horner, ed., *Education in New York State, 1784–1954* (Albany, 1954), pp. 16–17.

and where revenge was a common political tactic. Dewey came into office as Regents' Secretary during a period of intense party feelings. In 1889 most Albany watchers probably thought the position of Regents' Secretary not very promising. Dewey disagreed, and armed with a plan for educational reforms he immediately set out to prove them wrong.

The University of the State of New York had been incorporated in 1784 not as a teaching institution but as a supervisory and administrative body governed by an unsalaried board of nineteen Regents appointed by the legislature for life. The Board was empowered to charter New York schools and colleges, and by law was required "to visit and inspect all the colleges, academies and schools which are or may be established in this state." In 1790 the legislature created a "literature fund" for the Regents to assist New York's colleges and academies.[3] Then, in 1805, the legislature authorized proceeds from the sale of public land to be set aside for the support of common schools. In 1812 it passed another law that created New York's common school system, and fixed statewide district boundaries in which localities were required to make state funds available for common school teacher salaries. None of this enabling legislation, however, said anything about Regent powers.

In 1838 the legislature authorized New York's share of U.S. Treasury surplus funds to be distributed among the state's educational interests. Thereafter, common schools annually received $110,000, the Regents' literature fund $28,000, and school district libraries $55,000 for at least three years and subsequently either for the libraries or for teachers' salaries. Any excess reverted to the common school fund. Then, in 1854 the legislature tried to catch up with the rapid pace of New York common school development by establishing a Department of Public Instruction (DPI) with a superintendent who, among other responsibilities, was required to visit the state's common schools, monitor their curricula, management, and discipline, and report inspections annually to the legislature. He (always he) was also required to monitor teacher education programs in New York academies.

---

3. *Laws of New York,* 1787, Chap. 82; *Laws of New York,* 1790, Chap. 38. See also Charles E. Fitch, "The Education Department," in *Official New York from Cleveland to Hughes,* vol. IV, ed. Charles E. Fitch (N.Y., 1911), pp. 43–88.

The superintendent was appointed by the legislature for a three-year term and had power to form school libraries and regulate examinations for teaching certificates. He was also ex-officio member of the Board of Regents.[4]

As the common school system expanded, the Regents continued to grant charters and degrees, require annual reports from all chartered institutions, periodically visit and inspect chartered colleges and academies, and annually allocate money from the literature fund. It was inevitable that friction would develop between the Board and DPI. Generally the friction centered on control of academies and especially after 1875 the "academical departments" of union free schools that districts across the state were forming to extend public education to the secondary level. If these departments shared a building with elementary grades, a law gave DPI control over the physical plant, but made Regents responsible for admission requirements and curricula, except where they affected common school teacher education. Dual control also forced duplication of reports, inspections, and allocation of public funds. Many argued unification offered a solution to this problem, but attempts made in 1836 and 1869 failed because constituencies of both departments pressured politicians to kill unification bills.[5]

As the number of union free schools feeding graduates into the ranks of common school teachers increased dramatically between 1875 and 1890, the superintendent and his department gradually became more powerful than the Regents, and since the Board did not aggressively contest this growing power, many came to share Governor Hill's opinion that the university was a relatively useless place to park important men of literary bent for a lifetime appointment. On hearing of *Brooklyn Eagle* editor St. Clair McKelway's election to the Board in 1883, for example, a friend teased McKelway about being "received into the hoary and

4. Laws of New York, 1834, Chap. 241; 1838, Chap 237; 1844, Chap. 311; 1854, Chap. 97. See also Wayne W. Soper, *The Development of State Support of Education in New York State* (Albany, 1933), pp. 14–38.

5. Richard L. Canuteson, "A Historical Study of Some Effects of Dual Control in the New York State Educational System, 1854–1904" (Ph.D. diss., University of Michigan, 1950), pp. 150–51; Soper, pp. 39–40; and Frank G. Abbott, *Government Policy and Higher Education: A Study of the Regents of the University of the State of New York, 1784–1949* (Ithaca, 1958), pp. 59–60; 76.

toothless brotherhood of the Beatitude of Oblivion otherwise known as the University Regency." The *Albany Evening Journal* wrote in 1889, "The board contains a great many shelves where politicians in search of literary treatment can be safely stowed away, and where newspaper editors of susceptible variety can secure an enlargement of their literary forces."[6]

Regents were also uncertain about their role in links being formed between higher education and professional training. Members of old established and newly emerging professions were debating the most appropriate locus for training aspirants to their ranks. Some preferred to attach professional schools to universities, and many in the university community encouraged these efforts; others preferred private single-purpose proprietary schools that had served them well in the past. The former had not yet organized into a formidable lobby in New York in 1889; the latter had, however, learned to protect their interests by cultivating representatives in the legislature.

When State Librarian Henry Homes died on November 3, 1887, Regents Chancellor H. R. Pierson appointed a search committee with *New York Tribune* editor Whitelaw Reid as chair. On December 1 Reid contacted Dewey about the post. Dewey claimed lack of interest in the position, but said he welcomed "an opportunity to interest you if possible in attempting a larger work than has yet occurred to the Regents." Reid immediately arranged for Dewey to meet the search committee on December 20.[7] At the meeting Dewey waxed eloquent about the State Library's potential to foster the public library interests of the entire state. He discussed setting up a legislative reference service, a traveling library, and interlibrary loan programs, noted that a reference service operated out of State Library collections could serve all citizens of the state, and argued that the library ought to expand its hours of service and clientele served. Much of this he had already implemented at Columbia at no extra cost, he said, and there was no reason the State Library could not do the same. The committee was impressed, and decided to pursue Dewey. But one problem remained. The State Librarian's salary was less than

---

6. See August Schoonmaker to McKelway, 1/12/83, Box 1, McKelway Mss; *Albany Evening Journal*, 7/9/89.

7. See Pierson to Reid, 11/7/87; 12/9/87, Reel 166; Reid to Dewey, 12/16/87, Reel 56; Dewey to Reid, 12/2/87, Reel 135, Reid Mss.

Dewey commanded at Columbia. Pierson told Reid to keep communications with Dewey open while continuing to hold the State Librarian's post vacant, and suggested that Dewey be invited to address the June University convocation to elaborate the ideas they had just heard.[8]

On July 11, 1888, Dewey delivered a speech at the convocation elaborating his philosophy of library service and management. "The old library was passive, asleep. . . , *getting in* but not giving out. . . ; the librarian a . . . jailer to guard against the escape of the unfortunate under his care. The new library is active, an aggressive, educating force in the community, a living fountain of good influences; . . . and the librarian occupies a field of active usefulness second to none." Dewey was off and running at his rhetorical best, a child of the Burned-Over District who had committed his adult life to a crusade for education of the masses, especially through libraries. Public schools, he pointed out, were not designed to impart much "information or culture," but only "the simplest tools" to enable people to educate themselves "by reading." In previous generations people passed most of their information by conversation. No more, however. "Less and less from living voice, from pulpit or rostrum, and more and more from printed page, are people getting their ideas and ideals, their motives and inspiration. . . . Reading is a mighty engine." But reading the printed page was a two-edged sword, presenting those responsible for education with "a double reason for our missionary work; to give good reading for its own sake and also as the best means to drive out and keep out the bad." Supplying the "*best* reading" was the responsibility of public libraries, which, with the church and school, formed one of the three institutional pillars supporting education of the masses.

To answer this growing need, Dewey said, the Regents had a responsibility to inspect and charter public libraries like colleges and academies, and to establish a "system of university extension" run through local libraries by the State Library. The new system would help make public libraries "a new and mighty

---

8. Information about the December 20 meeting gleaned from subsequent correspondence. See Pierson to Reid, 1/4/88, Reel 166; Reid to Pierson, 1/5/88, Reel 56, Reid Mss; Pierson to Reid, 1/6/88; Reid to Dewey, 1/9/88, Box 71, Dewey Mss.

force in working out higher standards of good citizenship."
College teachers could be sent out "for a trifling fee" to give lectures at local libraries, which would have on hand the "best" reading to supplement the lectures. Those most interested, Dewey
said, could be encouraged to meet for "discussion and further
instruction" that subsequently might "be credited as a part of a
university course leading to a degree."[9] But New York had fallen
behind other states in advancing public libraries. By running
university extension through public libraries, however, New York
could become a leader if it acted quickly. "Gentlemen of the Convocation," Dewey concluded, "it is to-day your high privilege to
lead. To-morrow it may be your bounden duty to follow."[10]

Dewey's speech reaffirmed Regent commitment to bring him
to Albany. Existing correspondence does not suggest Regents
either were aware of, or if aware, cared much about the difficulties Dewey was then experiencing at Columbia, but the salary
problem persisted. Early fall brought some hope, however. At a
meeting in late September, several Regents met with Dewey in
New York. While no one present left a record of the meeting, subsequent correspondence indicates someone (evidence strongly
points to Dewey) suggested merging the offices of State Librarian
(still vacant), Regents' Secretary (occupied by an ailing incumbent), and Director of the State Museum (held by the seventy-
seven-year-old James Hall). The merger would allow Dewey to
run the kind of educational venture he outlined at his convocation speech from one office, and, perhaps most important, allow

---

9. Dewey had obviously given considerable thought to H. B. Adams's
suggestion at the 1887 ALA conference that public libraries become sites
for traveling university extension lectures. By that time, in fact, J. N. Larned
of Buffalo's public library had successfully experimented with a lecture
course on the "labor question." See J. N. Larned, "An Experiment in University Extension," *LJ* 13 (3–4/88): 75–76. See also Alexander C. Flick, ed.,
A History of the State of New York, vol. IX (N.Y., 1937), p. 70.

10. The speech was later printed in the convocation proceedings. A
copy can be found in Box P-46, Dewey Mss. Dewey had been introduced by
Chancellor Pierson as "one who believes that a library is educational, that
it is not simply a row of finely bound books, placed beyond reach for idle
administration, but an educator for men who are in search of education."
Before adjourning, the convocation also passed a resolution offered by
Union College President H. E. Webster calling on the Regents to begin inspection of libraries. See *Regents AR, 1888,* pp. 8, 11.

the Regents to consolidate appropriations to match Dewey's Columbia salary. Although no promises were exchanged, Dewey and the Regents left the meeting encouraged.[11]

The Regents moved quickly. On November 8 (three days after Dewey was suspended at Columbia) Pierson informed Reid that one Regent opposed making Dewey "*more* than Secretary of the Board and ex officio Director of the *State Library,* leaving the State Museum for *further consideration.*" Pierson said he agreed. Both knew Hall had powerful political friends in Albany, and they did not want to provoke a battle over his position. Reid then informed Dewey that Regents would probably agree to merging the positions of State Librarian and Regents' Secretary, but not Director of the State Museum. Reid also said some Regents thought Dewey's plans too ambitious.[12] Dewey rushed to respond. He reassured Reid he would not implement his plans faster than it was "wise to undertake them. . . . Give us two or three years on these lines, & we will lay forever that grim ghost that walks . . . with mutterings about abolishing the Regents as a useless body." Dewey then outlined his agenda as Regents' Secretary and State Librarian in what he called a "checklist" of "things to be done." The new State Librarian ought to develop the "ideal state library headquarters" and reorganize it for efficiency and ease of use. Here Dewey implied recataloging and reclassifying the collections. He also recommended that the State Library become the "very best working legislative library" serving "every officer of the state" quickly, and called for the implementation of an interlibrary loan program and a traveling library program "similar to what has proved so successful in Australia." The latter could be funded by the $55,000 the legislature annually gave to New York's district libraries, a program most thought wasteful and little used anyway.

Dewey reiterated his conviction that the State Librarian had an obligation to guide and supervise New York's developing

---

11. For correspondence leading up to this meeting, see Pierson to Reid, 9/19/88; 9/21/88, Reel 166; and Reid to Pierson, 9/20/88, Reel 57, Reid Mss. For evidence of the possibilities discussed at that meeting, see Henry Barnard to Dewey, 11/6/88, Box 94, Dewey Mss; and Pierson to Reid, 11/8/88, Reel 166, Reid Mss.

12. Pierson to Reid, 11/8/88, Reel 166, Reid Mss. See also Reid to Pierson, 11/10/88; 11/19/88, Reel 57; Pierson to Reid, 11/24/88, Reel 166; Reid to Dewey, 11/25/88, Reel 56, Reid Mss.

public library system by making "trained assistants" available who "can be detailed . . . to go to any town that may ask such help, & start a new library or reorganize an old one on the lines that will enable them to do the most good with their funds & opportunities." He indicated he wanted to bring his library school to Albany, but quickly added that it "can be so combined with your own library work as to impose a very slight financial burden" on the state. Finally, Dewey recommended the State Library begin a "state bibliographical bureau" that would harness the skills of library-school students to answer reference questions from New York's public school teachers, and that the State Library establish a state clearinghouse for duplicates.

Improving the profile and influence of the State Library was only half the work, however. Dewey also outlined for Reid what the new appointee ought to do as Regents' Secretary. He should retain and improve the University examination system, and confer University degrees on those who successfully passed them. He should make the University convocation into "the most important higher educational gathering of the year in America," and establish a university extension system to harness the potential of the local public library "with which it works hand in hand." All of these plans, Dewey reminded Reid, were intended to create a centripetal force to "weld together" the University's diverse interests "into one strong smoothly working organization." In 1888, Dewey argued, the system was "going on a centrifugal action," where its energy was dissipated, its plans easily stifled, and its future compromised by the whims and accidents of politics.[13]

The December 12 Board meeting began in routine fashion, but shortly after lunch Superintendent of Public Instruction Andrew Sloan Draper moved that the Regents create a new office of "Secretary to the Board and Director of the State Library," and pay its occupant an annual salary of $5,000. The Board agreed. Pierson then asked each Regent to write the name of potential candidates for the position on a ballot, and hand them to him. When he tallied them all, he announced that Melvil Dewey had

---

13. Copies of Dewey's lengthy letter to Reid, dated 11/25/88, are in Reel 135, Reid Mss; and Box 24, Dewey Mss. Regents initially balked at Dewey's hint of a training center for librarians. They dropped their objections, however, when Dewey reassured them it would not be a drain on the treasury. See Dewey to Butler, 8/26/26, Butler Mss.

been elected unanimously. Obviously, the process had been rehearsed. Dewey accepted the offer on December 19, and on the 27th left for Albany, telling a reporter of the *Albany Evening Journal* upon his arrival that he was assuming his duties unofficially the next day.[14]

Moving to Implement an Agenda
1889–1892

Dewey officially took office January 1, 1889. To effect reforms and implement his agenda, he quickly realized he had to deal with Draper, a Republican who had been appointed superintendent in 1886. Fortunately for Dewey, Draper wanted to cultivate a peaceful coexistence with Regents. "The line of demarcation" between DPI and the Regents should "be well defined," he said in a December 1, 1888, department circular, "to the end that there may be no divisions of responsibility and no possibility of clashing." He especially made reference to funds appropriated for New York's school district libraries. He estimated that since 1839 New York spent over $2,740,000 on books. During the next half century, the number of volumes reported in those libraries declined from 1,604,210 in 1853 to 737,716 in 1887. Obviously, he said, New York had a problem. When Dewey read the circular, he sensed an opportunity. Shortly after arriving in Albany he went to Draper to discuss school district libraries. They agreed to divide responsibilities for the largely dormant collections—part would go into school libraries (to be controlled by the DPI), part to public libraries (to be controlled by the Regents)—but Dewey was unable to get Draper to agree to split the legislature's annual $55,000 allocation with him.[15]

Dewey's first public appearance as Regents' Secretary and State Librarian took place at a board meeting January 9. He used it to profile his agenda and, in a speech intended for the public,

---

14. See *Albany Evening Journal,* 12/12/88; 12/13/88; 12/27/88; Albert B. Watkins to Dewey, 12/13/88, Box 74, Dewey Mss.

15. Copy of Draper's 12/1/88 circular in Gilman Mss. See also Dewey to Gilman, 12/15/88, Gilman Mss; Dewey to Poole, 12/15/88, Poole Mss; Gilman to Dewey, 12/20/88, Wyer Mss. Draper's report is summarized in *Eagle,* 12/16/88; his remarks are quoted from *Assembly Document No. 7, 1889,* p. 45. See also Canuteson, p. 241; *Regents AR, 1889,* p. 718.

especially emphasized New York's public libraries. After he finished, Regents approved a resolution that those public libraries
"found worthy of distinction" be officially recognized as part of the
University and given a seat in the annual convocation. They also
authorized the State Librarian to negotiate with Columbia to transfer the library school to Albany.[16] Dewey's plan was launched.

For the next few months Dewey worked to improve the
Regents' political position and solidify its powers, but he also recognized the need to cultivate a favorable press. Because his selection as Regents' Secretary was generally regarded as a Republican
appointment (he had been solicited by Whitelaw Reid) and
because Dewey himself generally voted Republican, he naturally
inclined towards the *New York Tribune,* widely regarded in the
Empire State as the voice of Republican orthodoxy. Dewey fully
realized what he was doing. In 1889 New York's Republican party
consisted of numerous factions. That Dewey had been sponsored
by Reid generally marked him as a member of Reid's faction, and
Dewey recognized that his subsequent activities would often be
judged by others—rightly or wrongly—as a product of orthodox
Republican politics.

On April 25 Dewey asked Reid to identify someone on the
Tribune staff to whom he could write in confidence. "I think it
likely that I shall now and then be able to send something that
you would like to use," he said, but "I should be unwilling to send
it except in this confidential way." Reid told him to write Donald
Nicholson, an editor who represented "discretion itself." Reid
then added, however, that State Geologist James Hall had recently visited him. Hall had opposed the transfer of the State
Museum library to Dewey's control (which the Regents had approved at Dewey's request January 9), and had heard about
Dewey's suggestion to merge the positions of Director of the
State Museum and State Library with Regents' Secretary. To ease
Hall's suspicions, Reid told Dewey he advised the State Geologist
"to get in close and friendly relations with you."[17]

---

16. See *Albany Evening Journal,* 1/10/89; 1/11/89.
17. Dewey to Reid, 4/25/89, Reel 135; Reid to Dewey, 4/27/89, Reel
59, Reid Mss. Dewey's efforts to establish confidential ties with a prominent
newspaper were not unusual in New York in the 1890s. For other examples,
see Harold P. Gosnell, *Boss Platt and His New York Machine: A Study of the
Political Leadership of Thomas C. Platt, Theodore Roosevelt, and Others*
(Chicago, 1924), pp. 130–38.

Dewey's most important work in the spring of 1889, however, was monitoring passage of a law he authored through the
legislature and getting it signed by Governor Hill. Four things
worked to favor Dewey's efforts. First, he was still enjoying a
"honeymoon" period generally extended to all new appointees in
the state bureaucracy. Second, he had quickly forged an ami-
cable working relationship with Draper that minimized conflict
between Regents and the DPI that might otherwise have drawn
public attention. This allowed him to work quietly behind the
scenes. Third, because most state politicians did not think very
much about the relatively powerless Regency, Dewey, who unlike
his predecessors had a clear plan, seemingly boundless energy,
and an irrepressible spirit of reform, was quietly able to work for
rule changes relatively unnoticed. Fourth, Dewey was working
with a Republican-controlled legislature that looked upon him as
a Republican appointee supported by the *New York Tribune.*
And because the bill required no new revenue, legislators took
little notice as it worked its way through both houses to the governor's desk.

The University Law of 1889 Dewey had crafted significantly
increased Regent powers. First, the law changed the University's
name from "The Regents of the University of the State of New
York" to "University of the State of New York," and gave it the
general powers of a corporation. Second, it extended University
powers "to maintain lectures connected with higher education in
this State," and to charter libraries, museums, summer schools,
correspondence schools, and "any other institution of higher
education." Third, it addressed the issue of professional education by stipulating that all students beginning medical school had
to take a Regents' examination unless they were already graduates of a University-chartered college. Fourth, the law transferred control of instruction in academies and the academical
departments of union schools to the superintendent in order to
centralize control of the training of common school teachers,
and gave DPI supervisory responsibility for teacher examinations and certification. Finally, it made the State Library and
State Museum integral parts of the University, thus positioning
each for the extension work Dewey was planning. That Governor
Hill approved the bill so quickly suggests he had not so much
questioned the Regents' existence in previous years as their well
deserved reputation for lethargy. That he approved it without

comment suggests he had conceded to Dewey's prediction of six months previous.[18]

For Dewey, passage of the law was a major accomplishment; it provided him with the basic structure he needed to implement his plans. He wrote Reid on July 1 that the new law "accomplished more than even I dared to hope we should attain in three to five years." Chancellor Pierson was also impressed with Dewey's success, but concerned about the Secretary's ability to independently work the legislature without Regent help. "He is aggressive, verbose, sensitive & very radical," Pierson wrote Reid, but there were other reasons Pierson worried. After Dewey got his new law, he unilaterally began lobbying for changes in the Regency's membership. When a vacancy arose in the summer, Dewey confidentially suggested to Reid the name of the individual he thought ought to be nominated. Although "as an officer of the Regents, I shall have no opinions, and expose myself to no criticism for electioneering," Dewey said, he did want Reid to know that the person named "is very deeply interested in our work and would give time and attention to it."[19]

The convocation for which Dewey had long been planning took place July 9. Chancellor Pierson opened it by acknowledging the increased powers and workload of the Regents brought by the recently passed University Law of 1889. The core of the convocation, however, centered on Dewey's address—"The Extension of the University of the State of New York." University extension had its origins in England only in 1873, Dewey noted, but by 1889 it had become so popular that over 60,000 British citizens had taken lecture courses offered by extension agencies at seven universities. New York needed similar efforts, he argued, that could be effected through Regent power to monitor public libraries. The latter would function as sites for extension classes and lectures and as repositories for interlibrary loan and traveling library reading materials necessary to support the classes

---

18. Laws of 1889, Chap. 529. See also Walter J. Gifford, *Historical Development of the New York State High School* (Albany, 1922), pp. 64–65; and Sidney Sherwood, *The University of the State of New York: History of Higher Education in the State of New York* (Washington, 1900), pp. 33, 44.

19. See Seth Low to Dewey, 5/8/89, Box 71; Dewey to St. Clair McKelway, 7/8/89, Box 91, Dewey Mss; Dewey to Reid, 7/1/89, Reel 135; and Pierson to Reid, 7/2/89, Reel 166, Reid Mss. See also *Regents AR, 1889*, p. 23; *Albany Argus*, 7/14/89.

and lectures. All of this, Dewey implied, could be accomplished for less than the $55,000 the state regularly expended on district libraries. Ultimately, he concluded, successful extension students ought to be able to get a certificate, perhaps someday even a degree.[20]

In deliberations following his speech, he forced an incident that revealed to the Regents a major character flaw Columbia trustees and ALA officers (among others) had discovered about Dewey earlier in the decade—a commitment to causes so deep he sometimes deliberately pushed the boundaries of his authority. The issue was Regent power to conduct examinations certifying successful candidates for professional practice in New York. Dewey wanted to strengthen Regent control over these examinations because they were effective tools to monitor the quality of proprietary schools he suspected were in too many cases more interested in making money than educational excellence. He was especially concerned about law and medicine, and at the convocation took advantage of what he perceived as an opportunity. After Lieutenant Governor E. F. Jones, who sat as an ex-officio member of the Board, expressed displeasure with Regents' law and medical examinations, Dewey drafted a resolution calling for increased control. Then, without identifying the author, he gave it to Chancellor Pierson to present to the Regents. Most thought the resolution came from Jones through Pierson, and during discussion Dewey did nothing to dissuade them of that assumption. Because Jones had not authored it, however, he was initially unaware Regents were connecting him to the resolution, so he was confused when several Regents criticized him for points of view expressed therein. Only after some discussion did Dewey admit his authorship of the resolution.

Although the resolution passed, Dewey's actions raised suspicion. Pierson worried about what he thought was a disturbing pattern in Dewey's behavior. Regent McKelway, like Pierson a Democrat, later scolded Dewey for his part in the misunderstanding. "The creation of the scene made the 'insult' personify [Jones] alone," he wrote, and warned Dewey against overstepping his bounds again by making hasty, impolitic moves, no mat-

---

20. *Regents AR, 1889,* pp. 73–113. Quotations taken from pp. 74, 78, 89, 91 and 92. See also *Albany Evening Journal,* 7/9/89, for accounts of this convocation.

ter how well intentioned. But Dewey would not apologize. "I think the very people who were inclined to attack us so savagely," he told McKelway, "will become our friends as they recognize that the Regents are no longer an ornamental body but a live body of earnest, manly men bound to guard jealously the higher educational interests of this great state."[21] Although the convocation concluded by endorsing Dewey's ideas, several Regents began to wonder if they had made a mistake by merging the posts of Regents' Secretary and State Librarian in order to hire Dewey.

After the convocation Dewey hustled to refine his plan. In early August he took a trip to England, in part to observe large British library systems, in part to observe extension services offered at Oxford and Cambridge.[22] In his absence, however, a small opposition formed against him. At root was what Dewey called "a base plot" by Chancellor Pierson. By this time Pierson was suspicious of Dewey's ambitious plans for university extension, and worried that Dewey was using the Regents to build a personal power base for a statewide higher education bureaucracy. He began lavishing "praise on my fitness for library work," Dewey later recalled, in order to induce him to resign as Secretary. Pierson then convinced Regents at their December 10 meeting to discuss control of examinations at their next meeting on January 30, 1890, and to pass a resolution that Dewey's extension plans not "supplant or rival the work of any other reputable agency engaged therein."[23] Dewey realized he was in trouble, and he knew the next Regents' meeting was shaping itself as a serious challenge to his tenure as Secretary. At that moment, however, fate intervened. Pierson died on January 1, 1890, thereby leaving only McKelway, one of the few Democrats on a Board dominated by Republicans, to press the issue. McKelway quickly recognized the situation and abandoned the effort. George W. Curtis, one of Dewey's strongest supporters, succeeded Pierson as Chancellor. For the foreseeable future, Dewey was safe.

21. See Dewey to McKelway, 7/10/89 and 7/15/89, Box 91; McKelway to Pierson, 7/11/89; McKelway to Dewey, 7/11/89, Dewey Mss; *BR Minutes,* 7/10/89, p. 539.

22. *Albany Evening Journal,* 7/24/89; NYSL *AR, 1889,* pp. xiv–xv.

23. Dewey describes what he perceived as Pierson's effort to have him removed as Regents' Secretary in Dewey to Curtis, 3/29/92, Box 91, Dewey Mss. See also *BR Minutes,* 12/10/89, pp. 562, 565.

With the threat of removal out of the way Dewey turned his efforts toward shoring up his political base and increasing the effectiveness of his office. For example, to monitor progress of all bills affecting educational interests he charged his Report Clerk to set up and maintain an up-to-the-minute file on proposed and pending educational legislation. Armed with this information, he then developed a network of New York's higher education administrators, and encouraged them to depend on his office for assistance. In January he told Seth Low, who was named Columbia's president several months after Dewey left, "you could always consider me ready to present [at the Capitol] any points you may wish to urge for or against any bill," and he volunteered to keep Low informed of legislation affecting Columbia's interests. Dewey recognized that the existence of a strong network would enable him to quickly mobilize educators to testify for or against relevant legislation at hearings. By spring the system was already showing results. "It is coming to be understood among our institutions," Dewey told the Regents after the 1890 Legislature adjourned, "that the Regents' office is protecting their interests against careless or mischievous legislation. . . ."

Always eager to make his office more efficient, in the spring of 1890 he reduced from twenty-seven to thirteen the number of separate Regents accounts. And while state salary averages tended to rise, University salary averages dropped from $1,500 to $800. Dewey accomplished this by using temporary help for peak periods and creating a secretarial pool where each secretary was expected to help others during slack time. His clear message to the Regents was that his was an efficiently run office unaffected by the spoils system.[24]

As Regents' Secretary Dewey especially worried about proprietary professional schools, and he looked to a fortified examination system he could control as the best means Regents had to check diploma mills. He once told Seth Low he preferred independent professional schools like law and divinity to attach themselves to New York's existing colleges and universities, and

---

24. *Regents AR, 1890,* pp. r19, r21, r22, r24. See also *Regents AR, 1893,* pp. r22–r35, r137; *BR Minutes,* 6/1/91, pp. 83–84; Abbott, *Government Policy and Higher Education,* p. 73. Responses his efforts received at the summer convocation indicated he also ruffled some feathers. See *Regents AR, 1890,* pp. 402–31.

he indicated he would always try to steer the former to the latter when they applied for university charters. This preference, he said, was born of suspicion about their material priorities. In one letter he called proprietary schools "cheap institutions that are doing so much to dilute New York's standards." In June 1891, he guided a bill through the legislature that denied a license to individuals wishing to practice medicine or surgery in New York after September 1, 1892, unless they passed Regents' examinations in anatomy, physiology, hygiene, chemistry, surgery, obstetrics, pathology, diagnoses, and therapeutics.[25]

Dewey began to lay the groundwork for university extension in early 1890. On February 19 he hosted a conference of expert observers on the subject. "The meeting is not public & is designed chiefly to guard the movement against getting into wrong channels or making a false step," he told Seth Low. In his annual report for 1890 he predicted the possibility of submitting "an enlarged University Law . . . in two or three years" that centered on university extension.[26]

A year later, however, he was already prepared to push a bill through the legislature. It called for increased appropriations for university extension and new money for organizing public libraries. Dewey still hoped he could convince Draper to share the annual $55,000 appropriated for district libraries, and he recognized that if the bill could be portrayed to the legislature as revenue-neutral, it stood a much better chance of passage. Despite the pressure, however, Draper refused to budge on the $55,000. Privately, Dewey began criticizing Draper, who by this time had begun to speak out against university extension. Characteristically, Dewey chose to interpret Draper's action as hostile; he wrote one friend in confidence on April 14 that Draper "is *knifing* us & says [the university bill] will *not* become law." To counter, Dewey asked his lobbying network to write strong let-

---

25. Dewey to Low, 3/5/91; 2/17/92, Low Mss. Laws summarized in *NYTr,* 6/20/91. See also *Educational Review* 4 (11/92): 309. This kind of action was usually supported by new professional associations and professional schools attached to universities. In August 1894, for example, the American Academy of Medicine commended the Regents on their actions governing preliminary education in medical schools. See *NYTr,* 8/31/94; and Haber, *Quest for Authority,* pp. 222–23. In 1893, 1895, and 1896 other minima were established for veterinarians, dentists, and accountants.

26. Dewey to Low, 2/7/90, Low Mss; *Regents AR, 1890,* p. r24.

ters of support to their legislators urging the bill's passage and
mobilized support from the New York Library Association (NYLA)
which he had recently organized. Under Section 3 of the bill, he
reminded librarians, he had included a subsidy for libraries
circulating "a higher grade of books."[27]

By April 20, however, the university bill became hostage to
a larger issue concerning the canal debt, and when it appeared
the bill would not pass before the legislature adjourned, Dewey
changed tactics. He organized his support network to push the
bill at a special session, removed public library appropriations
from it, and gave special emphasis to university extension. He
also solicited the governor's support. By April 27 Hill had told
Dewey that as long as the state's financial responsibilities would
only extend to covering expenses for extension supervisors, he
would sign the bill. With Hill's support to reassure an Assembly
controlled by Democrats, Dewey was able to push the bill through
in the legislature's final days. The law provided an appropriation
of $10,000, including $2,000 for a University extension department director; it also specifically prohibited use of the money for
lecturers or instructors, whose fees were to be borne "by the
localities benefitted." Dewey moved quickly to seal his victory.
He had already decided University Extension would become the
fifth department (Examinations, Executive, State Library, and
State Museum were the others) reporting to the Secretary.[28]

Although the 1891 convocation celebrated Dewey's victory,
New York's politicians still had not recognized that Dewey was
turning the University into a power base in the politics of higher
education. They continued to look upon the Regency as a relatively harmless (although recently more active) state agency,
and since Dewey and Draper had not quarreled openly, there was

---

27. See Dewey to Andrew D. White, 3/20/91; Sexton to White,
3/25/91; Dewey to White, 4/9/91; Dewey "To the Committee Representing
Colleges," 4/11/91; Dewey to Pres. C. F. Adams (of Cornell), 4/11/91; Dewey
to White, 4/14/91; 4/20/91, Reel 55, White Mss; Dewey to NYLA Executive
Board, 4/14/91, Box 71, Dewey Mss. See also *Eagle*, 4/5/91; and *NYTr*,
2/9/93. Dewey's role in organizing NYLA is covered on pp. 195–97.

28. Laws of 1891, Chap. 303. That Dewey was energizing the Regency
was evident in the remarks of a number of Regents. On December 29, 1891,
for example, one Regent informed a meeting of New York's Associated Academic Principals "the old tradition" that "the board of regents is a collection
of fossils" no longer applied. See *Regents AR, 1892,* p. 360.

no controversy in New York's educational bureaucracy to draw their attention. In addition, university extension had not yet impacted state education, and the foundations Dewey had laid for it and for checking professional proprietary schools had yet to yield results. In Albany, Dewey still enjoyed a honeymoon period, bolstered in part by Regents who watched their powers grow as a result of his initiatives, in part by a network of academy principals, higher education administrators, and librarians Dewey had developed whose voices were being represented more effectively and heard more frequently through his office.

Dewey spent the remainder of 1891 consolidating his gains. In fall he urged Regents to push for new laws setting higher standards for college and university charters, and revoking charters of "all fraudulent or discreditable institutions" on the University list. Here Dewey was after schools like the "New-York College of Magnetics," which taught that every disease humankind suffered could be cured by passing sunrays through red, white, and blue colored glass. Students who graduated from this three-month curriculum received a "doctor's" degree.[29] Dewey also began pushing an idea previously only hinted at: "There should be at least one place in each state or country where academic credentials and degrees can be earned on examinations, regardless of residence or how or where the candidate has acquired his knowledge." To implement this idea he called for a "joint board of examiners representing the best institutions of the state" to prepare and correct exams endorsed by the Regents' committee on higher examinations. He got even more specific when he joined the idea with his discussion of extension. "The public library, with accompanying guidance of private reading," he said, "is the very cornerstone of permanent extension work."[30] Dewey's intentions were now clear. He wanted to run extension through the state's public libraries to deliver higher education—including programs leading to university degrees—efficiently and cheaply to millions of New York citizens. The child of the

---

29. The Regents finally revoked the charter of the New-York College of Magnetics at their February 9, 1893, meeting. See *BR Minutes,* 12/14/92, p. 153; and *NYTr,* 2/9/93. For other examples of the diploma mills Dewey killed and the support he received from New York's higher education communities, see *School Bulletin* 20 (3/94): 113; and *Educational Review* 8 (10/94): 302.

30. *Regents AR, 1891,* pp. r52, r56–r58, r75.

Burned-Over District had taken his crusade for elevating the education of the masses to another level.

About this time, however, New York's political climate changed dramatically. Governor Hill left to become a senator, and although Democrat Roswell Flower was chosen to replace him in the November elections, Hill managed to have three contested Republican Senate seats overturned during his lame-duck period so the Democrats took control there too. Newspapers called his action the "Steal of the Senate"; Republicans were incensed, and retaliated. Machine Boss Thomas Platt took advantage of the anger and an economic depression and forged an even tighter Republican organization, and in 1893 Republicans regained control of the legislature. Beginning in 1897, however, he was forced to accommodate change brought by reformers based in business and the professions who felt traditional politics were not equal to pressures forced by immigration, urbanization, and industrialization.[31] For the remainder of the 1890s Dewey had to contend with all these contesting forces.

But if he had chosen, he could have left Albany. In spring of 1892, University of Chicago President William Rainey Harper offered him a job. If Dewey came, Harper said, he would merit a salary of $7,000, become "dean of the library school," and have responsibility for the University library and extension. The offer was tempting, but ultimately Dewey decided to stay in Albany. Several factors may have influenced his decision. First, Harper would not increase the salary at Chicago beyond $7,000, and Regents' Chancellor Curtis had promised privately he would do everything in his power to increase Dewey's salary at Albany.[32] In Chicago, Dewey would have to build from scratch; in Albany, he had already laid the groundwork. In Chicago, he would have

---

31. The standard history is Gosnell, *Boss Platt.* See pp. 37–38; 42–45, and especially Chap. 13. See also Richard P. McCormick, *From Realignment to Reform: Political Change in New York State, 1893–1910* (Ithaca, 1981), Chaps. 1 and 2; Robert F. Wesser, *A Response to Progressivism: The Democratic Party and New York Politics, 1902–1918* (New York, 1986), Chap. 1; and Bass, *Hill,* pp. 199–200.

32. At their September 29, 1892, meeting, the Regents voted Dewey a salary increase from $1,500 to $2,500 as State Librarian. Added to his base salary of $3,500 as Regents' Secretary, plus the extra $2,000 he received for running extension services, Dewey's annual income from state coffers totaled $8,000. See *BR Minutes,* 9/29/92, p. 146; 6/27/92, pp. 485–86.

to develop a working relationship with a new set of superiors; in Albany, he could build on existing Regent support which, Dewey noted, had changed so much since 1889 that "the element in the board that believes in protecting our strong and good institution, cutting off unworthy degrees . . . is now completely in the ascendant."

One other issue favoring Albany, unbeknown to either party, also played a role. Moving to Chicago would check a goal Melvil and Annie Dewey had set for themselves fourteen years earlier. In January 1892, the Deweys were close to selecting a site for their rest and recreation community in the Adirondacks, a short train ride from Albany but a long distance from Chicago. On February 3 Curtis thanked Dewey for his decision. "The enterprises which we have recently undertaken are especially yours and without you they could not prosper." Other Regents echoed these sentiments. The executive committee meeting held shortly thereafter, Dewey later described to a friend, was "the most satisfactory of any" during his tenure. "What Chancellor Curtis said did most to strengthen my position here."[33]

---

33. Curtis to Dewey, 2/3/92, Box 74; and Dewey to C. C. Soule, 2/13/92, Box 33A, Dewey Mss.

7

Moving the University
"Out of Innocuous Desuetude"

1892–1898

The University Law of 1892 and Its Impact
1892–1895

As spring approached Dewey prepared for the legislature's annual appropriations bills. In 1892 he had two goals: make University Extension a permanent line item in the state budget; get the legislature to approve annual appropriations enabling the State Librarian to match funds with local public libraries that agreed to acquire preapproved books. Dewey's aggressive pursuit of his goals, however, was beginning to meet some resistance. For example, when the Regents held their quarterly meeting in early February a "Committee Representing Colleges" unanimously opposed Dewey's recommendation that the University be authorized to grant degrees for successful completion of examinations run through University Extension. Their decision posed a setback for Dewey.[1] Although he countered that extension stan-

---

1. Dewey was far ahead of his time. The University began offering external degrees eighty years after he first suggested it. See Bruce D. Detlefson, *A Popular History of the Origins of the Regents of the University of the State of New York* (Albany, 1975), pp. 112–13.

dards would be made "as rigid as that given by any institution in the state," he changed no minds.[2]

University extension was also being questioned outside the university. In his inaugural address Governor Flower complimented the concept but said it was not a state responsibility. Nicholas Murray Butler wrote in a March *Educational Review* editorial that extension was "admirable" as "a matter of systematizing and carrying further along the work of the old lyceum lectures," but "as a substitute for a college or even an academic training, it is utterly useless and misleading." George Bacon, editor of the Association of Academic Principals' journal, *The Academy,* had a different slant. "One reason why there was such a good feeling towards the University Extension . . . was because the principals felt that it would furnish a good and harmless outlet for the superfluous energy of the Secretary."[3]

Despite the resistance, however, Dewey still managed to guide the University's appropriations bill through the legislature. Passage of the University Law of 1892 constituted another victory for the University, and especially for Dewey. Section 37 of the law promised financial support of New York public libraries only after a Regents' inspector made sure they were maintaining "a proper standard" by certifying that the "numbers of books circulated are of such character as to merit a grant of public money." Section 50 provided an appropriation of $25,000 to a Public Libraries Department within University Extension to be used for matching grants to public libraries chartered by the Regents in each school district.[4]

---

2. *Regents AR, 1892,* pp. r86–r93; BR Minutes, 2/9/92, copy found in Low Mss; *BR Minutes,* 2/11/92, pp. 110, 128. Seth Low had forecast opposition from New York's colleges and universities in December. Characteristically, Dewey ignored the warning signs. See Low to Dewey, 12/5/91; Dewey to Low, 12/7/91; 1/16/92, Low Mss.

3. *Educational Review* 3 (3/92): 297; *Academy* 7 (2/92): 41–42; Bacon to Dewey, 3/10/92, Dewey Mss. See also *Regents AR, 1892,* p. 311.

4. This section of the law was a clear compromise between Dewey and Draper. See NYSL *AR, 1892,* p. 57. The $25,000 was actually taken from the $55,000 New York had annually appropriated for school district libraries since 1838. Although the Regents were allocated $25,000 for the fiscal year only, and although the allocation could be renewed, the legislature's primary objective was to change the 1838 law to support only school libraries. It was expected that books in the old school district libraries

To qualify for an absolute charter a community needed to own books worth $1,000; five-year provisional charters were available for communities with as little as $100 worth of property. For buying books "approved for literary merit and educational value," public libraries could obtain up to $200 in matching funds for the first year, $100 in subsequent years. To help identify "the better class" of reading, Dewey later explained to New York's public librarians, communities could use "lists of approved books" appearing in sources like Regents' bulletins and circulars and the forthcoming *ALA Catalog* of 5,000 titles. Communities without public library service were invited to apply for "traveling libraries of 100 carefully selected books" that would circulate from the State Library for six-month periods.[5]

Passage of the University Law of 1892 stimulated the beginnings of an organized opposition to Dewey. Because a section of the law used school district lines to delineate boundaries in which chartered public libraries could act as conduits for university extension activities, DPI began to view extension as a potential threat to control of secondary education in New York. Dewey did not help matters when he reasserted the University's right to inspect academies and high schools (which irritated a lot of DPI officials who felt it an invasion of their turf), and routinely withheld funds in the University's literature fund from any high school not submitting an annual Regents' report (which irritated a lot of high-school principals who felt the Regents were unjustifiably harsh).[6]

This situation was exacerbated in April 1892, when Draper was forcibly "retired" from office at the end of his second three-year term because party control of the legislature had passed to the Democrats. He was succeeded by James F. Crooker, a partisan Democrat who cared little about secondary education and

considered not appropriate for school purposes would automatically go to developing local libraries. Academies, high schools, and academic departments of union schools could still apply for funds from the Regents' "academic fund," but those grants would be "spent only for books approved by the Regents office." See NYSL *AR, 1892*, p. 96; and *NYTr,* 9/11/92.

5. The contents of this law are conveniently summarized in a circular from Dewey entitled "State Aid to School Districts Wishing Good Public Libraries," Box 72, Dewey Mss. See also *Eagle,* 4/9/93; and *Regents AR, 1892,* p. r42, for explanations of the law.

6. Abbott, *Government Policy and Higher Education,* p. 62. For a discussion of the impact of regular Regent inspections of high schools, see Gifford, pp. 84–85.

thought most of New York's education budget ought to go toward improving the common school system.[7] Dewey suspected everything Crooker did was politically motivated. On August 9 he told Regent Anson Upson that for months Crooker "has been planning very adroitly to secure the control of this office" and that in the past "these people" had tried several approaches to get rid of him as Secretary, including showering him with lavish praise "on my great ability as a librarian," thus leaving the "impression that I ought to be in the state library rather than in the regents' office." He forewarned Upson not to be swayed by "sinister" moves generated by "an ulterior selfish purpose."[8]

In the fall of 1892, Dewey reported a revised plan for University Extension. Recognizing that New York's established higher education institutions were probably not going to allow Regents to grant external degrees in the 1890s, Dewey decided to change the term from "university" to "educational extension" and used his annual report to elaborate a scheme. New York's educational institutions could be divided into two groups, he said, "majors" (elementary, academic, colleges, universities, and professional and technical schools) and "minors" (libraries, museums, extension teaching, examinations, and associations). The former he referred to as "school education," the latter as "home education." Specific to "home education" he acknowledged the importance of "extension lectures," but emphasized that "free libraries and guidance to the best reading were more important elements of the plan. . . . Courses of reading, reading circles and clubs, home study from books without instructors, and similar agencies all belong to the library group" which, Dewey said, included "all education that comes from reading."

Dewey envisioned eight stages in this kind of extension work: (1) home study or reading, consisting of individual effort with no guidance; (2) club study, constituting group effort with no guidance; (3) correspondence teaching, in which individual

---

7. Department of Public Instruction. *Annual Report of the State Superintendent* (1893), pp. 18–19. Regent Charles Fitch called Crooker "the herald, if not the promoter, of the friction between the two education departments which subsequently became acute." See Fitch, "Education Department," p. 55.

8. Dewey to Upson (marked "Confidential"), 8/9/92, Box 91, Dewey Mss. See also *NYTr* 8/3/94, for speculation on the political reasons Crooker was appointed.

or group work would be connected to an instructor some distance away; (4) single lectures, designed to inspire and stimulate
groups rather than instruct; (5) a "course" (ten or more lectures); (6) a "sequence" (a series of related courses); (7) a "group"
(a series of related sequences); and (8) a "curriculum" (a series
of groups arranged into "a complete educational course"). By
Dewey's calculation, a graduate of the "curriculum" would have
taken four groups consisting of sixteen sequences, or 48 courses
(or 480 lectures), which would total 4,800 hours of work, thus
"corresponding exactly to four full years of solid school work of
1,200 hours each." People who completed the curriculum would
receive a credential engraved on steel and printed on parchment,
much like "the ordinary college diploma."

The system, as Dewey defined it, would be founded on three
kinds of reading—random, selected, and course reading. The
first two fit the home and club stages; the last fit the remaining
six and would be guided by bibliographies and the recommendations of extension instructors and librarians. To accommodate
students enrolled in the latter stages, Dewey announced intentions to add twenty to fifty "Regents' reading courses" to extension activities. "With our plan of university examiners, the New
York library association, and our public libraries department," he
said, "we have the best possible machinery for making, revising,
promulgating and administering these courses, while our examination department can with little extra labor or expense give the
official tests in every corner of the state." Dewey expected much
of this "home education" to be delivered through "centers" scattered throughout the state. Those remote from public libraries
would be sent traveling libraries as substitutes. To be officially
designated "Regents' Center," a site had at a minimum to "maintain a course of not less than ten weeks during the academic year
under direction of an accredited teacher giving each week not
only instruction, but also satisfactory class and paperwork."
Gradations went up from there. "Every successful center should
remember that a good public library is the very cornerstone of
university extension."

Dewey reminded the Regents that the 1892 law provided
$25,000 in grants to start public libraries, and that the "Public
Libraries Department" of the state library would "furnish lists of
model libraries of 100, 200, 500, 1,000 and 5,000 volumes, and
also lists of the best reference books for a beginning." These lists,

he added, would be used by state inspectors to check the collections of all public libraries seeking a charter from the University in order to obtain grants. "No library will be kept on the registered list as entitled to state aid or other privileges which does not remove promptly from its shelves any book which the state inspector reports as vicious," he said. "As to books which are simply weak or trashy, the local authorities will be advised, but must use their own judgement about retention in the library."[9]

Dewey was quick to launch Regents' Centers. Albany established the first on December 18, 1891. At opening ceremonies Dewey promised that university extension would provide "higher education for all classes, rich and poor alike." Eight more centers were established by the end of 1892, and by the summer of 1893 twenty-five "Regents' Centers" were offering thirty-four courses with a total enrollment of 13,190.[10]

Initial success with "home education" did not postpone the inevitable rift between Regents and the DPI brought by the University Law of 1892. Because Crooker proved every bit as aggressive as Dewey and unlike his predecessor much more political, conflict accelerated and intensified. And like Dewey, he did not lack a sympathetic press. On April 9 the *Brooklyn Eagle* entered the fray. "Centralizing academic examinations, . . . sending tramp libraries around the state, regulating degrees, wholesale booklending," and "getting public moneys for the fad of university extension," an editorial argued, showed the Regency's desire to "run" everything from a central office. On May 14 the *Albany Telegram* (which Dewey called Crooker's "official organ") ran an editorial attacking Dewey as "nothing short of a public calamity." The article claimed he boarded his own employees, and suggested his financial ties to the Library Bureau were suspect. Two weeks later the *Telegram* pointed to a public rift between Dewey and State Geologist James Hall.[11]

---

9. *Regents AR, 1892*, pp. r110–r137; 555.

10. *NYTr*, 12/18/91. See also Dewey to Low, 11/27/94, Low Mss, for evidence of Dewey's desire to establish Regents' Centers at New York City's established institutions of higher education.

11. *Eagle*, 4/9/93; *Albany Telegram*, 5/14/93; 5/28/93. See also Dewey to Hill, 4/5/93; and Dewey to John Boyd Thatcher, 11/7/93, Box 91, Dewey Mss, for his comments on the *Albany Telegram*. Crooker is quoted in New York [State] University, *Proceedings of the Convocation of 1893*, Regents Bulletin No. 22 (Albany, 1893), pp. 307–8.

Since he had been hired by the state in 1843, Hall had been accustomed to relative freedom in carrying out his responsibilities as director of the State Museum. But Dewey did not give any subordinate free rein, and after he took office checked any move Hall made that he thought inefficient or expensive. Because Dewey worried Hall's advanced age would prevent him from completing his work, he hired an assistant to take charge of the State Museum of Natural History in 1890. The State Geologist sensed a plot to supplant him. In February 1893, he told Regent Carroll E. Smith that Dewey "has for a long time been threatening me, and ever since he came into the Board I have had no peace." In April, the rift between the two became public when several of Hall's friends in the legislature introduced a bill to transfer the offices of State Geologist, Botanist, and Entomologist from the Regents to the governor. Terms of the bill allowed Regents to retain responsibility for the State Museum, but they would no longer have power to appoint or remove its officers. Ultimately, Hall got his way; the bill passed the 1893 Legislature and was signed into law. From that time on Dewey regarded his responsibilities for State Museum allocations as "merely clerical functions," and thereafter he avoided contact with Hall for fear of being accused of playing politics and exercising undue influence.[12]

But the rift with Hall was only a temporary sideshow to the looming battle between DPI and the Regents. At the 1893 Convocation, Crooker argued that New York ought to eliminate all state aid to University chartered institutions. The "unfortunate dual system now in vogue," he said, advantaged the urban and wealthy at the expense of the rural and poor. Regents quickly countered. "The University . . . is one of the most democratic of

---

12. See Hall to Dewey, 7/31/90; 4/13/93; 4/23/93, Folder 108; Hall to Smith, 12/4/91; 2/6/93, Folder 298, Hall Mss. See also Dewey to Reid, 10/28/90, Reel 135, Reid Mss; and New York [State], *Documents of the Assembly. 19th Session, 1896, Vol. 19. No. 89. Report of the Subcommittee of the Joint Committee of the Senate and Assembly Appointed to Investigate the State Departments, etc., April 24, 1896*, pp. 7–9. See also *NYTr*, 4/4/93; William S. Doane to Regents, 4/7/94, Box 73; and Dewey to T. Guilford Smith, 10/24/94, Box 91, Dewey Mss, for Dewey's summary of Regent troubles with Hall. For an interesting but brief discussion of Hall's career, see Robert K. Bruce, *Launching of Modern American Science, 1846–1876* (Ithaca, 1987), pp. 52–54.

education bodies," Regent Charles Fitch said, and to prove his point cited new programs like university extension services, traveling libraries, and since 1889 greatly extended services at the State Library and vast improvements in uniform examinations and inspections. Upson reminded his colleagues on the Board of new Regent powers Dewey had written into the 1892 University Law. "The time has passed when, as a board, we need to be placed or to place ourselves upon the defensive."[13]

Thus, the battle was publicly joined. On one side stood Crooker and the DPI bureaucracy, supported by a common school system defended by a group of legislators who mistrusted Regents as an entrenched group of educational aristocrats acquiring more and more authority over the state's educational system. On the other stood Dewey and the Regents, supported by higher education officials with a vested interest in preserving the status quo, and including such organizations as the New York Library Association and especially the Associated Academic Principals who looked upon the Superintendent and his department as a pack of politicians concerned mostly with being reelected. Both sides were quick to categorize "attacks" from the other as partisan politics.

For example, after the convocation Crooker sent out 10,000 copies of a pamphlet explaining his idea of a state education bureau. Dewey thought it a veiled attempt to take over the University and countered by forwarding copies to state educators, college presidents, and high-school principals. "The present superintendent has declared war against the high schools and all other higher educational interests of the state and is carrying it on after a most disreputable fashion." Some people criticized Dewey's tactics. Others held their own counsel. Andrew Sloan Draper refused to be drawn into the dispute. So did Nicholas Murray Butler. Dewey was the problem, Butler concluded. He had witnessed the irrepressible reformer's stubbornness at Columbia. "Sooner or later Mr. Dewey must go," he wrote Draper October 30, but he did not want Dewey to leave "under circumstances essentially political in their character." Rather, he advocated the solution Columbia found so palatable in 1888—"the

---

13. New York [State] University. *Proceedings of the Convocation of 1893*. Regents Bulletin No. 22 (Albany, 1893), pp. 324–26.

removal of Mr. Dewey by having him called to another sphere of work that he can honorably undertake."[14]

Over the winter the "war" between Dewey and Crooker subsided, but as both parties prepared for New York's Constitutional Convention of 1894, renewed conflict was predictable. Dewey took four steps to improve his position. First, he lobbied new Chancellor Anson Upson (Curtis had died in 1892) to make judicious appointments to University committee chairs. Second, he contacted Draper about the possibility that the coming convention might make the Superintendent an appointee of the Regents with "the same tenure of office as the secretary, thus taking it absolutely out of politics." The new arrangement would stop short of complete merger and make the Superintendent and Secretary "associates" in the state's educational system. Dewey said he favored Draper as the best candidate for the Superintendency under such an arrangement.

Third, Dewey encouraged Donald Nicholson of the *Tribune* to write an editorial on one of Crooker's most recent pamphlets, which Dewey regarded as part of a conspiracy to overthrow the University and combine all of the state's educational interests "in a single political department." If the *Tribune* wrote the piece, he said, it could become "a leader in this contest in which right is sure to win." And fourth, he intentionally structured the 1894 Convocation to inform delegates of the Constitutional Convention (which was meeting simultaneously in Albany) and invited people sympathetic to the Regents to give talks while delegates were in the audience.[15] But in summer 1894, everyone in Albany recognized that the convocation played second billing to the Constitutional Convention.

In 1886 New York voters had called for a constitutional convention by an overwhelming margin (575,000 to 30,000), but the convention itself was delayed as Republicans and Democrats

---

14. Dewey to "Dear Sir," 10/2/93; Draper to Dewey, 10/2/93, Box 74; Dewey to A. E. Winship, 10/21/93, Box 29, Dewey Mss; Draper to Butler, 10/27/93; Butler to Draper, 10/30/93, Butler Mss.

15. Dewey to Upson, 12/15/93, Box 91; Draper to Dewey, 1/8/94; Draper to Dewey, 2/27/94, Box 74; Dewey to Draper, 3/1/94, Box 91; Dewey to Nicholson, 4/2/94, Box 74, Dewey Mss. For an example of Dewey's efforts to drum up support for the 1894 Convocation, see Dewey to Syracuse University President James R. Day, 6/11/94; 6/25/94, Box 1, Day Mss; and Frederick Holls to White, 6/25/94, Reel 62, White Mss.

in the executive and legislative branches battled for advantage. Although Democrats laid plans in 1892 and 1893 to direct an 1894 convention, the surprising Republican victories in November 1893, gave the latter majority control. The Constitutional Convention convened in Assembly chambers on May 8. On the 22nd, the first full day of meetings, education received considerable attention. One delegate proposed to merge the dual system by having the Superintendent selected by the Regents, who would henceforth hold ten-year appointments. Another proposed to continue the University and the DPI as then organized, but called for the election of the Superintendent by the people for a four-year term. Several others introduced amendments designed to ban use of public school money for private school needs.[16]

Shortly thereafter the Convention president appointed a seventeen-member committee on education with Frederick W. Holls as chair. On May 27 Holls outlined his goals for the Convention to a friend. First, he wanted to eliminate public money to sectarian educational institutions. "The disproportion of money in favor of catholics in this state is positively scandalous." Second, he wanted to "put an end to the present dual system" by merging both educational departments under University control but subject the Regents to election by the legislature every ten years. "The Superintendent of Public Instruction is violently opposed to such a change," he said, "and he evidently has a good deal of influence behind him."

A month later he indicated he believed the committee ready to report an amendment giving Regents power to select a Superintendent and increasing their number to twenty-five but making their terms of office ten to fifteen years. "This will benefit our educational system and stop the wretched bickerings now going on between the Superintendent and the Regents." He also thought the committee would probably recommend in favor of giving all income from the U.S. Deposit Fund (which in 1894 amounted to $150,000) to the Permanent Literature Fund of the Regents, and add $50,000 to the principal. "This will make the Regents independent of the legislature, so far as this fund is con-

---

16. Charles Z. Lincoln, *The Constitutional History of New York, From the Beginning of the Colonial Period to the Year 1905; Showing the Origin, Development, and Judicial Construction of the Constitution*, vol. III (Rochester, 1906), pp. 30, 552–54.

cerned," and accelerate the "splendid work . . . being done under Mr. Dewey's direction." Ultimately, however, Holls could not carry his goals, and as time passed came to realize the best his committee could do was get the University recognized in the new constitution and obligate the legislature to support New York's common school system.[17]

For a time Dewey refrained from efforts to influence education committee deliberations, but by early August—as Holls seemed reconciled to compromise—Dewey could wait no longer. In characteristic fashion he began pressing. In a circular he implored Regents to "make it a personal matter" to carry through Holls's original recommendations. "The most critical days in the 110 years of the University are on us," he wrote. But Regents were not so quickly moved; they were beginning to recognize the exaggerated alarms Dewey routinely built into his epistles, and they worried that Dewey's inclination toward eleventh-hour activities would backfire by upsetting convocation politics. Several counseled caution. Charles Townsend advised against "too great activity on the part of the Regents in any effort to secure further power." Pliny Sexton wrote Dewey August 15: "The thing to do is to try no longer to influence, but rather to advise against further action by the present committee on education." Regents should be satisfied to "have placed in the Constitution the cornerstone of the University." Holls agreed. He warned Dewey that additional lobbying would be counterproductive. Regents ought to content themselves with "a great moral victory" of being constitutionally recognized. He knew Convention leaders would not support any amendments to committee recommendations on the convention floor, and he reported that "impetuous country Republicans" were looking for a chance to "whack at the Regents."[18]

---

17. Holls to White, 5/27/94; 6/26/94, Reel 62, White Mss.

18. Holls did not tell Dewey, however, that he at one time thought he had a committee majority behind a motion to grant the Regents power to appoint the Superintendent of Public Instruction, but that the swing vote was a Roman Catholic and leader of the antisectarian movement in the Convention. "Opponents of the Regents struck a bargain with him," Holls later told Andrew D. White, "agreeing to vote against the sectarian amendment if he would vote with them against the Regents." Holls describes the internal machinations of his committee in Holls to White, 10/27/94, Reel 62, White Mss.

When the committee report reached the Convention floor, an amendment was quickly presented which gave Regents power to appoint and remove the Superintendent of Public Instruction. Opposition was immediate. One delegate promptly moved to strike the entire section of the constitution having to do with the Regents, but was declared out of order. Another accused Regents of eyeing the DPI "as a cat does new milk." A third shouted that the "legislature, sir, which was good enough to elect the regents was plenty good enough, sir, to elect a superintendent." To rescue the committee report from what looked like certain death Holls declared that although he favored an amendment giving Regents power to appoint the Superintendent, he also felt it his duty to support his committee's compromise report and oppose the amendment. His move had the desired effect; the amendment was withdrawn. Convention leaders later told Holls that his action not only stilled opposition to the Regents, it also prevented a motion from being reintroduced and voted upon that would have deprived the Regents of constitutional recognition. Had Dewey injected himself into the process one can imagine a different result. Instead, the committee report passed 108 to 37.[19]

Ultimately, the Constitutional Convention of 1894 did not effect radical change in the State of New York. Delegates generally showed restraint. They gave constitutional recognition to civil service and education (including the University), enlarged representation in both houses of the legislature, and passed a new article on charities. They refused recommendations to lengthen terms of office for elected state officials, and voted 98 to 58 against a referendum on women's suffrage. With this slim scorecard of activity, Crooker and Dewey should have been pleased with results affecting their departments. For the former, the constitution recognized that "the Legislature shall provide

---

19. For a copy of Dewey's circular to Regents, see Dewey to Reid, 8/8/94, Reel 135, Reid Mss. See also Reid to Dewey, 8/9/94, Reel 67, Reid Mss; Sexton to Dewey, 8/15/94, Box 74; Dewey to Doane, 8/18/94; 8/30/94, Box 91; Holls to Dewey, 8/23/94; Dewey to Holls, 9/3/94, Box 74; Dewey to Holls, 9/5/94, Box 91, Dewey Mss; Holls to Dewey, 9/4/94, copy found in Butler Mss; Jacob Schurman to Holls, 9/8/94, Vol. 2, Letterbooks, Schurman Mss; Butler to Holls, 9/26/94, Butler Mss; Canuteson, p. 259. The debate over the education committee report on the convention floor is described in Holls to Dewey, 10/1/94, copy found in Butler Mss.

for the maintenance and support of a system of free common schools, wherein all the children of this State may be educated."

For the latter it provided that the state support a University controlled by a Board of Regents consisting of no less than nine members, but it also noted that the University's "corporate powers may be increasingly modified or diminished by the Legislature." Although Dewey may have been unhappy with the limited accomplishments of the Convention, Regents were not. They had entered the Convention from a position of strength (largely because Dewey had put them there), and by becoming a body sanctioned by the state constitution they were never again seriously threatened with abolition. By this time, *New York Education* later noted, Dewey had "dragged" the University "out of innocuous desuetude and made it a powerful educational influence."[20]

Although the remainder of 1894 and winter of 1895 were less eventful for Dewey, he continued to press his agenda. By this time he had considerably extended the University's reach; his office monitored almost 100 colleges and professional schools with a total enrollment of 25,000 students, nearly 600 academies, high schools, and academic departments with a student enrollment of 50,000, and 62 public and 533 academic libraries with a combined volume count of 2,000,000 (including the 800,000 volumes in school district libraries). Because he had fine-tuned his office's ability to monitor legislative action on education bills, he had effectively reduced their number and curtailed "tinkering" with general education laws.

Especially important to exercising statewide influence were several University departments. Because the "Inspection Division" required University-employed inspectors to submit an annual report for each institution the University chartered, Dewey was able to watch all of them much more closely than his predecessors and hold institutions to University-approved standards. The Examinations Department, which by this time had seven full-time employees, was also busy. Dewey predicted that the number of state examinations taken during the three periods during which they were offered in 1895 would exceed 1,000,000 at the 500 sites across the Empire State. The "Education Extension

---

20. John Hampden Dougherty, *Constitutional History of the State of New York* (N.Y., 1915), pp. 348–49; Soper, p. 33; *New York Education* 3 (1/00): 274.

Department," already three years old, boasted four divisions: Extension Teaching, Summer Schools, Study Clubs, and Public Libraries. Because Extension's Public Libraries Division was responsible for allocating matching funds and monitoring progress of the state's 723 public libraries, Dewey considered it especially important for quality control. "In the public library system we always look sharply at the results when the circulation increases with unexpected rapidity," he told Regents in 1895. "We have just succeeded in modifying materially the subsidy laws of the state to protect the free libraries against the temptation to increase the quantity at the expense of the quality of the reading furnished."[21] By combining Regent power to examine and his own power to subsidize, Dewey clearly hoped to control the books selected by local public libraries.

When it became obvious Crooker would not get a second term as Superintendent because Republicans had regained control of the legislature, Dewey asked Draper—at that time president of the University of Illinois—if he was still interested in a merged system that made the Superintendent and Regents' Secretary coequals. Draper expressed interest in returning to Albany, but wrote Butler on November 17, 1894: "The State Suptcy under present conditions is not large [enough] for me. If it could be put on an *educational* foundation with higher salaries and permanent tenure, . . . I should undoubtedly accept it."[22] Ultimately Republican legislators selected Charles R. Skinner, a former deputy whom Draper recommended. Dewey thought the appointment acceptable. Between 1889 and 1892 Skinner had showed sound leadership under Draper that suggested he placed DPI above politics; in 1896 he was even elected president of the National Education Association.

During the summer of 1895 Regents sought to address a problem concerning Dewey's salary. Because by law they could no longer combine the salaries of Regents' Secretary and State Library Director, and because Dewey was by law no longer allowed to draw $2,000 for directing Education Extension, the

---

21. Information taken from *BR Minutes*, 6/8/92, pp. 140–41; Dewey press release, *NYTr*, 3/14/95; and *Regents AR, 1897*, pp. r14–r15. Dewey uses the word "tinkering" in *Regents AR, 1894*, p. r39. See also *Regents AR, 1895*, pp. r93–r94.

22. Butler to Dewey, 11/14/94, Box 74, Dewey Mss: Draper to Butler, 11/17/94; Butler to Holls, 1/21/95, Butler Mss.

Board allowed him to pocket the extra $50 per month tuition charged nonresident students in the library school and authorized back payment of nearly $3,000 for "services and expenses" at the library school between 1889 and 1893 "at the rate of $50 per month."[23] No one else on the library school faculty benefited from the arrangement.

Challenges to Dewey's Power
1895–1898

Dewey had ample reason to be proud of his accomplishments as Regents' Secretary, but by this time his successes began to manifest themselves in a public arrogance fed by an increased sense of self-confidence. For example, every year he attended the conferences of the Association of Academic Principals. Up to 1893 he seemed willing to listen, and repeatedly offered to make the Regents' office servant to the needs of New York's principals. After 1893, however, he regularly lectured them on mixed messages they were sending him. He also spoke more surely of how the Regents would react to certain ideas, often using "we" when predicting their response.[24]

This self-confidence accelerated in August 1895, when Dewey successfully weathered a legislative investigation. The story begins the previous winter, when Dewey invited Henry I. Hazelton, a newspaper reporter for the Albany *State,* to interview him at his office. Hazelton came, but spent most of his time with James Hall. Then nothing happened for months. In the waning moments of its 1895 session, however, the legislature passed a joint resolution calling for an investigation of all state administrative offices during the summer. The subcommittee chairman assigned to investigate the University scheduled hearings to begin August 10.

On the 9th, however, Hazelton published a four-column piece in the *State* accusing Dewey of mistreating State Library books, cutting salaries by 50 percent, forcing employees to buy bicycles through him, boarding his own employees and visiting guests at his private residence, profiting from state contracts

---

23. For a record of the discussion concerning compensation for Dewey's services, see *BR Minutes,* 3/19/96, p. 335.

24. *School Bulletin* 20 (1/94): 65.

with the Library Bureau (of which he was president), and treating the State Geologist unfairly. Next day Dewey affected anger, and with column in hand demanded the right to be heard as the subcommittee's first witness. The stage was set for a confrontation newspaper reporters could not miss.

When the hearing convened at 10:00 A.M., Dewey began by taking the subcommittee and its press entourage on a tour of the State Library. He especially showed them the Capitol attic, where 100,000 volumes lay on the floor because the legislature refused to appropriate money for shelving. He then showed them the state's 1893 World's Fair exhibits that had cost New York $120,000, but were now in temporary crates because the University lacked appropriations to set them up in the State Museum. Upon returning to the hearing room after lunch, Dewey began to address the charges against him at great length "at the rate of 160 to 200 words per minute," one newspaper reported. Some of the *State*'s charges were true, he admitted. He was guilty of reducing the salaries in his department by 50 percent since 1889, but the savings allowed him to double the workforce within existing appropriations and thus keep pace with the department's increased workload. He was an agent for the sale of bicycles, but to encourage his employees to remain physically fit he had been advancing them the purchase price without interest if they repaid him $5 per month.

Rather than profiting from this practice, however, he said he had lost $300 in personal funds. To charges he had benefited financially from his connection to the Library Bureau, he indicated he never personally purchased anything from the Bureau for the University, and in fact had donated copies of the latest edition of his Decimal Classification to the State Library and personally reimbursed the Bureau $200.[25] And he denied the charge that he profited by boarding visitors with business at the State Library; always they were his guests. By this time Dewey had kept the subcommittee in its seats over four hours, and just as he was about to explain his feud with Hall, the chairman decided to recess until the next week.

The hearing sparked a lot of comment in the state press. "Everyone present seemed to be bewildered with the astonish-

---

25. Dewey was consistent here. He spoke to the issue in an annual report three years earlier. See NYSL *AR, 1892*, pp. 14–15.

ing rapidity with which Mr. Dewey unfurled his knowledge of the work," the *New York Tribune* reported. Most complimented Dewey for his pluck, persistence, honesty, and knowledge of his responsibilities, and most parroted the many improvements at the University and State Library since 1889 he had cited. They also generally agreed he ran an efficient office and did not deserve to lose his place. Some, however, also noted several Dewey mannerisms that tended to unnerve people. One was his penchant for superlatives, another his tendency toward histrionics. "There is a witchery about Secretary Dewey's eloquence and a magnetism in his presence," the *Academy* observed, "which silence the speech of those who differ from him, and which allow him to receive a false impression" of general agreement with his views. A third mannerism was his habit of wearing a thin-lipped smile while being "attacked." Seldom did Dewey laugh openly or heartily; seldom did he show his teeth. For some this habit suggested snobbishness. His enemies often interpreted the smile as a condescending gesture Dewey consciously used to discredit his opposition, to question their morality, and at the same time to communicate his amusement at their relative ignorance of the problem forcing the disagreement.[26]

Dewey resumed his testimony August 13 by explaining why he thought so many charges had been brought against him. Labor unions were part of the problem, he said. He had insisted that union members carry fifteen books instead of the three-book limit they set for themselves when the State Library moved its quarters up a floor in the Capitol building. But there were other reasons. When the subcommittee pressed him on his relationship with Hall, Dewey released information he had kept secret for five years. For years, Hall had been profiting from kickbacks by the printer doing his official reports and for years he had privately been selling fossils and other natural history specimens he

26. See *Academy* 7 (2/92): 41–42; *School Bulletin* 25 (1/99): 97; *New York Sun*, 8/4/95; 8/10/95; 8/13/95; *NYTr*, 8/9/95; 8/10/95; *Albany Evening News*, 8/8/95; 8/16/95; *Troy Press*, 8/6/95; *Albany Press and Knickerbocker*, 8/10/95; *Watertown Standard*, 8/10/95; *Utica Press*, 8/12/95; *Jefferson County Journal* 8/13/95. See also *Eagle*, 10/16/95; Dewey to Dana, 8/10/95, Box 4, Dewey Mss. Dewey's account books show that he loaned money to several NYSLS students (e.g., G. F. Bowerman, Minnie L. Vanderzee and E. L. Hanes) to purchase bicycles; they paid him back in installments. See FPA.

had collected while carrying out his state duties. Dewey claimed that under state law all specimens collected by the State Geologist were state property and could not be sold by state employees without proper authorization.

Hazelton testified next. Under cross-examination he was unable to substantiate his charges, and in the end admitted Hall had been his chief informant. When Hall was called, he refused to verify charges for which Hazelton said he had been the source, and under cross-examination when hearings were resumed on October 16, admitted he had at various times made duplicate specimen collections "at his own expense" and for his private use that he subsequently sold to museums. Hazelton returned for further questioning later in the day, and "after numerous questions he finally admitted that he had received money in connection with the attack on the regents." The *New York Tribune* reported that "this money had been paid to him through a third person, and he had no positive knowledge from whom it came." From that point on, the *Troy Press* said, the investigation "degenerated into a farce."[27]

Results of the hearings were conclusive: Dewey was exonerated, Hall and Hazelton discredited. The subcommittee, which issued its final report in late November, noted that none of the charges against Dewey had been substantiated, and that, in fact, Dewey deserved much praise for his management of the University. The committee also recommended that vacant space in the Capitol be turned over to the Library for relief of congested conditions. Finally, the subcommittee decided not to pursue State Geologist Hall. Dewey wisely chose not to object; he sensed Hall would soon bring about his own downfall.[28] Besides, the investigation had reinforced his position and temporarily silenced his enemies. In early fall he issued a pamphlet of reprinted press clippings reporting progress of the investigation, excerpts of letters of encouragement he had received while the investigation

27. *NYTr,* 10/17/95; 10/18/95; *Eagle,* 10/16/95; 10/17/95; *Buffalo News,* 10/17/95; *Troy Press,* 10/18/95; and *Albany Argus,* 10/20/95; 10/21/95. See also *School Journal,* 11/2/95; and *Educational Review* 11 (10/95): 311.

28. *School Bulletin* 22 (2/96): 82. On January 26, 1896, Hall was arrested in France trying to sell coins belonging to the Museum, and for trying to exchange some of the coins for a bottle of wine. See unidentified newsclipping in Box 73, Dewey Mss.

continued, and a copy of the final subcommittee report. He circulated scores to friends and supporters, and made sure every
Regent received a copy.[29]

As Regents' Secretary Dewey was obligated to defend academic requirements for a Regents' diploma, and over the years
many New York colleges used it as one of several credentials necessary for admission. Sometimes, however, an institution refused
to accept it. When that happened, Dewey usually fought back.
His dealings with Cornell University represent a case in point. In
the fall of 1895 the Regents decided to drop Greek and Latin
composition as separate requirements for a Regents' diploma.
Because Cornell was one of several colleges and universities
wishing to retain Latin and Greek composition as an admissions
requirement, it decided to drop the Regents' diploma as a necessary matriculating credential.[30] On February 18, 1896, Dewey
injudiciously wrote President Jacob Schurman that the "refusal
of Cornell to accept the standard Regents' diploma does it much
more harm than it does us." But Schurman was not intimidated.
"I have not supposed it was the function of the Regents to do this
sort of educational work," he protested. "I am sure it is the wrong
spirit; and, to speak quite frankly, I suspect their Secretary mis-
represents them." Schurman ripped Dewey on another issue in
April. In *Regents' Bulletin No. 34* Dewey badly miscalculated the
number of Cornell's class days in its summary data on New York
colleges. "The misrepresentation is so gross that it seems inex-
cusable." Dewey tried to justify the numbers and shift the blame.
He reminded Schurman that the Regents' form filled out by the
Cornell registrar required him to report the number of weeks in
the academic year. Dewey explained his office simply multiplied
by five the number reported. "What right had you to make an
arbitrary ruling that a college week was five days," Schurman

---

29. Copies of the pamphlet can be found in Box 76, Dewey Mss. In his
1896 Convocation address, Chancellor Upson praised Dewey, "who has
borne so much utterly undeserved obloquy," for courage and integrity. See
Regents AR, 1896, pp. 14–15; and *BR Minutes,* 11/21/95, p. 300. See also
Canuteson, pp. 270–72. Dewey sent a copy of the pamphlet to Draper,
attributing the source of the charges in the *State* to "the anonymous stories
that Crooker put in circulation." See Dewey to Draper, 10/28/95, Box 2,
Draper Mss.

30. See Gifford, pp. 150–51.

responded sharply, "when . . . at Cornell it is and has been six days?"[31]

Dewey's exchanges with Schurman showed he was losing his hold on the higher education lobby he had been cultivating since 1889; in fact, because of his recalcitrance, that lobby was beginning to develop a coherence independent of his office. At the end of 1896, for example, the Board had a vacancy which Nicholas Murray Butler wanted Frederick Holls to fill. Because Butler feared Dewey's public support would cost Holls votes, he told Dewey to take no part in efforts to get Holls appointed. But Butler's campaign ultimately failed; instead, Chester S. Lord, managing editor of the *New York Sun,* was elected in January 1887, in part, Butler said, "to help out [Benjamin] Tracy and Frank Platt in their fight for [George] Chase and his law school abuses."[32]

The law school "abuses" to which Butler referred were embodied in the Lexow-Austin New York Law School bill which the legislature had under consideration at the time, and which gave the proprietary school authority to bypass Regent control and conduct its own examinations and confer its own bachelor of laws degree. Spearheading the effort was George Chase, dean of the school whose application for a University charter had been approved in 1891. The story begins in early 1896, when Chase had been moved to act because of a recommendation to the Regents from Columbia, Syracuse, Rochester, Union, and New York University which read: "After January 1, 1898, the degree of LL.B. shall not be conferred because of graduation from any school which does not give at least 1,000 hours of actual instruction during its graduating course."[33] An unsigned note support-

---

31. Schurman to Dewey, 2/26/96; 3/13/96; 4/14/96; 4/18/96, Vol. 4, Letterbooks; 11/9/96, Vol. 5, Letterbooks, Schurman Mss. Three years earlier Seth Low had a similar exchange with Dewey about conforming to University forms. Low sent Dewey a personal letter threatening exposure to the Chancellor if Dewey persisted. See Low to Dewey, 2/23/93; 3/7/93, Box 13, Low Mss.

32. Butler to Dewey, 1/9/97; 1/15/97, Box 75, Dewey Mss. See also *Buffalo Express,* 1/11/97; *Buffalo Commercial,* 1/11/97; and *NYTr,* 1/22/97; 2/15/97.

33. See *School Bulletin* 22 (5/96): 98; and *Educational Review* 12 (12/96): 518–19; 13 (4/97): 411.

ing the recommendation sounded like Dewey. "Our best law schools will be seriously crippled in their recent earnest efforts to reach a higher plane if any school in the state . . . shall offer the same degree at much less than the minimum standard now generally adopted." In 1896 the New York Law School was operating in rented rooms and serving mostly part-time students employed in New York City law offices. As a result, it was politically well connected. Chase had the support of several powerful Republicans, including Clarence Lexow, George C. Austin, Benjamin Tracy, and Frank Platt, son of Senator Thomas Platt who controlled the state's Republican machine.

Chase formally objected to the recommendation on October 15. Because the Regents had already passed the recommendation to their Examination Committee, however, they asked the latter to hold a hearing on Chase's objection. Dewey immediately began preparing for the hearing by trying to mobilize his higher education network. "For two years I have been trying to induce Prof. Chase to raise his requirements to a respectable minimum, but he is evidently determined to make the last dollar possible out of his scheme," he wrote Low. He urged Low to attend the hearing as Columbia's representative, where he could join NYU's Law School dean "to attack in the most outspoken way the lower standards which the regents are tolerating."[34] On January 21, the Examination Committee gave each side an hour. Chase and Benjamin Tracy (Chase's counsel) spoke against the recommendation; law school deans from NYU and Columbia spoke for it. Thereafter the Committee went into executive session, and after deliberating for another hour voted in favor of a slightly watered-down version of the original: "After January 1, 1898," it read, "the degree of LL.B. shall not be conferred because of graduation from any law school unless the graduate shall have first passed the examination for admission to the bar of the state."

But Chase did not like the new version either, and when he returned home he drafted a bill incorporating the New York Law School with a special charter entitling it to give law degrees after two years of study; Lexow and Austin then agreed to sponsor it in the legislature. Within a short time, the bill "secured . . . the support of many members of both houses," the *Brooklyn Eagle* reported, "who argue that it will place within the reach of per-

34. *Regents AR, 1896,* p. r76; Dewey to Low, 12/15/96, Low Mss.

sons of moderate means the opportunity of securing admission to the bar in an institution where the tuition is not so great."[35]

For Dewey, this constituted war between politics and education, and like a righteous crusader he was ready to fight for the cause. He felt especially strongly about the need to establish "professional standards on a creditable basis" because in the growing number of late-nineteenth-century professions he saw solutions to America's pressing social problems. In fact, the motive for much of his effort to shore up inspections and insist on reports on standardized forms was to eliminate bogus diploma mills. But at the same time Dewey tended to categorize all proprietary professional schools as questionable, and manifested little sensitivity to the fact that for many people (especially Jews) who were denied admission to established colleges and universities, proprietary schools constituted the only vehicle into the professions.

Immediately after Lexow introduced the bill, Dewey penned a protest approved by the Executive Committee that was forwarded to the legislature February 22. Dewey fully expected Regents would sustain the resolution at their March 1 meeting. Finally, he asked New York law schools that met Regent standards to write their representatives to oppose the bill.[36]

But the Board meeting did not go as Dewey hoped. Regents spent the entire session in executive meeting on the Lexow-Austin bill. Initially they agreed to McKelway's motion to table discussion of amending the Examination Committee's January 21 resolution, and thereafter divided into two camps. On one side were Dewey and two members of the Regents' Executive Com-

---

35. *Eagle*, 2/24/97. See also 2/22 and 28/97.

36. *Regents AR, 1896*, p. r76; *BR Minutes*, 6/26/96, p. 352. Although Dewey was eager to use examinations to improve the quality of emerging professions, he and the Regents did have limits. Regent McKelway once complained to a convocation audience that "We did not ask to be even indirectly a doctor-factory; we have pointedly declined to be a chiropodist factory and a manicure factory; we came very near being made an undertaker-factory." See also *Regents AR, 1899*, pp. 262–63; and *BR Minutes*, 6/11/91, p. 65; 10/15/96, p. 372; and Low to Dewey, 8/8/96, Low Mss. Haber discusses the issue of discrimination and proprietary schools in *The Quest for Authority*, pp. 222–23, 228. For a flawed account of Dewey's position on chartering educational institutions for public accountants, see Paul J. Miranti, Jr., *Accountancy Comes of Age: The Development of an American Profession, 1886–1940* (Chapel Hill, 1990), pp. 50–67.

mittee, who argued the bill would cripple the effectiveness of the 1892 University Law. Everyone else stood on the other side. They argued that two years of legal study was sufficient to prepare for the examinations and said the school had been "badly treated" by an alliance of New York universities that wanted to establish three-year law school programs. They also argued that the Regents had no right to add conditions to a law school already chartered that had never abused its privileges, and condemned Dewey's efforts "to manufacture or to evoke expressions against the New York Law School by circulars to competing institutions."

Both sides engaged in what the *Brooklyn Eagle* later described as a "sharp, pungent and emphatic" discussion, but Dewey's opposition ultimately had the votes. By taking no action, Regents signaled the legislature it was free to act on the Lexow-Austin bill as it pleased. In a March 2 editorial, McKelway's *Eagle* called Board action an "unexpected rebuke . . . of the policy of tinkering and meddling" and condemned Dewey for organizing an opposition to "an independent law school . . . by methods akin to those of party machines."[37]

Ten days later Dewey wrote McKelway a private note. "I am more pained than I can well express to you at the attitude that you seem to have taken toward me"; he then asked for an explanation. McKelway responded: "The board was called to take a certain action when it should have been left free to determine its own course. . . . The office matter and . . . argumentation was all on one side." He clearly felt Dewey had set up the Regents. They had been fed information supporting only one position, McKelway said, and had not been told the law school bill had many powerful friends in the legislature and several on the Board. In addition, no matter what the Regents did, McKelway noted, the New York Law School would still "have its way under existing regulations." That Dewey had not told the Board this especially annoyed McKelway.[38]

---

37. *Eagle,* 3/2 and 3/97; *BR Minutes,* 3/1/97, pp. 393–95.

38. This information is patched together from the following: Dewey to Butler, 3/3/97, Box 91; Dewey to McKelway, 3/13/97; McKelway to Dewey, 3/15/97, Box 32; Dewey to George C. Austin, Box 29, Dewey Mss. See also Dewey to Low, 3/20/97, Low Mss.

Despite opposition from his own Board, however, Dewey would not retreat. He began writing "personal and confidential" letters to higher education officials across the state on his home stationery. He urged Vassar's President J. M. Taylor to fight the bill, but noted "my hands are tied by the attack of an individual regent." He told Seth Low that "this matter can be saved by earnest action," but that he was "writing no letters and taking no part in it lest I give grounds for the current argument that it is all a matter of personal prejudice with me." Syracuse's Chancellor James Day got a similar letter, but in it Dewey reported a rumor that the Platt machine intended to introduce a bill making the office of Regents' Secretary subject to legislative election. When Cornell's Schurman got a similar letter, he was not sympathetic. He coldly responded that colleges ought to determine their own entrance and graduation requirements, and that Regents were not qualified to make those decisions.[39] The Regents next scheduled meeting was March 18, and Dewey tried several tactics to get the Board to reverse itself. In hopes of increasing support for his position, Dewey wrote letters to Regents who generally missed the quarterly meetings to solicit their support and attendance. Then, at the meeting, he asked the Board to go into executive session so he could make his case off the record. The Board refused, and once again Dewey was rebuked.[40]

On March 24, the Lexow-Austin bill passed the Assembly 118 to 6, largely, Nicholas Murray Butler claimed, because the Platt machine was behind it. Still Dewey could not bring himself to give up the fight. Despite clear signals from the Regents to stop his opposition, on April 13 he privately mailed a circular imploring recipients to voice opposition to the bill at a final hearing before the governor on April 15. If enough people showed up, he suggested, the governor might veto the measure. He also apologized for having to send a personal note. "It is a great shame to be compelled to do these things," he concluded, "but unless somebody is willing to make sacrifices to protect general educa-

39. Dewey to Taylor, 3/13/97, Box 75; Dewey to Low, 3/13/97, Box 32, Dewey Mss; Dewey to Day, 3/11/97, copy found in Low Mss; Schurman to Dewey, 3/15/97, Vol. 5, Letterbooks, Schurman Mss.

40. *BR Minutes,* 3/18/97, p. 431–33; 4/18/97, pp. 437–41. For a summary of the meeting, see also *NYTr,* 3/20/97.

tional interests we shall go to pieces." At the hearing nine men testified against the bill, while only Frank Platt spoke for it. The governor signed the bill several days later.[41]

But Dewey had a hard time accepting the outcome. Because he continued to grumble that McKelway had been a source of misinformation throughout the fight, McKelway wrote a letter to the *New York Tribune* on April 22. The New York Law School proposed not to lower standards, he argued, but merely to "go alone, for it couldn't get on with the office of the Board of Regents and that office could not get along with it." Regents had not voted against the bill, he explained; some had personally been against it, but others refrained from action because they thought the matter solely a legislative responsibility. "A majority of the Regents— probably all—regretted and sought to correct the causes to which the bill owed its provocation," he said, but that apparently did not suffice. "There should never have been cause supplied to provoke the bill and to equip it with reason or with plausibility," he concluded, "and there won't be again."[42] McKelway was putting Dewey on notice. In 1889 McKelway was part of a small minority among the Regents who opposed Dewey's agenda. In 1897, however, on particular issues he had become part of a growing majority. In addition, Dewey's tactics to push his agenda were becoming increasingly fractious and embarrassing to the Regents, and they, in turn, were becoming increasingly impatient with his undisciplined irrepressibility.

Back at his office, however, some of Dewey's initiatives were flourishing by the summer of 1897; others languished. Development and proliferation of Regents' Centers, for example, stagnated. Dewey attributed this to "the difficulty of getting desirable lecturers." The "Inspections Division," on the other hand, had grown from three to six people in four years. "In the inspection division a specializing process is going on," Dewey said at the 1896 Convocation. Newest of the six was "Inspector for Literature," whose responsibility was twofold—"to work through our public

---

41. *NYTr*, 3/31/97; Butler to Low, 4/1/97, Butler Mss. A copy of Dewey's private circular dated 4/13/97 can be found in Box 1, Day Mss. See also Dewey to Butler, 4/15/97; Dewey to Reid, 4/15/97, Box 75, Dewey Mss; Butler to Low, 4/16/97, Low Mss; Reid to Dewey, 4/21/97, Reel 70, Reid Mss. See also *BR Minutes*, 4/8/97, pp. 437–41; *NYTr*, 4/16/97; *Eagle*, 4/8 and 16/97.

42. *NYTr*, 4/23/97. See also *Eagle*, 4/22/97.

libraries division and through the state library and study clubs springing up all over the state," and "to use our 640 secondary schools" to develop a "taste for literature." The Inspector's goal, Dewey said, was "to make New York known as reading more good literature than any other section." The position itself reflected Dewey's concept of librarianship's appropriate professional "niche."

To get "expert" opinion on quality literature Dewey looked not to librarians like Mary S. Cutler, who at the time was conducting a library school seminar on "book reading" one floor below Regent offices, but to Swarthmore Literature Professor Richard Jones, whom he hired as New York's first Inspector for Literature. When Dewey introduced him to Regents at the 1896 Convocation, Jones spoke about "the great work to which I have been called." What literature shall we read? he asked rhetorically. For young ladies not Boccaccio's *Decameron,* for young men not Robert Burns's *Jolly Beggars.* Great literature, Jones argued, contains "beauty and truth"; sin and evil were permissible, but retribution for that sin had to be the overriding message. George Eliot's *Adam Bede* met the test; Emile Zola's *Nana* did not. Neither did most French novelists and American naturalist authors.[43] It was obvious New York's first Inspector for Literature would exercise a conservative judgment, even for the times in which he lived. Dewey looked on approvingly.

With successes in some areas, failures in other, changing circumstances led Dewey to reorganize the University into five departments in 1897. A "college department" monitored state chartered colleges, universities, professional and technical schools, and all matters pertaining to degrees or licenses. A "high school department" included academics and academic departments of union schools. A "museum" department covered the State Museum and all the scientific interests of the University. A "library" department covered the State Library and all its interests, but also included a "Home Education Department" which assumed responsibility for all work previously done under the name of "Education Extension." An "administrative" department covered all work not assigned to any other department.

For Dewey, the creation of the "Home Education Department" signaled a retreat on extension. It had not been as suc-

---

43. *Regents AR, 1896,* pp. 135–37; 238; *1897,* pp. r9, r14–r15, r111. See also *New York Education* 1 (2/90): 335.

cessful as he hoped, and certainly not as quickly as he needed in order to maintain state funding. But his decision to place it in the library department made sense administratively, since he had consistently tied extension so closely to the state's public library interests. Besides, there he had an extremely loyal workforce with a history of making significant sacrifices for his educational reform interests. But other circumstances may also have factored into his decision. After eight years as Regents' Secretary he recognized that mere mention of his name often made people angry; he also recognized this effected delays in what he perceived to be an inevitable unification of the two departments. By this time he may also have surmised that a situation might arise in which it would be in his best interests to resign as Regents' Secretary but retain his post as Director of the State Library and Library School. If the "Home Education Department" was safely parked in the State Library he could protect it against opposition and foster its further development. Finally, in 1897 his interest in the Lake Placid Club (to be discussed in the Chapter 11) was commanding a lot of his out-of-office time; if he could drop the Secretaryship, he would have more time for the Club.

His public presence, however, remained irrepressibly optimistic. "Our chief lesson in home education is to be learned from the experience of the library school," he wrote in his 1899 annual report. "We are each year adding a little more both in the library school and in the summer library courses to interest young librarians in different phases of home education work, and to send them out with the idea that these interests are an essential part of the library province."[44] Library-school graduates, in other words, would become the soldiers in Dewey's crusading educational reform armies.

---

44. *Regents AR, 1898,* p. r86; *1899,* p. r41.

8

Overplaying Politics

1898–1899

L ike his fight with James Hall, Dewey's bouts with St. Clair
McKelway and George Chase were only temporary diversions from the University's ongoing battle with the Department of Public Instruction. The question of who controlled New
York's publicly funded high schools remained at the center of the
conflict; both departments claimed some jurisdiction. The situation was not helped when the legislature passed a law in 1895
giving the Superintendent power to supervise teacher training
courses in public high schools. In fall 1897, Dewey recommended
that Regents drop the examinations department and substitute
for it a distinct high-school department covering the 611 institutions for which the Regents claimed responsibility. When Skinner heard it he assumed Dewey wanted to extend Regent power
and swallow DPI. He had reason to worry. Between 1889 and
1896 the number of institutions reporting through Dewey to the
Regents had increased from 359 to 688. And the latter did not
even include the 329 chartered public libraries, the 200 study
clubs, and the 500 traveling libraries, all of which were under his
direct supervision.

Naturally Skinner opposed Dewey's recommendation; predictably Dewey interpreted his actions as trying to kill the University. "This of course means war," he wrote Nicholas Murray
Butler on February 12. "If he goes into this he will get whipped."

Skinner in turn wrote Butler "about Mr. Dewey's desire to extend his authority over the public schools of the State," and promised to fight any effort in that direction. He also deplored Dewey's unwillingness to compromise. "My belief today is that if Mr. Dewey cannot have the bill as he wants it he will not further its passage." Butler found the battles exasperating.[1]

Pressure to Unify
1898–1899

In March 1898 Charles Z. Lincoln, Chairman of the New York Statutory Revision Commission, presented another unification plan. He proposed to remove from University supervision all academic departments in union schools not distinctly identified as high schools. That would give DPI control of all state high schools and include authority to license high-school teachers. Although Lincoln's plan curtailed University powers, Dewey did not automatically dismiss it. "If I know that conceding no more than the best interests of the University would justify," he argued, "the desired end could be secured, I should as an individual vote heartily for that change."[2] His statement was a clear signal to Regents he was in favor of any unification plan he thought served the best educational interests of the state (but did not damage his own), and that he was willing to make personal and professional sacrifices to achieve it. What he did not expect, however, was that Regents would organize against him and use the power Dewey had won for them in the first half of the decade to check their Secretary's intractability.

In the fall of 1898, New York elected Theodore Roosevelt its new governor. Roosevelt played politics differently than his predecessors; often he chose the role of "honest broker" and used his office to bring warring parties together for a peaceful resolution to their dispute. As governor, Roosevelt had several issues he had to steer through a series of political interest groups.

---

1. *Regents AR, 1896,* p. 132; *1897,* pp. r39–r40; Dewey to Butler, 2/12/98, Box 75, Dewey Mss; Skinner to Butler, 3/17/98, Butler Mss. See also Gifford, p. 65; and Abbott, *Government Policy and Higher Education,* p. 79.

2. *Regents AR, 1898,* pp. 299, 300, 305. See also New York [State], *Documents of the Assembly. 121st Session, 1898, Vol. 12. No. 54. Report of the Commissioners of Statutory Revision, March 25, 1898.*

Among those drawing his primary attention were civil service, police commissions, the taxation of municipal franchises, and the Greater New York Charter. For Roosevelt, unification was desirable, but of secondary importance. He was not willing to spend a lot of political capital on its successful conclusion. The ramifications of all this for unification quickly became apparent when on January 10, 1899, Butler wrote Dewey that he had talked to Roosevelt about unification. "I begin to feel it increasingly necessary for outsiders to take hold of the situation and bring about legislation over the heads of the officers of the two departments." Butler reported that Roosevelt agreed with these views, and promised to participate. Two days later Roosevelt toured the State Library and visited several classes in the library school.[3]

On February 6 J. R. Parsons, director of the University's Examinations Department, hosted a working lunch attended by Roosevelt, Butler, Skinner, Dewey, and Syracuse University's C. R. Bardeen. The governor endorsed consolidation of the departments for economy and efficiency, and after he and Bardeen left, the four who remained discussed the matter further. Out of this meeting came the outline of a compromise. As Butler later described it to Bardeen, "I labored long and faithfully, and brought Skinner and Dewey nearer agreement than they had ever been before." Skinner accepted election of the Superintendent for a longer term by an enlarged Board of Regents. He also agreed to give up supervision of school libraries if granted power to inspect public high schools and certify high-school teachers. The Regents' examination system would remain "untouched," thus leaving in their hands a credentialing authority that governed entrance to state-chartered trade and professional schools. Dewey welcomed Butler's plan, but Parsons, who was becoming more vocal in unification discussions and represented Regent sentiments more closely than Dewey, "was frightened to death at it, and quite unwilling to accept any power of examination that was not coupled with inspection from his own office." Again negotiations were

---

3. Butler to Dewey, 1/10/99, Box 75, Dewey Mss; Ada Alice Jones to her mother, 1/12/99, Jones Mss. See also Butler to Bardeen, 1/11/99, Butler Mss. The standard history of Roosevelt's New York Governorship is still G. Wallace Chessman, *Governor Theodore Roosevelt: The Albany Apprenticeship, 1898–1900* (Cambridge, Mass., 1965). See also McCormick, *From Realignment to Reform*, pp. 157–63.

stalemated. When Butler later shared his frustrations with several legislators, they concluded that unifying the two departments would come only by outside force.[4]

On March 1 Roosevelt called a meeting between Skinner, Ainsworth, Charles Lincoln, Dewey, Parsons, and Senators Horace White and Timothy Ellsworth. For three hours the men discussed the merits of a bill White had written that gave a commissioner of education "supreme power" over departments of elementary and secondary education for a six-year term, and transferred control of school library functions in the state to the State Library. Both Ellsworth and White admitted, however, that the bill could not pass if either the DPI or the Regents opposed it. Again, Dewey did not object openly to the bill. He expressed willingness to support any effort to remove education from politics, although privately he said that because the White bill did not really remove the dual system, it represented his last choice among proposals being considered. He did blame Skinner for fussing over details, thus frustrating impatient politicians and inviting them to define less desirable alternatives. In a postscript to Butler he asked: "What would you think of Draper for commissioner?"[5]

As Dewey drew closer to supporters of the White bill, he inevitably pulled away from the Regents. At an April 6 meeting, Regents passed a resolution opposing the bill as "unnecessary, violent, revolutionary and unjust." They especially protested efforts to separate high-school academies from University control. Before adjourning, Regents appointed Pliny Sexton to chair a special committee to monitor legislative actions on the White bill. That the Regents did not routinely turn this responsibility over to Dewey was telling.

Several days later Roosevelt intervened by supporting an amendment sponsored by Senator Elon Brown that authorized the governor to appoint the first "Commissioner of Education"

---

4. See *School Bulletin* 25 (3/99): 131; Butler to Bardeen, 2/9/99; Butler to Fitch, 2/18/99; Butler to Skinner, 2/20/99, Butler Mss; Dewey to Draper, 2/14/99, Box 2, Draper Mss; Dewey to Skinner, 2/23/99; Skinner to Butler, 2/23/99; and Butler to Skinner, 2/24/99, Butler Mss. See also *BR Minutes,* 2/21/99, pp. 513–14.

5. Dewey to Butler, 3/1/99; Butler to Dewey, 3/2/99, Box 60, Dewey Mss; Skinner to Butler, 3/2/99, Butler Mss; and Butler to Dewey, 3/3/99, Box 75, Dewey Mss. See also Ainsworth to Butler, 3/4/99, Butler Mss; and *Educational Review* 17 (4/99): 409–11.

(who would thereafter be appointed by the Regents), and that increased the number of Regents by eight, thus creating one Regent's position for every judicial district in New York. Current Regents would not be removed, but their successors would be selected under rules of the amended bill. Roosevelt told Dewey Butler favored the amendment; but Parsons was "strongly against it."[6]

The Regents scheduled another meeting on the amended White bill, but in advance of their deliberations Anson Upson asked Dewey for his opinion. "It would be a great triumph to get unification," Dewey wrote, but he also acknowledged it would be impossible to attain "unless the regents will concede some modification in the life tenure hereafter." He reported that Roosevelt was willing to attend the Regents' meeting to urge their support for the amended bill, and Dewey supported Roosevelt. "We in the office are very hopeful that the regents will take this view and that we shall be spared the bitter warfare of a year which otherwise seems inevitable." He also said he had not discussed unification with anyone but Regents who visited his office, and he had instructed his staff to do likewise. Upson had reason to doubt Dewey's veracity. That same day Dewey wrote Andrew Sloan Draper, enclosing a copy of his letter to Upson and asking Draper if he would allow his name to be mentioned for the new post of Commissioner of Education if the bill passed. Draper cabled back: "If adopted the appointment would not be without interest to me."[7]

That Upson felt it necessary to ask Dewey his opinion is significant. Regents undoubtedly remembered Dewey's out-of-office tactics in attempts to kill the Lexow-Austin bill. Part of Upson's reason for soliciting Dewey's opinion may have been to measure the gap between him and the Regents, a gap which was making some Regents feel the Board's interests were not being

6. Dewey to Draper, 3/27/99, Box 2, Draper Mss; McKelway to Editor, *NYTr,* 3/3/99; *Eagle,* 4/7/99; *BR Minutes,* 4/6/99, pp. 517–18; copy of Regents' resolution on the White Education Bill, dated 4/6/99, found in Box 77, Dewey Mss; Roosevelt to Dewey, 4/13/99, Roosevelt Mss; Butler to Bardeen, 4/17/99, Butler Mss. See also Dewey to H. B. Adams, 3/8 and 3/28/99, Adams Mss.

7. Dewey to Upson, 4/21/99; Ainsworth to Butler, 4/21/99, Butler Mss; Dewey to Draper, 4/21/99; Draper to Dewey, 4/24/99, Box 75, Dewey Mss.

adequately and accurately represented by the Secretary on the question of unification. As time passed and the distance between Dewey and the Regents increased, Regents increasingly looked to Parsons for information from the Secretary's office. Parsons was eager to comply; he agreed with their position and shared their growing distrust for Dewey.

In the meantime Pliny Sexton, who chaired a special Regents' committee appointed to deal with the White bill, polled his colleagues to see if the collective opinion expressed in the Regents' April 6 protocol had changed because of Brown's amendment. By April 24, the day the Regents met in Albany, he had his answer: fifteen to one against the amended bill; the lone dissenter was Skinner. Sexton then labeled the bill "a vicious conspiracy to detach the High Schools from the supervision of the Regents." Not even direct intervention by Roosevelt, who attended the Regents' meeting and emphasized that unification would force no change in the state constitution concerning Regent responsibilities, changed their minds. That night, when the Senate finally killed the White-Brown bill, Regent Chauncey Depew told a *New York Tribune* reporter that the Board's actions had certainly demonstrated they no longer deserved a reputation as "one old fogy institution."[8]

At the University convocation June 26, unification was on everyone's mind. Reid spoke first and argued against merging the University and DPI under an elected Superintendent, noting that politics would greatly weaken the system of education in the state.[9] Other affected parties staked out their positions. "I know of no reason why high schools should not be under the exclusive

---

8. For evidence of Regent efforts on the amended White bill, see Sexton to McKelway, 4/20/99; 4/25/99, Box 2, McKelway Mss; and Sexton to Reid, 4/21/99; 4/24/99; 4/25/99, Reel 179, Reid Mss. See also *Eagle*, 4/25/99; and *NYTr*, 4/25/99.

9. While Reid spoke, a flyer circulated the audience containing statistics showing that in the previous three years Regents held fifteen meetings (eleven of which had a quorum), averaging 165 minutes each. That, the flyer concluded, meant Regents averaged less than 1.5 minutes per day on University matters. While the document was obviously intended to show how inactive Regents were, it also demonstrates to historians why without much direct supervision Dewey was able to fill a huge vacuum, control the Regents by tactical prodding and the selective dissemination of office information, and turn his office into a powerful force. A flyer outlining Regents' time commitments can be found in Box 11, Holls Mss.

direction of the department of public instruction," argued Superintendent Skinner. "Except for apportionment of money and inspection the direction is exclusive now." D. H. Ainsworth echoed
Skinner's tone. He attacked opponents of unification, singling
out McKelway for suggesting that talk of unification arose from
hungry politicians and Dewey for constantly criticizing the
quality of school district reports.

For the most part the convocation moved neither side to
compromise. Before convening, however, a group of school principals decided to ask Roosevelt to appoint a commission that
would devise a unification scheme for consideration at the next
legislative session. Roosevelt agreed; shortly thereafter he appointed a unification commission consisting of Frederick W.
Holls (chair), Daniel H. McMillan, Judge Joseph F. Daly, William
Kernan, Robert F. Wilkerson, Dewey, and Ainsworth. All except
Dewey and Ainsworth were lawyers; Holls and McMillan had
been members of the 1894 Constitutional Convention Committee on Education.[10]

But Regents were suspicious of Roosevelt's move and felt
unprotected. Sexton told Reid on July 4 that Dewey would not
represent Regent views accurately. McKelway teased that the
commission existed for "the amusement or relief of the governor," and argued that talk of unification was the result of "agitation" by Dewey and Skinner or Ainsworth. Regent T. G. Smith
agreed. He wrote McKelway on November 3 that "it probably
would never have come even to a commission if the two per-
sonalities had not been brought into contact." He advocated
patience and careful scrutiny. "Just what action it is best to take
perhaps we can determine in our November meeting."[11]

By the time the unification commission held its first public
meeting November 21, everyone suspected the motives of everyone else and all seemed especially suspicious of Dewey. DPI

---

10. New York [State] University, *Proceedings of the University
Convocation of 1899*, Regents Bulletin No. 48, Albany, 1899, pp. 213–14,
270–75, 313–16. Butler describes the rationale for the committee's composition in a letter to Holls. See Butler to Holls, 9/5/99, Butler Mss. See also
NYTr, 6/27/99; *Educational Review* 18 (12/99): 517; and *School Bulletin* 25
(7/99): 237–38.

11. Sexton to Reid, 7/4/99; 7/17/99, Reel 179; Reid to Dewey, 7/5/99;
Reid to McKelway, 7/27/99; Reid to Doane, 8/12/99, Reel 76, Reid Mss; T. G.
Smith to McKelway, 11/3/99, McKelway Mss. See also *Eagle*, 11/29/99.

officials believed Regents were primarily interested in protecting their life tenure and that Dewey was primarily interested in extending his control to elementary education. The legislature believed the fight was territorial, and that neither side was prepared to yield. Although legislators distrusted both sides, primarily they disliked Regents and especially Dewey, over whom they had little control. The Regents no longer had faith in Dewey to protect their interests, and suspected he was manipulating matters behind the scenes. Dewey had few friends left in Albany.

At the meeting Ainsworth pushed a plan that had prior approval from Holls, Wilkerson, and McMillan (who was absent from the meeting). He wanted to retire Regents over seventy-five, remove the lieutenant governor and secretary of state from the Board as ex-officio members, and authorize the governor to appoint at a salary of $10,000 per year a chancellor as head of a new State Department of Education created by merging the University with DPI. Although Dewey agreed with the first and second points, the third scared him; he did not want to report to the Regents through a superior, especially one appointed by a politician. Dewey still wanted a shared system under Regent supervision consisting of the Superintendent of Public Instruction, who would be responsible for elementary and secondary education, and the Regents' Secretary, who would be responsible for higher education, the library, and home education. But he masked his real objection by joining Daly to object publicly to giving the governor power to appoint the first chancellor. To counter, Daly proposed an amendment giving that power to the Regents. It failed two to four, only he and Dewey voting for it. The commission then voted three to three on the Ainsworth plan. William Kernan joined Daly and Dewey to oppose it. Dewey's opposition isolated him from the rest of the commission. Ainsworth told Butler in a confidential letter that the problem "is largely Mr. Dewey and his anxiety to protect himself and not be under any commissioner, chancellor, or other individual executive officer."[12]

On December 14 the Regents' Special Committee on Educational Unification forged its own plan of unification. It stressed the "independent and non-partisan character" of the University,

---

12. *NYTr,* 12/16/99. See also Dewey to Draper (2), 12/4/99, Box 75, Dewey Mss; and Ainsworth to Butler, 12/13/99, Butler Mss.

and called for the creation of the Office of the Chancellor whose occupant would be selected by the Board of Regents. Four officers would serve under the chancellor, each of whom would also be selected by the Regents. Dewey also spoke at the meeting. He "stated that he must not be considered in any decision made by the committee," the *New York Tribune* reported, and that he "was willing to surrender his office if such action was necessary in order to consolidate the school systems."[13] Publicly Dewey looked like a team player; privately he continued attempts to scuttle any effort to create a position superior to his own.

The unification commission met again on December 15 to consider Ainsworth's plan. This time because Kernan was absent and Wilkerson present, the vote turned. A majority of the commission (Holls, McMillan, Wilkerson, and Ainsworth) recommended creation of the position of chancellor of the whole system. The first chancellor would be appointed by the governor, succeeding chancellors by the Regents. The chancellor would have power to appoint and fix the salaries of the heads of the five divisions reporting to him, including bureaus for elementary, secondary, higher and home education, and for law, administration, and finance. In addition, Regents would be immediately reorganized into two groups: an "honorary" but nonvoting class over the age of seventy and an "active" class of members under seventy who would not be replaced until their numbers were reduced to fifteen. Thereafter Regent candidates would be appointed by the governor and confirmed by the senate. A commission minority (Daly and Dewey) agreed with the concept of appointing a chancellor, but advocated no change in the Regency. In addition, they recommended that only the Regents have power to appoint division heads and to fix their salaries.[14]

Once again, however, Dewey's public position differed from his true feelings. He had no objection to the appointment of a commissioner with responsibility for elementary and secondary education. He even had a candidate in mind for the post— Andrew Sloan Draper. What Dewey did not want, however, was the creation of a position through which he would have to report.

---

13. *NYTr*, 12/14 and 23/99.

14. A copy of this recommendation can be found in Box 11, Holls Mss. See also "Report of Commission on Educational Unification," 1/10/00, Box P-49, Dewey Mss; and *NYTr*, 12/16/99.

The Regents knew this, the unification commission knew this, the Department of Public Instruction knew it, and so did a number of legislators. Dewey did not seem to realize he was playing politics very poorly, in effect by his own actions sawing off the limb on which he was sitting.

Speculation and plotting swirled around him. The *Albany Argus* liked the bill because it promised to "abate the ancient war" between Skinner and Dewey, who "has reduced to an exact science by many years of patient manipulation that venerable if not particularly venerated body, the Board of Regents." The *Brooklyn Eagle* hated it because it "insured the choice of a Republican only" as chancellor and threatened to "dethrone" the Board. The *Eagle* also blamed Dewey. "This very talk about unification . . . started within the office," was engendered from "the office," and the "office . . . fomented quarrels with the Board" by which its powers were now being threatened. The "large majority of the board are in such a state of mind about the secretary that they can hardly talk about him, even among themselves," the newspaper claimed.[15] Dewey continued to be a flash point around which disagreement and controversy swirled.

Dewey's Resignation as Regents' Secretary
December 22, 1899

At 10:00 A.M. on December 22, 1899, the Regents met in a closed session. Most spoke in favor of the plan outlined by the Special Committee on Educational Unification; only Skinner objected, arguing instead for the Unification Commission plan. After the Regents approved the Special Committee's plan, Dewey asked to speak. He wanted to resign as Regents' Secretary, he announced. The effort to merge the Regency with the Department of Public Instruction had brought about "strained conditions" in which he "became a target for constant criticism from both sides of almost any question," and he wanted to "make a substantial concession toward educational harmony" by removing himself from those "strained conditions" and a heavy workload so he could return to libraries and home education, his "favorite field" of work. He complained that his position on unification had been regularly

---

15. *Albany Argus,* 12/18/99; *Eagle,* 12/17/99; 12/18/99.

misrepresented by all parties, and denied he had "fomented" any debate on the issue to increase the powers of his office. Regent Doane then moved the appointment of a committee to consider the resignation and report back to the Board. That afternoon Regents accepted Dewey's resignation, passed several resolutions recognizing his many accomplishments, and replaced him with J. R. Parsons, who had been Dewey's assistant for almost a decade.[16]

New York's press had not anticipated Dewey's move, in part because they believed he was always in quest for more power, in part because the resignation seemed so out of character for him, in part because they were unaware of a parallel move against him by a special Regents' investigating committee. The *Eagle* called Dewey's resignation "opportune," but generally editorials were gracious and complimentary. Several even accused Skinner and Ainsworth of driving him out of office. The *New York World* saw the problem as stemming from jurisdictional disputes. "There has been bad blood between Secretary Dewey and each succeeding legislature. There has also been a strained feeling between Secretary Dewey and the State Department of Public Instruction." *New York Education* offered the most balanced editorial. "It is probably true that the schools of the State owe no great EDUCATIONAL idea or impulse to him, but he has systematized those under his charge as few men could have done," the periodical argued, "and he has made the Board of Regents the efficient and useful organization that it is today."[17]

Although press coverage of the Regents' meeting focused on Dewey's resignation, another issue brought before the Board which received much less public attention may have had more to do with his decision than did his dispute with the Regents over unification. From 3:00 to 6:00 P.M. on December 21, the day before Dewey formally resigned, the Board reviewed a report from a special committee that had been asked to investigate complaints by the Senftner School about the activities of one of its competitors in Manhattan, the New York Preparatory School.

16. *BR Minutes,* 12/21/99, pp. 553–60. Copies of the Regents' minutes for this day can be found in Boxes 18 and 75, Dewey Mss. See also *NYTr,* 12/23/99.

17. See Albany *Argus,* 12/23/99; *Eagle,* 12/23/99; *New York World,* 12/23/99; *NYT,* 12/24/99; Syracuse *Post-Standard,* 12/27/99; *New York Education* 3 (1/00): 273–74.

Both proprietary schools sought to assist New York City students preparing for Regents' professional examinations, especially in law, medicine, dentistry and veterinary science. The Senftner School, however, had repeatedly claimed its rival was violating Regent rules. The history of the conflict dated back nearly six years.

On February 8, 1894, Regents had voted to give a three-year provisional charter to the New York Preparatory School, a private school founded in 1889. Almost immediately, however, Herman and Robert Senftner complained about improprieties by the New York Preparatory School in its advertising and the management of examinations, and asked for copies of application papers on which the school's provisional charter had been granted. Dewey responded on March 12 that although he would not supply the papers requested, Regents would monitor the school's conduct. The Senftners were not satisfied. On March 17 they reiterated their request for documents, and when Dewey refused a second time, they hired a lawyer. Between April 23 and May 2 Dewey and the lawyer had several exchanges, none of which resolved the problem.[18]

In September 1895 Asa O. Gallup—who was married to Dewey's niece—became president of the New York Preparatory School. Four months later the Senftners published a pamphlet addressed to the Regents detailing the history of their battle with Dewey, charged him with negligence and culpability, and accused the New York Preparatory School of "flagrant violations of the ordinances of the regents and improper use of the privileges conferred by its provisional charter." They charged that Gallup had opened and advertised a branch in Brooklyn which was in clear violation of Regent rulings.[19] This time their complaints caught Regent attention.

At their March 19, 1896, meeting, Regents had to act on the New York Preparatory School's expired provisional charter. When considering the school's object—"to establish and carry on secondary schools in New York and vicinity"—Regents agreed to grant a standard unregistered charter only if the words "and vicinity" were struck from the statement. They did not want the

---

18. *BR Minutes,* 12/13/93, p. 196; 2/8/94, p. 210; 6/4/94, p. 221; 12/21/99, pp. 534–35.

19. *BR Minutes,* 12/21/99, pp. 535–36. See also *Eagle,* 8/29/97.

school to open branches outside Manhattan, which at the time constituted the City of New York. After further prompting by the Senftners, the Board became even more specific at its next meeting when it amended the New York Preparatory School's charter to read "provided that no new branch shall be established without the previous written approval of the regents," and directed Dewey to tell Gallup the charter was intended to apply only to the City of New York.[20]

In February 1897 the Senftners issued a "supplement" to their pamphlet arguing that New York Preparatory School transgressions and abuses had not stopped. Dewey complained to his brother Manfred (Gallup's father-in-law) about "another long tirade from the Jews who have been attacking Gallup so bitterly," but on June 28 the Board decided to appoint a special committee consisting of Regents Reid, Stimson, and McKelway to investigate the matter. Since Reid was out of the country for most of 1898, however, Stimson and McKelway functioned as a two-man committee. On March 13, 1899, Parsons sent the committee "all the correspondence I find in the matter of the New York Preparatory School."[21]

Because of the committee's composition, Dewey felt unprotected. He told Gallup he worried about the Senftners case and began suggesting his nephew's talents might be better suited to business than education. At one time he mentioned employment at the Library Bureau; another time he suggested a position at his Lake Placid Club. Gallup was combative, however. "It is well known that this school has been founded—incorporated— reincorporated with stock and that it holds an absolute charter, has a seal, and a branch department in Brooklyn."[22] Gallup's perspective, however, was contrary to the facts. The New York Preparatory School had not received an absolute charter, nor had it been given permission to open a branch in Brooklyn. Gallup had either misinterpreted the information Dewey sent him about Regent actions since September 1895, or he had been

---

20. *BR Minutes*, 3/19/96, p. 306; 6/24/96, pp. 348–49; 12/21/99, p. 539.

21. *BR Minutes*, 6/28/97, pp. 447, 454; 1/30/99, p. 533; 3/13/99, p. 533. See also Dewey to Manfred Dewey, 6/16/97, Box 29, Dewey Mss.

22. See Dewey to Gallup, 3/7/98; Gallup to Dewey, 11/17/99; and Gallup to Dewey, 2/8/99, Box 75, Dewey Mss.

misinformed or not informed by Dewey. No other possibilities
exist to explain the discrepancy. Gallup seemed blissfully unaware of his own vulnerability.

When the committee delivered its findings to the full Board
December 21, it characterized the conflict between Dewey and
the Senftners as "unfortunate" and "unnecessary." On the one
hand it blamed Dewey for developing an attitude of "irritation,
distrust and disapproval" towards the Senftners. On the other
it blamed the Senftners for their "condemnation of the secretary and [their] admitted hostility to the New York Preparatory
School." As to the charges against the New York Preparatory
School, however, two were "well founded." To the charge that the
school engaged in misleading advertising, the committee noted
that because the school held only a "limited charter," to say it
held an "absolute charter" in its publication was a "deliberate"
violation of University laws and ordinances. To the charge that
the school had illegally opened a branch in Brooklyn, the committee cited Regent action on June 24, 1896, specifically pro-
hibiting the school from expanding beyond New York City, and
therefore said Gallup's claim that the "charter as at first issued
gave us power to open branches anywhere in the state" was "so
disingenuous as wholly to discredit Mr. Gallup before the board."
The committee concluded by recommending that the Board demand the New York Preparatory School close its Brooklyn branch
and "show cause why its present charter shall not be canceled."
It said nothing, however, about the fact that Dewey knew about
Gallup's activities, and did nothing to stop them.[23]

Because very little of this filtered into news coverage of the
Regents' meeting, almost no one publicly connected it to Dewey's
resignation. One person, however, refused to let it pass without
comment. On December 26, McKelway recounted the history of
the issue in an *Eagle* article entitled "Gallup's Methods Rebuked." He noted that after the five boroughs consolidated into
the City of New York on January 1, 1898, Gallup "received a suggestion from a source which need not be too clearly pointed out"
that the original grant could now be construed to cover the
Brooklyn branch. McKelway's reference to Dewey was unmistak-
able. So was his anger. The Regents had "been gravely compro-

---

23. *BR Minutes,* 12/21/91, pp. 540–41.

mised" by Gallup's action, he argued, a situation made much worse because that action "was apparently suggested, promoted, and protected."[24]

For eleven years Dewey had bragged to anyone within earshot that, unlike politically motivated people, he was above playing favorites. That he was caught in such a flagrant violation of this principle may have had more to do with his resignation than the issue of unification. If his resignation from Columbia eleven years earlier suggests a pattern, it is possible to conclude that Dewey in part traded his resignation for a muted investigation of his role in Gallup's school plans. But McKelway would have none of the self-sacrificing image Dewey tried to create at the Board's December 22 meeting. Always the maverick, he decided to run the story in the *Eagle*.

After reading McKelway's treatise, Dewey immediately protested to Reid. "The implication . . . that my resignation was due to some improper connection with Gallup's school is simply contemptible," he argued, "and I must rely on you . . . to set this right." He peppered his letter with phrases like "if you had all the facts before you" and "when all the truth comes out," but gave no details to counter McKelway's story. He concluded by promising a "memorandum of the facts" in a few days, and solicited Reid's assistance in efforts "to see to it that my good name is not smirched in this manner."[25] But Dewey never again addressed the subject, and the issue never caught the attention of the press beyond the *Eagle*. Shortly thereafter Gallup left the New York Preparatory School to become business manager at the Lake Placid Club. The career shift was hardly coincidental.

Although Dewey had removed himself from the debate on unification by resigning as Regents' Secretary, the controversy spun on without him. The Unification Commission Report that went to Roosevelt's desk January 10 did not carry a minority report. The Commission proposed to reduce the number of Regents from twenty-one to fourteen and to abolish the office of Superintendent of Public Instruction. In its place the state would create a Department of Education headed by a chancellor who

---

24. *Eagle*, 12/26/99. See also *NYTr*, 12/24/99.

25. Dewey to Reid, 12/26/99, Box 75, Dewey Mss.

would initially be appointed by the governor for an eight-year term, and thereafter by the Regents.[26] But the Regents opposed the Commission Report, and without Regent support the legislature could not muster enough votes to pass a unification bill.

The office of Secretary to the Board of Regents of the University of the State of New York that Melvil Dewey left on January 1, 1900, was significantly bigger and substantially more powerful than the one he inherited. In 1904 Vassar's J. M. Taylor reminded Dewey that the Regents "were doing exceedingly little" before he became Secretary in 1889 "and stirred that body into a prominence that it has had ever since." Between 1889 and 1899 student enrollment at state-chartered institutions had increased by 182 percent, faculty by 223 percent. The number of public high schools had increased by 250 percent. Professional education especially had boomed: up 80 percent in medicine, 59 percent in pharmacy, 136 percent in dentistry, 233 percent in law. New York, in fact, enrolled nearly 20 percent of the nation's law students.[27]

Superimposed upon this growth was a system of examination and licensing that accelerated the quality of professional practitioners to whom New York's citizens went for help, and reduced the number of incompetent practitioners throughout the state. Dewey had used Regent authority to inspect and establish standards for high schools and set minima for their teaching staff and libraries. He had also eliminated scores of diploma mills, and by forming a network among New York's institutions of higher education had given them a stronger, more unified voice in Albany. Before 1889 the Legislature "tinkered" freely with laws concerning New York education; thereafter legislators had great difficulty sneaking through bills that advantaged favored constituents. By 1899 the Regents had become a significant force to defend or oppose any proposed legislation. Dewey had made them into an executive body that acted in behalf of New York

---

26. See Parsons to McKelway, 1/2/00 (2), Box 2, McKelway Mss. See also New York [State], *Documents of the Assembly. 123d Session, 1900. Vol. 2, no. 17. Report of the Commission on Educational Unification, January 17, 1900;* and *Regents AR, 1899,* pp. r75–r78.

27. Taylor to Dewey, 2/15/04, Box 75, Dewey Mss. Statistics taken from *Regents AR, 1899,* pp. r31–r33. Dewey actually hand-signed 279,444 Regents' high-school certificates between 1889 and 1899. See Dawe, *Dewey,* p. 214.

higher education through the Secretary's office. In addition, the University had launched major initiatives in extension education, which Dewey had tied to a rapidly expanding public library community throughout the state. He had also raised the profile of the University Convocation and turned it into an event drawing national and international attention.

Although his legacy to higher education in the state of New York (and by New York's example to the rest of the nation) was substantial, Dewey has never been awarded the credit he deserves. "The University of the State of New York," the Carnegie Foundation for the Advancement of Teaching said in its 1908 annual report, "represents almost the only effective agency in any state of the Union which has the power to supervise or even to criticize institutions devoted to higher education and to professional training." The Foundation regularly complimented New York for its high standards.[28] Perhaps one reason Dewey's tenure as Regents' Secretary has been overlooked by historians is that he was both hero and villain, and as villain not a particularly attractive model for contemporary generations to emulate. Because he was so difficult to work with, Dewey took most of the blame for problems caused by the implementation of his system, and after he left office his contemporaries wished to forget more than to honor him.

On December 17, 1899, McKelway wrote a revealing column on the frustration Dewey's "queering personality" caused Regents during his tenure. On the one hand, Dewey "is a bright man of singular energy, marvelous intellectual fecundity, abounding and pervasive personality." On the other, Dewey had "an equal capacity to create or to occasion exciting situations, marked misinterpretations and extraordinary jealousies, and to explain them, or to explain them away, with results that are not impressive or permanent." While in office he committed no serious offenses, and his accomplishments had been impressive, yet he was "generally at daggers drawn with the Legislature" and "on the defensive with many state officers." Often, McKelway noted, Regents had been assured the opposition they drew was not necessarily directed at them as much as Dewey, and when they confronted their secretary with these allegations, he generally

---

28. Quotations taken from Abbott, *Government Policy and Higher Education*, pp. 72–73.

responded "that he is the most misunderstood, if not the most meritorious, man in the commonwealth." He had more "skill" in causing than avoiding difficulties. "He had been an electric current in a lethargic board, to which he has given a galvanic activity, with embarrassing results." The Board could not seem to live with him, nor without him. "He does not seem to have the faculty of keeping out of hot water, and he always seems to have several kettles on[,] which are filled with hot water to the boiling point for use in the cause of righteousness and of restlessness as a policy." He personified "the office," and as its resident became "indispensable, impossible, inevitable, and unmanageable."

A decade later Regent Charles Fitch was more generous. He called Dewey "an especially well-equipped and forceful executive, of rare initiative and constructive ability, jealous of the functions of the Board, and earnest, even aggressive, in asserting them." Despite "certain infirmities of disposition," Fitch concluded, New York was "under lasting obligation for what he accomplished in the advancement of her educational interests."[29]

---

29. *Eagle*, 12/17/99; Fitch, "Education Department," pp. 63–64.

9

Attending to Library Matters

1889–1904

What Dewey did as Regents' Secretary between 1889 and 1899 most people would have considered a full-time job. But Dewey also had responsibilities as State Librarian and Director of the New York State Library School (both of which he greatly expanded), and self-assumed responsibilities for other reform interests (most of which merited varying degrees of his time depending on opportunities he perceived). He was able to accomplish so much in part because of his tremendous capacity for work, in part because so many of his subordinates worked as hard as he did for his causes, in part because he was obsessed with office efficiency.

Dewey ran his office like a command post. Room 41A at the Capitol building seemed in perfect order; there he worked in a "kind of furious quiet." In a corner he located his self-designed desk (measured in metric, of course). Atop it he put a wrap-around bank of 120 pigeonholes, into which he placed shorthand notes on the back of "P-slips" (used catalog card stock). The arrangement, he later argued, allowed the "brainworker" to "acquire the easy habit of resting by change of work instead of idleness." He wrote notes in different colors from one of five fountain pens he carried in his pocket—each color designated for a particular department under his supervision. Subordinates were given open access to retrieve instructions or transmit messages via preassigned pigeonholes. Many times they delivered messages or picked up instructions while Dewey worked at his desk; often he did not even look up. "And the one thing that would provoke him most," one employee later recalled, "was to NEGLECT to look in our pigeonhole daily or even more." It was this level of intensity and efficiency that allowed him to handle personally the 555 pieces of mail his office averaged daily.

Later on, as demands on his time increased, he divided his day into blocks and assigned each department reporting to him a specific time period during which he could be approached. He then asked his staff to honor several rules. First, employees had to make sure their problem might not more properly be addressed by a department head. Second, employees were to have exactly in mind what they wished to discuss, and bring all necessary papers and references "marked, so that without loss of a moment you can present the case in fewest possible words." Third, they had to respect the privacy of a colleague already in Dewey's office by waiting "outside . . . till he is through, then come in promptly as soon as he turns to leave." Fourth, "make the statement too short rather than too long," since Dewey often was already familiar with the problem. Fifth, "as soon as the necessary points are covered promptly, give way for the next . . . to present his business." Finally, Dewey admonished "interviewees" to be frank. "Much as I enjoy meeting members of the staff socially, I admire and value most those who under any constant extreme pressure dispatch their business most directly and briefly and with the fewest words." But not everyone was happy with the system. Some disliked Dewey's obsessive behaviors. A subordinate once told Dewey "one of the principal criticisms against the office . . . is that it is constantly stirring up things and making changes all the while." Others marvelled at it. "He thinks of all the details," a library-school student recalled, "even teaches the sub-janitors how to dust books properly."[1]

---

1. Melvil Dewey, "Office Efficiency," in H. P. Dunham, ed., *The Business of Insurance,* vol. III (N.Y., 1912), pp. 3, 6; Dewey to State Library and Board of Regents' Employees, 12/7/97, Box 72; Gallup to Dewey, 7/18/94, Box 74; Katharine Sharp to her father, 10/19/90, Box P-52; and Oscar F. R. Tedder to Dewey, 11/2/31, Box 95, Dewey Mss. See also *Regents AR, 1895,* p. 128; *1897,* p. r89. Information on Dewey's work habits and office management taken from Grace Hewitt to Godfrey Dewey, -/-/32, Box 26; Dewey to "Friends," 6/14/21, Box 27; Dewey to R. S. Regan (3d Assistant Postmaster

Between 1889 and 1904 Dewey made his personal life as busy as his professional life. By 1890 he and Annie had purchased a large three-floor brick house at 315 Madison Street. The first floor was surrounded by three large porches and included a library, parlor, dining room, pantry, and kitchen. Melvil and Annie had separate bedrooms on the second floor, which also included two bathrooms and two guest bedrooms. Godfrey's bedroom was on the third floor, along with a billiard room and three more bedrooms. The large house allowed Dewey to host visitors and entertain guests; Annie's records show she averaged over six hundred guest meals annually. Shortly after the Deweys purchased the house, Annie's mother moved in. Eventually Walter S. Biscoe, May Seymour, and Florence Woodworth also moved in as permanent boarders; each paid $35 a month.[2]

The atmosphere Annie and Melvil Dewey developed at 315 Madison Street began to assume features of the home Joel and Eliza Dewey had created for Melvil as a child, with some modifications brought by the new concept of extended family Annie had experienced at Wellesley. It still embodied basic evangelical values of morality, piety, order, and self-discipline, but added Victorian family values of refinement, intellectuality, and education. Annie and Melvil also involved themselves in the community. Annie served as president of the Women's Auxiliary for Albany's Episcopalian diocese. Dewey became president of the Civic League of Albany.

Managing the New York State Library 1889–1904

The New York State Library was established in 1818 as a non-circulating library for the use of legislators and the visiting public. The State Librarian's position was a political football kicked between the two dominant political parties until 1844, when the legislature passed control of the Library to the Regents, and in particular to seven members who functioned as its trustees. Over

General), 4/15/29, Box 44, Dewey Mss; and Rider, *Dewey*, p. 124. A photo in Box 78, Dewey Mss, shows Dewey at his Capitol desk (see Plate 12).

2. Loomis recollection, 2/17/27, Box 19, Dewey Mss. See also Elva Bascom to Godfrey Dewey, 1/17/32; Account Books, FPA; Gunther, "Annie Godfrey Dewey," 358; and *School Bulletin* 18 (7/92): 123.

the next decade Regents determined that State Library collections should emphasize New York and United States history. In 1855 the Library moved into a separate building; Henry A. Homes was hired to help with the move, and in 1862 he became director of the General Library and his predecessor took responsibility for a separate Law Library. In 1883 the State Library moved "temporarily" into the new Capitol Building, still unfinished. The General Library, which by this time consisted of 127,000 volumes, was crammed into space originally planned for the Court of Appeals. "Temporary" stretched beyond 1883, until in 1888 Regents pushed for an increased appropriation to finish the library section of the building. Dewey's first official duty as Director was to move the Library into new quarters.[3]

Space allocated to the Library in 1889 seemed generous. It was located next to Senate and Assembly chambers, and initially shared office space with the Regents on the third floor, later on the fourth. The Law Library occupied space on the north end, the General Library on the south. The main reading room, seventy-three by forty-two feet with a concave ceiling reaching a height of fifty-six feet at its center, constituted the Library's central feature. Double tiers of galleries lined its perimeter, and portraits of icons fixed into the literary canon of Western Civilization (Shakespeare, Milton, Goethe, Schiller, Byron, and Longfellow) adorned available wall space. A huge oak circulation desk located just inside the entrance greeted 1,000 visitors daily.

Shortly after he arrived in Albany Dewey hired Biscoe to reclassify the Library's collections into the decimal scheme, and Woodworth and Cutler to move and manage the library school and its students in Albany. State officeholders throughout the building "did not quite like a troop of women from New York City taking possession every morning of their library," one student later recalled. But "all was in harmony in Mr. Dewey's library staff," another remembered; "all were loyal to him and his dreams." Dewey's subordinates eventually became known in Capitol corridors as the "Titans."[4]

---

3. For a more complete discussion of the history of the New York State Library, see Cecil R. Roseberry, *A History of the New York State Library* (Albany, 1970), pp. 53–80.

4. See Mary W. Loomis's recollection, dated 2/17/27, Box 19; and Joseph Gavin to Dawe, 7/22/32, Box 25, Dewey Mss.

When Dewey became director, the Law Library was under the able direction of Stephen B. Griswold, who in thirty years (1868–1898) increased its collections from 20,000 to 60,000 volumes. Records indicate Dewey generally left Griswold alone. In the General Library, Dewey replicated changes he had implemented at Columbia. For example, he laid carpets over parquet floors, and insisted employees wear rubber heels. He installed forty speaking tubes to link staff members to each other at various locations throughout the library, and over time replaced them with telephones. Dewey also experimented with library uniforms so patrons could quickly distinguish visitors from employees; initially employees were attired in dark blue, later in Quaker drab.[5] Dewey wanted his employees to be loud in neither voice nor appearance.

Because much of 1889 was spent moving State Library materials into new quarters, Dewey did not have much chance to implement his library ideas until 1890. During that year he inaugurated a Legislative Reference Section designed to collect documents and government publications for legislators' information needs, committed a separate alcove to educational materials and assigned Seymour to supervise it, and set up a Manuscripts Section under State Archivist George Howell, who was told to develop it into a state archives bureau and public records office. Dewey also expanded hours at the Library from eight to fourteen daily.[6]

In the summer of 1890 he decided to organize the New York State Library Association (NYLA). Threads leading to this decision are not hard to discern; the context in which Dewey conceived NYLA was fashioned by his plans for dual responsibilities as State Librarian and Regents' Secretary. As State Librarian he foresaw a system of New York public libraries delivering a vital form of education to Empire State citizens—both rural and urban. These libraries would look to the State Library for guidance and counsel on system, efficiency, and organization. There they would be shown that the "best" public libraries were organized by the Decimal Classification and managed efficiently with forms, appli-

---

5. Roseberry, pp. 63–64.

6. See, for example, Dewey to Governor David B. Hill, 4/14/90, Box 29, Dewey Mss. See also *Albany Evening Journal,* 7/23/89, for an interview with Dewey on the State Library's new quarters.

ances, and systems marketed by such agencies as the Library Bureau. There they would also find guidance in book and periodical selection. For most of these plans Dewey, as State Librarian, already had the authority to act.

As Regents' Secretary, however, Dewey also foresaw a system of New York public libraries functioning as chartered and certified University extension sites that would host University instructors who would take higher education throughout the state. These public libraries would also provide relevant reading materials and bibliographies, which would benefit from the interlibrary loan and traveling library systems Dewey projected for the State Library. For most of these plans Dewey needed enabling legislation and additional appropriations. But in 1890 Regents were still weak compared to the Department of Public Instruction, where the Superintendent had developed common school officials into a network of constituents ready to press politicians on educational matters affecting them. Dewey needed similar constituencies to influence politicians to pass his appropriations, so he established NYLA as an organized constituency to whom he could look for support for his agendas as Regents' Secretary and State Library Director.[7]

Against the advice of several Regents who suggested he wait a year, and in part because the New Hampshire Library Association had been incorporated in 1889 but had not yet organized, Dewey announced a meeting of librarians and other interested parties for just after the University's convocation on July 11, 1890. Proof of his plans for NYLA echoed in a preliminary circular he sent out—"to discuss some of the important New York library matters," he said, "which are soon to be submitted for action to the legislature and the regents." In the circular he identified several agenda items, including "What changes in library legislation should be asked at the coming session of the Legislature?" and even more important, "What changes should be made in the state district library system and the expenditure of the $55,000 a year now granted for it?"

---

7. In his efforts to organize New York's librarians into a political lobby, Dewey was several years ahead of other New York professionals. See McCormick, *From Realignment to Reform,* pp. 153, 264. See also Dewey to Reid, 11/10/90, Reel 135, Reid Mss, for a hint at his intentions for NYLA.

Forty-three people attended the three-hour meeting, including twenty women, four Regents, and a number of college professors and presidents. Although Chancellor George W. Curtis presided, Dewey had scripted the whole affair. He focused on the need to develop library leaders and raise the profile of librarianship's responsibility in the state's educational system, and to establish a "central bureau for library work." He noted that the University Law of 1889 had authorized the creation of (but not appropriations for) a duplicates department, and suggested the appointment of a State Library Inspector "who should give aid and advice whenever it was wished." He then read the law authorizing the New Hampshire Library Association and asked if New York ought to consider a similar move. After some discussion the group voted to establish NYLA which, a circular later explained, would "limit itself to advancing the library interests of New York state, leaving general library matters to the A.L.A." The group also elected Dewey president and set annual dues at $1.00.

For several years thereafter Dewey set NYLA's agenda and regularly scheduled meetings to coincide with University Convocation. Among "the first work to be done" by the Association he pushed for three lists—statistics on all New York libraries (to be reported on common University forms with common University definitions); a bibliography of all New York library catalogs, reports, and bulletins; and a register of all New York librarians and trustees. Dewey clearly intended to build a network. Once in place, he predicted to Regents they would soon find NYLA "their most powerful helper in all their library work." NYLA quickly became a model for librarians from other states, including Iowa and New Jersey, both of which established associations within a year.[8] Dewey was equally successful on other State Library matters, including both its on- and off-site activities. On site, the Library began publishing three annual comparative publications: (1) a summary of legislation in all states, including an index;

---

8. These events are detailed in *Regents AR, 1890*, pp. 147–50; NYSL *AR, 1891*, pp. 15–23; Richard D. Johnson, *This Larger Spirit: A Centennial Remembrance for NYLA* (Albany, 1990), pp. 11–12; and my own "Melvil Dewey and the Origins of the New York Library Association," *Bookmark* 48 (Winter, 1990): 81–85. Dewey recalled these events in Dewey to Frank K. Walter, 11/20/15, Box 1, Walter Mss. See also Dewey to Elizabeth Smith, 10/6/30, Box 29, Dewey Mss.

(2) a classified digest of the official messages of state governors; and (3) a review of legislative trends arranged by subjects. In 1891 Dewey won a $5,000 appropriation from the legislature to accession and maintain a collection of 2,500 volumes donated by the Albany Medical College. The gift became a magnet for others; the State Medical Society donated its library of 7,500 volumes and 3,600 pamphlets shortly thereafter. In 1893 Dewey acquired a Women's Library, originally assembled by a group of New York women for the World's Columbian Exposition in Chicago. When the Exposition closed, the library returned to New York, where Dewey gave it a separate alcove in the State Library.

In subsequent years Dewey also persuaded the Regents to fund a program of providing books for the blind in New York State, with the Public Libraries Division functioning as a clearinghouse for embossed print books. He established a Capitol Library that consisted of general interest materials available in a library corner to which all visitors had access, and when this library began to attract increasing numbers of young people Dewey had a Children's Library established initially at one end of the main reading room. After it became even more popular, however, he removed it in 1899 to a separate room on the fifth floor. Here he assembled a collection of 2,500 primarily English-language titles from the seventeenth to the twentieth centuries.

Because of Dewey's efforts collections quickly outgrew space available, and even the installation of mezzanines in the main reading room provided only a temporary relief. By mid-decade, Dewey presided over a library of 500,000 volumes, a number exceeded in the United States only by the Library of Congress, the Boston and New York Public Libraries, and Harvard University. He began campaigning for a separate building.[9]

Dewey was equally successful with the State Library's off-site activities. In 1893 he supervised the inauguration of a traveling library system. He appointed five members of his staff to a "book board" that included "the library examiner who has charge of the weekly reading seminar for training library school students in the systematic selection of books" and an assistant responsible for annotating traveling library catalogs. The board met weekly to identify appropriate titles for the collections and

---

9. NYSL *AR, 1891,* pp. 16–17; *1896,* p. 16; *1899,* p. 38; *Regents AR, 1900,* p. r24; *1903,* p. r28.

for citation in bibliographies of "approved" books the State Library disseminated to libraries across the state. "Partizan books" (which Dewey defined as "any book of a technically religious or controversial character") were "disallowed." Dewey was proud of the efficiency of the process. "Not more than two or three books in 100 are withdrawn from the list for further consultation," he noted in his 1896 annual report.[10]

Ultimately, the book board identified 1,000 volumes from State Library collections regarded as the most informative and the best recreational reading. These 1,000 volumes were then subdivided into lots of 100, and each of the resulting ten small libraries was placed into an oak bookcase with locking doors and sent for six-month loan periods. Small public libraries were eligible to receive traveling collections; so were remote New York communities submitting signatures of twenty-five resident taxpayers who agreed to pay a $5.00 transportation fee and promised "that a petition shall be made for a popular vote to be taken within two years . . . on the question of establishing a free public library."[11] The contents of the collections were carefully monitored; no more than 25 percent could be fiction, but 10 to 20 percent could be biography, travel, and history. By April 1894 the number of traveling library collections had grown to ninety (including sixteen sent to Regents' Centers) and their contents were expanded to include pictures, slides, and photographs. Three years later the number of traveling libraries had jumped to 1,000.[12]

Most of Dewey's accomplishments as State Librarian have been amply documented by historians, but what they have generally missed is an account of Dewey's efforts to maintain tight control from a central office over the collection development

---

10. Dewey's subordinates monitored these collections carefully. In 1899, for example, Myrtilla Avery of the Public Libraries Division wrote a rural New York librarian about one of the books in "Library 38" she wanted to withdraw because it "is not good enough to circulate." See *BR Minutes*, 11/22/95, p. 289; and *Regents AR, 1896*, pp. 475–76.

11. NYSL *AR, 1892*, p. 59. By 1901 Dewey dropped the number of signatures required to five, and switched to strong boxes instead of oak cases to save transportation costs. See *Regents AR, 1901*, pp. r26–r27.

12. NYSL *AR, 1893*, p. 47, 48; *1903*, pp. 37–38. See also Melvil Dewey, "Traveling Libraries: Field and Future of Traveling Libraries," University of the State of New York, Home Education Department, *Bulletin 40*, September, 1901, pp. 3–17.

(and thus much of the reading) of hundreds of small New York public libraries, and the example this set for public library development that led to the turn-of-the-century creation of public library commissions in many other states. While Dewey had made specific references to a "state library bureau" concept in his initial discussions with Regents in 1888, his plans began to take concrete form only after the legislature passed the University Law of 1892, and specifically after an allocation of $25,000 for public libraries became available October 1, 1892. On that day Dewey established the Public Libraries Division.

He had already prepared the New York library community for this moment by focusing part of the 1892 NYLA meeting on the question: "What kind of books circulated by some public libraries should the regents refuse to certify for subsidy?" John Crane of the Albany Young Men's Association Library argued: "Let every book which is objectionable and has not a high educational power be thrown out." Regent William S. Doane said libraries had a right to collect what they wanted, "but I should be sorry as a regent . . . to vote for the light literature." Dewey offered a solution. "My notion of this would be to make as good a select list as possible and send it to libraries." If libraries wished to purchase books not yet on the list, they would do so at their own risk. Should these books subsequently be judged "not good enough to go on the state list," the state would not recognize their circulation in the formula for determining state aid. A subsequent vote showed two to one in favor of basing state aid only on circulation of "the highest grade of books." Dewey had his mandate.

The $25,000 allocated for public library development by the legislature was intended for two purposes. First, to any community that raised at least $100 to start a public library the Regents would issue a matching grant up to $200 for the first year, $100 for successive years, "the entire amount to be spent for books approved by the regents." Application for successive grants would be based on circulation rates of the previous year, but only the circulation of "good books" would be counted. Second, to any public library chartered by the Regents and conforming to its regulations (or any community attempting to establish one either from scratch or by converting an existing social library), the State Library would loan "select [100-volume] collections of recent desirable books" for six-month periods. The intention here was to increase the availability of "good reading," discourage the circulation of "trash," and by withholding grant money directly prevent the acquisition of anything "vile," "vicious," or "pernicious."

Responsibility for the distribution of this money belonged to the "library inspector," part of whose duty it was to "personally examine the library and its work. . . . If he reports that the library in its administration and character of books is worthy of state aid," Dewey said, "the regents usually grant the request." That Dewey was concerned about the quality of reading (especially fiction) circulating in the social libraries that local communities wanted to turn into public institutions is evident from another responsibility he wrote into the inspector's job description. For any library applying for Regent money on the basis of book circulation, grants would "not exceed 10 cents for each volume of circulation" the library inspector "certified." In other words, books by Horatio Alger and Mrs. E. D. E. N. Southworth would not count in the formula for determining the size of state grants, no matter how many times they were checked out. On October 1 Dewey appointed William R. Eastman as the state's first library inspector.[13]

For the next year Dewey sold the program at library association meetings and school conventions. He had the Public Libraries Division issue circulars and pamphlets saying part of its object was "to provide annotated lists of the best books on all subjects, and in all practicable ways to assist communities willing to do their part in providing the best reading for their citizens." By October 1, 1893, Eastman had inspected 55 libraries in 30 counties; 43 of 44 applications had been approved for grants aggregating to $6,341. By 1903 the numbers had jumped to 330 inspections of the 1,160 libraries (553 of which were free public libraries) reporting on common University statistical data sheets; nearly half of New York's 337 chartered or registered free public libraries received grant money totaling $21,700 and "the whole" of that sum "was spent for books approved by the University," Dewey boasted.[14]

---

13. NYSL *AR, 1892,* p. 52, 53, 57, 72–81, 90–91.

14. See New York State Library. Extension Division, *State Aid to Libraries* (Albany, 1893); *Regents AR, 1903,* pp. r24–r25; NYSL *AR, 1903,* p. 36.

To identify the "best books" Dewey continued to push for an ALA "Catalog." In 1891 Regents authorized him to commit funds and staff time to the project, and several months later Dewey set the ALA 1893 World's Fair Conference as a target date for completion; he then gave Mary S. Cutler responsibility for meeting the deadline. For a while the *Catalog* (which was published in 1893) served as a useful collection guide, but it soon became dated. New books required new lists of "recommended" and "approved" titles, and because so many new public libraries were so small, bibliographies needed to be considerably downsized. Initially Dewey issued a series of subject-specific short annotated lists intended for wide distribution, but with Number 12 in his bibliography series he began an annual annotated "Best Books" list of 200 to 250 recently published titles put together by the Public Libraries Division's Book Board and including a graded system further refining recommendations by identifying the 20, 30, and 50 "best" books. Other numbers in the series included "Biography for Young People" by Bertha Hyatt, and a "Class List of a $500 Library Recommended for Schools." In time, most lists in the series adopted a grading system. Libraries seeking matching funds knew that if they purchased books from the State Library's graded and approved lists, they eliminated any question of the acceptability of their grant applications.

And Dewey's series soon generated interest outside New York. In 1899 the ALA Publishing Section began issuing printed cards containing citations and annotations drawn from the bibliographies. "No greater compliment could be paid to the bulletins than the recognition of practical value to all libraries," Dewey boasted in his 1899 annual report. In 1898 Dewey developed "fiction slips" to allow "those whose judgment is desired" (including Dewey's Literature Inspector Richard Jones) to comment on novels being considered for State Library traveling collections. Criteria for judging the "character" of each novel included "style, English, slang, vulgarity, profanity, trustworthiness, partizan moral tone, objectionable tendency, immoral [and] weak." And by 1897 Dewey's new "Home Education" Division monitored "over 400 registered study clubs" that under its supervision "were doing systematic continuous educational work for 10 or more weeks." Many of these clubs were being served by the University's 1,000 traveling libraries; most were run by women. "With three exceptions," Dewey boasted in his 1900 annual report, "every other state of the Union has within a half dozen years adopted our system more or less fully, because of its economy and educational efficiency."[15]

The traveling libraries accomplished their purpose as fore-runners of public libraries. Between 1893 and 1900 the number of New York communities establishing public libraries after re-ceiving traveling libraries increased from 29 to 175, their collec-tions from 70,000 to 600,000 volumes, and their circulation from 193,000 to 2,182,000. The 100-volume collections that stimu-lated this growth averaged 276 circulations in 1893, 360 in 1900. And the growth had not been inflated by the circulation of "trash," Dewey said. "Thousands of doubtful books . . . are dis-approved each year and better ones recommended in their places; and the local authorities are with hardly an exception not only content to receive, but are grateful for systematic and intel-ligent supervision which will not allow the taxpayers' money to be used for books of doubtful value or influence."

Statistics comparing New York's free public libraries be-tween 1893 and 1903 echo the point. In 1893 New York's 238 public libraries held 850,000 volumes and circulated 2,294,000 books; in 1903 New York's 553 public libraries held 2,792,000 volumes and circulated 10,870,000 books. From all these statis-tics, Dewey concluded, "There could be no better answer to the fear that proper supervision, while it might greatly improve the quality, might sadly reduce the quantity of reading." Some, however, chafed at the control. On August 5, 1904, Louis Sil-berman, a lawyer leading an effort to obtain a building grant for the Albany Free Library, reported to Andrew Carnegie that the library was "practically owned" by the Regents. "They designate the character of the books we should buy and the amount we shall spend . . . and dictate our course of work."[16]

---

15. *BR Minutes*, 2/12/91, p. 52; NYSL *AR, 1892*, p. 17; *1893*, pp. 123–24; *1898*, pp. 51–52; *1899*, pp. 9–10; and New York State Library. *Bibliography Bulletin* (Albany, 1899–1925). See also *Regents AR, 1900*, p. r21. Karen J. Bailey argues that study clubs provided opportunities for women to develop leadership skills. See her *The Clubwoman as Feminist: True Womanhood Redefined, 1868–1914* (N.Y., 1980), pp. 68, 98–101.

16. *Regents AR, 1900*, p. r22; *1903*, p. r25; Silberman to Carnegie, 8/5/04, 12/7/04, CLC. See also *Regents AR, 1901*, p. r28, where Dewey notes "we are no longer criticized for paternalism because of our active efforts to keep objectionable and weak books out of free circulation."

The New York State Library School
1889–1904

When the library school transferred to Albany in the spring of 1889, five instructors moved with it: Walter Biscoe, Ada Alice Jones, Florence Woodworth, May Seymour, and Mary Salome Cutler. Biscoe assumed responsibility for cataloging and classification in the library school curriculum and in the library, and during his long tenure there (1889–1929) contributed to the fourth through twelfth editions of the Decimal Classification. May Seymour took primary responsibility for editing new editions from the fourth to the tenth. Cutler took primary responsibility for the library school, however, and was named vice-director shortly after she arrived. At Dewey's direction, the relocated library school continued to monitor admissions by requiring examinations and personal interviews. Initially students were required to have only a high-school education. Still, almost half matriculated with a college degree, most of them women. By 1902, however, Dewey and his faculty raised standards by restricting admission for in-state applicants to graduates of University's chartered institutions. The move was a calculated risk. Under old standards the school had ten applicants for every opening. Under new the number dropped off considerably, but never below slots available.

On paper, the curriculum did not change much from Columbia. Like Columbia's trustees, Regents were willing to sanction the library school "provided no expense to the state is involved." Forced to run the school on a shoestring budget, Dewey once again compromised his agenda for formal library education. Saving the school by adapting it to tolerances of another indifferent environment was a higher priority. He pinched pennies where he could, and sometimes tried to increase revenue by expansion and outreach. Against the advice of already overworked faculty (who were not being compensated for services as instructors), Dewey began five-week summer sessions in July 1896, then extended them to six weeks in 1899.[17] But unlike Columbia, Regents authorized degrees of Bachelor of Library

---

17. See White, p. 63; Trautman, p. 24; NYSLS *AR, 1899,* p. xxxiii; NYSLS *Summer Course, April, 1899,* p. 8; *Regents AR, 1902,* pp. r36–r37; and Woodworth to Dewey, 7/26/94, Box 73, Dewey Mss.

Science, Master of Library Science, and the honorary degree of Doctor of Library Science.

For most of Dewey's tenure as director, the library school was located in Room 31; lectures were held in Room 31Λ, a "little cubby hole" that also housed an attractive fireplace around which students gathered as they listened to lectures. For his own lectures Dewey would rush in at the last moment, notes scribbled in shorthand on P-slips. He would begin almost immediately to pace back and forth and talk at the rate of 180 words per minute (some students actually counted), while students took notes furiously. Occasionally he would stop pacing, turn full square towards the class, draw his six foot frame erect before them, and while slightly tipping his head back, address them by looking down his nose. Students remembered the jutting chin, the cocked head, the flared nostrils as he pressed a point. He did not communicate in the cold manner of a stereotypical bureaucrat, however, and he made it a point to remember every student's face and name.[18]

The sudden way Dewey appeared and then disappeared added to his mystique among library school students, many of whom remained in awe of his influence and shared a sense of being a pioneer in library history. Consistent with his belief that library education had to inculcate the "library spirit," Dewey fashioned a number of his lectures to inspire, to push the cause of libraries as active agents of conservative reforms. One student took copious notes on Dewey's opening "Librarianship" lecture, from which, she later remembered, "my enthusiasm for my work has gathered momentum ever since." Another recalled phrases Dewey frequently used that "stuck in my mind." "Libraries, big and small, must be built around the P-slip"; "Secure a cataloger with a cataloging mind"; "Don't spend time or *fuss* over the ephemeral"; "work at 'concentrating cordiality.'" Over the years these kinds of stories were repeated hundreds of times in private conversations, at professional social occasions, and in formal presentations to large groups, and over the decades were undoubtedly embellished in library school classrooms. The stories also tended to drown out voices of students who did not like

---

18. Roseberry, p. 69; Asa Don Dickinson to Dawe, 6/27/32, Box 24A; E. L. Gant to Dewey, 11/10/31; Harriet Wood to Dewey, 12/10/31; Elizabeth Foote to Dewey, 12/10/31, Box 95, Dewey Mss.

Dewey. Charles McCarthy, for example, left the library school abruptly after five weeks because he "couldn't stand" Dewey's "rubbish." In the library profession, Dewey's disciples cultivated his image for generations; his detractors generally said nothing.[19]

Dewey continued the two-year program he brought from Columbia. In their "Junior" year, students took cataloging, shelf listing, accessioning, and "elementary library economy" during a twelve-week session that ended before Christmas. In January they took dictionary cataloging, in February classification, and in March and April library economy. May and June were assigned to apprenticeship work and some visits to other libraries. For "Seniors" the academic year extended to nine months. Students had two hours of daily supervised work somewhere in the Library, classwork on special subjects (classification, library economy, cataloging, and dictionary cataloging in the first five months; library economy and library work in the remaining four), a course in library history, and one hour of classwork daily—either a lecture or a seminar. Many of the lectures were delivered by invited visitors, most of whom were veterans like Cutter, Fletcher, and Hewins. Seniors were also expected to write a thesis that showed "independent thought and research," but by the late 1890s these theses evolved into specialized bibliographies, many of which became numbers in Dewey's "Best Books" series.

On the surface, the New York State Library School looked like an efficient operation run by cooperative hardworking pioneers in formal library education. Beneath the surface, however, rumblings of discontent centered around a philosophical disagreement between Dewey and Mary Salome Cutler, who, as vice-director of the Library School, had more freedom to innovate in Albany than she did at Columbia because Dewey was so preoccupied with other responsibilities. The focus of disagreement was a "Reading Seminar" she taught to a combined class of juniors and seniors. "The Seminar is that part of the work allowing freest scope for individuality," Cutler reported proudly in 1890. "Each student selects her own subject and treats it in her

---

19. Bascom to Godfrey Dewey, 1/17/32, FPA; Linn to Dewey, 12/10/31; Euphemia Corwin to Dewey, 11/16/31; Brown to Dewey, 11/11/31, Box 95, Dewey Mss. The comment by McCarthy is quoted in Edith Harper to Katharine Sharp, 3/8/08, University of Illinois Alumni Files, University of Illinois Archives. I am indebted to Professor Loriene Roy for bringing this letter to my attention.

own way. . . . This is the place to air pet theories." Although Cutler's description departed from the practical nature Dewey intended for the school, he did not openly object. Others did. An ALA committee assigned to monitor the library school criticized its curriculum for emphasizing "theoretical teaching rather than practical work."[20]

Cutler did not change, however, and by 1895 was moving even farther away from Dewey's blueprint. "To select good books wisely requires an abundance of time, knowledge of books, and sympathy with the popular taste," she told an NYLA audience in May. "Such reviews and criticisms as can be found in the *Literary World, Critic, Nation,* etc., will also be helpful." Reviews, in other words, were only a tool; knowing books and their potential audiences was more important. That same month she gave another address. The ALA motto—"The best reading for the largest number at the least cost"—she said, "smacks of arithmetic and commerce." The sentiment had a useful purpose, but it denied librarians "the philosophical insight which should grasp the higher motive of our profession" and connect it to the greater struggles of modern life. "It is sometimes said that the spirit of the library should be that of a merchant and his well-trained clerks, anxious to please their customers." She disagreed. "It should be rather the fine spirit of a hostess with the daughters of the house about her greeting guests."

The gender switch in these two sentences is significant; Cutler thought men's stereotypical orientation toward commerce and management exercised a cold and distant influence on librarianship, most evident in heavy reliance on published reviews. She thought women's stereotypical orientation toward family and domestic tranquility exercised a warm and direct influence on librarianship, most evident in knowledge of books they had read and of the community they wished to serve. That Dewey disagreed with her was obvious from an 1897 article he wrote for *Public Libraries.* "Look to your position as a high-grade business one," he said. The values Cutler expounded in speeches undoubtedly

---

20. Mary Salome Cutler, "Library School," *LJ* 15 (1/90): 24. See also NYSLS *Bulletin No. 1,* 8/91, pp. 30–40; and Dewey to Cutler, 8/10/93, Box 73, Dewey Mss, for evidence of Dewey's cursory attention to the library school before 1900. See also NYSLS *AR, 1891,* p. 21; and *Proceedings, 1892,* pp. 31–34.

surfaced in her Reading Seminar, where she had a captive audience of future professionals who, by the time they graduated, had seen much more of her than of Dewey. In 1897, Cutler married E. M. Fairchild, a Congregational minister from Albany much interested in promoting social morality through reading.[21]

Mary S. C. Fairchild's struggle to balance Dewey's emphasis on "commerce" with her own emphasis on "culture" was manifest in assignments to Reading Seminar students. In 1897 and 1898 the course treated book annotations "practically as well as theoretically"; students were required to submit a note "both descriptive and critical" of 100 books selected for discussion. But in 1899 she modified the assignment. Because she believed the librarian's essential need to acquire knowledge of a lot of books often forced "superficial" reading of too many "trivial, ephemeral and even worthless books," she worried "this tends to crowd out solid reading." To counter this, she argued, "every librarian should be master of the solid literature of some one field, however small." After 1899 students in her Reading Seminar could substitute for part of the 100 annotations an in-depth note on "any book of worth and permanent value" and have it count for at least two notes on books of lesser value."[22] This ran counter to Dewey's idea of limiting library education to the practical, avoiding issues of "general culture" best left to experts from other fields.

In 1899, Dewey was too preoccupied to contest Fairchild's direction, but after his resignation as Regents' Secretary, he began to reassert control over the school. His first move occurred early in 1900 when he gave Fairchild "direct charge" of developing a curriculum for library services to children. (Like many of his male peers in turn-of-the-century education professions, Dewey considered that Fairchild's gender made her "naturally" more qualified to evaluate children's than adult literature.) Because she had been working on this specialty for several years, however, Fairchild did not object. But she continued her public criticism of the "commerce" philosophy. In early 1901, Dewey moved more decisively; he decided to initiate a curriculum revision.

---

21. *LJ* 20 (1/95): 208; 21 (10/96): 446–49; 22 (1/97): 41; *PL* 2 (8/97): 267.

22. *LJ* 21 (10/96): 446–49; 22 (1/97): 41; NYSLS *AR, 1898,* pp. 132–35; NYSLS *Bulletin No. 6* (12/99): 278–79.

When members of the NYSLS Alumni Association heard about it, they appointed a committee to help. One member had a hidden agenda. "I wish that it might be known to the A.L.A. that the Alumni of the School are as a body ready to speak for it," Edith Clarke wrote a friend on March 31, "and stand as a factor to be considered in regard to it independently of Mr. Dewey." Clarke's loyalty to the school obviously exceeded her loyalty to Dewey. She was one of many alumnae much more attached to Fairchild who, they recognized, had "really run" the school since 1889.[23] In the spring the alumni committee sent out a circular soliciting opinions on the curriculum. It included predictable questions about entrance requirements, availability of electives, and the volume of time devoted to practical work. One question, however, struck at the philosophical difference separating Dewey and Fairchild. "If you could take your library school education anew, would you choose to have more time spent on technical training and in practical work? . . . Or, on the other hand, are the technicalities given too much attention at the expense of inspirational training, or of the learned, the theoretical, and the historical side of librarianship?" Responses showed alumni allied with Fairchild. They criticized the curriculum's emphasis on minutiae and the exploitation of student labor.

When the committee reported to Dewey, he thanked them for their efforts, said he welcomed any information that would help him improve the school, and then ignored their advice.[24] In September, Dewey made it very clear in the newly issued *Handbook of the New York State Library School* what direction the revised curriculum would take. In a section entitled "Practical vs. historical and antiquarian" he argued for "most attention to practical subjects, including traveling libraries. . . . This necessitates taking less time for subjects not so urgent or that can with less loss be deferred for personal reading or study after leaving school."[25]

---

23. NYSLS *AR, 1901*, p. 364; *LJ* 25 (12/00): 752; *Regents AR, 1902*, p. r37; Clarke to Harrison, 3/31/01, NYSLSAA Scrapbook.

24. See Sydney Mitchell, "The Pioneer Library School in Middle Age," *LQ* 20 (1950): 275; Alumni questionnaire and letter found in NYSLSAA Scrapbook. See also NYSLSAA Advisory Committee *Report* (Albany, 1905), copy found in Box 73, Dewey Mss.

25. NYSLS *Bulletin No. 9*, 9/01.

That Fairchild had lost became apparent when Dewey changed her beloved Reading Seminar into a course called "Selection of Books" in 1902. Emphasis was placed on training library school students to write annotations based solely on their reading of reviews in fifty periodicals, including subject-specific serials like *American Historical Review* and *Political Science Quarterly* and establishment literary organs like *Atlantic Monthly, Critic, Dial,* and *Saturday Review.* In part Dewey was motivated to change the course by another obligation he assumed for his Albany staff and students. In 1902 he also announced preparation under his direction of a new edition of the *ALA Catalog.* "With our work in the public libraries division, the selection of lists for schools, study clubs and State Library readers we have the most completely organized plan of systematic selection and annotation and it will be of great value to students in school during their course to become familiar with their work." The speed with which American librarians accepted this pattern of identifying "best reading" in subsequent years demonstrates that his efforts were largely successful. By the end of the decade the process had been institutionalized into professional practice by the publication of more bibliographic guides like the *Catalog* and its serial offspring, the monthly *Booklist* magazine issued by ALA.[26]

In the next two years Dewey added courses to the curriculum on bookbinding, public documents, typewriting, and state library commission work, and dropped courses on library language lessons, special subject libraries (e.g., law, medicine, music, theology, and art), reading and literary methods (including Cutler's seminar), and a thesis requirement for a BLS.[27] By that time his faculty had also produced a series of practical texts for their

---

26. NYSLS *AR, 1902,* pp. 214–15; NYSLS *Bulletin No. 10* (4/02), p. 443; *Bulletin No. 15,* pp. 252–62; NYSLS *AR, 1902,* p. 202. See also NYSLS *AR, 1901,* pp. 345–46; and Leon M. Solis-Cohen, "A Recent New York Graduate's View," *PL* 11 (3/06): 140–43. A listing of the periodicals Fairchild included in "Selection of Books" course can be found in NYSLS *Bulletin No. 12* 10/02: 131–38. The struggle between Dewey and Fairchild had generated sufficient heat for James I. Wyer to write Florence Woodworth that he had recently heard "Mrs. Fairchild had come to be persona non grata with Mr. Dewey." See Wyer to Woodworth, 9/24/01, Box 71, Dewey Mss.

27. NYSLS, *AR, 1905,* pp. 30–36.

students, including Dunkin V. R. Johnston's *Selected Reference Books* (1899) and Walter S. Biscoe's *Selected Subject Bibliographies* (1899), *Selected National Bibliographies* (1900), and *Lecture Outlines and Problems* (1902). In 1899 Dewey published his fourth edition of *Library School Rules: Card, Accession, Shelf* through the Library Bureau and in a conservative form of simplified spelling. "These are the A.L.A. condenst rules made clearer on many points," *Rules* began. Most of these works were picked up as texts for courses in other library schools across the country being established by former Dewey students who also mimed his curriculum. Eighteen years after the first library school opened, American library education remained very much a product of Melvil Dewey's practical mind.

Unification
1900–1904

The road to unification had not been smoothed by Dewey's resignation as Regents' Secretary. After January 1, 1900, Regents continued to resist attempts to eliminate their life tenure and entirely remove secondary education from their control; the Superintendent of Public Instruction continued to resist attempts to make his position subordinate to the Regents; legislators suspected the politics of both parties, and because they sensed an inability to compromise toward unification, they decided to force the issue. The unification law, which went into effect April 1, 1904, abolished the offices of Superintendent of Public Instruction and Regents' Secretary but created a Commissioner of Education. On April 6 Andrew Sloan Draper was sworn in as New York's first Commissioner and within weeks reorganized the University into three departments (elementary, secondary, and higher education), each of which would be administered by an assistant commissioner. The assistant commissioner for higher education would be responsible for professional and technical schools and divisions for libraries and museums; each division would function as a bureau and be administered by a director.[28]

---

28. See "Proposed Plan of Organization," *School Bulletin* 30 (4/04): 157–58; and "Dr. Draper's Appointments," p. 173. See also New York (State)

In effect, Draper's plan removed Dewey one step further from the center of power, and although the division of libraries would comprise school libraries, home education, the library school, and the State Library, Dewey's ability to set his own agenda would be significantly circumscribed by his distance from the Commissioner. Initially Draper worried about Dewey's reactions to his reorganization, but on August 26 he reported to new University Chancellor Whitelaw Reid he was "getting on with Mr. Dewey very satisfactorily," even though "it consumes rather too much productivity to keep him from doing things which will not go." Reid responded that Dewey "has as many crank notions as anybody outside of an asylum," but he was "so zealous, inventive, and in many ways useful that I am glad you are finding it possible to get on with him without too much friction."[29]

On October 4 Draper reported on Dewey's department to the Regents. He openly acknowledged Dewey's contribution to the state and praised the department under his supervision, but spent most of his time discussing its weaknesses. "I am . . . tentatively opposed to many of the projects which commend themselves to the intellectually prolific and widely experienced Director" and "unalterably opposed to undertaking projects involving energy and money on behalf of the State before they have been openly and authoritatively determined upon." By way of example he cited Dewey's goal of interlibrary loan to any teacher in the state. "There is much . . . unfortunate predisposition . . . to start something new simply because it is new." To counter this "predisposition" Draper recommended a reorganization of Dewey's department which refocused on State Library services in Albany and downplayed extension services outside the capital.[30]

For fifteen years Dewey had worked to expand State Library services and to institutionalize university extension in New York public libraries, but Draper clearly intended to cut

University, *Minutes of the Regents of the University, 1904* (Albany, 1905) pp. 25–31; and Draper "To the Board of Regents," 4/7/04, copy found in Reel 200, Reid Mss.

29. Draper to Reid, 8/26/04; Reid to Draper, 8/29/04, Reel 200, Reid Mss. See also Draper to Dewey, 8/25/04, copy found in Reel 200, Reid Mss.

30. A copy of this report to the Regents, dated 10/4/04, can be found in Reel 200, Reid Mss.

them back, and because he also wished to take extension work out of the State Library, he aimed at the heart of Dewey's Albany agenda. Indications of Draper's priorities began to appear quickly. Within days he moved control of the academic fund for the inspection of school libraries from Dewey's office to the Second Assistant Commissioner; he also questioned the efficiency of cataloging practices within the State Library.[31] At the time Dewey said nothing publicly, but no one who knew his past expected Dewey to take this without a fight.

31. Draper to Dewey, 10/5/04; 10/8/04, Box 75, Dewey Mss.

10

Working with the American Library Association

1889-1904

Even though Dewey's attention to Albany matters occupied most of his time between 1889 and 1904, he continued to influence greatly the direction and growth of the American Library Association. At the 1890 conference, for example, he was elected ALA president, placed on one of two committees responsible for planning ALA participation at the 1893 Chicago World's Fair, and made a member of the five-man executive committee of a newly established "Publishing Section." On July 11, 1891, however, he resigned the presidency for "reasons of health."[1] ALA met in San Francisco without him and elected Milwaukee Public Library Director Klas August Linderfelt—one of Poole's protégés—its president.

In the meantime problems began to surface between the two committees preparing for the 1893 conference. One committee—whose job it was to prepare an ALA exhibit—consisted of Dewey, Woodworth, and Cutler of the New York State Library, Frank P. Hill of the Newark Public Library, and Frederick Hild of the Chicago Public Library. Cutler chaired the group. The other was called the World Congress of Librarians Committee, a Chicago-

---

1. *LJ* 15 (12/90): 5; *Proceedings, 1890,* 87, 90, 94, 103, 105, 123, 129, 131, 140; Dewey to ALA Executive Board, 7/11/91, as found in *LJ* 16 (7/91): 200. Dewey's role in ALA activities between 1889 and 1904 is covered in more depth in my *Politics of an Emerging Profession* (1986), pp. 50–157.

based group Poole organized to plan an international meeting. Hild was supposed to coordinate activities between the two.[2] In late April 1892, an unexpected incident occurred that radically changed the situation and profoundly affected ALA. It had the effect of tipping the balance of power away from the old guard—whose mantle of leadership Poole had inherited in the mid-1880s—and toward Dewey and other librarians who sought greater efficiency and systematization in the profession. On April 28 Linderfelt was arrested for embezzling funds from the Milwaukee Public Library over a seven-year period. By May 10 he had resigned as ALA president,[3] and at the annual conference a week later ALA members decided Dewey should be the president to rescue the association from this embarrassment and lead it successfully into the 1893 Chicago World's Fair.

But the conference was significant for other reasons. Two hundred sixty people had registered; 150 (more than half) were women. A geographical analysis of conferees shows 200 from North Atlantic states, only twenty-nine from Great Lakes states. Fifty-eight attended from the New York State Library, including administrators, faculty members, and fifty-four current and former students. Little wonder control of ALA was passing to Dewey. He dominated the executive board and commanded the exposition committee through its chair, Mary S. Cutler, a subordinate whom he often called "one of his special lieutenants" in the 1890s. He also held an influential position on the board of the ALA publishing section. The Linderfelt affair had clearly hurt the old guard, who now had no one but Poole of sufficient stature within ALA to counter the momentum the energetic Dewey was creating. The only official link between Poole's Chicago-based committee and Cutler's Albany-based committee was Frederick Hild. The conference had not reduced the potential for conflict between the two groups, but it did effect significant changes in the balance of power among competing interests.

Less than two weeks after the 1892 conference, Dewey's leadership received two challenges from the old guard. Acting

---

2. Hild to Hill, 1/4/92, Librarians File, NPL; James to Dewey, 1/11/92; Harris to Dewey, 2/1/92; ALA circular, 4/1/92; Harris to Dewey, 5/5/92, Box 2, Dewey Mss. It was at this time that Dewey was being considered for a post at the University of Chicago.

3. Hill to Dewey, 4/29/92, Box 2, Dewey Mss; Hill to Cole, 4/30/92, Cole Mss, ALA; Hill to Bowker, 5/10/92, Bowker Mss.

on behalf of Poole's committee, Hild requested that Cutler step down as chair of the ALA exposition committee because he said as a woman she would not be as effective as a man. Dewey interpreted this not so much an issue of gender as ALA politics because Hild suggested Cutter (a member of the old guard) as Cutler's replacement. He immediately issued a circular soliciting the executive board and on June 22 announced the results. "We find ourselves unable with proper regard to the interest of the ALA to consent to the proposed change. This decision is clear, strong and unanimous."[4]

A second test came several months later when Dewey found out Hild and Poole were planning their international congress of librarians as "a rival meeting the week before ALA" that would "thus take the wind out of our sails." Dewey wanted a combined conference that scheduled ALA meetings in the morning and the international congress meetings in the afternoon or evening. His executive board, all of whom shared his ideas about the future of the profession, agreed. "I can't help thinking that if Poole or Hild had been elected [ALA] president," Frederick M. Crunden said, "there would have been no plan of this kind proposed." Hannah James was equally contemptuous. "I am thankful you are at the helm, with a crew that will follow you in the straight path. . . . All the storms we have will be of Poole's own raising—he'll soon find they will not wreck us!" On September 28 Dewey reported to the Chicago committee that the ALA executive board unanimously agreed there should not be two separate conferences. He followed his letter with a personal visit in mid-October, and forced Poole and Hild to agree to schedule ALA meetings simultaneously with the international congress. The former would meet six to nine days in single sessions each morning; the latter would meet in the afternoon. Dewey had successfully met both challenges.[5]

---

4. H. P. James to Dewey, 6/16/92; Hild to Dewey, 6/16/92; F. M. Crunden to Dewey, 6/17/92; Cutter to Dewey, 6/19/92, 6/20/92; Dewey to "Members of the ALA Columbia Exposition Committee, 6/22/92; Crunden to Dewey, 6/26/92; 7/5/92, Box 3, Dewey Mss; Cutter to C. Alex Nelson, n.d. (attached to letter dated 4/1/93), Poole Mss.

5. Hild to Dewey, 8/8/92; 8/29/92; Dewey to "Standing Committee," 9/5/92; Dewey to Hild, 9/5/92; Hill to Dewey, 9/9/92; Crunden to Dewey, 9/12/92; James to Dewey, 9/19/92; Document entitled "ALA Columbia Meeting, 1893, by Melvil Dewey," Box 3, Dewey Mss. See also *LJ* 18 (2/93): 44–45.

As Dewey led the ALA into the Chicago conference, both the association and the profession had obviously changed. The organizational composition of the American library community had altered significantly over previous years. For example, Illinois librarians were discussing the possibility of following New York's lead and organizing a state association, the Colorado Library Association held its first meeting in 1892, and by that time the Minnesota Library Association had already met a second time. In addition, the Drexel Institute of Philadelphia announced it was opening a new library school; its curriculum was modeled on Albany's, and its first director was Alice Kroeger, a member of Dewey's class of 1891. Another school had already been in existence at Pratt Institute since 1890, that one run by Mary W. Plummer, one of the seventeen women in Dewey's first Columbia library school class. The profession's leadership was also changing.

By his own admission, Winsor spent most of his time on historical scholarship, very little on librarianship, and was "not now enough in the swim of such things" to make a difference in ALA. In the Midwest, Poole—now at Chicago's Newberry Library—was being openly criticized by his own board of trustees for spending too much time on materials acquisition, not enough on efficient library administration.[6] With Linderfelt gone and Hild humbled by his two recent defeats, the only other non-eastern librarian with enough stature to contest Dewey's growing influence was Frederick M. Crunden. But Crunden was a staunch Dewey ally who regularly agreed with the direction Dewey wanted to take the association.

Crunden represented a new breed of librarians championed by Dewey who were anxious to put "the best reading" (identified for librarians in such sources as the forthcoming *ALA Catalog*) into the hands of more Americans (". . . for the largest number") as efficiently as possible (". . . at the least cost"). Dewey's position had been secured in 1893 by a group of allies on the ALA executive board, by a loyal group of influential and hardworking subordinates at the New York State Library and the New York State Library School, and by the ever increasing number of

---

6. Winsor to Poole, 3/20/93, Poole Mss; Cutter to Bowker, 3/2/93, Bowker Mss. Edith E. Clarke, Poole's cataloger at the Newberry, noted the library's internal problems in Clarke to Dewey, 7/5/93, Box 3, Dewey Mss.

Dewey library-school graduates who assumed positions in libraries across the country.

Excitement hung in the air when ALA members gathered in Chicago for their World's Fair conference. Dewey opened it on July 13, but declined to give a formal address. Instead, he asked ALA Secretary Frank Hill to report on ALA's "Model Library," a 5,000-volume collection of "best books" that the association recommended for every library and that was simultaneously being published in book form by the Bureau of Education. Hill said the Library "will probably interest more members than will any other exhibit at the fair." Thus, sixteen years after he first advocated the concept Dewey watched the *ALA Catalog* become a reality. And it was only made possible because he could combine the authority of his position as New York State Librarian with loyal subordinates who were already doing the necessary spadework in a series of activities Dewey had initiated for his University and State Library extension plans. Although awkwardly titled *Catalog of "A.L.A." Library,* the publication was jointly sponsored by ALA and the U.S. Bureau of Education. One-half of its citations were classified by DC, the other half by Cutter's Expansive Classification (EC). The "Model Library" itself consisted of 5,000 volumes shelved in six separate types of bookstacks donated by library suppliers from around the country, including one set from the Library Bureau, which had recently opened an office in Chicago.

After opening remarks the conference settled down to a pattern of activity Dewey had deliberately programmed into the schedule. By assigning specific subjects to specific authors, he hoped that the published proceedings would ultimately serve as a "handbook of library economy," another goal toward which he had been working for over a decade. He had already arranged for the Bureau of Education to publish the handbook and distribute it along with the *ALA Catalog* free to requesting libraries and librarians. Because of this goal, the conference devoted most of its attention to shelves, fixtures, binding, furniture, accession policies and procedures, and librarians' salaries. Spirited discussions focused upon technique, not theory, upon practical matters, not abstract thought addressing issues of meaning and discovery.

By most accounts the Chicago conference had been the most successful in ALA history. Because of Dewey's leadership,

ALA could claim numerous accomplishments, including publication of the *ALA Catalog* and the forthcoming *Handbook of Library Economy,* closer ties between ALA and the Bureau of Education, and a series of successful exhibits. By Dewey's design, practical matters had dominated the program. The conference was his show. He had organized it; his people had carried out his dictates. Poole and his western associates were not highly visible at association meetings, a striking fact considering that the conference was held in their own backyard. In 1893 ALA was proud of its president.

ALA's next conference met in Lake Placid, a resort village in New York's Adirondack mountain range. Dewey had pushed for the site, which was near property he and Annie recently purchased to develop the private rest and recreation resort for middle-class professionals they had been talking about since 1878. In 1894 the Deweys were looking for partners willing to invest in the venture, and locating the ALA conference there they thought would give them an excellent opportunity to let Lake Placid's beauty sell itself to the kinds of people they hoped to attract. The conference itself went very smoothly and included ten sessions and two separate section meetings—the College Library Section and the Publishing Section. In the latter Dewey (who had been elected section president in 1893) reported no progress on publishing the *ALA Manual,* but noted the *ALA Index* was beginning to show a profit, and sales of J. F. Sargent's *Reading for the Young* had almost matched publication expenses. A *List of Subject Headings for a Dictionary Catalog* was nearly ready for the printer, and an annotated list of books for girls' and women's clubs that the section planned was almost ready for publication. Dewey's efforts to centralize and standardize were finally beginning to pay dividends. Before adjourning, the section directed its executive board to "prepare for private circulation an annotated list of undesirable fiction."

Dewey did not attend the 1895 ALA conference in Denver, and did not participate in electing a slate of officers for the forthcoming year who largely came from the West. Nor did he participate in the discussion of a constitutional amendment on electing officers that followed the actual elections and reflected a growing sectionalism within ALA. He did, however, send a report for a cooperation committee he chaired, and urged several initiatives.

He promoted a plan for printing catalog cards to be distributed by the Library Bureau, and called for the organization and co-ordination of state and local library associations and for inter-changeable membership among them. He also pushed for the compilation of "a list of 500 books for the use of small libraries, many of which are simply dazed and confused by the wealth of the A.L.A. Library," and cooperative selection and annotation of books based upon a model provided by the Massachusetts Li-brary Club fiction list.[7]

The election of officers and the subsequent dispute on the constitutional amendment caused some consternation among the membership. Incoming Secretary H. L. Elmendorf of the St. Joseph, Missouri, Public Library, wrote Dewey he feared "it was a mistake to make the new organization so decidedly western." Incoming ALA President John Cotton Dana of the Denver Public Library agreed, but Dewey replied to both, "I believe it well to have tried a decidedly western organization. We want to make the ALA national and not let the idea get abroad that it is a New England affair."[8] Despite Dewey's reassurances, however, sec-tional dissension increased as ALA significantly expanded its membership beyond North Atlantic states, where librarians felt they had different priorities than their East Coast colleagues. One manifestation of these differences was evident when Dana and Theresa West of the Milwaukee Public Library visited Bow-ker in New York in October and identified "our desire for some means of communication with the smaller libraries." Specifi-cally, they wanted "a circular of information on the starting of li-braries in small towns." Bowker showed no interest.

Because Bowker was not interested, Dana asked George Meleney of the Library Bureau's recently opened Chicago office if he could help. Meleney expressed interest, but said he would have to check with Dewey. By Christmas 1895, Dewey and Meleney decided to issue a new periodical entitled *Public Li-braries* from the Bureau's Chicago offices. It would be cheaper than *Library Journal* and would address the needs of the smaller public libraries of the Midwest that were beginning to proliferate.

---

7. Dewey to Dana, 8/10/95, Box 4, Dewey Mss: *Proceedings, 1895,* 4, 36, 52, 59, 66, 67, 84, 86, 88, 89.

8. Elmendorf to Dewey, 9/2/95; Dana to Dewey, 9/4/95; Dewey to Dana, 9/10/95; and Dewey to Elmendorf, 9/12/95, Box 4, Dewey Mss.

Dewey advised Meleney to put together an editorial board of "ten or a dozen of your best people" from libraries west of the Alleghenies, and recommended Lutie Stearns of the Wisconsin Free Public Library Commission as managing editor, although he wanted her to change her first name because he thought it would reflect poorly on the journal—just as "if Mr. Dana printed on his letterhead 'Tootsie C. Dana,'" he told Stearns. He also suggested that the first number of *Public Libraries* carry Dana's recently completed *Library Primer.* Meleney agreed with all Dewey's recommendations, but when he attempted to negotiate a salary with Stearns, she demanded twice as much as he was willing to pay and refused to change her first name. Mary Ahern of the Indiana Public Library Commission got the job instead.[9]

By February 1896, news of plans for a new periodical reached Bowker. Still angry over the duplicitous way in which Dewey had introduced his now infrequently issued serial *Library Notes* nine years earlier, Bowker wrote Dewey on March 7 that this new periodical "limits the field of the *Journal* seriously and prevents the development it should have in importance, extent and circulation." Dewey responded that the "new western monthly" should not be regarded as a "rival" to *LJ,* but a complementary publication.[10]

The first issue of *Public Libraries* appeared in May and carried Dana's "Library Primer." Its subscription price was one dollar per year, four dollars less than *LJ.* An introductory note said the periodical would fill "the need for a publication which shall give special attention to the more common details and trials of the small and new public libraries." *Public Libraries* quickly became a voice for the Midwest/rural library advocates who were dissatisfied with a *Library Journal* they claimed heavily favored Northeast/large research and urban library advocates. For Dewey, *Public Libraries* also promised to fill a need he had intended for

---

9. The chronology of events is reconstructed from the following: Parker to Dewey, 12/9/95, Box 62; West to Dewey, 4/23/96; Dewey to West, 1/31/96; Dewey to Meleney, 2/4/96; Stearns to Dewey, 2/20/96; Dana to Dewey, 3/4/96; Ahern to Dewey, 3/16/96, Box 4, Dewey Mss.

10. Tessa Kelso to Bowker, 2/4/96; Dewey to Bowker, 3/9/96; Bowker to Reuben G. Thwaites, 3/18/96; 3/27/96; Bowker to Davidson, 3/20/96; Bowker to Elmendorf, 4/2/96; and Bowker to Dana, 4/2/96, Bowker Mss; Bowker to Dewey, 3/7/96; Dana to Dewey, 3/11/96; Bowker to Dewey, 3/18/96; Elmendorf to Dewey, 3/19/96, Box 4, Dewey Mss.

```
┌─────────────────────────────────────────────────────────────────┐
│                                                                   │
│  Library Bureau                                            189     │
│    215 Madison St.                                                │
│    Chicago.                    Inclosed find ONE DOLLAR for which  │
│                                                                   │
│  please send PUBLIC LIBRARIES to the following address for one year│
│                                                                   │
│  (10 numbers), beginning with _____No. 189                  │
│                                                                   │
│                        (Name)_____    │
│                                                                   │
│                        (Address) _____    │
│  ──────────────────────────────────────────────                  │
│                                                                   │
│                              Chicago, _____  189      │
│  Received payment as above.                                       │
│                                  LIBRARY BUREAU.                  │
│                                  Per_____     │
│                                                                   │
└─────────────────────────────────────────────────────────────────┘
```

R. R. Bowker, publisher of *Library Journal,* was not pleased when Dewey launched *Public Libraries* in 1896. Dewey argued that it would not compete, but he set its subscription rate at one dollar, four dollars less than *LJ.* The new journal increased Midwest library visibility.

Notes, which by this time was being issued infrequently. Within a year Dewey decided to let *Public Libraries* "absorb" *Notes,* and the latter ceased publication.[11]

When ALA met in Cleveland in 1896, Dewey was not highly visible. Other, younger members of the association—especially from the Midwest—assumed leadership roles on issues Dewey had been pushing for decades. In the fall of 1896 Dewey was one of three people invited to appear before Congress's Joint Committee on the Library in Washington, D.C., which had been charged to inquire "into the condition of the Library of Congress." Dewey made such an impression on congressmen with his vision for a "national library" that newly elected President William McKinley flirted with the idea of nominating him as Librarian of Congress. At the time, however, Dewey expressed no interest in leaving Albany.[12]

Also in 1896 the Publishing Section agreed to prepare printed catalog cards for the Library Bureau if the Bureau would

11. Dewey to Meleney, 4/3/96; 4/10/96; Dewey to Ahern, 4/11/96; Dewey to West, 4/27/96; Dana to Dewey, 5/14/96, Box 4, Dewey Mss; *LJ* 21 (5/96): 216; "Prospectus," *PL* 1 (5/96): 3.

12. Details about Dewey's appearance before the Committee and McKinley's subsequent inquiries about appointing him Congressional Librarian are discussed more fully in my "Herbert Putnam's Appointment as Librarian of Congress," *LQ* 49 (1979): 255–82.

market and distribute them. Boston Athenaeum Library Director William C. Lane would supervise their preparation from a room that the Athenaeum provided ALA free of charge. The section then hired Nina Browne of the Library Bureau, one of Dewey's former students, to do the cataloging. The section also issued supplements to *Reading for the Young* and Caroline Hewins's *Books for Boys and Girls: A Select List*. Dewey's pressure to centralize continued to bear dividends as many of his disciples loyally carried out his "world work."

ALA President William Howard Brett opened the 1897 ALA conference at an informal gathering at the Pennsylvania Historical Society in Philadelphia on June 21. In his presidential address Brett took a retrospective look at the association that had first met in Philadelphia just over twenty years before. During the evening session Dewey offered his own perspective on the association's history. Between 1876 and 1886 ALA had fostered the development of library methods to augment the impact of libraries at minimal cost, he said. Between 1886 and 1896 ALA had raised the profile of the public library as an essential part of the nation's educational system. In 1896, ALA was entering a "filtration period" which promised to filter bad literature and expose the public only to the good. Here Dewey undoubtedly had in mind the kind of centralized book selection system he was constructing in Albany and extending through selection aids published, in press, and contemplated by the ALA Publishing Section he chaired. Characteristically, however, he said nothing about criteria for distinguishing good from bad; he continued to believe those decisions should be left to outside experts.

The desire to celebrate ALA history was evident in the slate of officers members elected for the coming year: for president, Justin Winsor; for vice presidents, Rutherford P. Hayes, Hannah P. James, and Frederick Crunden; for secretary, Dewey; for treasurer, Gardner Jones; and for recorder, Helen Haines. Dewey then introduced a constitutional amendment to increase by 25 percent the number of elected members of council, a body still without function that ALA had authorized several years earlier at Dewey's urging. In addition, Dewey recommended that each state or local library association be entitled to "one councillor of its own selection, and to one additional for each full 100 members."

Dewey's motive was not immediately apparent, but by expanding council membership, it is likely he hoped to minimize the possibility of splinter groups forming separate rival library associations. The amendment would provide a constitutionally sanctioned superstructure under which specialized library interests could find common ground. It also allowed for differences in geography as well as types and sizes of libraries. Not coincidentally, it had the potential for extending his influence on ALA's future direction by engaging former students and soulmates in his practical library service philosophy in pushing his agenda. At this time he was not concerned with defining the council's function or role within ALA. He was more concerned with preserving the unity of the association itself. Dewey asked for a vote approving the amendment so that the association could discuss it at the next conference. Conferees agreed.[13] Dewey still had a lot of clout in ALA.

When Winsor died on October 22, 1897, however, Dewey unwisely chose to inject himself into routine efforts to fill the vacant presidency because he worried about growing sectionalist feelings in ALA. Precedent suggested the office should go to Rutherford P. Hayes, ALA vice president from Ohio who had received the most votes in the previous election. That had happened in 1892 when William I. Fletcher succeeded Linderfelt (albeit for only a month until ALA elected Dewey at its subsequent conference). Dewey had wholeheartedly supported that move, but in 1897 he chose a radically different approach. On November 12 he wrote ALA executive board members that "after careful study" of the ALA constitution he concluded "it is the duty of the executive board to elect a president for the balance of this year," but until that election, as ALA secretary he would be in charge of the association. He then suggested Boston Public Library Director Herbert Putnam would be Winsor's "natural successor in the presidency which had gone to Boston for the year." Dewey wanted to retain the sequence that had evolved in the 1890s of shifting the ALA presidency annually from East to West and back again.

But ALA Recorder Helen Haines, at the time *Library Journal* associate editor, resisted. Haines normally consulted Bowker on all ALA matters, and Bowker may have cautioned her against

---

13. *Proceedings, 1897*, 95, 99, 103, 155, 173. See also *LJ* 22 (7/97): 339; (11/97): 686; *PL* 2 (11/97): 448–49; Dewey "To the members of the A.L.A.," 6/30/97; James to Hayes, 12/4/97, copy found in Box 4, Dewey Mss.

trusting Dewey. She ultimately decided to request every board member's interpretation of the ALA constitution "before giving a final vote on the subject." Hannah James was equivocal, but not so suspicious. Although she thought the first vice president "had to be considered," she acknowledged "I'm pretty pleased at the idea of Putnam." Hayes did not equivocate; he challenged Dewey directly. While he did not dispute the need to elect a new president, he reported his "understanding of the constitution" that "from the time of the death of Dr. Winsor until the election of a president, I am the chief executive of the Association and that official notices of all kinds should be sent out by my direction."[14]

Dewey responded quickly, haughtily, decisively. "You are partly right and partly wrong . . . I can easily understand how one who has only recently been active in the association might get a wrong impression, and so give you the points with some detail." Citing his extensive experience in ALA and his authorship of its constitution, he indicated the presidency was mostly ceremonial and that the real center of ALA activity had always been the secretary's office, from which "all needed notices are sent out." He then indicated the executive board could elect a new president by mail if the vote was unanimous and asked Hayes to send a nomination. He also continued to press for Putnam. On November 23 he reported to the board that four votes had been cast for Putnam and "three have not yet voted." Since no other nomination had been made, he asked: "Shall we make the vote unanimous electing Putnam, or nominate someone else, or leave the place open till later?"[15]

James repeated her vote for Putnam; so did Haines. Brett balked, however, in part because he shared Hayes's anger over Dewey's imperious move. Dewey's contention that the secretary was the "real executive head of the Association," he said, "seems to me absurd." Hayes also took issue with Dewey's interpretation of the ALA constitution. He told Dewey he was regularly receiving telegrams and letters urging him as ALA's "chief executive

14. *PL* 2 (10/97): 400–1; Wire to Dewey, 10/26/97; Dewey to "Executive Board of the ALA," 11/12/97; Haines to "Executive Board of the ALA," 11/14/97; James to Dewey, 11/15/97; Hayes to Dewey, 11/15/97, Box 4, Dewey Mss.

15. Dewey to Hayes, 11/16/97; Dewey to ALA Executive Board, 11/16/97; 11/23/97, Box 4, Dewey Mss.

officer" to protest a recent effort to remove the Superintendent of Documents, and he felt he had to respond on behalf of the association. He then repeated his understanding of the situation. "From the death of Mr. Winsor until the election of his successor I am president and chief executive officer of the Association."[16]

Dewey's response three days later was nasty. "Of course, you are totally wrong . . . , but if it amuses you it does not hurt anyone else. Your self-appointment as 'chief executive officer' is purely a figment of your imagination." In a postscript he added, "Merry Christmas." When Dewey sent copies of his letter to other ALA board members, Haines showed it to Bowker, who called Dewey's comments "doubly unnecessary," and wrote in an *LJ* editorial that "Mr. Hayes, as the present vice-president, has very properly assumed the duties of the presidency pending a settlement of the question." Bowker also indicated that although the executive board favored Putnam as president, the issue of whether the office was vacant had to be settled first.[17]

Dewey immediately tried to use Bowker's editorial to his advantage. He wrote another circular to the board, claimed *LJ* had endorsed Putnam, and called for a unanimous vote to elect him. Haines responded immediately that the *Journal* had endorsed no one, and that she would refuse to vote until the vacancy question was settled. Her letter placed Dewey on the defensive. He first wrote Bowker, "I am awfully sorry about the LJ episode, but you evidently do not quite understand my attitude." He explained he had intended to circulate Putnam's name to board members privately, but the whole episode had become "very humiliating to Hayes who has made a great goose of himself." With Haines he was more aggressive. "Mr. Hayes and the others have sent in their votes for Mr. Putnam, but I cannot announce it till you definitely give your vote again." Still Haines hesitated; she suspected Dewey had not been forthcoming. "I should greatly regret to have my vote counted as a telling one," she wrote. Only after Hayes told Bowker he had voted for Putnam did Haines send Dewey her vote, but she indicated it was

---

16. James to Dewey, 11/26/97; Brett to Dewey, 11/26/97 (2 letters); Haines to Dewey, 11/27/97; Hayes to Dewey, 12/2/97, Box 4, Dewey Mss; Hayes to Brett, 11/20/97, Brett Mss.

17. Dewey to Hayes, 12/5/97; Bowker to Dewey, 12/24/97, Box 4, Dewey Mss; *LJ* 22 (12/97): 735.

| William H. Brett | Rutherford P. Hayes |

In ALA election politics of 1897, Dewey managed to offend both Past ALA President Brett and Vice President Hayes, who believed himself automatic successor to deceased President Justin Winsor. For that, Dewey referred to Hayes as "a great goose" with a "screw loose."

cast on the assumption hers was the final vote that would make the election unanimous.[18]

But Haines was in for one more surprise. When Bowker asked Dewey for official notification of the election, Dewey replied Brett still had not voted. "You stated that my vote was the *only* one not received on the presidential question!" Haines fired back. She was now certain Dewey had tricked her into voting for Putnam. Dewey responded sheepishly. "You were right," he admitted, but Brett "had written three letters, all of them very strongly supporting Mr. Putnam as his first choice . . . and while he had voted three times I did not have the official vote which of course he had a right to change at the last minute. Both statements, you see, were correct."

18. Crunden to Hayes, 12/3/97; Crunden to Dewey, 12/3/97; James to Hayes, 12/4/97; James to Dewey, 12/4/97; Hayes to Dewey, 12/8/97; Hayes to Dewey, 12/11/97; Dewey to Hayes, 12/14/97; Haines to Dewey, 12/28/97; Dewey to Bowker, 12/28/97; Dewey to Haines, 1/3/98; Haines to Dewey 1/5/98, Box 4, Dewey Mss; Brett to Hayes, 12/10/97; Brett to Dewey, 12/10/97, Brett Mss.

To Brett he was demanding. "Everything is blockaded because you do not vote . . . at least be courteous enough to tell us." Brett was equally incensed, calling Dewey's communication "entirely out of place." Nonetheless, he acquiesced and made Putnam's election unanimous. When Dewey then asked Putnam to accept the appointment on January 18, Putnam balked. He had never authorized Dewey to campaign on his behalf, disliked the circumstances leading to the election, and worried Hayes had been unfairly treated. Dewey tried to assuage Putnam's anxiety by indicating "there is a screw loose in Hayes' makeup," but only after Hayes sent a friendly letter to Putnam offering "an expression of his personal desire that I should accept the presidency" did Putnam finally change his mind.[19]

The incident was over, the matter settled, and the *Library Journal* applauded Putnam's election to the ALA presidency in its February issue. But a residue of bitter feelings remained, mostly directed at Dewey. The suspicions he had raised in pushing Putnam's election did not quickly dissipate. People felt manipulated. While Dewey may have felt he was working for the good of ALA, many ALA officers suspected he was working for the good of Melvil Dewey. From that time on Dewey's direct influence on ALA affairs began to diminish. *Public Libraries,* which had been one of Dewey's staunchest western supporters because of parallel philosophies of library service and a coterminous interest in small public libraries, openly declared "a mistake has been made" in the way Putnam was elected. Frederick Crunden, a westerner who had backed Dewey on numerous occasions, wrote a friend: "I think all the members of the ALA are pretty well agreed that we must, as far as possible, eliminate politics from the Association."[20] As in 1880, Dewey had overstepped his bounds. He undoubtedly thought his ends justified his means, but his means alienated close friends and ALA leaders on both sides of the Alleghenies.

At the subsequent annual conference held at Chautauqua in early July, the board voted to assign a constitutional revision

---

19. Bowker to Dewey, 1/10/98; Haines to Dewey, 1/10/98; 1/12/98; Dewey to Haines, 1/17/98; Dewey to Brett, 1/14/98; 1/17/98; Dewey to Putnam, 1/18/98; 1/28/98; Putnam to Dewey, 1/26/98, Box 4, Dewey Mss. See also Haines to Brett, 1/17/98, Brett Mss; and *LJ* 23 (1/98): 22–23.

20. *LJ* 23 (2/98): 47; *PL* 3 (2/98): 46, 47; Crunden to Carr, 1/16/98, Carr Mss; Ahern to Dewey, 1/13/98, Box 4, Dewey Mss.

committee the task of "defining the duties of president and secretary" and "specifying procedure in case of vacancy in the presidency." Putnam's presidential address avoided the controversies surrounding his selection. At one of the sessions he invited discussion on the constitutional amendment Dewey had proposed in Philadelphia. Elmendorf agreed the council had been "largely an ornamental body," but unless the amendment defined its duties more precisely, "it seems unnecessary to increase its size." Dewey answered that the proposed amendment was a response to "some older members of the Association" who had suggested membership ought to be restricted. Enlarging the council would enable ALA to recognize a group for "conspicuous public services. Beyond that, the query of how much the council shall do is still an open one." Crunden agreed with Elmendorf, and moved that the proposed amendment be referred to a constitutional revision committee for further review. His motion passed.

As in previous years the conference also scheduled time for section meetings, but the Chautauqua conference was unusual because it offered more meetings that were more active. Dewey, who had planned the program as ALA secretary, believed the association should stretch to cover specialized interests materializing within the profession. To ignore them, he argued, would lead to smaller groups organizing outside ALA control, thereby muting the association's claim as national voice for library interests. Because the Chautauqua conference hosted sectional meetings for librarians interested in large libraries, small libraries, state libraries, and college and reference libraries, it showed Dewey's hand throughout—tight schedule, short papers focusing on practical library problems, participation by as many members as possible, and restricted forums. Henry J. Carr of the Grand Rapids (Mich.) Public Library later complained that this focus was too restrictive.[21]

But Dewey had another motive. Subsurface grumbling, cloakroom comments, and guarded complaints had been too frequent over the last several years; the issues sparking them threatened to shred the ALA fabric. By keeping the conference moving, by allowing minimal time for debate, and by providing

21. *LJ* 23 (7/98): 271–72, 283–94; *Proceedings, 1897,* 125–26, 137, 154–56; Dana to Putnam, 7/12/98, Dana Mss; *PL* 3 (7/98): 242–43, 250; Carr to Lane, 1/14/98, Carr Mss.

separate forums for growing special interest groups, Dewey had effectively split dissident groups and deprived them of opportunities to join forces against the parent organization. Dewey acted to preserve the unified ALA momentum he had helped to build over the past decade; because of his efforts it remained the national voice for library interests.

Although Dewey's planning proved successful in keeping ALA unified, he himself continued to lose influence. For the next several years his voice was generally absent from conference proceedings, and much between-conference correspondence among ALA officers failed even to mention his name. He attended ALA conferences regularly, but was elected or appointed only to peripheral positions of leadership from which he espoused his causes. In September 1901, however, he was appointed for a three-year term to the Publishing Board (it had changed its name from Publishing Section several years earlier), and when Education Commissioner William T. Harris told the board the Bureau would not be able to publish a new edition of the *ALA Catalog* the following spring, Dewey suggested to Putnam (who by that time had been appointed Librarian of Congress) that LC undertake the project.[22]

Putnam agreed, and Dewey announced the effort at the 1902 ALA conference. At that same conference ALA announced a grant of $100,000 from Andrew Carnegie as an endowment fund for its Publishing Board. Dewey quickly saw an opportunity. He suggested that "a part of Mr. Carnegie's gift . . . be used to help on the ALA Catalog." The Board approved his request to employ a full-time assistant at $100 a month. On November 15 he issued a circular outlining the general plan for a catalog of 8,000 titles particularly adapted to "very small libraries" because citations would be ranked and annotated; he also urged the publishing board to adopt the Decimal scheme as the *Catalog*'s standard arrangement.[23]

To coordinate "the general editorship of the publication," on July 10, 1893, Putnam asked W. Dawson Johnston to repre-

---

22. *PL* 6 (11/01): 536–37; Harris to Dewey, 3/28/02, LCE-NA; Dewey to Putnam, 4/16/02, "Dewey File," Putnam Mss.

23. Dewey to ALA Publishing Board, 7/3/02, Lane Mss; Fletcher to Bowker, 9/29/02; Dewey circular entitled "A.L.A. Catalog of 1904," 11/15/02, as found in Bowker Mss; Dewey to Wellman, 11/18/02, SPL Archives; *LJ* 27 (12/02): 989, 1016; Dewey to Putnam, 12/1/02, "Dewey File," Putnam Mss.

sent LC in the joint effort. Knowing how Dewey often interpreted orders to his own advantage, Putnam was very precise with Johnston. The final source of authority, Putnam argued, should be the ALA Publishing Board. Johnston contacted Dewey four days later, indicated that Putnam wanted all material ready for press by November 1, and asked Dewey to assemble a corps of experts who would select and describe titles included. Next day Dewey welcomed Johnston to the project and offered to add his name on the *ALA Catalog* title page as associate editor.[24] It appeared the project was off to a harmonious start. Not for long, however.

On September 9 Putnam noticed that in an August letter Dewey had written about the arrangement of the *Catalog* "as if settled." Putnam sensed trouble; the question of arrangement would not be determined "until passed by the Publishing Board," he told Johnston, and directed his subordinate to investigate. Johnston then questioned Dewey on his assumption that the *Catalog* would be arranged in DC order. Dewey responded sharply on September 29. "Your unfamiliarity with the previous history of the *ALA Catalog* has led you into an impossible position. I will try to get you straight on this matter." Dewey then recounted the *Catalog's* twenty-five-year history, and since Johnston could not dispute Dewey's interpretation Dewey was free to select any "history" he wished to reinforce his point of view. He especially emphasized *Catalog* arrangement and concluded that because the Regents had invested so much time and energy the *Catalog* had to be in two parts; one a dictionary catalog, the other a classified catalog "in DC order . . . it is now too late to discuss radical changes for the edition."[25] Dewey then wrote Publishing Board chairman Fletcher that Johnston was trying to change the rules in the middle of the game without mentioning that Johnston was questioning his insistence on a Decimal arrangement. And without investigating the issue further, Fletcher sided with Dewey, "So far as I can learn we of the Board are with you." Thus reassured, Dewey wrote Johnston that "no trifling with the matter

---

24. Putnam to Johnston, 7/10/03; Johnston to Dewey, 7/14/03; Hastings to Johnston, 7/16/03; Lane to Johnston, 7/17/03; Dewey to Johnston, 7/17/03, Johnston Mss.

25. Seymour to Johnston, 8/17/03; Putnam to Boyd, 9/9/03, as quoted in Boyd to Johnston, 9/21/03; Dewey to Johnston, 9/29/03; Johnston to Dewey, 10/5/03, Johnston Mss.

will be tolerated. . . . I can rely on [the Board] to stand loyally by me."

When Johnston took the matter back to Putnam, the Librarian of Congress felt he had to acquiesce. He could not fight Dewey without support of the Publishing Board, and since LC was committed to publishing the *Catalog* for ALA, he could not retreat. He decided to neutralize the situation by relieving Johnston of any connection with the *ALA Catalog* and hiring Theresa West Elmendorf (she had married H. L. Elmendorf in 1896) to serve as liaison between the Publishing Board and the Library.[26]

Then in March Fletcher discovered Dewey had misrepresented the Publishing Board's position to Johnston and Putnam, and protested Dewey's insistence on Decimal order. Dewey would not retreat, despite the fact that he had been caught unfairly manipulating the situation. "We want a dictionary catalog and a DC Catalog because most libraries use one or the other," he told Fletcher. "It is no expression as to their merits, but a mere adoption of what is most used." Naturally, Fletcher was angry. "The Publishing Board has been going on the assumption it had entire jurisdiction, by a majority vote, over the ALA Catalog," he complained to Putnam. "Your communications . . . indicated that you had the same idea. Now Mr. Dewey claims for himself practically the ownership of the entire project and a right to direct as to its form, etc." Although Fletcher proposed a meeting to resolve the problem, Dewey wrote board members he would not compromise. The board was forced to acquiesce if it wanted the *Catalog* published at all.[27]

Although Dewey ultimately won the battle, it was a Pyrrhic victory. In order to make sure the classified section of the *ALA Catalog* was only in Decimal he had used arguments and tactics

---

26. Fletcher to Dewey, 10/15/03; Dewey to Johnston, 10/17/03, Dewey Mss: Dewey to Putnam, 11/8/93, copy in Johnston Mss; Dewey to Theresa West Elmendorf, 11/16/03, "Dewey File," Putnam Mss; Lane to Johnston, 12/28/03, Johnston Mss.

27. Dewey to Fletcher, 4/5/04, "Dewey File"; Fletcher to Putnam, 5/24/04, quoted in Boyd to Putnam, 5/26/04; Dewey to Fletcher, 5/24/04, quoted in Boyd to Putnam, 5/27/04, Putnam Mss; Dewey to Hiller C. Wellman, 5/24/04, Wellman Mss; Fletcher to Putnam, 5/25/04, as quoted in Boyd to Putnam, 8/1/04, Putnam Mss. See also Dewey to Putnam, 8/10/04 and 9/10/04, "Dewey File," Putnam Mss, for evidence of some of the adverse ramifications Dewey experienced because of this "victory."

similar to his justification for mixing ALA and Readers and Writers Economy Company funds in 1880, and for manipulating the election of Winsor's successor as ALA president in 1897. In the process he had alienated members of the ALA Publishing Board and the Librarian of Congress. He had also unfairly manipulated one of Putnam's subordinates. Putnam, Lane, Fletcher, and Johnston had experienced the same Dewey intransigence that Winsor, Bowker, and Poole had experienced decades before. After 1904 they all became much more cautious of the New York State Librarian.

Dewey did attend the ALA conference in St. Louis in October 1904, but was not a force in its proceedings. He did, however, push one cause. The previous February he had complained to Putnam: "I grow more and more impatient . . . that a very small minority of the ALA doubt the wisdom of increasing its membership and talk about getting unwieldy." He thought a natural solution was a "library century, league or academy, strictly limited to 100 to do the work of a smaller body" within the larger association. When he introduced his idea for an ALA academy (which included a recommendation for the creation of a "distinctly national library school") at the conference, the ALA council delayed action by appointing another committee of five to report at the next meeting.[28] ALA was not in a hurry to jump for another Dewey scheme; perhaps members recognized and welcomed Dewey's waning influence within ALA, and sensed his scheme as an effort to regain a measure of control. At the end of 1904, Dewey's star was continuing to descend on the ALA horizon.

---

28. Dewey to Putnam, 2/3/04, "Dewey File," Putnam Mss; *PL* 9 (5/04): 238; (6/04): 274–75; *LJ* 29 (6/04): 300; *Proceedings, 1904,* 257. See also *PL* 9 (1/04): 16–18.

11

Other Interests

1889–1910

The Library Bureau
1889–1910

After accepting the offer to become Regents' Secretary and New York State Librarian in 1888, Dewey recognized that his future dealings with the Library Bureau would be limited and he sought to put the appearance of distance between himself and the Bureau. For example, he responded to a library school applicant on December 22, 1889: "You quite mistake my connection with the Library Bureau. I have long since turned over the active management to Mr. Parker & Mr. Davidson, who are constantly improving this work." To Parker he explained he could not have the State Library place large orders with the Bureau because "if one wished to be malicious he could say that I was buying of my own concern. . . . I simply cannot & will not risk having my work & influence crippled by any such gossip."

Although Dewey drew no salary as president, he and his family automatically earned 6 percent (7 percent beginning in 1891) on the company's annual profits from majority stock they owned. Dewey rolled all of it back into company stock to maintain family control. He made no secret of his motive. To Bureau Vice President J. S. Lockwood on July 24, 1889, he wrote "how much I should regret if its educational side became overshad-

234

owed by a money-making notion." Dewey hoped Lockwood would become his ears to Parker and Davidson's plans and would act as a brake against a materialistic "tendency" to "drift away" from "library interests."[1]

By the time Dewey reached Albany, the Library Bureau had incorporated under the laws of the State of Massachusetts. A copy of a contract dated August 7, 1891, shows that W. E. Parker and H. E. Davidson were employed as managers by Bureau directors who at the time of incorporation were Melvil and Annie Dewey, Annie Jackson, W. S. Biscoe, and Parker and Davidson. The latter two were each paid $125 per month, but at the end of the fiscal year, after distributing 7 percent dividends on the capital stock owned by the directors, they split 80 percent of the remaining profits minus the $125 per month they had previously been paid.[2]

Throughout the 1890s Dewey's relationship with Parker and Davidson was testy. As long as Parker and Davidson followed Dewey's direction, matters remained peaceful. When either pushed the Bureau in directions that threatened Dewey's library, metric, and spelling reform interests, he resisted. And when either complained that serving Dewey's pet reforms was costing the Bureau money, Dewey used his control of majority stock to force his will. Still, the Bureau continued to grow, primarily because Davidson began selling library card stock for commercial record-keeping indexing systems. Businesses adopting the cards found they were able to reduce record-keeping time by up to 50 percent; and as word of these benefits spread in the business world Davidson increasingly tapped into a new market that significantly tested the Library Bureau's capacity to respond.[3]

Naturally Davidson and Parker were eager to accommodate that market. In April 1891, the Bureau opened offices in New York. By January 1893, they were ready to open offices in Chicago and had plans to open offices in London and Philadelphia. Business was growing so rapidly Bureau directors voted to increase

---

1. Dewey to Lockwood, 7/24/89; Dewey to Parker, 12/6/89; Dewey to Helen Sperry, 12/22/89, Box 91, Dewey Mss. See also Lockwood to Dewey, 6/30/90, Box 62, Dewey Mss; NYSL *AR, 1892,* pp. 14–15.

2. Copy of this contract can be found in Box 62, Dewey Mss.

3. See Library Bureau, *The Story of the Library Bureau* (Boston, 1909), pp. 5–8; Joanna Yates, *Control through Communication: The Rise of System in American Management* (Baltimore, 1989), pp. 56–57.

capital stock from $15,000 to $30,000 in the summer, and to $50,000 in October—all this in the middle of the Panic of 1893.[4] Dewey agreed to these recapitalizations for several reasons. First, they allowed him to expand "family" control without having to invest more money. Second, they gave Davidson and Parker some flexibility to expand into promising markets without compromising Dewey's control or requiring more personal investment. Third, the $50,000 recapitalization led to a renegotiated contract in November, in which Dewey was designated to receive a cash payment of 20 percent on company profits.

He had specific intentions for this money. In the summer of 1893 he and Annie had found a location for the private club they had planned for since 1878 at Lake Placid, New York. In order to start their scheme, however (which is discussed more fully at the end of this chapter), they needed capital. The Library Bureau's recapitalization promised to supply a substantial fraction of the sums needed. Dewey guessed right; in 1894 he received dividends of $3,650; in 1895 $5,750. Parker did not discourage the Deweys from investing their Bureau dividends in their Lake Placid venture, but he did restrict Dewey's access to company accounts. Rather than agreeing to Dewey's requests for loans directly from the Bureau, he suggested Dewey borrow from a local bank against his Bureau stock.[5]

By the beginning of 1894 the Library Bureau had successfully moved into new office supplies markets. Sales grew from $35,000 in 1889 to $193,000 in 1893, most of which came from catalog card stock, cabinets, and trays sold to businesses, not to libraries. Naturally Parker and Davidson wanted to push into these new markets even more, but Dewey continually hesitated, fearful that if he lost control of the majority of the Bureau's stock his reform schemes would be buried in a quest for company

---

4. See George Meleney (of the new Chicago office) to Dewey, 3/9/93, Box 3; E. W. Sherman to Dewey, 7/10/93; Parker to Dewey, 8/28/93; Davidson to Cedric Cheevers, 9/29/93, Box 62, Dewey Mss.

5. "Memorandum of a Contract," 11/20/93, Box 62; "Confidential Statement of the Library Bureau," 1901, Box 64; "Library Bureau Stockholders Records," 7/31/95, Box 100, Dewey Mss. See also Parker to Annie Dewey, 9/19/93; Parker to Dewey, 10/6/93, Box 62; Cutler to Dewey, 9/7/93; 9/17/93, Box 73; Dewey to Godfrey Dewey, 1/2/17, Box 23, Dewey Mss; and Dewey's personal account book, FPA. Page 19 lists LB stockholders and the amounts they held between 1888 and 1895.

Known in the 1880s for library-economy devices and contraptions, the Library Bureau prospered in the '90s on the strength of card stock, cabinets, and trays sold to businesses. By 1910, when Dewey gave up his last interests in it, the company had 3,000 employees in thirty-two cities.

profits. Parker pressed. "Why can you not be satisfied in the future to link your interests with Davidson's and mine," he wrote on February 6; "Will it not retard the growth toward which we are tending . . . to attempt in your family to hold the majority of stock?"[6]

Dewey would not listen. Although he needed more money for Lake Placid, he could not bring himself to share control of the Bureau. Instead, he played angles. Sometimes he got his brother to guarantee loans against Bureau stock that banks had initially refused because it was "unlisted"; sometimes he tried to convince "family" members to increase the number of shares they owned; sometimes he tried to convince common stockholders not members of his "family" to trade for the preferred stock he owned. Parker and Davidson did not know how heavily or to whom Dewey's majority LB stock was collateralized.[7]

Dewey also continued to use his majority control to push pet reform schemes. In late 1893 he forced the Bureau to join the cooperative cataloging efforts being run through the ALA Publishing Section. Parker objected. "Criticisms are beginning to come in as to methods of cataloging on little points." The Bureau had no time for the correspondence such quibbling necessitated, he said.[8] A year later Parker disagreed with Dewey's decision to retain stocks of metric materials. The stuff did not sell, he argued, and warehousing goods that did not move represented "one of the most potent menaces to our business." But Dewey would not budge, and Parker and Davidson could do nothing because Dewey had the votes.

By the middle of 1895 Dewey had also involved the Bureau in cooperative efforts with the Massachusetts Library Club to

---

6. See Parker to Dewey, 2/6/94, Box 62, Dewey Mss. Treasurer's account of sales and profits for the years 1889–1893 are in Davidson to Dewey, 6/20/94, Box 31, Dewey Mss.

7. See Parker to Dewey, 7/10/94 (2); 7/13/94; 10/10/94; and 10/17/94, Box 62, Dewey Mss. See also George Champlin to Dewey, 7/24/94, Box 62; Dewey to J. E. Rothery, 10/20/94; Dewey to Tessa Kelso, 12/10/94; Dewey to Rothery, 12/11/94; Dewey to Champlin, 12/18/95, Box 91; and Biscoe to Dewey, 9/4/95, Box 30, Dewey Mss. For evidence of Dewey's practice of using LB common stock as collateral for cash loans, see Dewey to H. P. James, 3/17/97, Box 31A, Dewey Mss.

8. The Library Bureau relinquished this responsibility in September 1896, when the ALA Publishing Section agreed to take the printed card project over. Parker had told Dewey that it was one of the few Bureau departments that regularly lost money; he recommended on September 1 that unless the matter reversed itself or the ALA took it over, "we shall drop it." See Parker to Dewey, 9/1/96, Box 62, Dewey Mss; William Coolidge Lane to Bowker, 9/11/96, Bowker Mss; *LJ* 21 (10/86): 474.

issue its "Monthly List of Selected Fiction." He followed this initiative by having the Bureau publish a number of titles for the ALA Publishing Section in the 1890s, including Caroline Hewins's *Books for Boys and Girls,* Augusta H. Leypoldt and George Iles's *List of Books for Girls and Women and Their Clubs,* John F. Sargeant's *Reading for the Young* and *Catalog of Historical Fiction for Young People,* and Sophie Cornu and William Beer's *List of French Fiction.* The latter represented an effort to acquaint librarians with authors considered more acceptable than Emile Zola, Guy De Maupassant, and Alphonse Daudet.[9]

But Davidson and Parker recognized that Dewey's ability to control was becoming more tenuous, in part because they knew Dewey's Lake Placid ventures made constant demands on him for more capital, in part because they knew Dewey could not risk any publicity concerning his connection with the Bureau while he was a New York State public servant. In late 1897 they found a way to break Dewey's stranglehold. By asking Dewey to include them in his "financial family," they got him to agree to setting up a trust on October 1, 1898, in which four major investors (Dewey, Davidson, Parker, and New York businessman Atherton Loring) controlled a majority of LB stock and by their four votes thus controlled the company. Dewey would remain president.

Because Dewey believed he could control Parker and Davidson, he convinced himself the Bureau would not change much in the near future. As members of his "family," he fully expected Parker and Davidson to honor commitments to his reform initiatives and to follow the directions he had outlined for the Library Bureau fifteen years earlier. Others saw the situation differently, however. When Bowker heard of the new contract, he wrote Davidson: "I congratulate you and Mr. Parker most cordially on the fact that you are now in a position to reap the permanent benefit from the business."[10] Conflict was inevitable.

---

9. See Parker to Dewey, 12/14/93; 11/3/94, Box 62, Dewey Mss. See also circular dated 5/1/95 entitled "Monthly List of Selected Fiction," Box 4; Parker to Dewey, 11/21/95; Davidson to Dewey, 1/20/96, Box 62, Dewey Mss; and "List of Publications of the A.L.A. Publishing Section," *LJ* 24 (4/99): 192.

10. Bowker to Davidson, 9/28/98, Bowker Mss. A copy of the contract dated 10/1/98, is in Box 100, Dewey Mss. See also Parker to Dewey, 9/9/98, Box 63; entry in LB stockholders book dated 9/23/98, Box 100; and Parker to Dewey, 7/10/00, Box 63, in which Parker explains business arrangements with Loring in more detail.

In the summer of 1900 Davidson, Parker, and Loring decided to raise the Bureau's capital stock another $100,000. Dewey vehemently objected, arguing his interpretation of the October 1898 agreement that neither Parker nor Davidson would vote against him in Library Bureau matters and both would recognize and honor the many sacrifices he had made for the company. Parker scoffed at Dewey's contention "that no action of the trustees should ever be taken which did not meet with your approval," and reminded Dewey he and Davidson had made many more sacrifices for the Bureau over the previous ten years, during which time its ledgers reflected "how little you have done for it."[11] Still Dewey refused to accept the new situation. He convinced himself that Loring had launched a "conspiracy" to wrest control from him, and that Davidson and Parker were being duped by Loring's pure business interests into departing from the Bureau's "original intent." At first, he bluffed. He told his partners that if he detected any move to eliminate him from management of the Bureau he would block it by invoking the power of his "financial family" which, he claimed, controlled 756 shares of the Bureau's total 1,500. He did not, however, acknowledge that part of those 756 shares were bound by contract into the trust, control of which Dewey shared with three other directors. And because control of the block of stock he owned had been split, he could not by law claim majority control.

Davidson and Parker quickly called his bluff and decided to take advantage of the situation to eliminate Dewey's obstructionist tactics once and for all. On July 28 they directed Dewey to "wire your assent" to two statements, one to the Library Bureau stockholders and directors that "it is your wish not to be elected on the board of directors," the other to the directors "that you do not wish to be elected president. This, it seems to us, will be better than for you to resign." Dewey's response was strongly argued but weakly defended because it fell back on his interpretation that the 1898 contract "requires that any [LB] action shall be approved by all three of us. . . . I shall hold you responsible to the fullest extent for any violation of our agreement." But Parker and Davidson would not be bullied. "We believe it is not in your power to in any way dictate what the policy of the corporation

---

11. Parker to Dewey, 6/16/00; Parker to Dewey, 7/10/00, Box 63, Dewey Mss.

shall be," they argued. Because they regarded Dewey's letter as an ultimatum, they said, they would thereafter act through their attorney and advised Dewey to do likewise.[12]

Finally Dewey recognized he had been beaten. Although he continued to claim what he believed were his rights, he also let Davidson know that for the right price he might sell his interest in future profits of the Bureau. Davidson, Parker, and Loring felt no need to appease him, however. In the first place, together they controlled the trust and they all agreed on the need to drop Dewey's unprofitable ventures and move into more lucrative markets. In the second place, they knew that Dewey's Lake Placid interests consumed more and more of his capital, and that under the right circumstances, he would be willing to part with his Bureau stock.[13] In May, they informed all Library Bureau stockholders that Bureau directors intended to carry through a reorganization. Davidson later revealed to Bowker that reorganization was "the only means of arriving at a satisfactory settlement with Mr. Dewey and eliminating him from the management pertaining to the Library Bureau." On August 28, 1901, the Bureau reorganized and reincorporated under the laws of New Jersey. Officers included Davidson (president), Loring and James S. Cobb (vice presidents), and Parker (secretary-treasurer). Dewey was finally out.

Although the new arrangement gave Dewey $40,800 in preferred stock and $9,200 in common stock, his relationship to the reorganized Bureau was like that of every other stockholder. In 1902 Davidson offered to sell Dewey's stock off privately in blocks worth $5,000, as Dewey needed the money for his Lake Placid venture. Dewey agreed, and by this plan slowly sold his way out of the Library Bureau. By November 1904 he was down to $24,000; in December 1908, to $20,000.[14]

---

12. Davidson and Parker to Dewey, 7/28/00; Dewey to Davidson and Parker, 8/1/00; Parker and Davidson to Dewey, 8/3/00; and Davidson to Dewey, 8/10/00, Box 63, Dewey Mss. See also list of LB stockholders for 7/12/00 in Box 62.

13. "Notes on Library Bureau Contracts," 8/31/00, Box 63, Dewey Mss. See also Arthur Russell to Davidson, 9/1/00, copy found in Box 63; Loring to Dewey, 10/3/00; Dewey to Loring, 10/5/00; 10/21/00, Box 63, Dewey Mss.

14. The reorganization is detailed in a flyer in Box 63, Dewey Mss. See also Davidson to Bowker, n.d., Bowker Mss; *LJ* 27 (12/02): 1036;

Without him, Bureau growth accelerated significantly. By 1909 the Bureau had ten factories, offices in thirty-two cities in North America and Europe, three thousand employees, and annual sales in the millions of dollars. In addition to card index sales to the private sector, it continued to supply a growing library market with material such as circulation records and accessions books, and quality furniture such as circulation desks and card catalogs. In 1910 Dewey finally sold the rest of his Library Bureau stock for $25,000. Grace Hewitt, Dewey's personal stenographer at Lake Placid at the time, recalled his reaction to the sale years later. "I shall never forget the look of deep regret when he came back to his study and said the deal had been closed and he had $25,000 for immediate use to apply on Club bills." It was "the greatest sacrifice Dr. Dewey ever made." Nonetheless, to the end of his association with the Library Bureau, the irrepressible reformer remained loyal to his dreams. "I put all my Library Buro sales of stok into LPCo preferd & never yet casht a dividend chek," he told Placid Company Directors on September 5, 1930. No money made by interests he had started, in other words, had ever gone into his pocket for mere material gain; all of it was eventually channeled into the education reforms for which Dewey had spent a lifetime crusading.[15]

Metric and Spelling Reform
1889–1904

When Dewey was eliminated from the Library Bureau's management team in 1901, he took his metric and spelling reform interests with him. Parker and Davidson did not resist; both had been losing propositions. In fact, efforts towards metric reform

---

Davidson to Dewey, 6/30/99; Whitman to Dewey, 3/8/01; 4/9/01; Dewey to Parker, 5/7/03; Davidson to Dewey, 5/25/03; Dewey to Parker, 10/27/03; 2/1/04; 11/3/04, Box 63; Dewey to Davidson, 12/26/08, Box 64, Dewey Mss. See also Dewey to "Library Bureau Preferred Stockholders," 2/19/07, Box 64, Dewey Mss. Dewey explained the timing of his shifting family investments from Bureau to Lake Placid Company stock in Dewey to Godfrey Dewey, 1/2/17, Box 23, Dewey Mss.

15. Hewitt to Godfrey Dewey, -/-/32, Box 26, Dewey Mss; Dewey to Placid Company Directors, 9/5/30, FPA. See also *The Story of the Library Bureau*, pp. 20–25.

had languished while Dewey was in Albany. In 1888, the American Metric Bureau was almost defunct, a part of the Library Bureau in name only. It did not survive the latter's 1901 reorganization. Although Dewey continued to hold the position of Secretary of the American Metrological Society, the Society met infrequently and mostly without Dewey. Until 1901 the Library Bureau had continued to print proceedings of its meetings, but sold very few copies. When individuals inquired concerning metric conversion, Dewey regularly and characteristically responded with enthusiasm and often encouraged them to take a leadership position. No one took his advice, however, and on those few occasions during the 1890s when members of the AMS petitioned Congress to adopt metric as a standard system of weights and measures for the United States, Dewey did little more than write supporting letters.[16] In 1904, America was no closer to metric conversion than it had been in 1889.

Spelling reform, however, showed more promise. When Dewey moved to Albany in 1888, he had already been neglecting the Spelling Reform Association for several years, even though he was still its secretary. Because the press's image of spelling reformers as unconventional people pressing "crackpot" schemes persisted, Dewey believed conferences that brought them all together reinforced this negative image. He preferred instead a slower paced, more conservative reform based on a small number of phonetic principles approved by the American Philological Association, which news media, book publishers, and various government agencies could more easily adopt. He also thought SRA interests were better served when executive board meetings were attached to conferences of scholarly organizations like the APA. But Dewey seldom attended these either. Because he did not have the time, what Dewey really wanted was someone he could control who would do for spelling reform in the 1890s what loyal subordinates were doing for his library reform interests in the 1880s and 1890s.

Then, in the spring of 1895, he thought he found "the man we have been looking for." Robert M. Pierce, who had been

---

16. Dewey to Augustus DuBois, 12/6/89; J. K. Rees to Dewey, 12/19/89; 1/6/90; 3/19/92; Dewey to Rufus P. Williams, 2/7/02; Dewey to Henry D. Hubbard (Secretary, National Bureau of Standards, Treasury Department), 10/1/02; Dewey to J. H. Gore, 4/21/03, Box 66, Dewey Mss.

introduced to Dewey by publisher Henry Holt, agreed to become
SRA secretary if the organization paid him a salary of $720 and
made him editor of *Spelling*. "He has enough of the missionary in
his disposition," Dewey told SRA officers on March 11, "to be
willing to do what I did 15 years ago, do a great deal of hard work
for no compensation beyond actual living expenses." Dewey
offered to give Pierce free working space in the Library Bureau's
New York offices. The SRA board quickly consented, but only on
condition that Dewey stay on as secretary and Pierce be made
corresponding secretary. Pierce agreed to the arrangement and
moved quickly; by March 14 he had set up offices and was ready
to commit himself to the cause.

Just as quickly, however, it became obvious Dewey under-
estimated Pierce's independence and overestimated his own
ability to control Pierce's missionary spirit. When Pierce recommended SRA reduce costs by paring *Spelling* to sixteen pages,
Dewey objected. A few less pages would not substantially reduce
costs, he argued. Rather, Pierce ought to devote his attention to
increasing membership.[17] This Pierce resisted. Why not make
Spelling into a pamphlet and use the time normally invested in
publishing the journal for other matters? he asked. After all, the
SRA had only thirty-five members, and dues were only a dollar a
year. "Do not plan to give up Spelling," Dewey argued. "That I
shall maintain if I have to pay the bills myself as a quarterly."
Again he told Pierce to devote most attention to memberships,
and with his letter included a copy of Lindsley's tachigraphy. "Go
over this as rapidly as possible," he wrote on March 25, "as I have
matter to write you every day if I could do it in shorthand." The
patterns of communication reflected in this move are telling;
Dewey apparently intended to issue orders to Pierce just as he
issued orders to May Seymour, Florence Woodworth, and Walter
Biscoe. He expected Pierce to follow them, and although he
would tolerate some questioning he would tolerate no refusal.
Understandably Pierce bristled under these conditions. He complained to March that Dewey's "method is terribly curt and dic-

---

17. See Fernald to Dewey, 3/3/95, Box 84; Dewey to Scott, 3/11/95,
Box 87; Dewey to March, 3/11/95, Box 87; Dewey to "Officers of the S.R.A.,"
3/11/95, Box 87; Pierce to Dewey, 3/14/95, Box 84; Dewey to Pierce, Box 87,
Dewey Mss. See also Dewey to Eggleston, 3/15/95, Box 84, Dewey Mss;
Dewey to Eggleston, 3/18/95, Eggleston Mss.

tatorial," and objected to Dewey's "display of sharp criticisms
. . . and a sort of spred eaglism about what the past 19 years had
proved." He also said he would refuse to tolerate "this absurd
policy which seems to Prof. Dewey's mind to be quite the proper
and usual manner of talking to people who happen to be considered in his power."[18]

But by this time Dewey had already decided Pierce had to
go, and began to make Pierce's life miserable by withholding
office supplies that the SRA had routinely purchased through the
Library Bureau. When Pierce complained, Dewey said he would
get no more until he pledged "not to incur any bills or claims of
any name or nature for the S.R.A. or for any of its officers or
members in connection with this work." Pierce responded on
April 19 that he did not have to make pledges because he had no
authority to encumber SRA funds anyway, and he continued to
object to Dewey's tone. "I ask that you giv me no more cause for
further discussion," he concluded. Dewey then began working on
March. "I am afraid we have gotten in a scrape," he said, "and
through my fault." He complained about Pierce's "half-dozen
letters filled with the most disagreeable sneers at everything that
has been done by the S.R.A.," and gave a unique interpretation
of Pierce's April 19 letter by accusing Pierce of "declining to
agree not to run up bills against the S.R.A." Pierce had to go, he
said. Dewey's tactics worked; Pierce was in a no-win situation,
and he resigned May 6.[19]

In 1897, however, spelling reform began to pick up momentum by garnering support from groups with no connection to
Dewey's SRA. On February 18, the National Education Association's Department of Superintendence adopted a resolution
introduced by E. O. Vaile (editor of *Intelligence,* a Chicago-based
educational periodical) that called for use of simplified spellings
of twelve words (e.g., "program" instead of "programme," "thru"
instead of "through," and "catalog" instead of "catalogue"). At the

18. Pierce to Dewey, 3/19/95, Box 90; Dewey to Pierce, 3/25/95, Box
87; Pierce to Dewey, 4/15/95, Box 90; Dewey to Pierce, 4/16/95, Box 87;
Pierce to Dewey, 4/19/95, Box 84; Pierce to March, 4/19/95, copy found in
Box 90, Dewey Mss.

19. Pierce to March, 4/27/95, Box 90; Dewey to Pierce, 4/27/95, Box
87; Pierce to Dewey, 4/29/95, Box 84; Dewey to March, 5/1/95, Box 87;
Pierce to Dewey, 5/6/95, Box 84; Pierce to March, 5/6/95, copy found in Box
90, Dewey Mss.

1897 convention of the National Association of American Manufacturers, Andrew D. White told an audience: "I believe that the highest interest of Christian civilization and of humanity would be served by making the spelling and pronunciation of the English language phonetic." He argued that with spelling reform China and Japan would become English-speaking and Christianized countries within fifty years, and that this would "throw open those vast countries" to American trade. By the end of 1898 the *Standard* and the *Century* dictionaries had begun using new spellings of several words, and *Webster's* had begun issuing an appendix identifying changing practices.[20] Dewey was encouraged, but because he was preoccupied with other matters in 1898 and 1899, he made no effort to move center stage.

Into the vacuum stepped E. O. Vaile. In 1900 Vaile asked the NEA to appropriate $1,000 a year for five years, and put it at the disposal of a spelling reform committee consisting of W. T. Harris, Nicholas Murray Butler, and such prominent people as Thomas R. Lounsbury of Yale, William Dean Howells of the *Atlantic,* and Benjamin E. Smith of the *Century Dictionary.* The NEA approved the motion in principle, but delayed action until the following conference. Dewey immediately saw possibilities in harnessing Vaile's energy and commitment, but worried about Vaile's missionary fervor. In February 1901, he encouraged Butler to lend his cooperation to Vaile's initiative; he also wrote William Rainey Harper, Andrew Sloan Draper, Brander Matthews, and Henry Holt, all of whom, he told Butler, would make "sure that nothing visionary or undignified will be proposed" if they agreed to join an NEA commission.[21]

When NEA failed to fund the commission at its 1901 conference, Vaile shopped for opportunities elsewhere. On January 30, 1902, he told Dewey he had just contacted Andrew Carnegie—for some time known to be a simplified spelling advocate—to underwrite the commission he was proposing and included a copy of his letter to Carnegie. At this point, however, Dewey

---

20. See Tauber, "Spelling Reform," pp. 132–33; Butler to Dewey, 4/5/97, Box 75; and newspaper clipping entitled "Speech to the Convention of National Association of American Manufacturers, 1897," found in Box 89, Dewey Mss. See also Dewey to Alfred Andrews, 11/23/98, Box 84, Dewey Mss.

21. Dewey to Butler, 2/21/01, Butler Mss; Holt to Vaile, 2/19/01, copy found in Box 84, Dewey Mss.

decided to inject himself into the situation, and by stealth quickly and effectively usurped Vaile's initiative. On February 18 he told Vaile: "I have written Mr. Carnegie and shall see him at dinner on Mar. 13, but we very likely can't enlist him." Dewey's letter belied his real purpose; he wanted to find out for himself if Carnegie had any interest in a national commission on simplified spelling, and at the same time he wanted to eliminate Vaile from the negotiations. That same day he wrote Carnegie. He praised Carnegie's commitment to public libraries, but argued "the chief obstacle to getting the greatest good from public libraries" was "the absurd spelling of English" that, he claimed, wasted three years of the average school child's life. "I sincerely believe that the greatest service that can be rendered the race today," he said, was "the support for a few years of an office where a first class man" could "conduct a wise, conservative campaign for the simplification of English spelling."[22]

It is not clear what happened at the March 13 dinner, but in subsequent correspondence describing it Dewey claimed to have obtained Carnegie's promise of $10,000 a year for ten years to fund a central New York office and an executive secretary, if the latter could assemble a governing commission of twenty prominent officers who would "keep in the background the overzealous reformers," avoid the phrase "spelling reform," and adopt use of simplified spelling of the twelve words Vaile had gotten the NEA Department of Superintendence to approve in 1897. Dewey promised to organize a meeting of prominent people to consider Carnegie's offer.

The meeting took place in New York on February 21, 1903, and included representatives of four dictionaries (G. C. Merriam, Funk and Wagnalls, the Century Company, and Macmillan), March of Lafayette College, Lounsbury of Yale, Butler and Matthews of Columbia, Calvin Thomas in his capacity as president of the Modern Language Association, and of course Dewey, who presided. Dewey had structured the meeting by sending out a tentative agenda two days earlier. In it he suggested that the group shun use of the word "reform" in its title, that it avoid "entangling alliances" with publishers, that it open offices in New York, that it elect a board of nine to guide the commission, and

---

22. See Dewey to Vaile, 1/22/02; Vaile to Dewey, 2/15/02; Dewey to Vaile, 2/18/02; Dewey to Carnegie, 2/18/02, Box 84, Dewey Mss.

that it find "if possible for secretary a strong young man who can give his whole time to the work."

At the meeting all expressed agreement with Dewey's agenda, which then provided the foundation for a series of resolutions passed during the afternoon session. In addition, attendees elected Butler chairman of the committee, Dewey secretary. Thus Dewey had maneuvered himself into a position to influence a pet reform. If the commission was going to have a paid secretary to direct a national spelling reform campaign, he was now well placed to be a top candidate. On March 31 he boasted to a friend, "Mr. Carnegie has just given me $10,000 for expenses for ten years of an office for a vigorous campaign in favor of a simplification of English."[23]

After the meeting, Dewey forwarded copies of the minutes to Carnegie. He reminded Carnegie of the oral commitment he had made the previous year, and asked him to send a statement confirming his offer as soon as possible. Carnegie's reply, however, took Dewey by surprise. He told Dewey he had read the minutes, but then argued "the vital point" was not discussed. "You said you could get the signatures" of prominent people "to agree to use improved spelling of at least ten or twelve words," he complained. "The money I agreed to give as needed was to be spent in circulating the knowledge of this fact and to develop the work in other ways by hastening the general use of new spelling." Where Carnegie wanted individual commitment and practical results, Dewey wanted a bureaucracy organized from a central office that would publicly legitimize educational change.

Dewey quickly responded it would be difficult to get the signatures without a central office, and the existence of an office would make the quest for signatures much easier. But Carnegie would not yield. "You stated that you could get the signatures of the leading educationalists . . . to agree to use improved spelling in a number of the worst words. Until that is done, I have nothing to do in the promises." By that time a story was circulating to national newspapers that Carnegie would establish an institute to facilitate "easy acquisition and worldwide use of English," and that he had put $100,000 in Dewey's hands "as expenses for ten

23. Circulars, Dewey to "Language Board," 2/10/03; 2/19/03; Minutes, "Language Board Conference" at Columbia College, 2/21/03, Box 87, Dewey Mss. See also Dewey to Harris, 2/16/03; Harris to Dewey, 2/19/03; Dewey to Paul Passy, 3/2/05, Box 85, Dewey Mss.

years of an office for a vigorous campaign for simplification of spelling." Dewey's complaints to friends that Funk and Harris had leaked the story did not help matters. Carnegie would not release the money until his conditions were met, and when interested parties asked Butler, Lounsbury, and Calvin Thomas when the "institute" would get under way, they could only look to Dewey for an answer. The situation was stalemated, and became embarrassing to all identified with it.[24]

And Dewey was most embarrassed. In a May 25 circular he tried to cover himself by shifting blame to Carnegie. Because "we have to humor his peculiarities," he said, Carnegie's gift would probably not be forthcoming until the end of the year. "His idea seems to be that we ought to put our main strength on inducing the largest number of people possible to break the ice by adopting the 12 NEA words." In June Dewey appealed to Carnegie again, begging him to identify the number of names he wanted. Twenty of "the best men," Dewey argued, would be better than "200 weaker ones." "Get the twenty names," Carnegie replied. "All depends upon who they are. I cannot be hurried into this. I do not see how an office is to be of much use." Carnegie wanted names; Dewey wanted an office. Carnegie wanted a limited campaign; Dewey wanted a broad campaign. "He is a canny Scotsman who will have his own head," Dewey wrote I. K. Funk on July 16. Dewey continued to press Carnegie, but seemed unwilling to come up with the twenty names Carnegie insisted upon without also extracting a promise to fund a central office. But to no avail. "Surely, you know by this time that I have made up my mind," Carnegie wrote Dewey January 14. "There is no use in trying to get me to change this."[25]

In March, however, Dewey's luck appeared to change. Vaile had been working closely with the NEA's Department of Superintendence to endorse association use of the twelve words, and

24. Dewey to Vaile, 3/3/03, Box 84, Dewey Mss; Dewey to Carnegie, 3/26/03; Carnegie to Dewey, 4/1/03; Dewey to Carnegie, 4/2/03; Carnegie to Dewey, 4/7/03, LB 95, Carnegie Mss. See also *Philadelphia North American,* 4/5/03.

25. Dewey to "Members of the Conference on Language Commission," 5/25/03, Box 87; Thomas to Dewey, 5/26/03, Box 84, Dewey Mss; Dewey to Carnegie, 6/19/03; Carnegie to Dewey, LB 97, Carnegie Mss; Dewey to Funk, 7/16/03, Box 87, Dewey Mss; Dewey to Carnegie, 12/23/03, LB 102, Carnegie Mss; James Bertram to Dewey, 12/30/03, Box 84; Dewey to Carnegie, 1/12/04; Carnegie to Dewey, 1/14/04, LB 102, Carnegie Mss.

at the NEA national conference got the department to recommend consideration of a commission for more active work.
Dewey, who had access to NEA power brokers through Board and
Appropriations Committee member Nicholas Murray Butler,
sensed an opportunity. He went back to Carnegie. If he came up
with a draft pledge statement Carnegie approved, would Carnegie authorize $500 to circulate the pledge from a central office?
Yes, Carnegie said. Dewey immediately circularized those attending his February 1903, meeting, and put his own spin on the interview. Carnegie "only asks as a condition of his first substantial
check that 20 strong names be added to his as really using these
words," he wrote, then added: "He is willing to pay all expenses
of a first class man with needed assistants to push the work."[26]

Dewey then encouraged Butler to help him draft an acceptable pledge to be presented at the next NEA meeting, and convinced him to take the draft to Carnegie for comment. When
Carnegie approved in late April, the stalemate finally broke, and
the plan Dewey and Butler had hatched became evident the beginning of May as Butler prepared to attend the NEA conference. In
response to Vaile's proposals for an NEA simplified spelling commission, Butler would recommend instead that the NEA establish
"an English Language Board . . . to do for the English language,
spoken and written, what the French Academy does for the French
language." It was Dewey's responsibility to hold Vaile's enthusiasm
in check so he would not wreck the plan Butler worked through
the NEA. Dewey informed Vaile of Butler's intentions May 7 and
said he thought the NEA would vote for the proposal and that Carnegie would approve it as a vehicle for the campaign he offered to
fund. He did not tell Vaile Carnegie had already preapproved it,
nor did he identify his own role in developing the proposal.[27]

Vaile sensed the ruse, but miscalculated its origin. "It is an
underhanded piece of business," he argued. "All the work I have

---

26. Dewey to Carnegie, 3/14/04; Bertram to Dewey, 3/16/04, LB 103,
Carnegie Mss; Dewey to B. F. Smith, 3/17/04, Box 85, Dewey Mss; Dewey to
Carnegie, 3/17/04, LB 103, Carnegie Mss; Circular, Dewey to "Carnegie
Spelling Conference," 3/24/04, Box 85, Dewey Mss. See also Dewey to
Butler, 3/23/04, Box 87, Dewey Mss.

27. Dewey to Gilman, 4/16/04; Dewey to Vaile, 4/22/04; Charles C.
Walcott (Secretary, Carnegic Institute) to Dewey, 4/26/04; Dewey to Vaile,
5/13/04; Vaile to Dewey, 5/13/04, Box 85, Dewey Mss; Butler to Vaile,
5/7/04, Butler Mss.

done, and the expectations that have been raised, will count for nothing." He complained to Dewey about "the readiness with which you fall in with Butler's plan" and soundly criticized Butler. "At this juncture you suddenly find time to come out of your tent, to take advantage of the situation which I have developed and to propose a plan of your own materially different from mine and which will certainly neutralize and defeat the purpose for which I have been working all these years." But his complaints were in vain; Butler had Carnegie's approval of a pledge that if signed by the ten men named to the commission would be followed by the release of $500 for its organizational setup. And because Butler also held a seat on the NEA Board of Directors and the NEA Appropriations Committee, he had much more influence in the NEA than Vaile.[28]

It took Vaile some time to reconcile himself to this power play. He never did find out that Dewey had been behind the move within the NEA to work the compromise between Carnegie's wishes and his own plans for Carnegie's money for simplified spelling. And to make sure Vaile did not sabotage negotiations, Dewey slowed them for the remainder of 1904, awaiting a more propitious moment when he felt secure enough to launch the new venture, perhaps sometime in early 1905. And because Dewey was willing to wait, so were Butler and Carnegie.

The Lake Placid Club
1893–1904

Early in their marriage, Annie and Melvil Dewey decided to purchase a summer home and organize a community around it as soon as they could afford it. Their reasons were myriad. Both manifested the Victorian Protestant's need to establish contact with nature; both had allergies exacerbated by summer urban living; both believed sincerely in the benefits of healthful living in a setting of lakes, forests, rivers, and mountains; and once Godfrey arrived, both committed themselves to making sure their offspring would experience healthy summers. Both were also committed to establishing and fostering a model community

---

28. Vaile to Dewey, 5/13/04; 5/16/04, Box 85, Dewey Mss; Vaile to Butler, 5/18/04, copy found in Box 85, Dewey Mss.

developed for the recreation and rest of professional people that would become an example to the nation of how households should be run efficiently, inexpensively, and in accordance with the best principles of the domestic sciences advocated by home economists. Annie took a personal and professional interest in this. Like Catherine Beecher and her sister Harriet Beecher Stowe, Annie believed that domestic reform could best be accomplished by running the home as efficiently as possible. A part of the motivation for creating Lake Placid was the Deweys' belief that occupations requiring "brain work" put people at higher risk of nervous prostration that, if not checked, would lead to fatigue and even death. This belief was grounded in conventional nineteenth-century medical wisdom.[29]

The model community concept also fit the Deweys' evolving views of a civilized morality manifest in Christian domesticity that relied heavily on rituals, customs, and hard work, all of which bound inhabitants together. They also worried that immigration was eating away at the Protestant popular base and that the rise of the robber baron threatened the concept of stewardship and the philosophy of individualism. Annie and Melvil Dewey's model community would have none of it. The privacy which their community would afford its middle-class members was to be social, not personal, to avoid the outward manifestations of upper-class formality without abandoning its traditional WASP culture. It was to be an organized opportunity to avoid contact with the kinds of people (working class, African-American, Jewish) that professionals were expected to assist as part of their professional responsibilities. It purposefully and by design would exclude cross-class (and other types of) social interaction.[30]

---

29. See Charles E. Rosenberg, "The Place of George M. Beard in Nineteenth-Century Psychiatry," *Bulletin of the History of Medicine* 36 (1972): 245–59; Carroll Smith-Rosenberg, "The Hysterical Woman: Sex Roles and Role Conflict in Nineteenth-Century America," *Social Research,* 39 (1972): 652–78; Barbara Sicherman, "The Paradox of Prudence: Mental Health in the Gilded Age," *Journal of American History* 62 (1976): 890–912; and Rosalee McReynolds, "The Sexual Politics of Illness in Turn-of-the-Century Libraries," *Libraries & Culture* 25 (1990): 194–217.

30. Melvil's religious and family upbringing fostered this sense of corporate community; in fact, Dewey directed most of his reform efforts towards cultivating the sense of corporate community he thought was being threatened. The theme of "corporate community" in Progressive America is well developed in Thomas Bender, *Community and Social Change in*

Every summer the Deweys went to a different resort area in search of the best place to locate their model community; in 1890 they visited Lake Placid in the Adirondacks. Because Dewey lived in Albany and occupied a state post from which he could closely observe legislation, he undoubtedly watched as the 1892 Legislature passed a bill creating an Adirondack Park from huge chunks of Hamilton, Herkimer, St. Lawrence, Franklin, Essex, and Warren Counties. What property remained would inevitably become more valuable—and more insulated from others. Lake Placid, New York, located 1967 feet above sea level in the "High Peak" area of the Adirondacks and ringed by Marcy (5,344 feet), Algonquin (5,112 feet) and Whiteface (4,872 feet) Mountains, became one of the park's few unprotected pockets, and in the late nineteenth century represented potential for becoming a hub to the protected wilderness.[31]

By 1893 Melvil and Annie were ready to move on their dream. Initially they bought a ten-acre plot on the west shore of Mirror Lake, on which were located most of the area's summer resort hotels and the village's Main Street. They quickly changed their minds, however. In the summer of 1893 they formed a corporation to purchase seventy acres of undeveloped land on the high eastern shore of Mirror Lake and called it "Morningside," after which they named their corporation. The Deweys intended to buy up property, "hold it as a private park, make it as beautiful as our means would allow, and secure the cost of maintenance from ground rents for cottages or clubs who would consider a location in a private park much more desirable than elsewhere."[32] In the fall of 1893 the Deweys took out an option on a large house called "Bonnie Blink" (which Dewey quickly

America (Baltimore, 1978). Domestic efficiency is discussed in McDannell, *The Christian Home*, p. 28, 34, 106. Perceived threats to late 19th-century American Protestantism are discussed in Robert T. Handy, *A Christian America: Protestant Hopes and Historical Realities* (N.Y., 1984), pp. 64–68. See also Stephanie Coontz, *The Social Origins of Private Life: A History of American Families, 1600–1900* (London, 1988), p. 272.

31. For background information on Lake Placid, see Mary MacKenzie, "History of the Village of Lake Placid, New York," *The Placid Pioneer* (Autumn, 1970): 1; and Arthur W. Hayes, *Lake Placid: Its Early History and Developments from the Time of the Civil War to the Present Time* (Lake Placid, N.Y., 1946), pp. 35–36.

32. See Dewey to Mabie, 9/15/96, Box 58, Dewey Mss. See also Rider, *Dewey*, p. 107.

changed to "Bonniblink"), located on property immediately next to theirs. Bonniblink had fifteen bedrooms, a large stone fireplace, three toilet rooms, and five water closets on two of its three floors. It also had public rooms and servants' quarters. With a building to house large numbers of people on grounds they owned, Annie and Melvil began to organize a private club.

Their first step was to mail a circular entitled "An Ideal Summer Home" to a select group of friends. "We are intensely interested in getting for neighbors people whom of all others we would prefer," he wrote.[33] Within months he, Annie and other members of his "family" like Florence Woodworth (all of whom formed the Morningside Company) had made twenty different purchases totalling 100 acres, upon which were several clubhouses. He improved the shoreline, and cleared brush from the land to give the grounds a parklike appearance. The Company also purchased three new boathouses and several boats, and installed new docks and landings for member use. It extended Bonniblink's piazza, improved its tennis courts, and was in the process of laying out a golf course. In addition, Dewey noted that other Club members owned 500 hundred acres on Moose Island and the east and west shores of Lake Placid, and 250 acres west of Mirror Lake on both sides of the Placid outlet. While the Club itself owned no land, he reminded people, the fact that its leading members did protected it "against undesirable neighbors and for its future development."[34]

By the summer of 1895 Dewey was issuing invitations on letterhead stationery to join the "Placid Club," an organization of which he was president, Cornell Professor Jeremiah W. Jenks vice president, and H. Wade Hicks of Cornell's Christian Association secretary. In a letter of April 29 to President Merrill E. Gates of Amherst he listed people planning to spend summers at Placid, including Jenks, Herbert Baxter Adams, H. A. P. Torrey

---

33. See "An Ideal Summer Home," undated circular, Box 58; Dewey to Crunden, 11/3/93, Box 3; Dewey to J. F. Rogers, 2/27/94, Box 91, Dewey Mss. In the latter Dewey recounts the chronology of his original purchase of 70 acres in summer 1893.

34. Dewey to Bradford, 1/2/94, Box 91; "Invitation to Privileges of the Placid Club," undated, Box 58; Dewey to Gates, 4/29/95, Box 58, Dewey Mss. Quotation concerning "undesirable neighbors" taken from page 8 of 1895 Placid Club member's handbook, copy of which is found in LPEF Mss. Florence Woodworth began buying Lake Placid land in January 1895, for monthly payments averaging $25. See Account Book, FPA.

of the University of Vermont, Lydia Godfrey (Annie's sister) of Wellesley, and Professor Herman H. Neill of Amherst. When he sent University of Chicago Political Science Professor J. Lawrence Laughlin an invitation, Laughlin initially balked when he saw Jenks's name. "Socially," he said, the "Cornell Professor whom you mention . . . would not be agreeable to me. . . . If more of his kind come I think I should be more comfortable elsewhere." Dewey recognized the code his WASP culture used to mask its anti-Semitism, and reassured Laughlin that Jenks was no Jew. Laughlin joined the Club shortly thereafter. When Dewey later told Jenks about the incident, he speculated the Club would lose $15 for every dollar it gained if it took in Jews. "We shall get a bad name by taking them in. I have some Hebrew friends who are very charming," he said, "but I should not dare break the rule" barring them from Club membership.[35] He did not mention he and Annie had made the original Club rules.

For much of 1895 Dewey wrote scores of people to consider membership in the Club. Pamphlets accompanying the letters identified the professional posts of all Placid Club officers and outlined the Club's objective—"by cooperation to secure for its members, at actual cost, the privileges of an ideal summer home in ideal surroundings." "Ideal" was defined as quarters quiet after 10 P.M., offering home comforts and rest rather than excitement, and without elaborate social features like special dress for dinner. Among early entertainments listed was "Float Night," when guests decorated floats and illuminated boats and canoes, sailed them all on Mirror Lake, and ended with a group sing around a lakeshore fire. The latter quickly became a weekly event, one of which soon evolved into the annual Iroquois Indian Council Fire in which almost all Club members participated in Indian costume. The pamphlet also said that the Company promised over time to lease or buy more land, buildings, and equipment, to maintain cottages, and to provide meals, rooms, and recreation, but that individual Club members would not be permitted to own land independent of Club control. "None of the central land is for

---

35. Laughlin to Dewey, 5/8/95, Box 58; Dewey to Jenks, 5/31/95, Box 91, Dewey Mss. For a description of Jenks's sociocultural and religious views, which were very much like Dewey's, see Clarence J. Wunderlin, Jr., *Visions of a New Industrial Order: Social Science and Labor Theory in the American Progressive Era* (N.Y., 1992), pp. 15–22.

sale, as it was bought and is held to protect the club against undesirable neighbors and for its future development." In November Dewey announced the Club would open for the winter season
by making rooms available in Bonniblink and Seven Gables, both
of which had been winterized.[36]

The pamphlet's optimism, however, masked early financial
problems emanating from two sources—Dewey's unconventional
business practices and a dispute between the Deweys and the
Club's first officers. Because Dewey sensed tremendous potential
in the Lake Placid Club he regularly overextended himself financially by building a complex set of interconnected obligations.
For example, his conviction that the club idea would be a quick
success led him to pay for certain improvements by encumbering funds anticipated from an increased membership. In 1895 he
also set up a dummy corporation called the Placid Boat Company, through which he channeled purchases by Club members
for items like furniture and boats. He then joined the Placid Boat
Company's bank account with his own, and drew money from it
to accelerate his acquisition of property. His goal was to generate
a Club membership of 100, which, he believed, would put the
Club on a firmer financial foundation. And because of his obsessive desire to buy up land around the Club's grounds to keep
away "undesirables," he encouraged Club members to lease adjacent land and promised to pay them for it at market value plus 8
percent in five years.[37]

The dispute with Club officers can be traced to conflicting
goals. In order to protect their interests and guard against the
possibility that the Deweys would sell the land out from under
them, Club officers felt the Club needed to own the property on
which it existed; but the Deweys felt they needed to own the
property to make sure their goals for the Club were never modified. At a business meeting late in 1896, several Club officers
recommended that the Club incorporate and proposed that

36. Scores of letters inviting people to consider Club membership
can be found in LB 7/2/94–11/5/95, Box 91, Dewey Mss. See also Placid
Club 1895 Member's Handbook; and Godfrey Dewey, "Sixty Years of Lake
Placid Club, 1895–1955," (Lake Placid, N.Y., 1955), p. 3.

37. See Jared Newman to Dewey and Jenks, 8/30/95, Box 51;
Newman to Dewey, 10/28/95, Box 58, Dewey Mss. For an account of how
Dewey used the Placid Boat Company in his business transactions with the
Club, see Jenks to Dewey, 2/20/97, Box 49, Dewey Mss.

Dewey sell some land to Club members under Club restrictions. Because they also thought the Club should have some control over Club property in order to raise capital necessary to improve the physical plant, they asked Dewey to discern the market value of the property he and Annie owned. Dewey, who had been very uncomfortable with the direction of the conversation, responded by insisting the property was not for sale. Club officers persisted. Was there not some price at which the Deweys would give up their plan? Dewey's anger flashed; he suggested Club officers' action and persistence amounted to a form of "blackmail." The meeting broke up on sour note. Club officers, especially Jenks, were suspicious of the Morningside Company's financial status. Dewey sensed a conspiracy to subvert the plans he and Annie had for the Club, and he was especially suspicious of Jenks.

An open fight was averted, however, when at a June 1 meeting both sides reached an "understanding." Dewey agreed "to consider" selling the Club any land he and Annie owned at appraised value. In 1896 Club officers had no experience with Dewey's tendency to interpret any "understanding" to his own advantage, and then hold to that interpretation against any opposition. In Dewey's eyes, the agreement changed nothing between the Company and the Club it supported.[38] Not so for Club members. In anticipation of future purchases, they incorporated as "Placid Club Morningside" on April 25 and began ordering furniture and other goods worth over $10,000 through Dewey's Placid Boat Company. They then elected a board of trustees and three weeks later trustees elected officers. As these meetings took place, Dewey gave the impression he felt comfortable with the direction the Club was taking.[39]

Unbeknown to Club trustees, however, Dewey had figured out several ways to subvert their intentions. First, the money they paid the Placid Boat Company for goods and furniture Dewey used to buy options on more property, all the while holding Boat Company creditors at bay. By the beginning of summer properties Dewey bought in the name of his Morningside Company

38. This "understanding" is summarized in Place to Dewey, 9/21/96, Box 58, Dewey Mss.

39. See Jenks circular entitled "Placid Club," 3/18/96, Box 58; Placid Club Constitution dated 4/17/96, copy found in Box 47; Dewey to Albert Shaw, 4/27/96; Dewey to Clark, 4/29/96, Box 91; and Jenks to "Dear Sir," 5/13/96, Box 53, Dewey Mss.

tripled the size of its shoreline access, added 300 acres of forest, and included several new buildings. All of these acquisitions pushed the size of the tracts available for Club use to nearly a thousand acres. In addition, he began constructing a new dining room at Bonniblink capable of seating 100 people. In effect, Dewey was using his Placid Boat Company accounts to obtain Club members' money to purchase control of enough adjacent property to deny them opportunities to buy it. Second, Dewey also actively campaigned for people close to him to invest in his Company. Hannah P. James, for example, committed $435 to build and furnish a lodge. In return, Dewey promised her use of the lodge free of charge until 1899, when he would repay her $435 investment plus 8 percent. It was a standard set of terms under which Dewey enrolled people close to him whose interests he wished to control, and another means to check efforts by Club members to buy Company land.[40]

Then on September 2, Dewey wrote Club treasurer Jenks with an offer to sell the Club all the land his Company owned at cost, except for several tracts "not intended for Club ownership." The latter included areas Dewey had planned for a new club-house larger than Bonniblink, and golf links. Club officers were startled by Dewey's offer. It was their "understanding" that Dewey had been purchasing property "for the Club, and in its interest, and that you had no other conflicting plans." Dewey's September 2 offer did not accord with their interpretation of the June 1 "understanding." It appeared to them Dewey was now willing to sever his connections with the Club, and start another Club on property his Company retained after dealing the remainder to Placid Club Morningside. But Dewey obviously took a different slant on the June 1 "understanding." What followed thereafter was a battle of interpretations.[41]

---

40. See Holls to Dewey, 8/29/96, Box 14, Holls Mss; Dewey to Sprague, 4/24/91, Box 91; James to Dewey, 6/1/96; 6/6/96; 7/7/96; 7/16/96, Box 4, Dewey Mss. See also Dewey's handwritten receipt of the $435, dated, 7/15/96, which outlined the terms of his agreement with James, in Box 4; Jenks to Dewey, 2/20/97; 2/27/97; 3/9/97, Box 49, Dewey Mss.

41. The chronology leading to this late-summer dilemma has been reconstructed from subsequent correspondence. See especially Jenks to Dewey, 9/9/96, Box 48; and Dewey to Mabie, 9/15/96, Box 58, Dewey Mss. See also Place to Dewey, 9/21/96; and a circular sent by Club trustees Mabie, Jenks, Place, Shaw, Kates, and Mairs "To the Members of the Placid Club," dated 3/12/97, Box 58, Dewey Mss. The circular gives some of the background from the perspective of Club officers.

For more than a month the two sides battled. Jenks claimed "the sole cause of the misunderstanding between you and the Club is . . . your way of doing things." Dewey, on the other hand, argued that because "it was *my private property*" he could protect the Club "against sanitariums, cheap boarding houses, stables and other undesirable neighbors." Club officers tried to buy the eighty-five acres under and around Bonniblink, but Dewey refused to sell it.[42] In mid-October, however, Dewey proposed an alternative. He offered to pay off all Club debts, relieve members of personal responsibilities and refund everyone's money if the Club agreed to surrender any claims to buying property, and allow him to continue the Club under his original plan. Because their loyalty to the Club was not great enough to counter the prospect of a prolonged fight, and because Dewey's persistence and intransigence had simply worn them down, Club trustees agreed to accept. On January 16, 1897, Dewey and Club officers reached tentative agreement on a final settlement. Club trustees consented to sell all Club property to Dewey's Morningside Company at 80 percent of its net cost (or $6,400). In return, Dewey forgave notes totalling $4,650 and agreed to pay the balance of $1,750 directly to the Club to settle the dispute.[43]

Even before the agreement was signed, however, Dewey organized a new entity—the Placid Park Club. Trustees included Melvil and Annie Dewey, Hannah James, W. E. Parker and H. E. Davidson. "Bonniblink" was changed to "Lakesyd," and each new member was requested to sign an agreement. "I understand that my election is to the social and cooperative privileges of the Placid Park Club," the agreement read, "and not to the responsibilities and powers which by the constitution are limited to the life members, who are the owners and managers of the entire club property."[44] A March 12 circular to Placid Club Morningside members explained the new circumstances. Inserting the word "park" into the title, the circular said, would be "more suggestive of the original plan to keep the whole of Morningside as a private park."

---

42. Jenks to Dewey, 9/9/96, Box 48; Dewey to Hamilton Mabie, 9/-/96, Box 32; Place to Dewey, 9/21/96 (2), Box 58, Dewey Mss.

43. The formal agreement was signed March 12, 1897. See Trustees Circular "To Members of the Placid Club," 3/12/97, Box 58, Dewey Mss.

44. Copy of an undated circular titled "Important to Members" listing Placid Park Club officers can be found in Box 52, Dewey Mss. See also "Placid Park Club Members Agreement" LPEF Mss; and *Placid Park Club Handbook,* 1897, pp. 6–7.

Actually, Dewey's choice of title was more calculated. By giving the new club a name so similar to the old, he intended to capitalize on the Placid Club's growing reputation when he approached potential new members. And once he got their attention he could promise a club *and* location. In March 1897, Placid Club Morningside could only offer a club. The circular pressed the point. "The new club believes that its members will dislike to give any of their vacation hours to details of club housekeeping or to financial cares," Dewey wrote, "and will much prefer to leave both discussion and action on these matters to the few life members who furnish all the capital and take all the risk."[45] Dewey then invited Placid Club Morningside members to join the Placid Park Club. Most did. Membership records for 1898 show Place, Jenks, Shaw, Laughlin, and Mabie on the list.

One thing did not change, however. When Albert H. Harris of New York City requested a cottage for his family for August 1899, Dewey responded that the Placid Park Club did not admit Jews. "Personally, many of my choicest friends are Jews," he wrote August 6, "but the majority of the club made the rule and we have no power to vary from it, so of course it ends the matter." His answer to Harris was evasive. Dewey's victory of 1897 guaranteed that no rule passed the Placid Park Club without his support. No matter the wishes of individual members, Annie and Melvil Dewey would control the Club on their terms. "It is like Paradise Regained that Mr. Dewey and I are now free to carry out this experiment in altruism in our own way," Annie Dewey wrote Lucy Salmon on May 17, "free from the spirit which so nearly wrecked everything last summer."[46]

---

45. That Placid Club Morningside trustees recognized what Dewey was doing is evident from a separate notice they attached to their own March 12 circular. "The Trustees of the Club have, and have had, no part in forming Mr. Dewey's plans set forth in his circular letter of March 12, 1897, to the members," it stated. See Dewey "To the Members of the Placid Club of 1896," 3/12/97, Box 47; and Club trustees Mabie, Jenks, Place, Shaw, Kates, and Mairs "To the Members of the Placid Club," 3/12/97, Box 58, Dewey Mss.

46. Dewey "To the Trustees of the Placid Club," 4/13/97, Box 49; Butler to Dewey, 5/28/97, Box 75; Mabie to Annie Dewey, 6/2/97, Box 20A; Shaw to Dewey, 7/26/97, Box 49; Annie Dewey to Salmon, 5/17/97, Box 19, Dewey Mss. A letter of 12/9/98 from Jenks to Dewey lists the following as members: Lucy Salmon, Ira Place, M. Hayward Post, James B. Reynolds, Hester P. Jenks, Albert Shaw, Daniel C. Young, Hannah P. James, Emily I. Alexander, Mary W. Plummer, J. L. Harrison, John B. Clark, Herman M.

Plate 16. Dewey's woes were mounting in 1905, and there were more to come after this July trip to Alaska, following ALA's conference in Portland, Oregon. Since January he had faced widely publicized charges of anti-Semitism at his Lake Placid Club; his wife was seriously ill; he was under pressure to resign as New York State Librarian; his financial situation was precarious. And during the postconference trip he behaved toward women in a manner that would later cause a stir. In this photo, he posed with other early ALA presidents, including (from left) John Cotton Dana, Ernest Cushing Richardson, Frank Pierce Hill, Frederick Morgan Crunden, and Henry James Carr.

Plates 17–19. Two domestic scenes at Lake Placid Club (below): With Annie, ca. 1911, and Godfrey, ca. 1907. In 1911 a matter of Club financing "drove a wedge between Dewey and his son, from which neither fully recovered." Godfrey devoted much of his life to spelling reform and was instrumental in bringing the 1932 Winter Olympics to Lake Placid. (Opposite) Part of the Club property in 1922 (across lake).

Plate 20 (below).   Annie at play at Lake Placid, about five years before her death in 1922. The "passenger" is unidentified.

Plate 21 (right).   Apparently Dewey in costume for a Lake Placid Club event, ca. 1912.

Plate 23 (below).   Dewey at Lake Placid in 1924, a year the Club was enjoying unprecedented success.

Plate 22 (above).   Kate Crunden and R. R. Bowker, two players in Dewey's life, at a 1923 ALA Conference. It was Crunden who warned Dewey in 1903 that Henry Leipziger, in a show of "bad taste," was planning to retaliate for being barred from the Lake Placid Club as a Jew. Leipziger did indeed trigger the petition that led to Dewey's decline in Albany. R. R. Bowker, publisher of *Library Journal,* was often at odds with Dewey, but in the end lauded him for his forethought, energies, and "inventive genius."

Plate 24 (below).   A 1927 photo labeled "A happy trio of Deweys" and marked on the reverse, "A Merry Xmas." The women appear to be, on Dewey's left, his daughter-in-law Marjorie, and on his right, Emily Beal Dewey, whom he had married in 1924, twenty-one months after Annie's death. Emily had been a good friend of the couple and a Club staff member. She was a devoted companion and business partner in Dewey's last years.

Plate 25 (right).   A later photo of Emily Beal Dewey.

Plate 26. Litlloj or "Lake Placid South," the Florida resort venture and last home of Melvil and Emily Dewey.

Plate 27. "Mr. Dewey and his Dot," a trademark developed by OCLC Online Computer Library Center, Inc., to market the Dewey Decimal Classification. OCLC purchased Forest Press, publisher of the DDC for eight decades, in 1988. Under OCLC supervision the DDC has prospered and expanded in its formats and applications. The cartoon figures, created by OCLC staff artist Mickey Hawk, appear as characters in a range of promotional materials. © OCLC Online Computer Library Center.

In 1899 Dewey claimed assets of $44,000 worth of Library Bureau stock and $30,000 worth of real estate in Albany (including 315 Madison Avenue and five other houses). His largest interests, however, were in Lake Placid, where he owned $21,000 worth of personal property and $49,900 worth of real estate. He identified Annie Dewey's assets at $30,000, spread over Library Bureau stock and property in Albany and Lake Placid. Taken together, Melvil and Annie Dewey's estate consisted of 1,671 acres and 45 buildings. The Deweys claimed liabilities of $40,000 in real estate loans, and $18,000 on a loan due Vassar College. As the twentieth century approached, Melvil and Annie Dewey owned considerably more than they had twenty years earlier. While they could justifiably claim wealth, they continually rolled their income back into their pet reform schemes. In fact, Dewey regularly overextended himself by using (and often mixing) family assets as collateral for short-term loans to fund improvements already undertaken. Because they were so impatient to realize their goals, the Deweys perpetually lived on the edge of solvency. On May 7, 1903, for example, Dewey pressed William Parker to sell some of his Bureau stock quickly so he could meet his weekly payroll at Lake Placid. "It keeps me shaking out all my old clothes looking for stray pennies," he quipped, "and I have nearly worn out the clothes."[47] Still, the Deweys pushed forward, firmly convinced that because their course was right, any sensitive creditor or business associate would readily understand and forgive their unconventional practices.

Progress in developing the physical plant and the club accelerated at the turn of the century. In 1900 ownership was

---

Biggs, Elizabeth Harvey, Homer Folks, Mary Harvey, E. R. L. Gould, Jared Newman, Chauncey P. Biggs, D. W. Burdick, D. O. Esbaugh, J. W. Jenks, Clarence Sears Kates, Charles H. Wilcox, Mrs. S. E. Tuckerman, H. E. Davidson, Melvil Dewey, Lydia Godfrey, F. W. Holls, W. B. Holland, W. E. Parker, May Seymour, Florence Woodworth, Myrtilla Avery, J. Lawrence Laughlin, Helen Moore, Francis H. Stoddard, Hamilton Mabie, Thomas B. Adams, N. M. Butler, Edwin H. Mairs, and William J. Milne. It is probable that the dues of several people in the list (like Butler) were carried by Dewey in order to boost the image of Club membership that Dewey wanted to create. See also Albert Harris to Dewey, 8/5/99; 8/6/99; and 8/8/99; Dewey to Albert Harris, 8/7/99; 8/8/99, Box 70, Dewey Mss; and *Placid Park Club, Morningside, Lake Placid, New York,* p. 19.

47. A copy of Dewey's 1899 financial statement, labeled "Personal" and found in correspondence of 1898 and 1899, can be found in Box 38, Dewey Mss. See also Dewey to Parker, 5/7/03, Box 63, Dewey Mss.

formally consolidated under the name "Lake Placid Company," and the Club itself reassumed its original name—"Lake Placid Club." Common stockholders drew no dividends; all earnings were rolled back into improving and expanding the physical plant. A Lake Placid Club promotion pamphlet dated March 5, 1901, noted that the "chief charm and safeguard of the club" was based on an "invariable rule that satisfactory introductions must precede all first visits." References had to be obtained from "university or college officers, clergymen, librarians, and well known literary and professional men" who constituted Club membership. By that date the Club had an Advisory Council (elected in part by the membership, in part by the trustees) whose job it was to resolve "questions involving social privileges of members, initiations, amusements, entertainments, house rules, ethical standards and such other matters as are chiefly determined by personal preferences."

The Club handbook for 1901 also identified that "club plans are shaped by prominent workers in the new science of home economics, who hold their annual conferences at the club." Annie Dewey had joined with Ellen H. Richards of the Massachusetts Institute of Technology to organize a Lake Placid Conference on Home Economics in 1899, an event that with two exceptions was made annual thereafter until 1910 and eventually led to formation of the American Home Economics Association in 1908. The Deweys liked the kind of people the conference brought to the Club—middle-class, mostly WASP, women forging a new profession serving the interests of the masses. Melvil regularly greeted conferees and frequently lectured on libraries and home education. Annie Dewey was more active, in large part because she looked to develop a model community of home economics efficiency at Lake Placid. "A leading purpose is to show practically that the most attractiv home and table may also in the highest degree illustrate the teaching of modern science as to health and home comforts." For a while, Dewey even considered Richards' recommendation to move "Domestic Economy" (640) from a subheading under "Useful Arts" (600) in the Decimal Classification to a more prestigious location in "Sociology" between "Political Economy" (330) and "Law" (340).[48]

---

48. Membership pamphlet dated 3/5/01, Box 1, LPEF Mss; Lake Placid Club *Handbook, 1901,* pp. 5–6; copy of Club employee contract

As for the Club itself, added to the annual "Float" and "Iroquois Indian Council Fire" nights and the weekly lakeshore fire was a regular Sunday evening gathering to sing favorite Protestant hymns. In 1903 the Club introduced the automobile to the Adirondacks by purchasing three cars, one of which was a three-cylinder Thomas Flyer with a canopy top. Godfrey Dewey became the Club's chief mechanic and chauffeur; in 1904 he made the trip from Albany to Lake Placid in only twelve hours, a speed so rapid local papers commented on the marvel of it all.[49] In October 1904, LPC Treasurer Asa O. Gallup mailed a circular to members and guests of the Club on the occasion of its tenth season. He noted that the Club now boasted its own fire department and a new fire engine, an eighteen-hole golf course, and a new Club launch that was the largest and fastest on the lake. Four new cottages would be ready for the next season, but Gallup also reminded members and guests that certain quarters would be open during the winter. The only thing preventing even greater growth was lack of capital. "If every club member would invest $1,000 in the company's first mortgage 5 per cent gold coupon bonds or in its 6 per cent preferred stock," Gallup said, "it would provide capital for all needed additions and improvements."[50] Because of Dewey's persistence and irrepressible spirit, the Lake Placid Club had survived its first decade and his dream was still intact. But as a result of past behavior his world was about to change radically, and not for the better.

---

dated 3/5/02, Box 1, LPEF Mss; Dewey to Gallup, 11/12/01, Box 53, Dewey Mss. See also a typescript copy of Annie Dewey's 1903 speech to the Conference on Home Economics entitled "The Ethical Side of Home Economics," Box 23, Dewey Mss. See also *Lake Placid Club Yearbook, 1928* (Lake Placid, N.Y., 1928), p. 3; "Notes on Lake Placid Co Financial Program for 1910," n.d., FPA; "Home Economics," *American Kitchen Magazine* 13 (1900): 177–79; 223–26; Laura Shapiro, *Perfection Salad: Women and Cooking at the Turn of the Century* (N.Y., 1986), pp. 176–82; Emma Seifrit Weigley, "It Might Have Been Euthenics: The Lake Placid Conferences and the Home Economics Movement," *American Quarterly,* 26 (1974): 79–96; and Comaromi, p. 252. Ultimately, Dewey decided to keep "Domestic Economy" at 640, but in the next edition expanded the schedule to eleven pages.

    49. Godfrey Dewey, "Sixty Years of Lake Placid Club," pp. 5–6; Carroll, *Lake Placid,* p. 34.

    50. Circular, Gallup "To Members and Guests," n.d., Box 1, LPEF Mss. The first winter season is described in *LPC News* 3 (12/20/29): 420.

12

"Jew Attack"

1905

Beginning in 1899, the New York Library Association held an annual "Library Week" at Dewey's Lake Placid Club the end of September. All NYLA members were invited, and those attending were also invited to use Club services and facilities while on Club grounds. At the 1903 "Library Week," New York Public Library Circulation Committee member Henry M. Leipziger and a friend were waiting in the "Lakesyd" lobby when his friend picked up a 1901 Club catalog. As he paged through it, his eye caught a paragraph he then showed to Leipziger. "No one shall be received as member or guest, against whom there is physical, moral, social or race objection." The paragraph concluded: "It is found impracticable to make exceptions to Jews or others excluded, even when of unusual personal qualifications."

Leipziger flushed. In previous years he had asked Dewey several times about Club membership, but Dewey repeatedly told Leipziger he had no control over admissions and advised him to write the Club for membership literature. On one occasion, Leipziger had written the Club to request rooms for himself, his sister, and his mother, but was turned down because he needed a personal privilege card from a member. Not until his friend showed him the 1901 circular did he fully realize why he was being denied. He responded loudly that he "would trouble the place no longer," and left Club grounds an angry man.

A year later Leipziger was spending his summer vacation at the Lake Placid Inn, a public hotel a short distance from Club grounds, when on a village street he met Kate Crunden, wife of the St. Louis Public Library Director. When she asked Leipziger if he would be coming to "Library Week" in September, he responded angrily he could not: "Mr. Dewey had barred all Jews from the club no matter how unusual in personal qualifications." "That seemed to hurt him," Crunden later told Annie Dewey, and then she related what she described as Leipziger's commitment to getting Dewey fired as State Librarian. Shortly thereafter she also told Dewey about the "bad taste" Leipziger "had just shown in displaying his temper," and warned Dewey to watch for retaliation. Dewey had already heard the same from other quarters, however. On several occasions in previous months Leipziger had been overheard to say "We now have a Jew on the Board of Regents [Edward Lauterbach, appointed in 1904] and I will show Dewey that he can not leave me out." But Dewey ignored Leipziger's threats.[1]

In the fall of 1904 Leipziger took his complaint to Louis Marshall, a prominent Jewish New York City lawyer. Marshall shared Leipziger's disgust for anti-Semitic practices in Adirondack hotels, but was especially angry that a private club excluding Jews was being run by a public official. He believed that because of Dewey's public position his exclusionary practices gave other clubs and hotels additional courage to make "restricted" part of the Adirondack lexicon. He decided to make an issue of Dewey's connection to the Club by filing a petition with the Regents calling for Dewey's removal. First, however, he settled on a plan. "I am starting now on the warpath," he wrote Edgar Nathan on November 28. He began gathering Club documents, publications, and stationery, and wrote the New York Secretary of State for a copy of the Club's articles of incorporation. He also asked a friend,

---

1. Evidence presented here is compiled from two sources: Kate Crunden to Annie Dewey, 1/23/05, Box 70, Dewey Mss; and a lengthy transcript of a Regents' Library Committee hearing held in Albany 2/2/05, and found in Reel 201, Reid Mss. Rules barring Jews were commonplace among Adirondack resorts at the turn of the century and long thereafter. See, for example, Stephen Birmingham, *"Our Crowd": The Great Jewish Families of New York* (N.Y., 1967), pp. 146–47; Harvey Kaiser, *Great Camps in the Adirondacks* (Boston, 1982), p. 135; and William Chapman White, *Adirondack Country* (Syracuse, 1985), pp. 138–39.

William C. Taylor, to write the Club asking for information about membership and organization.

Taylor initiated a correspondence with Club Treasurer Asa Gallup, who first sent him literature, but in answer to a second inquiry enclosed a personal letter identifying its President as Melvil Dewey, "probably the most famous librarian in the world." Taylor then wrote Dewey at his State Library office. He quoted Gallup's compliment and asked if he would be liable for any Club debts should he wish to join. Dewey responded from his office six days later, assured Taylor he would be liable for no Club debts, then commented on Gallup's compliment. "He clearly meant it simply to show that in its founding and management it had always been in the hands of cultivated people with high standards, and not of hotel keepers or mere moneymakers."[2] After he received Dewey's response, Taylor turned all the correspondence with the Club and Dewey over to Marshall.

By the end of December Marshall was ready. He drafted a petition to the Regents calling for Dewey's dismissal, and on December 20 circulated it to several prominent New York City Jews for comment and signature. To Jacob Schiff he also wrote: "I have discussed the matter with Mr. Lauterbach, who assures me that the proceeding meets with his entire approval, and that it will receive most favorable consideration."[3]

On January 3, 1905, Marshall sent the petition signed by himself, Schiff, Nathan, Adolph Lewisohn, Daniel Guggenheimer, Isidor Straus, Henry B. Ickelheimer, Nathan Bijur, Cyrus L. Sulzberger, Adolph S. Ochs, and Abraham Abraham to Regents' Chancellor Whitelaw Reid with copies to Commissioner Andrew Sloan Draper and Dewey. "For some years," the petition said, "Mr. Dewey has been the leading and guiding spirit of the Lake Placid Company," which had wide-ranging business interests and several internal departments. One was the "Lake Placid Club,"

---

2. Information gleaned from Edgar Nathan to Marshall, 11/28/04, Box 151; Marshall to Nathan, 11/28/04; Marshall to New York Secretary of State John F. O'Brien, 12/3/04, Box 1573, Marshall Mss; Taylor to Gallup, 11/28/04; Taylor to Dewey, 12/7/04; Dewey to Taylor, 12/13/04, Box 70, Dewey Mss; Regents Library Committee Hearing, 2/2/05, Reel 201, Reid Mss.

3. Marshall to Schiff, 12/20/04; Marshall to Cyrus Sulzberger, 12/22/04, Box 1573, Marshall Mss. See also Marshall to Simon Rosendale, 12/27/04; Marshall to Ochs, 12/20/04, Box 1573, Marshall Mss.

which "constitutes the hotel, for the conduct of which the corporation was organized." For years the Club had been issuing circulars and publications, and because all its literature was written in simplified spelling the literature itself represented "irrefragable evidence . . . Mr. Dewey is the author."

Petitioners then quoted the paragraph Leipziger found so objectionable. They also noted 750,000 Jews lived in New York State, Jews who paid taxes from which Dewey's salary was being drawn, Jews who were being insulted by his exclusionary practices. Petitioners were not taking issue with the club's exclusionary practices, they said, but when "a high public official" could "spread broadcast through the land a publication which tends to make of the Hebrew an outcast and a pariah of the State," Regents had an obligation not to "allow an infamous precedent to be established."

Chancellor Reid recognized the hot potato just dumped in his lap. Although Marshall asked that the petition be discussed at the next Regents meeting, Reid decided to accept the petition and assign it "informally and unofficially for the confidential consideration of the Library Committee."[4]

The petition became public when it was formally presented at the January 18 Regents' meeting, and for the next several days New York's newspapers were filled with the story. Most reported the incident dispassionately by sticking to details outlined in the petition. Officially, the Regents and Draper would say nothing to the press pending the hearing before the Library Committee. Albert Vander Veer, Chairman of the committee that also included St. Clair McKelway and Pliny Sexton, did ask Dewey to submit a statement replying to Marshall's petition, and scheduled a closed hearing for February 2.[5]

Dewey prepared the statement, but on January 23—two days before he sent it to Vander Veer—he issued a copy to the press. Several papers, including the *New York Times,* the *Albany Evening Journal,* and the *Buffalo Express* ran the reply verba-

---

4. Marshall to Reid, 1/3/05, Box 1574; Reid to Marshall, 1/6/05, Box 16, Marshall Mss; and Reid to Draper, 1/6/05, Reel 93, Reid Mss. Both the *NYT* and the *NYTr,* 1/21/05, reprinted the petition in its entirety.

5. See *Albany Sunday Telegram,* 1/22/05; *Saratoga Sun,* 1/23/05; *Ithaca News,* 1/21/05; *Utica Herald-Dispatch,* 1/21/05; *Rochester Union,* 1/21/05; *Elmira Gazette,* 1/21/05. The *Albany Argus* could get no immediate statements from the Regents, Draper, or Dewey. See *Argus* 1/23/05.

ASK REGENTS TO DEPOSE STATE LIBRARIAN DEWEY

His Company Runs Hotel, Called a Club, Which Bars Jews.

OFFICE AS ADVERTISEMENT

So Used in Circulars Sent Out Describing Enterprise, the Petitioners Allege.

Through Chancellor Whitelaw Reid on Wednesday was presented a petition to the Regents of the University of the State of New York asking for the removal of Melvil Dewey, State Librarian. The petition, which was referred to the Library Committee for investigation, was as follows:

"Your petitioners respectfully ask for the removal from office of Melvil Dewey, the present State Librarian, whose tenure of office is dependent upon your action.

"We are not unmindful of the serious nature of our application, and will, therefore, proceed to state the facts on which we base the conclusion that he has disqualified himself from continuing as the incumbent of the important position which he occupies.

"Mr. Dewey is the President of the

DID NOT USE POSITION TO BOOM CLUB---DEWEY

State Librarian's Defense Against Charges of Jews.

ADMITS JEWISH EXCLUSION

But Declares the Lake Placid Club Strictly a Social Organization, and Not a Hotel in Any Sense.

Special to The New York Times.

ALBANY, Jan. 24.—Melvil Dewey, Director of the State Library, to-night made the reply which he had sent to the Library Committee's Board of Regents, in answer to a request from the committee by Jewish citizens that, while using his official position to advertise the Lake Placid Club, he was a party to a rule of that Jews should not be received at the club's hotel. Director Dewey's answer to the committee is as ...

... the request of the Chairman I submit statement about the petition for ... oval because Jews are exclud ...

Charges of anti-Semitism were splashed across the headlines—including those of a *New York Times* story of January 21, 1905—as petitioners called for Dewey's dismissal from public office. The newspaper ran Dewey's response on January 25.

tim. In it Dewey was unrepentive. Yes, it was true the Club had not admitted Jews from its founding, but Dewey said the paragraph quoted in Marshall's petition was designed to clarify Club rules to avoid embarrassment, especially for Jews who might think they merited consideration because they were "cultivated and desirable." Dewey then referred to a "threat" made to a Club member by a New York Jew "from which this petition has doubtless come. . . . to punish me because he was excluded." Dewey never condoned race or faith prejudice "officially," and as evidence, indicated he had over the years invited many Jews to his home. He also argued that from its origins the Club had been a social organization "limited to its members and those regularly introduced as in other clubs." Even Marshall's petition recognized the Club's right to restrict membership. "Except for the exclusion of Jews," he concluded, "all allegations enumerated in the petition do not accord with the facts." Dewey may have convinced himself, but he did not convince Marshall. "Dewey has played into my hands," Marshall told a friend, "and I shall prove not only that he is a fool, but a liar as well."[6]

Public pressure began to build against Dewey from a variety of sources. In a January 25 letter to the editor of the *New York Tribune* Rabbi Bernard Drachman called Dewey's statement "about as painful a bit of reading as it has ever been my misfortune to peruse." The *Middleton Daily Times* called it "racial tommyrot." The *Brooklyn Eagle* took a different approach; it castigated Dewey for the amount of time he spent away from Albany managing and monitoring the Club.[7] Dewey had no immediate public defenders except for Funk and Wagnalls' I. K. Funk, the Protestant publisher of the multivolume *Jewish Encyclopedia* just then coming out, who had worked with Dewey on the *Century Dictionary* and was an ally in Dewey's efforts to get Andrew Carnegie to fund a simplified spelling office. "He has exhibited, in all my dealings with him, not the slightest trace of Jewish prejudice," Funk told the *Sun* February 1, and warned that "the success of this anti-Dewey petition will be a defeat for the Jew" because it would actually increase race prejudice.

Privately, Funk was feeding Dewey information given him by Isidore Singer, editor-in-chief of the *Jewish Encyclopedia.* On February 2 Funk hinted that Marshall and his cohorts had laid a trap for Dewey by means of a decoy letter. "Trace this hint . . . I think you will find that a trick has been played on you." Funk also said that many "prominent" Jews had thanked him for writing the *Sun.* He further suggested to Dewey that Singer was especially supportive. Because Funk's correspondence convinced Dewey that Marshall and his cohorts had only limited support

---

6. Copy of Dewey's statement, dated 1/25/05, in Box 70, Dewey Mss. See also Marshall to Wollman, 1/25/05; Marshall to H. W. Rosenbaum, 1/25/05; Marshall to Lowenstein, 1/27/05, Box 1574; Marshall to Dewey, 1/27/05, Box 151, Marshall Mss.

7. Drachman "To the Editor of the Tribune," *NYTr,* 1/29/05; *Middleton Daily Times,* 2/1/05; *Eagle,* 2/1/05. See also *Syracuse Post Standard,* 1/20/05.

from New York's Jewish community for their "attack," he felt confident going into the hearing.[8]

The Library Committee met in closed session on February 2. Marshall represented petitioners; Dewey represented himself. Marshall began his examination by asking Dewey about stock he owned in the Lake Placid Company and the Lake Placid Club. Dewey explained he and his family owned one share more than the controlling vote on both preferred and common stock, and that they were under contract to maintain that control with "certain other people who invested their money on that condition." Who owns the buildings on which the Club stands? asked Marshall. The Company owns everything, Dewey replied. Does the Club have books? asked Marshall. No, responded Dewey, the Club had a council of seven members who "meet and discuss questions of policy and pass questions of votes and transmit them to the superintendent to be carried out." How many members at last count? About 148 families, paying dues of $10.00 per year. What is done with the dues? The money was used for Club entertainments. Who keeps track of that money? The Company and its employees. Was the Club a department of the Company then? "It would be truer to say that the Company is a department of the Club."

Marshall then switched his line of questioning. "Who passes on the persons proposed for membership in the Club?" The Council, Dewey replied. Any member could issue a "privilege card" to a personal friend good for two weeks. Two members by written consent could introduce a personal friend for one year. No one was elected to membership "until he has spent one year at the Club." Who prepared the Club literature? "A half-dozen different people." What about the exclusionary paragraphs quoted in the petition? "I think it was originally written by Professor Jenks of Cornell." What about the spelling of the words "consumptiv," "thru," and "offensiv"? "I hope I am to blame for that," Dewey answered. "You have impressed your individuality upon it to that extent?" Marshall asked. "I think so," Dewey admitted.

---

8. Funk "To the Editor," 2/1/05, New York *Sun,* 2/2/05. See also Funk to Dewey, 1/30/05; Dewey to Funk, 2/1/05; Funk to Dewey 2/2/05; Dewey to Funk, 2/4/05, Box 70, Dewey Mss. The colorful history of the publication of the *Jewish Encyclopedia* is nicely detailed in Shuly Rubin Schwarz, *The Emergence of Jewish Scholarship in America: The Publication of the "Jewish Encyclopedia"* (Cincinnati, 1991).

Marshall then focused more carefully on the rule excluding Jews. Had it been strictly enforced? Yes, Dewey responded. Did Dewey host professional conferences at the Club? Indeed, answered Dewey, and because invitations were sent to every member of the associations, "Jews have never been discriminated against." Outside of these conferences, Marshall continued, Jews were not permitted at the Club? "Even after all this most unfortunate discussion," Dewey responded, "I do not think they would elect a Jew to the Lake Placid Club." Even Mr. Lauterbach? Marshall asked. Even Mr. Lauterbach, Dewey responded. But Dewey owned a controlling interest in the institution, and still "you would not feel that you could change" the attitude of the Club, even for Mr. Lauterbach? "No, I would have no right," Dewey answered; it was a Club rule.

Again Marshall switched his line of questioning. Did Dewey transact Club business while in Albany? Yes, Dewey replied, but the vast majority was conducted out of his private home at 315 Madison Avenue. And what if someone inquired of Dewey at his office about Club dues and rules? Normally, Dewey said, he would forward all inquiries to Lake Placid. "Invariably?" Marshall asked. "Perhaps not invariably—if the inquirer were a person well known to me I might write him a letter." Then Marshall sprung his trap. "Do you know Mr. William C. Taylor of New York?" Dewey smiled; Funk had forewarned him about this. "I have heard of him." Marshall quickly produced the exchange of correspondence between Taylor and Gallup, and Dewey jumped at the chance to explain. The only time Gallup ever mentioned that Dewey was State Librarian in Club correspondence was when Taylor asked directly who Dewey was, he said. He now understood the purpose of Taylor's inquiry. "It is a decoy letter . . . and we fell into the trap. . . . You will pardon my laughing. It was certainly a very clever decoy." Marshall retorted, "Sometimes these things are necessary with certain people."

Marshall then pressed Dewey on his accusation that the petition was the result of one Jew's revenge. Dewey responded he was sure Leipziger was the source of the problem, but Marshall asked whether Dewey thought any of the petitioners also had a legitimate complaint about the Club's exclusionary practices. Dewey sidestepped the question. He cited a letter published in the New York *Sun* the previous day by Isidore Singer, "one of the most prominent Jews in the City of New York," deploring petitioners' action, then asked Marshall, "Is Mr. Taylor a Jew?" When Marshall responded "No," Dewey replied, "I thought not. Mr. Gallup and I fell into that trap without suspicion. It was very cleverly done (smiling)." Marshall bristled: "But I do not look at it in so jocular a vein as you do, Mr. Dewey." Dewey then played to his audience. "I have no desire to make light of the matter, Mr. Marshall. I feel the seriousness of it, and deplore the annoyance to the Regents, more than I can say." After Marshall presented copies of correspondence between Dewey, Taylor, and Gallup, he told the Library Committee he had no further evidence to offer.

Vander Veer then asked Dewey if he had anything to say. Dewey began by disavowing prejudice against Jews. "I have never in my life had any of this feeling. I have always despised it." He told the committee he had originally invested in Lake Placid because the allergies he and his wife suffered forced them to seek a more hospitable environment for two months each summer. Once they decided on a club structure rather than a hotel, he and his wife felt they had to honor Club rules as determined by a membership board. He hinted at a concession to the unpleasant situation in which he found himself by indicating that although he would still be willing to serve as a Club director in the future, he would not accept reelection as president of the trustees. Thereafter he turned to Marshall. "I may smile, Mr. Marshall, but you have hit me very hard. It was cleverly done and I give you all credit. I have always said the Jewish race was the smartest on earth." He told the Committee he had gone as far as he thought Club members would allow him, and apologized that the Regents "have had the humiliation of this discussion. I think if Mr. Marshall had gotten the facts instead of having me pilloried as an anti-Semite, he would have found that I am absolutely free from prejudice." But Marshall would not let Dewey's conclusion go unchallenged. Dewey was not a "mere member" of the Lake Placid Club, he said, "he is the Club—the whole institution. He holds the controlling vote." He should not be allowed to "shelter himself behind his wife's petticoats, or behind the corporation form of his institution" and still disseminate race hatred.

When both parties had finished, McKelway moved to go into executive session and asked Commissioner Draper to remain for the discussion. Three hours had passed since the closed hearing had started.[9] As Marshall and Dewey left the room, reporters were waiting to catch their reactions. Dewey made no comment, but referred reporters to his January 25 statement. Marshall was not so circumspect. "Dewey backed down completely," he told a *New York Times* reporter. "He said he really liked Jews and was willing to discontinue his official connection with the Lake Placid Club. With his wife and family he holds the controlling interest."[10] Two hours later Regents and Commissioner Draper emerged from the conference room. Draper told reporters the Regents had discussed all the evidence, but "they desire time for reflection." He predicted a report on the charges no earlier than April 1. McKelway took another approach. "Is the State entitled . . . to the whole of Mr. Dewey's time, less a reasonable vacation?" he asked a *New York Herald* reporter rhetorically.[11]

In subsequent weeks matters took several curious turns that demonstrated complexities in people's understanding of issues being debated. Dewey found allies in Funk and Singer, who were concerned that Marshall represented a group and a cause that threatened to inflame rather than check anti-Semitism. Funk warned Dewey that "in Mr. Marshall you have a very able lawyer as an opponent, and he is no doubt a bitter hater." Singer was even more critical. "This Marshall is the evil genius of NY Judaism," he said. Singer believed Marshall represented the interests of wealthy Jews while he himself was more concerned with the little people "upon whom these mighty men looked

---

9. Transcripts of the hearing can be found in Reel 201, Reid Mss; Box 14, McKelway Mss; and Box 70, Dewey Mss.

10. Privately Marshall told Cyrus Adler that Dewey was "crawling and sliming in the most humble mood, and I succeeded in making him feel small enough to go through the smallest key-hole, to the amusement of those present at the hearing." See Marshall to Adler, 2/3/05, Box 1574, Marshall Mss. When Dewey returned to his office, he wrote the Committee a letter further explaining his inability to use his controlling vote to reverse Club rules. "One of the best corporation lawyers in New York" advised him he could be "legally estopped from doing it by dishonorable treatment of the minority stockholders" who disagreed with any rule change. See Dewey to Library Committee, 2/2/05, Box 70, Dewey Mss.

11. See *NYT,* 2/3/05; *Albany Evening Journal,* 2/3/05; *Albany Times-Union,* 2/3/05; *New York Herald,* 2/3/05. In an editorial *Harper's Weekly* defended Dewey by acknowledging Jews did not easily fit into polite society. See *Harper's Weekly* 49 (2/4/05): 150.

down." Because of Singer's support, Dewey had ample reason to believe American Jews were not united against him. He traced his real troubles to "practical politics," for which this "attack" was only a cover.[12]

Privately, Funk and Singer began campaigning in Dewey's behalf. Singer wrote Nathan Bijur that Marshall had erred in sending the decoy letters to Gallup and Dewey. Funk wrote Marshall directly (with copies to each of the petitioners) that he believed the incident had rekindled race prejudice. He noticed at a recent dinner of New York clergymen "this Dewey matter was talked over, and much feeling was expressed. Old stories against the Jews were resurrected." Funk also indicated that some of his hopes for reducing anti-Semitism were founded on publication of the *Jewish Encyclopedia*. The kind of racism invited by the "Dewey matter" would hurt the encyclopedia's prospects. He recommended that Marshall and his cohorts withdraw their petition and simply declare that bringing the issue to the public was their real goal.[13]

Other support for Dewey came from Herbert Putnam, Librarian of Congress, who had read McKelway's comments in the newspapers. Although he did not feel he could speak for himself or the nation's library community on charges of anti-Semitism, he did write Chancellor Reid that accusations Dewey neglected his work were "as ridiculous as its motive appears to be contemptible. Mr. Dewey eats, drinks, sleeps, and talks library and library-work." The Regents would be making a terrible mistake if they fired Dewey, he said. Two days later Reid asked Putnam for permission to present his letter to the Regents. Putnam agreed, but told Reid Dewey knew nothing about it. While Putnam was writing Reid confidentially, Dewey was confiding in friends. He wrote James Day of Syracuse University that "a small company of wealthy Jews have boasted they will punish me." He thought

---

12. Dewey to Funk, 2/3/05; 2/4/05: Funk to Dewey, 2/4/05; Singer to Dewey, 2/8/05, Box 70, Dewey Mss. See also Singer "To the Editor," *New York Globe,* 2/8/05; and Andrew Raymond (President of Union College) to McKelway, 2/11/05, Box 3, McKelway Mss. Raymond argued that Dewey was "a positive force in the right direction and I want to do something if possible to prevent his removal from the office of State Librarian."

13. Singer to Bijur, 2/9/05, Box 70, Dewey Mss; Funk to Marshall, Box 151, Marshall Mss.

it incredible so few could so besmirch the "vast work" of a life of beneficial service.[14]

By February 10 rumors began to circulate that the Regents would meet February 15 to decide Dewey's fate. If true, the move meant trouble for Dewey. Fearful of the danger inherent in this "snap meeting," he encouraged his friends to accelerate efforts on his behalf. He got some help from Singer, who recommended that Dewey compile a pamphlet reprinting relevant documents Singer could send to members of the Jewish Publication Society. On February 10 Dewey begged Nicholas Murray Butler for support. "It seems a crime to wreck my life work here." He also enclosed a copy of the forty-page pamphlet he had compiled for Singer which, he said, he was sending "to a half dozen personal friends," and a circular entitled "Action on Petition to Remove State Librarian," which he was sending to scores more. The former was put together by Gallup; the latter was more personal. "My enemies will make a supreme effort for my harm" at the next Regents' meeting, he said, and asked all circular recipients to come to his aid and save the "work to which I have given the best 17 years of my life." Butler replied three days later he did not know enough about the situation to involve himself and assured Dewey the Regents would not "do anything that is inequitable."[15]

Singer was not idle either. He suggested Dewey prepare a private but unsigned letter thanking him for his February 1 *Sun* article, state the "facts" of the case, and have two hundred copies run off. Dewey should then send the package to him, and he would then forward copies of the letter with a personal note to fifty "eminent rabbis and 150 laymen throughout the country." Next day he wrote petitioner Isidore Straus. "Louis Marshall is a stiff lawyer and a bitter hater," he told Straus, and all Jews would suffer if he was allowed to push for Dewey's removal at the February 15 Regents meeting. Dewey's "2000 colleagues throughout the country in their professional and confessional

---

14. Putnam to Reid, 2/9/05, Box 2, Putnam Mss; Reid to Putnam, 2/11/05, Reel 93, Reid Mss; Dewey to Day, 2/9/05, Box 79, Dewey Mss.

15. Singer to Dewey, 2/10/05; Singer to Leipziger, 2/10/05; Dewey to Singer, 2/16/05, Box 70, Dewey Mss; Dewey to Butler, 2/10/05; Butler to Dewey, 2/13/05, Butler Mss. Circular dated 2/10/05 also in Butler Mss. A copy of the 40-page pamphlet can be found in Box 1574, Marshall Mss. An expanded version is in Box 53, Dewey Mss.

quality," he argued, "will undoubtedly take his part of the decision of the regents over against him, and without going into any details start a campaign against the Jews, first in the library rooms themselves, and then outside of them."

Marshall was fully aware of what Singer, Funk, and Dewey were doing. On February 11 he wrote Funk he welcomed an opportunity to have the hearing testimony made public at the next Regents' meeting. Revenge was not the goal of petitioners, he said, but justice. He and his group would not turn the other cheek. "From Mr. Dewey there is no word of regret for the wrong that has been done; no apology, no recantation; nothing but patronizing and nauseating slobber." As for Funk's clerical friends, Marshall said, they "stand by and raise not one word of protest, of indignation, or of admonition, but, on the contrary, voice the gospel of hate, of intolerance, and of bigotry. No; the petition will not be withdrawn."[16]

Dewey spent February 11 writing letters to petitioners. To convince them to remove their name from the petition, he included copies of the forty-page pamphlet, and echoed Singer and Funk's concern that the whole incident threatened to increase precisely the kind of feelings petitioners were struggling to reduce. Next day he suggested to Singer that if pressure were brought to remove Leipziger as Assistant Superintendent of New York City schools, Leipziger might be inclined to clear himself of any connection with the petition.[17]

February 13 witnessed a flurry of correspondence as the Dewey forces continued to fight for leverage with the Regents.

---

16. Singer to Dewey, 2/10/05; Singer to Straus, 2/11/05, copy found in Box 70, Dewey Mss; Marshall to Funk, 2/11/05; Marshall to Abraham, 2/11/05, Box 1574, Marshall Mss.

17. Dewey's activity on February 11 is evident in correspondence from Bijur to Dewey, 2/14/05; and Singer to Abraham, 2/14/05, copy of which is in Box 70, Dewey Mss. See also Dewey to Singer, 2/12/05, Box 70, Dewey Mss. Singer forwarded copies of Dewey's letter and statement to Abraham and Lauterbach on February 14. To the former he wrote: "Please, withdraw your name from a document which certainly will be made the pivot of the first anti-Semitic campaign in the United States." To the latter he indicated he "would bring his campaign machine to a stop" if Lauterbach would telegraph that the petition was withdrawn. "It would be a misfortune to have an anti-Semitic campaign start," he forewarned. See Singer to Abraham, 2/14/05; and Singer to Lauterbach, 2/14/05, copies found in Box 70, Dewey Mss.

Dewey asked James Day to contact Regent William Nottingham on his behalf, and write T. Guilford Smith, Daniel Beach, and Albert Vander Veer, all of them Regents who "would lay great stress on anything you might say." To Regent Charles A. Gardiner he reported the split in the Jewish community, and asked only for "fair play." To Singer he noted that Presidents Raymond of Union, Taylor of Vassar, and Day of Syracuse were all backing him, and that the latter had predicted "a tremendous protest from all over the state against this persecution." He also reported feedback that the petition reflected "the worst tactics that could possibly have been adopted by friends of the Jews," and concluded that "Marshall may have lighted a prairie fire that will do endless damage before it can be put out." Dewey's staff certainly sensed the turmoil. "There are earthquake rumblings around Mr. Dewey again," Ada Alice Jones wrote to her sister; she had been with Dewey sixteen years, "feeling always that I was living near a volcano."[18]

Dewey's hopes that petitioners would abandon Marshall were ill-founded. On February 14 Bijur wrote Dewey he had been inclined to remove his name from the petition if Dewey had made "such amends as might be possible under the circumstances." The letter and statement Dewey had sent him on the 11th, however, showed Dewey "preferred to stand upon disproof of the allegations. Viewed as an attempted denial," he said, "your answer seems to me to be an incomplete, inconsequential and irrelevant address, in involved terms, to everything except the substantial fact charged." Sulzberger sent a similar letter. "I regret to say that instead of a frank and manly admission of error, I find a mass of shuffling evasion and deception."[19]

On February 14 McKelway published the correspondence between Funk and Marshall in the *Brooklyn Eagle*. In an accom-

---

18. Existing correspondence does not reveal the cracks in the petitioners' coalition that Singer sensed. Abraham Abraham complimented Marshall on his "forcible" answer to Funk, whose letter "adds insult to injury." He promised to send copies of the Marshall-Funk correspondence to McKelway. See Abraham to Marshall, 2/13/05, Box 14, Marshall Mss. See also Dewey to Day, 2/13/05, Box 2, Day Mss; Dewey to Gardiner, 2/13/05; Dewey to Singer, 2/13/05, Box 70, Dewey Mss; Ada Alice Jones to Helen, 2/13/05, Jones Mss.

19. Bijur to Dewey, 2/14/05; Sulzberger to Dewey, 2/15/05, Box 70, Dewey Mss. A copy of Bijur's letter can also be found in Box 151, Marshall Mss. See also Singer to Abraham, 2/14/05, Box 70, Dewey Mss.

panying editorial the *Eagle* avoided taking sides, lamented that the Regents had been unwillingly sucked into the dispute, but suggested that they would probably have to make a decision on Dewey based not on "racial consideration" but on whether he could run both the State Library and the Lake Placid Club. That same day the *Sun* published an impassioned letter from Singer. He appealed to individuals associated with the petition to abandon their effort, but especially he wanted readers and Regents to know that "a dozen of Jewish individuals" did not represent the 750,000 New York Jews. If given time and opportunity, he said, he would "offer a counter-petition signed not by eleven, but by 11,000 Hebrews, not only of this, but of all forty-five States of the Union." In an accompanying editorial the *Sun* echoed Singer's sentiments, and concluded that the movement against Dewey "is ill advised and unfortunate."[20]

The mood was tense when Regents convened on February 15 to discuss the petition against Dewey. The controversy had been in the New York press for several weeks, and the issue had forced a visible split in the American Jewish community along lines of wealth. Quietly operating behind the scenes and laced throughout private correspondence were animosities against Dewey for past and present improprieties, for previous political positions he had taken, for his self-righteous attitude and seriously flawed personality, for his irrepressibility, and for his refusal to admit any error. Some quarters believed the wrong decision would bring the nation's library community to Dewey's aid; a letter from the Librarian of Congress tended to reinforce that belief. Some quarters believed a wrong decision might usher in a series of race riots and occasion an American Dreyfus affair. Some quarters believed the Board had no business deliberating Dewey's private matters. Finally, it was also obvious that an insidious anti-Semitism lurked behind the position of many of Dewey's Gentile supporters. All of this probably was on the minds of Regents as they sat down to discuss the problem.

Chancellor Reid opened the meeting, attended by McKelway, Beach, Sexton, Smith, Vander Veer, Lauterbach, Nottingham, Charles S. Francis, and Eugene A. Philbin. Draper was also

---

20. *Eagle,* 2/14/05; New York *Sun,* 2/14/05. The *Albany Evening Journal* reprinted excerpts from the correspondence on February 15. See also anti-Dewey letter from a "Citizen" "To the Editor," *NYT,* 2/15/05.

present. Although initially Dewey was not present, Reid had with him a letter Dewey sent to Vander Veer asking permission to address the Regents before they considered the Library Committee's report. Vander Veer noted that because all Regents had received a transcript of its February 2 hearing the Library Committee did not think it necessary to submit any recommendation to the full Board. The committee did, however, cite six "facts": (1) Dewey was president of the Lake Placid Company; (2) the Company was active and organized into several departments; (3) the Lake Placid Club was a separate entity, although bound to the Company by agreement made for the mutual advantage of both; (4) the Club was open to all who met its standards; (5) the Club did exclude Jews from membership; and (6) "the regulation excluding Jews is not due to any personal prejudice on the part of Mr. Dewey." Reid then called for Dewey.

Melvil Dewey was a shaken man when he entered the room. He knew his library career was in jeopardy; he was also carrying a heavy personal burden. Annie had recently been admitted to the famous Battle Creek Sanitarium in Michigan, where doctors found hardening of the arteries and told her she had only a short time to live.[21] "I want to say," he began, "that I am deeply humiliated that I should not have been bright enough in this circular printed in 1901 to have realized that some day it would cause this criticism." Dewey still would not or could not admit injustice in Club rules; the error, he perceived, was not in the rule, but the manner in which it was communicated. As close as he could come to an apology came several sentences later: "I am profoundly sorry, I would be very glad to apologize to any Jew whose feelings were hurt by that. . . . And I apologize to the Board of Regents for the annoyance that it has caused them, most sincerely." He also indicated he had recently declined to be re-elected president of the Lake Placid Company. As a result, he assured the Regents, he had "disassociated myself so far as possible from the Lake Placid enterprise so as to relieve you from any further embarrassment with regard to that." For the remainder of his presentation, he addressed the question of how much time he spent on State Library duties.

---

21. Florence Woodworth had accompanied Annie to Battle Creek, and kept Dewey informed of his wife's health. Letters from Woodworth to Dewey dated February and March 1905 can be found in Box 21, Dewey Mss.

After Dewey finished, several Regents asked him questions. Beach in particular wanted to know about the evolution of the 1901 Club circular. Dewey retraced its history, and noted that the exclusionary clause had been changed twice since that circular. On the first occasion reference to Jews was dropped so that since 1902 the clause read: "No one will be admitted to whom even a small minority would object. This excludes rightly any one against whom there is any reasonable physical, mental, racial or social objection." And in recent weeks, Dewey said, Club directors voted to eliminate the word "racial" because they thought "social" sufficient to cover the matter. When no one else asked questions, Reid excused Dewey. As he left the room, Dewey explained he would personally rather resign than subject himself to further attack, but because he owed a responsibility to 100 staff members at the State Library, fifty students at the State Library School, and the entire library profession, he felt compelled "to stand some humiliation rather than sacrifice the work." Some Regents may have thought his self-assumed magnanimity somewhat disingenuous.

When Dewey left, Reid read the letter he had received from Putnam, then passed around a series of letters from people who supported and opposed Dewey. In the "prolonged discussion" that followed, Regents agreed they could not justifiably connect the private Lake Placid Club acts cited in Marshall's petition to Dewey's public duties as State Librarian. Ultimately, however, the Board approved a motion by McKelway to censure Dewey for his part in the 1901 Lake Placid Club publication, to rebuke him publicly and formally for his conduct regarding it, and to admonish him that "further control" of this private business was "incompatible" with a public position serving the educational interests of the state. Thus they agreed to let Dewey survive as State Librarian, but not without a public scolding.[22]

---

22. A copy of the minutes of the Regents' February 15 meeting can be found in Box 151, Marshall Mss. A transcript of Dewey's comments (not included in the official minutes) can be found in Box 70, Dewey Mss. A copy of the Regents' agreement that they could not tie Dewey's private acts to his public duties (also not included in the official minutes) can be found in Box 151, Marshall Mss. That the Board was glad to be rid of the matter was obvious from a letter Reid wrote Draper on March 16. "It was a situation which might easily have become ugly," he said, and he complimented the Board on taking the only right course. "I thought Dewey would submit to it

Next day the Regents made public a copy of the minutes of their meeting, which included the Library Committee report and the censure vote. Reactions were mixed. Among state newspapers none summarized Dewey's comments (most did not even refer to them); none noted the Board's conclusion that it could not tie issues raised in Marshall's petition directly to Dewey's official performance. The library press was equivocal. After reciting Dewey's many contributions and his importance to the profession, *Library Journal* said it was glad the "attack" on him "by leading Hebrew citizens" of New York was over. *Public Libraries* was less circumspect. Charges of "undue absence" from the State Library were "unfounded," and "personal prejudice is the last accusation to bring against Mr. Dewey." The editor concluded: "Do the regents expect the public to take them seriously?"[23]

Petitioners seemed satisfied. Marshall thanked Reid for "the very satisfactory and gratifying disposition of the matter as embodied in the resolutions adopted," and thanked McKelway for his "great courtesy to me in connection with this most trying affair." To his uncle he wrote he preferred Dewey "should be disciplined rather than removed, as I did not care to make a martyr of him." He told Isidor Lewi that the results of Regent deliberations were "a great triumph for justice," that not "a single one of the signers of the original petition wavered in his purpose," and that it was not "worthwhile" to pay "any attention to Singer or his lucubrations." He also summarized his interpretation of Regent action: Dewey

> was guilty and the Regents proceeded to mete out punishment, first, by censuring the publication which was the basis for our proceedings; second, in severely and

'in good temper.' My only fear has been that even then, he would hardly fully appreciate the gravity of it or the necessity of getting out from responsibility for his Lake Placid enterprise." See Reid to Draper, 3/16/05, Reel 94, Reid Mss.

23. For examples of newspaper coverage, see *NYT,* 2/16/05; *Albany Argus,* 2/16/05; *Albany Evening Journal,* 2/16/05; New York *Sun,* 2/16/05; *NYTr,* 2/16/05; *Schenectady Gazette,* 2/16/05; and *Syracuse Post-Standard,* 2/16/05. See also *LJ* 30 (3/05): 135–36; and *PL* 10 (3/05): 126–29. Mary Ahern, *PL*'s editor and frequent visitor to the Lake Placid Club, had supported Dewey since the story broke. See Ahern to Dewey, 2/13/05; Dewey to Ahern, 2/16/05; Ahern to Dewey, 2/20/05; Dewey to Ahern, 2/22/05, Box 70, Dewey Mss.

publicly rebuking the librarian; third, in admonishing him that he must cease his connection with an institution conducted on the lines that the Lake Placid Club has heretofore been conducted, or else leave his post as librarian.

Marshall himself received praise for his efforts. H. W. Rosenbaum was "delighted" with the punishment given that "nauseating slobberer"; Regent Nottingham indicated the Board "were all indignant at the position in which the Librarian had placed himself."[24]

Once the Board's decision was made public, Dewey considered the incident over, and sent a circular to LPC members dated February 20 that explained his view of the incident. He was very careful to point out no Club rules would change. In a letter to *Public Libraries* editor Mary Ahern two days later he complimented her for understanding "the Jew case exactly right," and explained that "Gallup is adding 2 or 3 things to the pamphlet to go to members. He wants to say some things which you are evidently going to say either [in] this or the next PL, and it would be much better to quote from you. . . ." Dewey also made feeble attempts to repair bridges, but in his characteristically insensitive and unapologetic manner. On February 24 he complimented Lauterbach on the "dignity and fairness" with which "you met the most unpleasant incident thrust upon us by people who may have felt justified because they assumed certain false rumors to be true," and then asked Lauterbach for an interview to discuss plans he had for the future of the State Library. Lauterbach never answered.[25]

---

24. Marshall to Reid, 2/16/05; Marshall to McKelway, 2/16/05; Marshall to Lewi, 2/16/05; 3/6/05; Marshall to Bernard Lowenstein, 2/23/05, Box 1574, Marshall Mss. See also Nottingham to Marshall, 2/17/05; Rosenbaum to Marshall, 2/16/05, Box 16, Marshall Mss; Philip Cowan to Marshall, 2/17/05, Box 14, Marshall Mss.

25. Dewey circular, 2/20/05; Dewey to Ahern, 2/22/05; Dewey to Lauterbach, 2/24/05, Box 70, Dewey Mss. See also Dewey to C. F. Birdseye, 2/24/05, Box 70, Dewey Mss. Lauterbach forwarded a copy of Dewey's letter to Marshall, with a note saying he had not answered Dewey. See Lauterbach to Marshall, 3/13/05, Box 15, Marshall Mss.

13

Disgraced, and Banished for His Sins: Dewey's Downfall

1905–1906

Because Dewey recognized his hold on his position in Albany was tenuous at best in mid-1905, he looked to increase options for the future. He pushed two prospects—spelling reform and the creation of a library academy. Concerning the former, he looked to Carnegie. On April 17 he assured the philanthropist twenty people would commit themselves "as soon as they know your attitude," and asked Carnegie to repeat "what you have said 2 or 3 times to me" that upon submission of a "satisfactory list of strong names pledged to use the new spellings" he was ready to pay expenses of a central office. That Dewey had something in mind was evident from his actions at a May 3 meeting at Brander Matthews's house in New York. Dewey moved that "in the opinion of the conference, the plan should include an office in New York, a paid secretary, a stenographer and such other assistance as may be needed," and that its "first work . . . should be to secure the adoption of the Twelve Words by individual periodicals and publishers." Dewey later summarized the meeting for Carnegie. "I submitted our correspondence and a clear statement of your ideas and preferences and those present were absolutely unanimous in agreement with you." That Dewey did not mention potential candidates for secretary was telling; his silence suggests he considered himself a candidate. Circulars from the committee which met at Matthews's house were sent out May 18, accompanied by a preprinted "Promise as to Twelve Words." Correspondence showed Matthews as chair of the group, C. P. G. Scott as secretary. "With the fund supplied by Mr. Carnegie," the circular explained, "it is proposed to organize a board, to engage a secretary, and to enter on an active campaign to win a wider acceptance for these simplifications."[1]

The "library academy" project held less promise because Dewey could not easily tie it to external funding. His model was the French Academy, originally established in 1634 to purify the French language and maintain French literary standards. Dewey admonished library peers to sell the idea to colleagues because "it can do no harm and may do a large good." At a Council meeting April 1 he argued that ALA had to grow, but it needed a "manageable body" like an "academy" to discuss important library problems. He then convinced the Council to consider the matter and have him report at the forthcoming conference. The *Library Journal* objected to the project; it would create a separate body independent of ALA, *LJ* argued, that would eventually usurp some of its powers. In addition, it would tend to retain older members and retard the recruitment of new, countering the welcome trend that the ALA constitution inaugurated by making council members ineligible to succeed themselves.[2]

By this time, however, Dewey's attention was being diverted back to the Lake Placid Club. In late March, Asa Gallup completed compilation of the pamphlet to which Dewey had referred in previous correspondence, and mailed it out with the Club's annual circular to LPC members and numerous others Dewey had preselected. The pretense for compiling and circulating it was to provide background information concerning a rule change to remove the words "Jew" and "racial" from Club literature. In

---

1. Dewey to Carnegie, 4/17/05; "Minutes of a Conference on Simplified Spelling," 5/3/05, Box 85, Dewey Mss; Dewey to Carnegie, 5/8/05, LB 124, Carnegie Mss; Circular (marked "Confidential") from Matthews's Committee to "Dear Sir," 5/18/05, copy found in Box 88, Dewey Mss; Dewey to Butler, 5/22/05, Butler Mss; and C. P. G. Scott to Dewey, 5/25/05, Box 85, Dewey Mss.

2. Dewey to "Committee on the Library Academy," 2/4/05; 3/2/05, Box 6, Dewey Mss; Dewey to "Committee on the Library Academy," 3/28/05, Thwaites Mss; *LJ* 30 (5/05): 268, 289–90; *PL* 10 (3/05): 140–43. A recent study of the French Academy of Sciences is Maurice Crosland, *Science under Control: The French Academy of Sciences, 1795–1914* (Cambridge, Mass., 1992).

a preamble Gallup explained: "The public attack on the Club's membership rule makes it desirable that each member should see the statements before voting on the wording of this rule which the council is to submit for use hereafter." The original forty-page pamphlet had contained verbatim transcripts of the petition, a copy of what appeared to be the prepared response Dewey submitted to the Board, letters to the New York *Sun*, letters from I. K. Funk and Isidore Singer in support of the Club's right to exclude Jews, and similarly supportive editorials in the *Saratoga Sun*, the New York *Sun*, and *Harper's Weekly*. The expanded edition also included verbatim transcripts of additional supporting documentation, including a February 16 letter John Cotton Dana sent to the *Brooklyn Eagle*, Herbert Putnam's February 9 letter to University Chancellor Whitelaw Reid, editorials in the March issues of *Public Libraries* and *School Bulletin*, and a brief editorial from the *Utica Press*.[3]

On May 17 Louis Marshall wrote Regent Edward Lauterbach that he had heard Dewey was circulating a pamphlet concerning the petition. "I am disposed to keep close watch on the gentleman, who is evidently trying to make capital out of his own disgrace." After Lauterbach sent Marshall a copy of the pamphlet he obtained from Commissioner Andrew Sloan Draper, Marshall pointed out that Dewey's "answer" to petitioners' accusations reprinted in the new version "is entirely different from that which he presented to the Board." For example, he included several pages of new matter that reflected a split in the Jewish community not part of the original hearings, and on page 19 had written: "The Club Council after this outbreak will probably avoid the word Jew in any rule again, but will surely maintain its absolute right to reject from membership any person not desired at the Club." Did not Dewey promise, Marshall asked, to withdraw from leadership in the Club? Dewey was "willfully defying the Board of Regents" because the pamphlet showed he still controlled the organization. In addition, the pamphlet portrayed the petitioners as "animated by petty spite and narrowness," depicted the Regents' proceeding as "preposterous," and conveyed the impression that Dewey's rebuke was "remarkable" and that the public should not take it "seriously." Marshall then quoted a sentence

---

3. A copy of the 40-page pamphlet can be found in Box 151, Marshall Mss; a copy of the 56-page pamphlet can be found in Box 53, Dewey Mss.

written by Gallup on page 56: "The Jews are too important an element nowadays to be discriminated against by anybody who holds a public position. Jews may be despised, but their votes are respected." On June 21 Lauterbach replied he had just received a letter from Regent St. Clair McKelway concerning Dewey's pamphlet. McKelway advised a meeting "in order that some course of action may be adopted." Shortly thereafter, the Regents scheduled a meeting for June 30 to discuss the pamphlet, and asked Dewey to respond to Marshall's charges.[4] Dewey was in trouble again.

Dewey outlined his response in a June 27 letter to his lawyer (and former Amherst classmate), C. F. Birdseye. Marshall's accusations "garbled" the record, he said. "Some of it reads like a strong case," he wrote, "but checked up by facts there is nothing the regents can seriously criticize." To the accusation that he added material to his initial statement Dewey said it encompassed supplements given to the Regents for their February 15 hearing. He had had no contact with the press since that meeting, and the circular about which Marshall was complaining was simply Gallup's composition to help LPC members vote on new Club rules. "I have in good faith carried out my statement to the regents," he told Birdseye, and "disconnected myself officially wholly from the Club." He asked Birdseye to inform Lauterbach "*strongly* and *vouch for the truth* of it that I shall not under any circumstances revive this matter."[5]

Next day Dewey sent a similar statement to Draper. The pamphlet had been circulated only to "those directly interested in the club rules," he said; if copies had fallen into other hands it was not by design. In addition, he had "loyally accepted the regents' public rebuke," and because he had made no comment to the press since, he now protested the attempt to reopen the issue. He asked that his letter be read to the Regents if the subject was brought up at a future meeting, and included with it a statement from Gallup in which he explained that except for a file copy all the 1901 circulars had been removed, that all

---

4. Marshall to Lauterbach, 5/17/05; Box 1574; Lauterbach to Marshall, 5/20/05, Box 15; Marshall to Lauterbach, 6/1/05; 6/17/05, Box 1574, Marshall Mss. Copies of the last two can also be found in Box 70, Dewey Mss. See also Lauterbach to Marshall, 6/21/05, Box 15, Marshall Mss; Dewey to James H. Canfield, 6/30/05, Box 70, Dewey Mss.
5. Dewey to Birdseye, 6/27/05, Box 70, Dewey Mss.

letterhead stationery identifying Dewey as company president had been destroyed, and that he had been "solely responsible" for the compilation and distribution of the pamphlet.[6]

Although the Regents met on June 30 with Dewey present, the official record does not indicate they discussed Marshall's charges. Subsequent correspondence, however, indicates Lauterbach made a motion to demand Dewey's resignation, but it failed to carry a majority. Instead, Regents made it known they thought it in Dewey's best interests to resign "at no very remote date," but they were not going to force the issue immediately. Dewey said he understood their position, and indicated he would probably resign in the near future. As he later described it to others, however, the meeting took on a different profile.

He told James H. Canfield of the Columbia University Library, for example, that "regents were unwilling to have on record [that] the Jew attack" was discussed. It was "4 hours fight and tussle," and "no action." He also said he was reconciled to keeping quiet, but added "I have no notion of continuing very long in a place where I am subject to such attacks." He planned to stay on as State Librarian "to the end of the next school year," then "devote myself to the larger things of library work without the 'ball and chain.'" He told Mary Ahern that "Draper I think has made a deal with the Jews for support in the legislature, the price being that he will assent to my overturn," but he said nothing about the timing of his departure. He was more forthcoming with Regent Pliny Sexton: "Personally I should prefer to resign in October to take effect during the fiscal year as soon as I could close my work without serious injury, perhaps as early as April."

Based on this evidence alone it is obvious that sometime in summer Dewey decided to resign, but it is also obvious from other correspondence that only one thing kept him from making that decision public—the disposition of "his" library school. If Dewey had to leave the State Library he wanted to take the school with him. Because it represented the last institution he controlled in the American library community, he did not want to give it up. As a result, the question of what to do with the library school—a question only Dewey was raising—became a pawn in the timing of his decision to announce his resignation.

---

6. Dewey to Draper, 6/28/05, Box 70; Gallup to Dewey, 6/28/05, Box 49, Dewey Mss.

First evidence of his tactics surfaced in a conversation he had with Draper in early July concerning the future of the library school. But Draper was not as eager to deal the library school in 1905 as Columbia was in 1888.[7]

Relocating the library school was much on Dewey's mind when he attended the ALA conference that opened July 4 in Portland, Oregon. At the time his wife was still ill, and nothing about her health had changed to suggest the doctors' prognosis was inaccurate. In addition, at their June 30 meeting several Regents had clearly indicated they preferred Dewey's resignation as State Librarian. Nor was he any closer to becoming a paid secretary of a Carnegie-funded simplified spelling board. The weight of these problems affected his demeanor and behavior, but characteristically he pushed forward. At the conference Dewey advocated the establishment of an "American Library Institute" (ALI). Conferees voted to sanction an institute to consist of "100 persons chosen from English-speaking America," and stipulated that "the ex-Presidents of the A.L.A. be the first members . . . with power to add to their number, to organize and adopt needed rules." Dewey was thus successful in gaining ALA approval for an elite body to which members would have access only by selection. Its purpose was vague, but its existence was a compliment to Dewey's persistence in the face of some opposition and much indifference. Later in the conference Dewey spoke on "Unity and Cooperation in Library Work," and suggested the possibility of moving the New York State Library School to another site. He also indicated he still hoped ALA could tap Carnegie for a donation to endow "a permanent headquarters that shall undertake the work that belongs to librarianship."[8]

Dewey was probably fishing for opportunities here. Just as he angled for a position as paid secretary of a Carnegie-sponsored simplified spelling organization, he also probably envisioned himself as a paid secretary of a Carnegie-endowed ALA or, more likely, a Carnegie-endowed American Library Institute run something like the recently established Carnegie Institute in Wash-

---

7. Funk "To the Editor," New York *Sun,* 9/8/05; Dewey to Canfield, 6/30/05, Box 71; Dewey to Canfield, 8/14/05, Box 73; Dewey to Funk, 9/17/05, Box 85; Dewey to Ahern, 8/28/05; Dewey to Sexton, 9/18/05, Box 70, Dewey Mss.

8. *Proceedings, 1905,* 180–84.

ington. Given the circumstances he had left in Albany, the scenario makes sense. At its first meeting of the conference, the executive board directed ALA ex-presidents to draft an ALI constitution to define the organization. Dewey won his conference goal, and was later elected ALI's first president. After the conference he joined friends and associates on a postconference cruise to Alaska for some much needed rest and relaxation. Between his wife's precarious health, their precarious financial situation at Lake Placid, and his own precarious position at Albany, Dewey reached out for comfort and support from his closest friends and let down his guard on controlling his behavior toward women in public. Only later would he realize that many in the post-conference party thought he had greatly overreached the bounds of social propriety.

Resignation
1905

When he returned to Albany, rumors of his impending resignation began to appear in the press with greater frequency,[9] but Dewey seemed to ignore the rumors. He was more interested in moving the library school. On August 14 he told Canfield the library school ought to have "a university connection" and asked Canfield if Columbia might want it back. He also reported conversations with universities in Chicago, Wisconsin, and California "and 2 or 3 others" that, he said, "would mightily like to have the school transferred there," then bent the truth by saying Draper was willing to let it go. "All of this is unofficial, but I have assurances that justify this letter to you." On August 14 he wrote B. I. Wheeler, president of the University of California, and again bent the truth. He noted that as ALI president he could report "we [sic] are studying these problems in a broad way and it is clear that either Berkeley or Stanford is the one place for the one great library school west of the Rockies." He said Wheeler ought to consider the New York State Library School because it was the

---

9. *Albany Evening Journal*, 8/17/05; *Jamestown Post*, 8/26/05; Johnstown (NY) *Republican*, 9/15/05. On August 21 Marshall asked Lauterbach, "Have you any confirmation as to the report that Dewey's resignation is in the hands of the Board of Regents?" Marshall to Lauterbach, 8/21/05, Box 1574, Marshall Mss.

only one with "any men on the faculty." Most others were "training schools for young women, taught by two or three women."[10]

While Dewey secretly tried to peddle his school to another
institution, his problems at Albany did not go away. As long as he
held onto the position of State Librarian, his tenure remained a
point of contention between two factions of New York City's
Jewish community. One side worried that a successful campaign
to dump him would make him a martyr, usher in violence, and
accelerate anti-Semitism. The other side worried that an unsuc-
cessful campaign would send a signal it was acceptable for public officials to be openly anti-Semitic in their private business
affairs. The dispute flared again in early September. On September 8, the New York *Sun* ran a letter from Funk, who asked if it
was "wise for the Jews" to create the impression among "thousands of educated men" that they forced the resignation of "the
most energetic and most resourceful librarian in the world." Next
day the *Sun* ran a similar letter from Singer, and on September 10 the newspaper itself ran an editorial supporting both
men's positions.[11]

Other newspapers addressed the issue in editorial columns.
The *Boston Herald* agreed with Funk and Singer that "the threatened union" of Jews to remove Dewey would likely be counterproductive. On September 14 the *Rochester Herald* called the
Sun's discussion a "remarkably good-tempered and sane editorial disquisition," and warned the "Seligmans and the Loebs and
the Schiffs . . . not to perpetuate in this new country the racial
animosities of the old." The Johnstown (N.Y.) *Republican* sensed
that "politics are entering into the state department of education." The *Sun* ran a letter from "One of the Committee" suggesting that New York Jews "stand seriously in need of wisdom
and prudence in dealing with unsound and unsafe counsel controlled by political ambition."[12]

---

10. Dewey to Canfield, 8/14/05, Box 73; Dewey to Wheeler, 8/14/05,
Box 65, Dewey Mss. Two days later he received a letter from James I. Wyer
encouraging Dewey to consider moving the library school to the University
of Wisconsin. See Wyer to Dewey, 8/16/05, Box 73, Dewey Mss. There is no
indication in any published proceedings that the American Library Institute ever discussed the issue of locating a library school west of the Rockies.

11. New York *Sun*, 9/8/05; 9/9/05; and 9/10/05.

12. *Rochester Herald,* 9/14/05 (quoting *Boston Herald* in its own
editorial); Johnstown (N.Y.) *Republican*, 9/15/05; New York *Sun*, 9/15/05.

Marshall reacted to the news coverage quickly. In a letter to Lauterbach he called Funk an "insidious" enemy to Jews, Singer an "arch anti-Semite," and the *Sun* "that distinguished anti-Semitic organ." He noted how similar these tactics were to those Dewey and his allies had used to discredit petitioners' charges in January and February and reminded Lauterbach that the "evidence" Funk, Singer, and the *Sun* cited had been pulled from a pamphlet Dewey claimed had not been widely circulated. He then urged Lauterbach to "push the matter to its logical conclusion." Lauterbach assured Marshall on the 11th that the Regents would discuss the matter at their next meeting on September 20.[13] Draper responded more publicly to the mounting newspaper cacophony by issuing a press release on September 14. A reorganization of the State Library was being planned, he indicated, and announced for the first time that the Regents had "unanimously agreed" at their June 30 meeting that "it was desirable that Mr. Dewey's official connection with the library should terminate at no very remote date. This decision was at once communicated to him and acquiesced in by him with apparent favor."

"Laughable," the *Albany Argus* quipped, then quoted Dewey in a recent article in the New York *Herald:* "It is not true that I have resigned. . . . If I am ousted it will be on a purely political issue." On September 16 the *Sun* forecast "more and more dangerous examples of this trick to provoke race animosity as a means of forwarding political and personal schemes," and on the 17th the *Argus* reported that neither Draper, Lauterbach, nor Marshall would respond to Dewey's *Herald* statements. The *Argus* did quote Funk, however, who said Draper was wrong; Dewey had not resigned because of race prejudice at the Lake Placid Club and in fact was being driven out "because he stands in the way of certain political bosses who want to use the State library for political patronage."[14]

---

13. Marshall to Lauterbach, 9/8/05; 9/11/05; Marshall to Lewi, 9/11/05, Box 1574; Lauterbach to Marshall, 9/11/05, Box 15, Marshall Mss.

14. Draper's press release is quoted in the *NYTr,* 9/15/05; Johnstown *Republican,* 9/15/05, and the *Albany Argus,* 9/16/05. The latter also quoted the statement Dewey sent to the New York *Herald.* See also New York *Sun,* 9/16/05; and *Albany Argus,* 9/17/05. Funk did not issue his statement until after he had contacted Dewey on the 16th. He wanted to make sure Dewey had not resigned, as Draper suggested, and asked for more facts concerning

During all this time Dewey continued to peddle the library school without authorization from Draper or the Regents. He again asked Canfield about moving it to Columbia, indicating that the school "is my baby, and I am pretty particular who adopts it." But Canfield's conversations with Columbia's President Nicholas Murray Butler were discouraging. Dewey also contacted Charles W. Needham, President of George Washington University. "Chances are more than 9 out of 10 it will be changed to a university connection within a year," he said, and suggested Boston, New York, and Washington represented "the most desirable places."[15]

Eventually news of his campaign reached library-school faculty and alumni. On September 8 Alumni Association President Robert Shaw asked if rumors about the school's impending move were true. Others knew more about Dewey's tactics. On September 17 Florence Woodworth told Dewey of a conversation she had with E. M. Fairchild, husband of Mary S. C. Fairchild, who was at the time quite ill. Woodworth said Fairchild thought Dewey "unwise to precipitate at this juncture [the] question of moving the school," and resented Dewey's implication that his wife would go with the school if it moved. Fairchild felt it was best for Dewey to resign quietly since his "usefulness" in the State Library "was at an end," and if Dewey persisted "in raising a fight," he and others would reveal certain things about Dewey's administration.

About this time Isabel E. Lord, a Pratt Institute employee, contacted Regent McKelway on behalf of the alumni association concerning rumors that Regents were going to discontinue the school or transfer it from Albany. She had reason to suspect Dewey because she overheard him discussing the possibility in Portland. She was also angry with Dewey for his behavior on the postconference cruise to Alaska, although the reason for this anger did not surface until the following summer. When McKelway assured her the subject had never been brought up at a

---

"the previous complaints against you. Were these not wholly of a political nature, or springing out of politics?" See Funk to Dewey, 9/15/05, Box 70, Dewey Mss.

15. Dewey to Canfield, 8/18/05, Box 73; 9/14/05, Box 30A; Dewey to Butler, 9/14/05, Box 70; Canfield to Dewey, 9/15/05, Box 73, Dewey Mss. See also Dewey to Needham, 9/13/05; Dewey to Wyer, 9/8/05, Box 73, Dewey Mss.

Regents' meeting, Lord's suspicions were confirmed. She became convinced Dewey was acting in his own interests and not those of the New York State Library School. McKelway's suspicions were also aroused. After more than fifteen years of observing the tactics of this irrepressible reformer, he quickly recognized a familiar pattern of behavior.[16]

Because of his allergies, Dewey intended to stay at Lake Placid through the first week in October. Before he left Albany in August he had asked if Regents could schedule a meeting on October 15 so "I could [then] submit my resignation" in order to "avoid some of the serious injury to the state's library interests likely to come from any sudden overturning of the administration." He did not learn until September 15, however, that Lauterbach was pushing the Regents to "accept" his resignation at their September 20 meeting.

He looked to two people to protect his interests. First, he asked C. F. Birdseye to go to Albany and outline terms under which he would resign to as many Regents as possible before the meeting. "If I leave I want the assurance that the school can be cordially cared for in the place I select for it. It was my creation and it will go to pieces unless I take care of it." He noted that Mary Fairchild was very ill and unable to run the school, and rather than kill it, "they owe it to me to let me take it when I leave." He did not want to leave Placid, but did ask Birdseye's advice if the Regents requested his presence. "I insist on the right to be heard on library matters before action is taken." He wrote Funk that same day that he was reconciled to the Board's decision. "It is a supreme effort of Draper . . . to jam action through. He confidently expects to do it. I shall do nothing and personally wish it were over with."[17]

Second, on September 18 he told Pliny Sexton he would be unable to attend the meeting, and asked Sexton to make sure State Library interests were not polluted by politics. He also told

---

16. Shaw to Dewey, 9/8/05; Dewey to Shaw, 9/14/05; Woodworth to Dewey (marked "personal"), 9/17/05, Box 73; and long-hand memorandum from Woodworth to Dewey, 9/17/05, Box 21, Dewey Mss. For a description of the substance of Lord's letter to McKelway, see McKelway to Lord, 9/21/05, copy found in Box 73, Dewey Mss. See also Dewey, "Future of Library Schools," *PL* 10 (9/05): 435–38.

17. Dewey to Birdseye, 9/8/05; 9/17/05, Box 70; Dewey to Funk, 9/17/05, Box 85, Dewey Mss.

Sexton that the "extremely discourteous treatment" Draper accorded him since June had convinced him the Commissioner "had combined with the Jews for my overthrow." When he "inquired" about the future of the library school, Dewey said, Draper assumed "a very offensive manner" and "glared at me as if a bootblack had intruded." He was prepared to submit his resignation, he told Sexton, but he hoped the Regents would allow the library school to be transferred to a university.[18]

On the evening of the 19th Dewey was asked to come to Albany for a breakfast meeting in Sexton's office the following morning. Somehow Dewey found the wherewithal to risk his health and make the trip. There he met with "five of the oldest and strongest Regents" to discuss the situation, and together, he later explained to friends, they came to an agreement that "more mischief could be prevented and more valuable interests protected by avoiding the impending conflict and putting my unreserved resignation in the hands of the Regents." With Dewey's resignation in hand, Sexton then went to the Board meeting, where Regents agreed with Draper's reorganization of the Education Department and a redistribution of responsibilities in the State Library. The Home Education Department was given its own chief, made a division of the Department of Education, and had its name changed to the Educational Extension Department. Supervision of school libraries was made a separate division of the Education Department and placed under the Third Assistant Commissioner of Education. The First Assistant Commissioner assumed responsibility for the business affairs of the State Library and the new Educational Extension Department. The reorganization thus left the State Librarian with responsibility for the State Library only. The structure Dewey had built and sustained against significant opposition over the previous fifteen years was thus effectively dismantled. Had Dewey chosen to fight for his position and won, he would have occupied a post greatly reduced in power and influence. Instead, Dewey submitted his resignation as Director of the State Library and the Home Education Department "to take effect in each case at the pleasure of the Regents." He did not resign as director of the library school.

The Regents accepted his resignation effective January 1, 1906, "with grateful recognition and sincere appreciation . . . of

18. Dewey to Sexton, 9/18/05, Box 70, Dewey Mss.

the value of his services to the cause of public education and of library development." They also decided that in view of Dewey's "offer to continue to assist . . . in the conduct . . . of the library school," the date of his resignation as director "be left for later determination." The question of Dewey's future relationship to the library school may have been a temporary compromise worked out between Dewey, Sexton, and the rest of the board in order to obtain Dewey's resignation at the meeting. Dewey certainly viewed the arrangement as an invitation to continue his efforts to move the library school; the Regents viewed it otherwise, however, but said nothing in public. On September 21 McKelway reassured Isabel Lord that "the Board of Regents has no intention or desire to discontinue or to transfer from Albany the State Library School."[19]

Private reaction to Dewey's resignation was mixed. Katharine Sharp, a former student who directed the University of Illinois Library and Library School, congratulated him on his new freedom. Other librarians did the same, but coupled it with regrets on the loss of his leadership to the profession. No one from the library community mentioned the petition of New York Jews, or took a position on Lake Placid's anti-Semitic practices. Clergymen, members of the SRA, and several other unsolicited letters did address the issue, but supported Dewey's position. Whitelaw Reid's reaction was philosophical. He was relieved "to have the situation cleared up," but took some responsibility that it had taken so long. Still, Reid said, he did not regret bringing Dewey to Albany. "I think when the balance is fairly struck it will still be found that the State is considerably the better off for having had him."[20]

Press coverage of Dewey's resignation generally stressed the politics, and viewed Dewey's connection with the anti-Semitic practices of the Lake Placid Club as mere pretext for getting rid

---

19. Dewey explained the chronology of his resignation in a circular to friends dated 9/21/05, Box 70, Dewey Mss. See also Dewey to Commissioner of Education and the Regents of the University, 9/20/05, Box 70, Dewey Mss; *LJ* 30 (10/05): 800; and McKelway to Lord, 9/21/05, copy found in Box 73, Dewey Mss.

20. Sharp to Dewey, 9/23/05, Box 70, Dewey Mss. This is one of many positive letters located in Box 70 that Dewey received upon the announcement of his resignation. See also Reid to Draper, 11/27/05, Reel 96, Reid Mss.

of him. Reaction in the state press was probably influenced by New York's political climate in the fall of 1905, when Charles Evans Hughes was conducting investigations showing collusion between Empire State politicians and the insurance industry. The *Argus* led the way with a September 21 headline "Odell-Draper Combine Ousts Melvil Dewey." Next day it ran an even longer article, listing all State Library employees (and their salaries) likely to be replaced by political appointments after January 1. The New York *Herald* was less judgmental, but the implication that Dewey's resignation was largely a matter of politics was clearly threaded throughout its coverage. Dewey made no comment to any newspaper. The library press reflected similar reactions. The *Library Journal* simply reported Board action and Dewey's resignation. *Public Libraries,* however, echoed the *Argus.* "The Jewish people of New York who have been used as a lever in this matter . . . will be found shortly asking themselves Why?"[21]

Although his resignation was now public, the disposition of the library school, as far as Dewey was concerned, was still an open question, and he pushed hard. On September 1 he sent *Public Libraries* an article entitled "The Future of Library Schools." In it he wondered about the wisdom of keeping the library school in the middle of a political atmosphere and noted "my willingness to see the original school transferred to a satisfactory university connection." On September 22 he asked C. W. Bardeen of Syracuse about moving it there. Although he had "no official authority" to negotiate for the state, and although some Regents seemed committed to keeping the library school in Albany, he said, Draper, his subordinates, "and the rest of the Legislature . . . will insist on moving it so we must settle this question soon." Dewey claimed "a half dozen places want it."

But some people suggested Dewey pushed too hard. On September 24 Florence Woodworth warned Dewey the alumni were getting uneasy about constant rumors Dewey was unilaterally trying to move the school. Next day Dewey received a letter from Lord and Shaw, who reported the results of Lord's visit with Regent McKelway and enclosed a copy of his written response.

---

21. *Albany Argus,* 9/21/05; 9/22/05; New York *Herald,* 9/21/05; *LJ* 30 (10/05): 800; *PL* 10 (11/05): 470–71. For a summary of the Hughes investigation, see McCormick, *From Realignment to Reform,* pp. 193–205. Dewey's resignation was not part of the shift in politics McCormick describes here.

They also reported a conversation Lord had with Draper, who confirmed that the school was "an integral part of the state educational system and that the Board had never otherwise considered it."[22] It was obvious from their response they now fully recognized the school's existence had never been in jeopardy, and that the only threat to its removal was coming from Dewey, not the Regents. And the information Lord obtained directly from those in power was considerably different than the information Dewey was disseminating. Lord's initial suspicions had turned to open distrust.

Characteristically, Dewey chose to interpret Lord's actions as disloyalty to one of the causes he had championed and for which he had "sacrificed" most of his adult life, and continued efforts to move the school. On September 25 he corresponded with Martha Van Rensselaer about transferring it to Cornell, and on October 24 told James Day that Syracuse was still among the possibilities. At the University of Chicago, he used a former student to float a trial balloon and provided her with the kind of information he thought would catch the institution's attention. "Mr. Dewey has been made the President of the new national institute of librarians which will meet annually to discuss the great library problems," Irene Warren wrote Dean George Vincent on November 15. "The University has the opportunity, I believe, if it should see its way clear to establish a graduate library school now, to turn the tide of affairs in such a way that Chicago may become the library center of the country."

By that time, however, word had circulated from several sources (including the NYSLS Alumni Association) that the school's future was not uncertain. On November 16 Herbert Putnam told Dewey about a conversation he had had with Draper, who "was emphatic to me" that the school "was not to leave New York State. He said this with such emphasis as to lead me to infer that he supposed that I should like to get it to Washington." Putnam probably suspected Dewey had told Draper—and others—that Putnam wanted the school. Over the previous decade Putnam

---

22. Dewey to Bardeen, 9/22/05; Woodworth to Dewey, 9/24/05, Box 73, Dewey Mss. Dewey's article was published in the *PL*'s October issue, previously cited. See also Lord and Shaw to Dewey, 9/25/05, Box 73, Dewey Mss. (This information was probably communicated to the NYSLS Alumni Association Executive Board at the NYLA meeting in Lake Placid September 23–30.)

had witnessed enough Dewey intrigues to give the possibility credence. On December 30 George Washington University's Needham reported to Dewey a recent conversation he had with Draper concerning the library school. "I conclude it has been determined to keep the school at Albany."[23]

Ultimately, Dewey had to accept the inevitable. On December 12 he received a letter from the First Assistant Commissioner of Education that outlined a prearranged procedure concerning Dewey's relationship to the school. First, the Regents would accept his resignation as director to take effect January 1; second, they would invite him to continue lecturing "for the remainder of the year, or for so long as we may mutually think is advisable, and assist us in fulfilling the pledges of this Department." The Regents reaffirmed their commitment to the library school December 13, then on December 14 accepted Dewey's resignation as director. At the same meeting they announced they had hired Edwin H. Anderson, a graduate of the library school, to become the next State Librarian of New York.[24]

Dewey was no more successful with simplified spelling, but—as with the library school—not for lack of trying. On November 23 he asked Brander Matthews, "Have you not yet found the angel from heaven for whom we are looking and praying to take care of the office?" He was more explicit in a letter to B. E. Smith. "After Jan. 1 I shall be my own master, thank the Lord, and ready to do my full share for the good cause." He said he knew Smith shared his conviction that simplified spelling needed a strong hand at the center, but because "I cannot find anyone we can get that I should feel like trusting without considerable steering at the first," he was "quite willing to give a good deal of time to helping" launch the office. "We must have a thoroughly efficient executive on salary to turn the crank in an active campaign." Dewey also wrote Carnegie in a transparent attempt to "prove" he was not anti-Semitic. "I know your interest in com-

---

23. Dewey to Van Rensselaer, 9/25/05, Box 73; Day to Dewey, 10/18/05; Dewey to Day, 10/24/05, Box 70; Dewey to Warren, 11/3/05; Warren to Vincent, 11/15/05; Putnam to Dewey, 11/16/05, Box 73, Dewey Mss. See also Needham to Dewey, 12/20/05; Dewey to Needham, 1/2/06, Box P-53, Dewey Mss.

24. Dewey to Sexton, 12/9/05, Box 75; Rogers to Dewey, 12/12/05, Box 71, Dewey Mss; and NYSL *AR, 1906,* p. 184. A copy of Dewey's resignation can be found in Box 70, Dewey Mss.

bating narrowness and bigotry in religion," he said, then suggested Carnegie give $10,000 to Isidore Singer to assist him in publishing the *Jewish Encyclopedia.*[25]

But Dewey was not at a December 18, 1905, meeting at Brander Matthews's house in New York, at which participants discussed Carnegie's grant. All present agreed that "the more obvious anomalies of our orthography" had to be removed "if our speech is to be made fit for service as a world-language." Several days later C. P. G. Scott told Funk he and Matthews had just had "a satisfactory session" with Carnegie, and they expected to be able to make a report in the near future. Dewey was, however, at a January 12, 1906, meeting in New York at which a committee of eleven voted to enlarge its membership into a "Simplified Spelling Board" and elect nineteen people to "preferred" membership. Although he was among the nineteen, he was not elected to serve as an officer of the Board, nor as a member of the Executive Committee. Matthews was elected chairman, Scott secretary, and Charles E. Sprague treasurer. All three joined Funk, Henry Holt, Benjamin Smith, and William H. Ward on the Executive Board.[26]

On March 12 the *New York Times* carried a story entitled "Carnegie Assaults the Spelling Book." The article identified important people who had signed the pledge to use the twelve NEA words and explained that "an office will be opened in New York to serve as headquarters for the work." It also noted that the newly formed "Simplified Spelling Board" (SSB) did not intend any "violent alteration" of the language, and would not advance any "extreme theories." Its sole purpose was to "expedite that process of simplification which has been going on in English, . . . notably in the omission of silent and useless letters." On March 23 the Board issued a list of three hundred words it wanted "pruned," and asked people who signed the pledge to begin using the recommended spellings of these words in their correspondence and formal writing. Pledge cards were to be

---

25. Dewey to Matthews, 11/23/05; Dewey to Smith, 12/8/05; Dewey to Carnegie, 12/8/05, Box 85, Dewey Mss; Dewey to Carnegie, 12/20/05, LB 123, Carnegie Mss. See also Scott to Funk, 12/27/05, copy found in Box 85, Dewey Mss.

26. See Brander Matthews, *These Many Years: Recollections of a New Yorker* (N.Y., 1917), pp. 441, 443–44. See also Scott to Funk, 12/27/05, copy found in Box 85, Dewey Mss; Scott to Carnegie, 1/3/06; 1/15/06, LB 124, Carnegie Mss.

returned to the SSB secretary at its main office, 1 Madison Avenue.[27]

Although Dewey continued to support efforts of the Simplified Spelling Board and to attend its meetings, he was not central to its subsequent activities. His name had probably become anathema to Carnegie, Matthews, Scott, and Sprague, none of whom likely wanted the Simplified Spelling Board tainted by giving leadership to someone so controversial and difficult to work with as Melvil Dewey.[28] Names like Mark Twain, Richard Watson Gilder, Andrew D. White, and William James were given more prominent billing. In 1906 President Theodore Roosevelt became a member of the Board, and when he ordered the Public Printer to adopt SSB recommendations that fall, he projected the issue into the political arena and onto a much larger stage. Here the opposition became more intense, as the American literary establishment began to marshal its forces. Dewey was not involved in these debates, and although he continued to remind spelling reformers and SSB members he was the one who had originally cultivated Carnegie, he had to content himself with a peripheral role.

Dewey's fortunes did not improve in other areas, either. On February 27 E. H. Anderson told Dewey that because a "complaint has been made to the Commissioner" that the DDC was being revised on state time, and because "this criticism has been current among librarians generally and among members of the State Library staff in particular for several years," he came to the conclusion that "this work should be done anywhere rather than in this library." Three months later Dewey signed an agreement with May Seymour, who resigned her position at the State Library to move to Lake Placid. There she agreed to devote half her time to the DDC and half to Lake Placid Club publications. In return, Dewey promised she could live on Club grounds free of charge and earn half the net proceeds from the seventh edition and any later editions "she may get out."[29] The DDC was on its own.

---

27. *NYT,* 3/12/06; 3/13/06; 3/22/06; and 4/1/06.

28. Box 87 in the Dewey Mss contains the first page of a multipage letter to Dewey on SSB stationery dated 1/18/17 which reads in part, "You are aware that there is a lack of enthusiasm for you . . . on the part of one or two members of the Exec. Com." The remaining pages of the letter are missing.

29. Anderson to Dewey, 2/27/06, Box 71; copy of agreement between Dewey and Seymour, dated 5/1/06, Box 81, Dewey Mss.

"The Fairchild-Lord Plot"
1906

Dewey's connections with ALA and NYLA were also severed in 1906, but not by his own volition. Others forced him out. The catalyst was his behavior on the 1905 ALA postconference trip when he violated standards of Victorian social conduct by publicly hugging, squeezing, and kissing several ALA women, especially Mary Downey of Ottumwa, Iowa, and Theresa Hitchler of the New York Public Library Cataloging Department.[30] That Dewey regularly had engaged in this type of behavior since the 1880s is evident from correspondence and documentation in the Dewey Papers and elsewhere. Some ALA women, like Florence Woodworth, May Seymour, and later Katharine Sharp, accepted it in their relationship with Dewey; others did not. Before 1905, however, those who objected said nothing about his harassing behavior and simply chose either to endure it or avoid him. After 1905, however, several decided to protest openly.

But in order to understand the timing and intensity of their reaction, it is also important to reconstruct the milieu in which this all took place. In July 1905, Dewey was emotionally drained. He was still the subject of a campaign to remove him from office, and had only recently decided to succumb to Regent pressure to resign. In addition, his wife was still suffering from an extended illness, and the prognosis that she would not live long had not been changed. In this particularly trying time, Dewey probably felt the need to reach out for comfort, and this may explain why his social behavior toward women on the postconference trip was especially unacceptable. That he engaged in it while acting as though he owned the New York State Library School by openly pushing for its removal from Albany upset several people. Some loyal NYSLS alumnae, including Isabel Ely Lord and Mary W. Plummer, were already predisposed to dislike Dewey because of the cavalier way in which "he" was treating "their" school, which

---

30. Florence Woodworth, who was not on the trip, later described Dewey's behavior in a shorthand draft of a letter to J. H. Canfield, dated 7/10/06. It is possible Dewey provided Woodworth with details. Although it is obvious from Canfield's response to Woodworth that she sent him a letter on that day, I was unable to find a copy to check it against her shorthand draft, which is in Box 81, Dewey Mss.

since 1889 they recognized had really been run by Fairchild, not Dewey. Most had much more loyalty to Fairchild.

Additional evidence suggests that some of their anger can be traced to Dewey's unilateral decision in 1902 to minimize Fairchild's curricular emphasis on books and restore his own emphasis on technique. In addition, Dewey had just embarrassed the profession with the national exposure he received because of his Lake Placid exclusionary practices. All of this probably combined to convince Lord and Plummer that Dewey was a liability to ALA and NYLA, and both began to make their feelings known to others. But it was Dewey's objectionable behavior on the post-conference trip that served as the catalyst around which others rallied. And when Lord found out in early fall that Dewey was trying to relocate the school without Regent permission, she and Plummer became even more angry. Plummer was especially vocal that NYLA should never again meet at Placid. Characteristically, Dewey chose to interpret all these activities as a "conspiracy" against him (which in his mind also included Mary S. C. Fairchild and her husband), and in this interpretation he was joined by Seymour, Woodworth, Sharp, and his wife Annie.

First evidence of this behind-the-scenes brouhaha came on June 10, 1906, when Florence Woodworth told James H. Canfield that an ugly rumor concerning Dewey's social behavior at the 1905 conference was circulating the state library community and threatening to disrupt the forthcoming ALA conference. She asked his help, and suggested he talk to Lord. To Dewey she wrote, "My advice is to keep perfectly quiet" pending Canfield's response. But Dewey ignored her advice; two days later he wrote Canfield that because of the damaging information certain people (whom he did not identify) were bandying about and threatening to circulate at the ALA conference, he was going "to drop out of all offices, committees, etc. as rapidly as can be done without its looking like losing interest," and in the future devote himself to his own work. He said he was angry with "those who feel [so] antagonistic that anything they can do to injure me seems a pleasure. My thought is to put this clear statement in your hands and rely on you to state my position and vouch for its sincerity." He also said he "would not accept any library position in the country," then concluded by saying that although he and Annie planned to attend most future NYLA and ALA meetings, it would be only to renew old acquaintances and reminisce about good times past.[31]

Canfield was confused. "I have not the slightest intimation as to what is brewing," he wrote May Seymour, and asked further information. In the interim, however, he decided to talk to Lord. But Lord also avoided specifics except to say "rumors have been rife ever since the Portland meeting." Although she knew of no effort "to give this talk publicity," Bowker, she told Canfield, "knew all about the matter" and could give him much more information.[32] On June 15, however, he received a letter from Annie Dewey (who by this time had recovered from her illness and returned to Lake Placid) that added more detail to the situation. "I learn that Miss Seymour has written you concerning another scheme to injure Mr. Dewey." She enclosed with her note a copy of a letter she was sending to Lord, and continued: "If this gossip should be circulated at the ALA, as threatened, I would like to give you authority to use this letter as you judge best. Otherwise, I hope the subject may never again be mentioned."

In her letter to Lord, Annie Dewey acknowledged that "long absences from home" the past few years together with "some criticisms of Mr. Dewey's unconventional ways" had been so misunderstood "as to occasion gossip, which would seem to have a basis of truth." Yes, he had entertained library-school students and other guests at their home in Albany while she had been away, but "women who have keen intuitions know by instinct that they can trust Mr. Dewey implicitly." She acknowledged that because Dewey was "so sure of his own self-control . . . unconsciously his manner has grown more and more unconventional and familiar." She also acknowledged that "he has been frequently warned of the danger" of passing "the bounds of convention." Still, because his motives were so pure, because he knew Annie "was absolutely free from jealousy, he has doubtless gone farther than with a wife who felt it necessary to watch her husband." But, she told Lord, their marriage was unique because it was based "on an intellectual companionship and congenial

---

31. Woodworth to Dewey, 6/10/06, Box 7; Canfield to Seymour, 6/12/06, Box 81; Dewey to Canfield, 6/12/06, Box 7, Dewey Mss. See also Dewey to H. J. Carr, 6/28/06, Box 7, Dewey Mss.

32. See Canfield to Seymour, 6/14/06; 6/16/06, Box 81, Dewey Mss.

friendship stronger than the usual tie." Although other interests, especially those at Lake Placid, had kept her from attending ALA conferences, these absences had simply been "misunderstood." She then asked Lord to convey the contents of her letter to "all who may know of this matter from your standpoint," thus correcting "any wrong impressions. . . . No good purpose is served by scandal," she argued, and because her husband "is now out of the library field and has no intention of actively entering it again," nothing would be gained by spreading rumors. At the bottom of her letter she penned in longhand, "I should add that Mr. Dewey knows nothing of this letter. The responsibility is wholly mine."[33]

Unbeknown to Canfield, Annie also wrote E. M. Fairchild who, she believed, was the real source of the "conspiracy." On June 19 she sent him a copy of her letter to Lord, but in a personal note characterized by "righteous indignation" elaborated her feelings. Since the day Dewey removed Fairchild's name from a list of proposed library school lecturers several years earlier, "you have plotted and schemed in underhanded ways to injure him. You have poisoned your wife's mind and made her disloyal to her executive head." She accused him of "intense egotism and conceit" and of plotting for Dewey's position. She demanded that Fairchild inform members of New York's Education Department of the truth concerning the 1905 postconference trip, especially of the fact "that you now know however careless and unconventional his manner," Dewey was "free of any impure motives or actions. They have been wholly the interpretation of your own idle imagination." And if he did not stop the rumors, Annie Dewey threatened, she would tell Dewey and "set him right at your expense."[34]

By this time Bowker and Canfield were trading information. On June 19 Bowker told Canfield he had known nothing of the accusations until June 12, when he learned what Lord had told Anderson, and as far as he knew, no one else knew about them except Anderson, Hill, Canfield, and himself. "How far the talk has gone among the women I do not know, but I think that the question . . . should be handled in consultation by the three or

---

33. Annie Dewey to Canfield, 6/15/06; Annie Dewey to Lord, 6/15/06, Box 7, Dewey Mss.
34. Annie Dewey to Fairchild, 6/19/06, Box 19, Dewey Mss.

four men who have been taken into confidence." Apparently
Bowker believed women were less capable of handling such a
delicate situation, and incapable of understanding it objectively.
He told Canfield he had been aware of previous "incidental criticism of uncalled for familiarity," and although he had always regarded it as "trifling," he did not think "any of us can usefully
correspond as to the details of these statements, which indicate
conduct beyond what you have or I had in mind, but, I should
add, short of the extreme." Still, the problem had been extreme,
extreme enough that he had agreed with Mary Plummer that
NYLA should not meet in Lake Placid in 1906. Bowker wrote
Anderson the same day, enclosing a copy of his letter to Canfield
and suggesting that the three men meet prior to the ALA Conference to discuss the matter.[35]

Despite efforts to contain rumors, however, word leaked
out. On June 21 longtime state library employee Helen Sperry
told Dewey "everybody in the library seems most intelligent on
the subject," and because of the rumor mill Dewey and his wife
had "scarcely been out of my mind since Miss Seymour enlight-
ened me as to the last hateful project that is afloat." She could
understand why "such a venomous crusade" might be started
had Dewey still been State Librarian, "but why, when you are out
of their way, they should stoop to such damnable, debasing
schemes is utterly incomprehensible." She thought she knew the
real reason, however:

> They are simply reading into your nonconventionalism
> all the turpitude that such unconventionality would mean
> in their own cases with unexplored sensual reminders
> hidden back of eternal forces.[36]

Canfield wrote Annie Dewey on June 25 that he had just
had "long conferences" with Bowker, Anderson, and Hill. There
was "no question," he said, "that Mr. Dewey's language and action
have thoroughly alarmed and distressed and annoyed at least
three library-world women—two of whom [are] certainly of the

35. Bowker to Canfield, 6/19/06; Bowker to Anderson, 6/19/06,
Bowker Mss. See also Bowker to Canfield, 6/22/06, Bowker Mss, for an
indication of correspondence attempting to set up a meeting between the
two men and Anderson before the ALA conference.

36. Speery to Dewey, 6/21/06, Box 7, Dewey Mss.

highest character and reputation and standing, and not known as hostile to him before this time." There was also "no question that this information is in the hands of those who *are* hostile to Mr. Dewey, and that in their final use of it they will be rather indifferent as to the results." Canfield said he believed all parties wanted to avoid publicity, but "in their overwrought nervous condition, even a half-dozen people are likely to do great harm." Given these circumstances, Canfield and "two or three" others urged Dewey to stay away from the forthcoming ALA conference. Some people would regard Dewey's absence as an admission of guilt, Canfield acknowledged, but "those who wish him harm have the advantage of thorough preparation—we have none." If Dewey stayed away, if he refrained from becoming "a storm center," Canfield and others could make "further quiet inquiry" at the conference, report back to the Deweys after it was over, and they could then "take up the entire matter leisurely and in any way which may seem best to you both."[37]

By this time Annie Dewey had received a response from E. M. Fairchild, fully rejecting her tone and accusations. On the contrary, he argued, he had done a "great service" for the Deweys that had actually "put off this evil day several years for you." In 1903 a member of the State Library staff had come to his wife and "charged Mr. Dewey with improper conduct toward another member of the staff." Fairchild indicated his wife discussed the matter with him, and together with Reference Librarian D. V. R. Johnston convinced the staff member that "none of the rest of the staff wanted an attack of that kind made" and managed to "secure a promise that she would drop the matter." Fairchild said he had never made the incident public, not even during the height of Dewey's troubles in 1905 when it would easily have been made into a scandal by his enemies. Fairchild also said other incidents had been alleged. For example, at one time a group of female students reportedly "avoided going driving with Mr. Dewey because they did not like appearances."

Dewey's troubles, Fairchild argued, could not be traced to anything he did but to "overanxiety on Mr. Dewey's part to keep fast hold of his library friends professionally at the Portland

---

37. Canfield to Annie Dewey, 6/25/06, Box 20, Dewey Mss. See also Bowker to Helen E. Haines, 6/25/06, Box 38, Bowker Mss, in which he refers to a meeting with Canfield on that day.

meeting, and, principally from his friendly treatment of the library women on the 'post conference' trip." The heart of the problem, as far as he was concerned, was "a general movement to reestablish book knowledge and culture as an essential of the American librarian." He implied Melvil Dewey was against it; that was evident from his "work." He said his wife had been for it; that was evident from her Reading Seminar and speeches she had made in previous years. Because of her strong convictions she had almost left the library school in 1902 when Dewey changed her Reading Seminar into a "Book Selection" course. Fairchild told Annie he did not think Dewey "had committed any serious immorality," and that he himself had never been a candidate for Dewey's position.[38]

On June 27 Annie responded to Canfield's letter of the 25th. By that time the Deweys seemed very eager to put the matter behind them and still save face. "It is impossible for either Mr. Dewey or myself to attend" the ALA conference, she wrote, largely because their work at Lake Placid was at "its most critical stage." She also enclosed a copy of her letter to Fairchild, and said "this Fairchild-Lord plot" had been the result of bad feelings created in 1901 when in "his outspoken way" Dewey "took [Lord] to task . . . because she threatened to take a position offered her in a department where she 'could get more money,'" Fairchild and Lord were at the center of the "scandal," she argued; their motive was revenge. "That Mr. Dewey has been most unwise in his unconventional manner with women I do not in the least excuse," she concluded, "but this is not the way a man with evil intentions goes about it. I trust this unpleasant episode will clear the air."

Dewey added even more paranoia to this interpretation on June 29. "This plot is old enough to be addled," he wrote Canfield. "It was hatched soon after Miss Cutler's marriage. It has been worked in my own library where 5 or 6 were tainted." He said he was proud of his enemies, however, most of whom he considered grafters and professional politicians in search of half-truths on which to hang him. All of this, he said, he had "discussed fully with Mrs. Dewey and the ladies of my family, Misses Sharp, Seymour and Woodworth"; all had agreed to ignore their enemies. "If you knew the whole truth," he said, "you would

---

38. Fairchild to Annie Dewey, 6/23/06, Box 20; Fairchild to Woodworth, 6/27/06, copy found in Box 7, Dewey Mss.

understand my contempt for these scandalmongers who distort innocent things out of the ordinary into plain evil doing. . . . I suffer for my carelessness during 30 years in ALA," he concluded, "and for my conceit that I was so different from most men and had so much more trust in women. Pure women would understand my ways."[39] Apparently women who did not understand were in Dewey's mind something less than "pure."

Although the Deweys did not attend the ALA conference in early July, Dewey did submit reports of his ALA work in the form of letters to the committee chairs. To Henry Carr Dewey indicated his desire to abdicate leadership of the American Library Institute, and suggested Canfield as his replacement.[40] The published proceedings make no reference to the controversy surrounding Dewey, but private correspondence sent him during and shortly after the conference shows it was a primary subject of discussion in cloakrooms and hallways. Helen Sperry reported to Annie Dewey her "indignation at the malice of your enemies (which has kept my nerves continually on the stretch since I came to this meeting)." But Dewey's primary "ears" were Woodworth, Seymour, and Sharp. Seymour reported that "four prominent women in the ALA" were "ready to testify to [Dewey's] improprieties and two . . . would resign from ALA" if Dewey did not stop. She also said Ahern had been made "the recipient of several tearful confidings from girls [Dewey] had disturbed," but despite the fact Ahern "disapproved" of Dewey's behavior, she "understood the situation and quieted their fears."

Sharp indicated that she, Seymour, and Woodworth "do not confer together *conspicuously,*" and reported that in her judgment cloakroom sentiment was running against Dewey's enemies, who were circulating widely. "Some say they will go home if the annoyance does not stop." Sharp then commented on people the Deweys obviously held suspect in the "Fairchild-Lord plot." "Miss [Lutie] Stearns and Miss [Alice] Tyler [of the Iowa Library Commission] are alright and each is the center of strong feeling. Miss Ahern and Miss Downey are o.k.; Dr. C[anfield] had been warned about Miss A. but I told him I thought she was true in this." Isabel Ely Lord, however, "is everywhere. Has been

---

39. Annie Dewey to Canfield, 6/27/06, Box 19; Dewey to Canfield, 6/29/06, Box 7, Dewey Mss.
40. Dewey to Carr, 7/10/06, Box 7, Dewey Mss.

nominated to council and cannot be defeated without explanation." In a second letter written after the conference Sharp reported that the "better element is disgusted and that sentiment is spreading," then concluded: "Don't worry about anything. The worst is over now." Canfield wrote Dewey July 5. Dewey's absence, he said, relieved his enemies "of any sense of repression whatever, and they talked themselves out accordingly. As far as I could discover the older and better known members—both men and women—were simply annoyed and repelled by this gossip."[41]

The end of the 1906 conference also signaled the end of Dewey's active participation in ALA matters. In exchange for a quiet departure he was spared an ugly and public exposé of one of his major flaws. Characteristically, however, he would not or could not blame himself for his predicament. Instead he was disappointed that members of his profession had not come to his aid in his time of crisis. He also felt the association he had created, for which he had "sacrificed" so much, had abandoned him. Although Dewey continued his interest in ALA's progress throughout the remainder of his life, and although he regularly contributed his ideas by means of correspondence with various ALA luminaries, he was never again a power player in ALA politics. By 1906, many ALA members (and especially many female ALA members) were tired of dealing with an overenthusiastic administrator who seemed unwilling to compromise and incapable of changing his behavior. They concluded that their association was better off without Melvil Dewey, and few sought to keep him actively enrolled in its progress.[42]

But by that time Dewey had cemented his influence into the practice of librarianship and permanently affected its position among all information professions by making its highest priority service to the authority of others' expertise. Over 1,400

---

41. Sperry to Annie Dewey, 6/28/06, Box 21; Seymour to Dewey, 7/2/06, Box 81; Sharp to Dewey, 7/1/06; Canfield to Dewey, 7/5/06, Box 7, Dewey Mss.

42. Dewey attended only three more ALA conferences before he died: 1918, 1921, and 1926. Without Dewey's active leadership, the American Library Institute became an organization in search of a function. After an insignificant existence extending over three decades, it finally expired in 1941. See George B. Utley, "American Library Institute: A Historical Sketch," *LQ* 16 (1946): 152–59.

This impressive notice of election to the Italian Bibliographic Society reflected Dewey's stature abroad as well as in the American library community.

communities received grants from Andrew Carnegie between 1890 and 1915 to build new public libraries. As they joined hundreds of others already in existence that wished to make their institutions more responsive to the pressures they perceived emanating from industrialization, immigration, and urbanization, they all cast about for guidance in selecting and organizing collections of books for their physical plants, furnishing them with the latest equipment, and staffing them with personnel possessing the most up-to-date skills in efficient library managment.

For organizing their collections the vast majority found the Dewey Decimal Classification the most suitable and widely accepted. For selection of the "right" books the vast majority found the *ALA Catalog* and its serial offspring, the monthly *Booklist* magazine ALA began publishing in 1905, ready to provide guidance. For furnishing their libraries, the vast majority found the Library Bureau had the best circulation desks, library supplies, and especially card catalogs into which they placed the 7.5 × 12.5 cm cards containing the kinds of systematized bibliographic information Dewey had convinced several ALA committees to adopt since 1877. And for helping them manage their plants some were able to afford graduates of Dewey's library school or one of its clones; most, however, hired local women willing to work for less money who possessed the right "character" and could pick up the necessary skills either by reading the textbooks library-school faculty published or by attending summer institutes sponsored by a growing number of state public library commissions seeking to duplicate what Melvil Dewey did for New York between 1889 and 1905. After 1905 no American librarians—and by extension no American library users—could say they and their institutions had not been affected by the legacy of this irrepressible reformer.

PART THREE

The Lake Placid Years

1906–1931

14

Building an Efficient
WASP's Nest

1906–1925

When Dewey moved to Lake Placid permanently in May
1906, he did not reduce his intensity for reform. Instead, he rechanneled his energies to more singular
interests. From then on, all other reform interests assumed avo-
cational status; from then on, making the Lake Placid Club a
success occupied most of his attention. He and Annie were determined it would become the nation's model rest and recreation
community based on Protestant values and Victorian standards
of social conduct. They dedicated themselves to making it a leading example of healthy and efficient living, but never at the expense of "culture and refinement." Under their direction, the
Lake Placid Club continued to ban consumption of liquor and
tobacco, forbade gambling, lotteries, and raffles, and respected
the Sunday Sabbath. One former employee, however, suggested
an additional less altruistic motive—Dewey also wanted to build
a community wealthy Jews would covet but could not join.[1]

Dewey ran the Lake Placid Club and Company like he ran
most of his other private enterprises. Much consisted of "smoke
and mirrors" accounting. Generally, his dreams and goals greatly
outpaced his financial resources, but by constantly pushing
the latter and persuading close disciples of his lifework schemes

---

1. Colburn interview, 5/13/1985.

315

to invest in the former, he achieved amazing results. Several times his propensity to push his financial limits brought him to the brink of bankruptcy; oftentimes it brought him into conflict with his creditors; regularly it manifested itself in reliance on old friends whose loyalties Dewey had been exploiting for years.[2]

Because of the unpleasant experiences of 1895 and 1896, the Deweys determined never to mix the Lake Placid Club with the Lake Placid Company. The Company was the business corporation organized to finance the Club; it owned all property, took all financial risks, issued securities, and assumed responsibility for all liabilities. The Deweys were always majority stockholders. The Club, on the other hand, represented the social organization which in effect rented what the Company owned; the Club owned no property and took no financial risks. Individual Club members were encouraged to purchase Company-issued bonds or nonvoting preferred stock aimed at improving the physical plant, but the financial responsibility of ownership and operation remained in the hands of common stockholders— the Dewey family. Oftentimes people confused the Club with the Company; regularly the term "Lake Placid Club" was used for either—or both.

"Wheels within Wheels": Expanding the Physical Plant and the Debt 1906–1921

As soon as he moved to Lake Placid Dewey began acting on building plans. Beginning that summer, he and Annie formed a routine. They met at breakfast every morning, where they discussed problems and progress on Club improvements. Thereafter, Annie circulated Club grounds in a white smock she designed with different colored pockets, each of which held a different colored notebook for specific subjects, departments, or individuals. Melvil walked Club grounds carrying a six-foot rule he designed

---

2. May Seymour moved to Placid in August 1906; Katharine Sharp moved in August 1907. Dewey described some of this on the occasion of Seymour's death in a circular to "Friends," 6/14/21, Box 27, Dewey Mss. See also Laurel Grotzinger, *The Power and the Dignity: Librarianship and Katharine Sharp* (Metuchen, N.J., 1966), p. 273.

that was tapered at the bottom. Because the thick end had higher gradations for large measurements, the thin end lower gradations for small measurements, Dewey figured he never wasted time by grabbing the wrong end.[3]

Since 1900 the Club's summer occupancy had run nearly 100 percent, but in 1906 Dewey was more immediately concerned with the three remaining seasons, and especially winter. He sensed great potential for winter sports, especially sledding, skating, and skiing. He immediately launched a winterization program for several buildings to promote winter occupancy. Forest Towers was built for the 1905–6 season, but quickly proved too small. Dewey then built Forest Hall and connected it by means of glass-enclosed piazzas to several other buildings so guests had direct inside access to the Club's public rooms, 103 bedrooms, 47 baths, and 45 open fires.

Dewey also pushed to increase occupancy for the other two seasons when guests could, he said, witness "the miracle of opening spring" or the "brilliant splendors" of an Adirondack autumn. But no matter when they came, Dewey reminded them, they could breathe the air that came to Club grounds after traversing 4,000,000 acres of pine forest. "Evergreen forests have a powerful purifying effect on the surrounding atmosfere," *Lake Placid Club Notes* reported in March 1907. Air was "made antiseptic by some element which is not only fatal to germ life, but at the same time is stimulant and tonic to normal fisiologic processes."[4]

In the fall of 1907 Dewey's plans were in full evidence. He was preparing to enlarge the Club for the 1,000 summer guests he expected in 1908, up from the 200 it had hosted in 1900. But to do so he had spent more than $275,000 on improvements in 1906 and 1907, including a new laundry, powerhouse, icehouse, and cooler. In 1906 the Company had sold $70,000 worth of real estate to cover part of the cost of these improvements,[5] but this

---

3. Colburn Interview, 5/13/1985; Gunther, "Annie Godfrey Dewey," p. 366; Dawe, *Dewey,* p. 110.

4. See *LPC Notes,* no. 4 (5/06): 6; *LPC Notes,* no. 9 (3/14/07): 1–4; LPC *Handbook* (1914): 91; 287; Godfrey Dewey, "Sixty Years," pp. 6–7; and George Carroll, *Lake Placid: The Adirondack Village That Became World Famous* (Glens Falls, N.Y., 1968), pp. 29–30.

5. Some of this money came from the sale of land on the 500-acre Moose Island (located in the middle of Mirror Lake) to a community of Jews that included E. R. A. Seligman and J. Benjamin Dimmick. Perhaps Dewey

hardly offset the cost of investments plus debt repayments of $200,000 on land optioned in 1896 and 1897.

In addition, the fall season had been so rainy that the guest rate was down, and the Panic of 1907 had depressed real estate values (the sale of which constituted a large part of the working capital on which Dewey counted) and bankrupted several people who held Company securities. In order to protect Company interests, the Dewey "family" had to buy the securities at auction using money originally targeted for capital improvements. In addition, sales of real estate, bonds, and preferred stock languished as a result of the Panic. Dewey's only recourse was to borrow; in the next two years the Company became heavily mortgaged, and by 1909 Dewey had once again backed himself in a corner.[6]

On the surface the Club's future looked bright. In 1909 Dewey bragged that a Club consisting of five acres, one building, and an annual income of $5,000 in 1895 had in fifteen years grown into a Company owning 6,000 acres, 225 buildings, and an annual income of $500,000. The Company operated three of the four sawmills in Essex County, and the only creamery and certified milk plant within 35 miles. Its 21 farms supported 260 milk cows and a poultry plant housing 5,000 leghorns. It paid over $7,000 in local taxes, and in peak season employed 500 people, including 100 boys who caddied Club golf courses. And Club members, Dewey noted, spent thousands of dollars in local Adirondack communities, especially during summer.

Privately, however, Dewey worried about Company debt. Initially he took several minor steps to address the problem. First, the Deweys vacated their own cottage so it could generate rent by Club members, and moved to rooms in another building. During peak season Dewey even slept on a couch in Annie's room to release another room to generate rent. Second, he borrowed some money from his brother Manfred and Ginn Brothers, his original business partners in 1876. Third, he raised membership dues to make the Club self-supporting. Because the Company

---

surmised that Jews might be appeased by his magnanimity yet contained by the island's geography. See Dewey to Seligman, 3/22/06; and Dewey to Dimmick, 3/22/06, Seligman Mss. Eventually, the Company bought the island back. See LPC *Handbook,* 1914, pp. 17, 697.

6. See undated circular, "Why the Club Is Short of Funds after Its Most Successful Year," Box 52, Dewey Mss; and Dewey "To Preferred Stockholders of Lake Placid Co.," 9/1/08, LPEF Mss.

had covered Club deficits totalling $75,000 for ten years, he told members, associate member and season golf tickets would increase 20 percent and regular member table discounts of 20 percent would be reduced to 10 percent eleven months of the year, and altogether in August.

This last step, however, also forced Dewey to explain the Company's financial situation to Club members. In recent years, he said, the Club's growing popularity had encouraged Company owners to expand. Raising $200,000 in preferred stock in 1900 and $200,000 from bonds in 1904 had helped, but not enough to cover the cost of improvements needed to meet demand after 1907. As a result, "we have greatly overworked our capital so that we sometimes have to delay payments as long as business friends will let us." Among creditors, Dewey admitted, the Company had a "reputation of being 'slow pay.'" To remedy the problem, the Company had to take three steps: it would (1) build no new cottages or commence no additions to existing buildings for the foreseeable future unless someone advanced the money as a loan to be paid directly from earnings, not from working capital; (2) raise capital by issuing more bonds and an additional $300,000 worth of preferred stock; and (3) improve its standing with local banks by moving Asa Gallup from Company treasurer to "clerk."

Dewey did not elaborate the last step, but Gallup's poor credit with upstate New York banks had been an open secret for several years. His entreprencurial spirit had always been more personally materialistic than Dewey's. Since 1900 he had observed how Dewey's successes with the Club increased the value of adjacent land, and in 1905 he took a part-time position with a local real estate company to take advantage of the potential. Here he renewed a close working relationship with Albany businessman Samuel S. Hatt, whose fortunes suddenly turned sour in the Panic of 1907; so sour, in fact, that in 1909 all New York banks refused to honor notes endorsed by him or any of his business partners. Inevitably, Gallup's association with Hatt became part of the upstate New York economic climate in which Lake Placid Company finances were perceived. Dewey hoped Gallup's demotion would help the Company's financial profile.[7]

---

7. "Notes on Lake Placid Co Financial Program for 1910," n.d., FPA. See also Gallup to Dewey, 12/9/11, Box 52; and undated Dewey memoir, Box 58, Dewey Mss.

Efforts to make the Club solvent were successful. By November 1910, increased fees enabled the Club to erase its deficit. Company accounts continued to show heavy debts, however, and in summer 1911, several creditors lost patience with Dewey. They demanded he either repay them immediately or create a Lake Placid Company voting trust so they could be assured its finances would be managed more responsibly. But Dewey would not abdicate Company control to a voting trust; he undoubtedly recalled how Davidson and Parker had used that tactic to wrest control of the Library Bureau from him. Instead, he contacted Club member George Plimpton, who advised a "long-term compromise settlement" with creditors.

When Dewey approached creditors to negotiate the arrangement Plimpton recommended, however, they were adamantly against it. At first Dewey thought part of the reason for their opposition was Gallup's control of $25,000 in Company preferred stock that Dewey could not pledge as collateral. To eliminate this problem he offered Gallup a ten-year option to buy 49 percent of Company stock if Gallup released control of the stock to him. Gallup gladly accepted Dewey's offer; in it he saw opportunities to improve his own prospects and quickly told Hatt about his new arrangement. When Dewey returned to his creditors with Gallup's guarantee, however, they still refused to renegotiate. Dewey sensed something else had triggered their refusal. For the time being, however, he could do nothing about it; instead, he went back to Plimpton for further advice.[8]

This time Plimpton was more forthright. He pressed Dewey to accept a plan to form a "Finance Committee" of four to function as a voting trust, to oversee Placid Company finances, and to represent the Company to local banks. All Lake Placid stock would be put in escrow, and the 49 percent on which Gallup had recently been given an option (Plimpton scolded Dewey for this move) would be put up for sale. In addition, Plimpton insisted that Dewey get his son Godfrey to return control of the $10,000 in Company common stock his parents had given him for graduation from Harvard in 1910 in order that Dewey could guarantee absolute control of 51 percent of the stock. To all of this Dewey agreed, but only if he and the trust shared veto power. The trust could take no action on Placid finances without Dewey's vote;

---

8. Plimpton to Dewey, 8/21/11; 9/5/11, Plimpton Mss.

Dewey could launch no new ventures without approval of the voting trust.

After Plimpton acquiesced, Dewey asked Godfrey to relinquish control of the common stock. He was "shocked," however, when Godfrey refused unless Dewey replaced it with $40,000 in preferred stock. Ultimately, Dewey had no choice but to agree to Godfrey's terms if he wanted to conclude the arrangement with the Finance Committee and appease his creditors. (Understandably, the whole episode drove a wedge between Dewey and his son, from which neither fully recovered.)[9] Dewey then quickly returned to Plimpton with Godfrey's assurances, and together they formalized the agreement setting up the voting trust.

Plimpton then urged Dewey to make up a clear and simple budget for the forthcoming year that the trust could show to creditors, and warned Dewey against two character flaws—do not make "so many 'wheels within wheels,'" he said, and do not incorporate "gush, enthusiasm and promises" into the budget plan. "All such things are not going to pay the bills. You must remember that your credit is mighty poor."[10] By the beginning of December all of his creditors agreed to extend Dewey's repayment timetable under the new voting trust, and the Company's financial situation not only stabilized, it considerably improved for the rest of the decade. Dewey had weathered another crisis.

Three months later, however, he accidentally discovered how lucky he had been to close the agreement in late 1911, and how close he had come to losing his beloved Lake Placid Club. In the spring of 1912, Sam Hatt was arrested for illegal business practices. Because Gallup was bedridden at the time with a serious illness and Dewey worried that Gallup's connections to Hatt might damage the Company's financial situation, without permission he began looking through Gallup's papers. What he found shocked him. By piecing together bits of information he came to realize that after he had demoted Gallup from Company treasurer to clerk Gallup went back to Hatt, and together they devised a plan to take control of majority stock and turn the

9. See undated note in Box 58, Dewey Mss (which Dewey wrote more than a decade later and in which he recalled the chronology of events surrounding the creation of the voting trust); Dewey to Dun and Bradstreet, 2/6/23, FPA; Dewey to Godfrey, 9/11/31, Box 23, Dewey Mss.

10. Plimpton to Dewey, 11/2/11, 11/3/11; 11/24/11, Plimpton Mss.

Company into a profit-making resort in order to rescue themselves from debt. Unbeknown to Dewey, his offer to Gallup to buy 49 percent of Company stock had actually played directly into their hands.

When Gallup gave Hatt a list of Company creditors in late August, Hatt visited each, hinted at the Company's shaky financial base, and represented himself as an associate of a Company partner with an option to buy 49 percent of its stock. He also hinted at their plans to turn the Club into a profit-making resort. Because of Hatt's activities in August, Dewey's creditors came to believe the Company was about to be taken over. Dewey surmised that was why he had met such strong opposition from creditors when he asked them to extend his repayment timetable. He guessed that Gallup and Hatt hoped creditors would press for immediate payment, drive him into a corner, and create a situation in which he would lose control of voting stock to Gallup and Hatt. Dewey also realized that had Gallup gone to Godfrey (who at the time controlled 10 percent of Company common stock) and convinced Godfrey to join them in turning the Club into a resort, and had they then arranged financing to exercise Gallup's option to buy 49 percent of Company common stock, Gallup and Godfrey could have taken over the Lake Placid Company. Unwittingly, however, Dewey had foiled Gallup's and Hatt's plans by agreeing to form a Finance Committee as a voting trust that satisfied Dewey's creditors.

The realization of how close the Lake Placid Company had come to takeover triggered two responses. Dewey became even angrier with Godfrey for holding his control of Company common stock hostage to "selfish" goals; he was indignant with Gallup for conspiring to subvert "family" interests. For the time being he decided to suppress his anger with Godfrey, but act on his discovery of Gallup's conspiracy with Hatt. When he confronted Gallup with the evidence, Gallup admitted complicity. Dewey in turn told the Finance Committee and in June the Committee fired Gallup. Dewey had fully concurred with their decision.[11]

---

11. This information and chronology pieced together from Gallup to Dewey, 12/9/11, Box 52; undated Dewey memoir, Box 58; Dewey to Finance Committee 1/23/12; 3/25/12; Dewey to Mr. Bosworth, 7/31/19, Box 52; Dewey to Marissa Green, 2/5/13, Box 38, Dewey Mss; and Dewey to Nicholas Murray Butler, n.d., Butler Mss. See also Dewey to Finance Committee, 10/26/18, Box 52, Dewey Mss; and Fremont Rider, *And Master of None: An*

But the realization of how close he had come to losing the Club did not deter him. Characteristically, Dewey pushed forward. In January 1913, he set a goal of doubling Club membership and filling Club quarters during slack seasons. By that time the Club had 76 residence houses and four central clubhouses. The Lakesyd Clubhouse, oldest and largest, contained eighty-four sleeping rooms and six dining rooms large enough to accommodate five hundred people. The Forest group, which centered around Forest Hall, served as headquarters for winter activity. The Iroquois Group, set off to the side, was reserved for the "more quiet and retiring."[12] Winter season occupancy continued to grow; in February, Dewey counted a Club family of 223. Part of the reason was the installation of two starting platforms erected above the lake for toboggans and coasters; one stood forty-two feet high, the other twenty. Both channeled riders onto the frozen lake and "clear across to the village."

Although he wanted to double membership, he still refused to compromise Club customs. In a June 1914 issue of *Club Notes* he reminded all Club members that "whatever fashion allows drinking, smoking and gambling by women yung or old wil no more be tolerated at this family club than wud contajus diseases." He also said that "dansing without vulgar extremes" was welcome at the Club, but families who refused to stop their children from dancing "cheek to cheek" were asked to leave. Club employees, whose behavior was subject to the same regulations as guests, were directed not to accept tips, and Club members were encouraged not to offer them.[13]

Nor were basic admissions standards changed. "No one will be received as member or guest against whom there is any reasonable physical, moral, social or race objection," Dewey wrote in the 1914 *Handbook,* "or who would be unwelcome to even a

---

Autobiography in the Third Person (Middleton, Conn., 1955), pp. 231–32. Late in 1913 Hatt was sentenced to thirteen years in prison. Shortly after he was fired Gallup moved to suburban New York City, where he became manager of a small hotel. Although he retained the ten-year option to buy 49 percent of company common stock, he had no financial means to exercise that option. When Gallup died in 1917, the option passed to his estate.

12. LPC *Handbook,* 1914, pp. 91; 474.

13. *LPC Notes,* no. 48 (2/13): 406–10; no. 63 (3/13): 417–18; no. 65 (6/14): 518; 521. See also a Dewey private circular dated 7/3/20, LPEF Mss; and Dewey to Finance Committee 7/20/20, Box 52, Dewey Mss.

small minority." The standard applied not only to candidates for election to Club membership, but also to member guests. "We have many Southern members," Dewey noted, "so negroes can be admitted only to servants quarters." Eight years later he reminded Club officers that "no Jews or negros were elijibl for Club membership," and that "new-rich groups" like "many Cubans" would also be denied because of "lack of refinement." To simplify matters, Dewey divided Club applicants into five classes. Those designated "A" were "admirably suited to further the ideals of the club" and were sought for membership. Those designated "B" had some desirable distinctions advantageous to the Club, and their applications were welcomed. "C" individuals represented the "common client" whose membership was considered neither advantageous nor disadvantageous. "D" designees manifested deficiencies meriting further investigation. "E" people were "unsuitables who . . . must be excluded for the protection of the rest."[14]

The Club's object had not changed either—"to secure among congenial people and beautiful natural surroundings all advantages of an ideal vacation or permanent cuntry home, with highest standards of helth, comfort, rest and attractiv recreations both summer and winter." In part the Club functioned as a laboratory for members of the American Home Economics Association, which continued to meet there for annual conferences until 1908, when conferences outgrew the Club's ability to accommodate them. After 1908, however, the Club continued to host the annual meeting of the AHEA's Household Administration section, which was a particular interest of Annie's because she wanted to apply its "science" to her administration of the Club. By that time lists of directions Annie had prepared for Club waitresses, chambermaids, and other employees had been gathered together in a small booklet and adopted by the AHEA as a text for home economics classes across the country.[15]

Until November 1, 1916, Annie Dewey chose all Club furniture and draperies, managed the Club table, and had responsi-

14. LPC *Handbook,* 1914, pp. 1, 5, 18, 27, 468, 478–79, 482; T. Morris Longstreth, *The Adirondacks* (N.Y., 1917), p. 247. See also Dewey note to LPClub officers, 9/5/22, LPEF Mss; and *LPC News* 2 (9/7/28): 7.

15. See "Home Economics," *LPC Notes* no. 50 (April, 1911): 309; Annie Dewey, "Standards of Living in the Home," *Outlook* 101 (6/29/12): 486–94. See also Cornelia Marvin to Annie Dewey, 2/8/11; Annie Dewey to Marvin, 2/16/11, RG/L-8, OSA; and Gunther, "Annie Godfrey Dewey," p. 360.

bility for the Club's domestic science practices. After that date, however, her failing health and diminished eyesight forced her to relinquish responsibility to trusted subordinate Emily Beal, who continued Annie's litmus tests of efficiency. For example, because Club managers assigned families to particular tables in lodge dining halls, Beal decided to change napkins only once per day. Dewey calculated it saved the Club approximately $2,900 per year. During World War I, Dewey ordered the dining rooms to serve guests smaller portions "with entire freedom to order more if wanted." Most did not ask for more, and Dewey discovered this practice reduced waste by two-thirds and saved $50,000 annually. In addition, he instructed cooks to push vegetables, not meat; the former were healthier, the latter was more expensive. Dewey later calculated this practice saved the Club another $5,000 annually.[16]

His passion for "efficiency" also drew Dewey to one of his few post-1906 efforts at reform off Club grounds. On March 12, 1912, several New York City businessmen organized an Efficiency Society "to promote efficiency or percentage of result obtained relative to effort expended in every activity of man and in everything he employs." The Society had intentions of expanding the concept of efficiency to all areas of human endeavor and far beyond Frederick Taylor's scientific management, which at the time was being widely applied to American industry. It quickly drew over seven hundred members (among whom were Melvil and Godfrey Dewey). Because Society officers were so optimistic about the future, however, they began encumbering funds on projected membership increases.

On May 27, Dewey addressed the Society on "Ofis Motion Study," and told his audience most offices could save 15 percent of their time by using short words and eliminating useless syllables. In September 1913, Dewey hosted a Society conference on Club grounds; Annie organized a "Ladies Meeting" devoted to "Home Economics," and the Club put on a "Special Efficiency Dinner" at Lakesyd. Several months later Dewey again addressed the Efficiency Society, this time on "How the Professional Man Can Keep His Own System." In February 1914, he was made Chairman of a "Languaj Committee" (he insisted on the spelling)

---

16. See copy of Dewey's speech before the Home Economics Association, 1/9/15, Box 41, Dewey Mss; and *LPC Notes,* no. 87 (11/16): 625.

and began taking a more active role in Society affairs. He hoped this position would allow him to coordinate efforts of the SSB and SRA and accelerate wider adoption of simplified spelling. The Society held its second meeting at the Club September 17–20.[17]

But by this time the Society was struggling, and from a high of 856 early in 1914 began losing members rapidly. It had been unable to issue its journal in a timely fashion and was anxious about the image of inefficiency this projected to the outside world. Some talked of merging with other efficiency societies, but Dewey resisted. The Society had a vital and unique role to play in the efficiency movement, he argued. Perhaps he spoke too forcefully. In January 1915 he was elected president. At the time the Society was in serious financial difficulty and organizational disarray with no clear purpose and a rapidly decreasing membership list. At a June 21 meeting, membership voted almost indifferently that "the work of the Society should go on in some way," but seemed incapable of being more specific. The Society held its third and last annual meeting at Lake Placid September 17–19.[18]

In January 1916, the Society began negotiations along with the National Institute of Efficiency to become constituent parts of the National Efficiency Society in Washington, D.C. By 1918 negotiations had been completed, and the Efficiency Society over which Dewey had presided apathetically for three years largely disappeared into the pages of history. For a time the Lake Placid Club sponsored a small chapter with ties to the national organization, but even this disappeared from Club activities after 1922. On February 12, 1923, Dewey answered an inquiry from a former member that the Society was "not ded, but sleeping quyt soundli," and that he hoped in the near future "to revive" it. He never did.[19]

---

17. *Transactions,* I, p. 41; *Bulletin of the Efficiency Society* 2 (5/13): 5; *NYT,* 5/28/13; *Greater Efficiency: Journal of the Efficiency Society* 3 (2/14): 79; 83; Dewey to Scott, 2/24/14, Box 86, Dewey Mss. Text of Dewey's speech in Box 40, Dewey Mss.

18. Much of the correspondence between Dewey and Efficiency Society officers detailing its problems is in Box 39, Dewey Mss. See especially H. S. McCormick to Dewey, 3/2/15.

19. See Dewey "To the Efficiency Society," 7/18/15; Dewey to William B. Howland, 1/22/16; Dewey to Charles Dexter Allen, 2/12/23, Box

Dewey did not so readily drop other reforms, despite stronger criticisms. In all Club publications Dewey continued to use simplified spelling. Occasionally, it cost him members and subjected him to ridicule and scorn. Club member Alonzo G. See chided Dewey for his rigid adherence to "manufactured spelling." One guest, he teased, saw "Stud Prunes" on the menu and asked if these were specially prepared for men. "I suspect you are heartily ashamed of the mongrel spelling yourself," See continued, but "lack the courage to let go." Lake Placid's William J. Blunt lived up to his name. "Your rotten way of spelling the English language certainly amuses me," he wrote in 1914. "Have a little sense and don't make an ass out of yourself." But Dewey refused to modify his practices; all Club publications continued to use simplified spelling. Guests were reminded to close their doors "tyt" at night and were served "cofi" every morning.[20]

The fiscal constraints effected by the Finance Committee did not forbid Dewey from expanding his plant by exploiting his friends. In November 1913, for example, he convinced May Seymour to buy a 143-acre farm abutting Company property at $60 per month to cover principal and interest. The Company then agreed to rent the farm for $60 per month, and supplement it with an 8 percent annual dividend on the principal she had invested. Seymour then promised to turn the deed over to the Company when she had recovered her investment.[21] The agreement was tidy; Dewey got to use Seymour's good credit to increase the buffer between Club grounds and the outside world. And because striking the agreement required no action from the Finance Committee, Dewey did not risk their veto.

Another tack he used regularly was to convince friends to reinvest the interest (and sometimes the principal) he owed on loans they extended him by agreeing to accept preferred stock in lieu of cash. Although he and Annie Dewey guaranteed the stock against loss, this practice allowed him to make transfers on

39; and notes on the meetings of the Lake Placid Efficiency Club, Box P-21, Dewey Mss. See also Samuel Haber, *Efficiency and Uplift: Scientific Management in the Progressive Era, 1890–1920* (Chicago, 1964), pp. 72–74, for an abbreviated summary of the Efficiency Society's history.

20. See A. G. See to Dewey, 11/16/20; Blunt to Dewey, 9/19/14, Box 86, Dewey Mss. See also E. V. Lucas, "Turning East and Turning West," undated typescript found in Box P-68, Dewey Mss.

21. Copy of this agreement, dated 11/3/13, is in Box 81, Dewey Mss.

paper alone. During the next four years he worked out similar arrangements with May Seymour, Florence Woodworth, Mary
Sharp (sister of Katharine L. Sharp), Margaret Linn, Mary Ahern,
Theresa West Elmendorf, and Walter S. Biscoe and his sister.
Although he often referred to the women in this group as his
"widows," most had never married. And their loyalty to him continued to feed a rumor mill quite active in the nation's library
community.[22]

In 1920 May Seymour had a large cottage called White
Birches built on Club grounds, and made it large enough to accommodate her in one section, and Melvil and Annie Dewey in
another. White Birches quickly became the Deweys' social center; they regularly entertained there, and turned it into a family
circle much like Albany's 315 Madison Street house. Mealtime
was unique. One Club member who regularly attended later recalled that seldom was a meal "not interrupted by dictionary
research. We argued constantly about pronunciation and deriva-
tions, and I can still see Dr. Dewey dashing from the dining room,
his napkin sailing from his vest, in his search of accuracy in his
favorite Funk and Wagnall's unabridged." Dewey's extended
family quickly adjusted to Dewey's "habit of peripatetic meals."[23]

Club Successes and the
Lake Placid Club Education Foundation
1921–1926

On December 10, 1921—Dewey's seventieth birthday—the ten-
year option held by Asa Gallup's estate expired. Subordinates
scheduled a birthday party to celebrate that evening, and in the
afternoon Dewey met with his creditors. At the meeting, the
Finance Committee was dissolved and Dewey received all shares
of legally endorsed voting stock. Creditors explained, however,

---

22. See Dewey to Biscoe, 2/14/17, Wyer Mss; Circular, Dewey "To the
Personal Friends to Whom I have given a bonus that brings their net return
up to double savings bank interest," 9/7/18; Dewey "To the Directors,"
4/7/22, LPEF Mss. See also Dewey circular, 6/14/21 (on the occasion of May
Seymour's death), Box 27; Dewey to Mina Gallup, 2/7/25, Box 38, Dewey
Mss.

23. Margaret Miller to Dawe, 8/3/32, Box 24A, Dewey Mss; Colburn
Interview, 5/13/1985.

that they thought it wise to continue the practice of telling him under what conditions they would lend him money to guard against Dewey's habit of overextending himself and to check what some suspected were overly ambitious plans for the future. Dewey immediately bristled, and with tears in his eyes responded, "You're telling me the conditions?" He proceeded to lecture them on the sacrifices he had made for the Club since 1895 and the contributions it made to the Adirondack economy, then stormed out of the room.

Deo Colburn, who had been present and remained there after Dewey left, recalled the quandary in which creditors found themselves. Would Dewey show for his birthday party later that evening? They dispatched Colburn to find out. When Colburn located him, Dewey chuckled. "I've got 'em now," he said, and told Colburn he would see the bankers at 6:30. It was a risky move, but Dewey was committed. He had just rid himself of a financial albatross that greatly limited his flexibility, and he was committed not to let it happen again. At the meeting he told the bankers *he* would set conditions for loans, and then agreed to accompany them to his birthday party. Faced with this *fait accompli,* they decided to let the matter pass without comment.[24] True to form, Dewey interpreted their silence as consent.

Dewey's ambitious plans became obvious one week later when he promised to turn over all Club voting stock, valued at $420,000, to a "Lake Placid Club Education Foundation" as soon as it was fully and formally organized. To this Foundation Dewey also pledged $300,000 from his and Annie's estate, $20,000 from the estate that Katharine Sharp had willed to the Club, and $40,000 from the estate of May Seymour. The decision to create a Foundation had evolved over a long period of time. Much of the groundwork for its charter was accomplished during mealtime discussions at White Birches. Deo Colburn later recalled how Dewey checked all important words against the dictionary to make sure the charter's clauses said exactly what he wanted.[25]

In a sense, the Foundation served as the culmination of reforming efforts that characterized Melvil and Annie Dewey's marriage, and reflected their irrepressible desire to see these

---

24. Colburn Interview, 5/13/1985.
25. Dewey to Foundation Trustees, 9/3/28, LPEF Mss; Colburn interview, 5/13/1985.

efforts extend beyond their deaths. The charter required a board of trustees to elect officers to run the Club and fix prices at 5 percent above expenses. Foundation trustees could pay for needed improvements from the 5 percent, but any remaining sums were to be distributed for educational purposes. Here Dewey was very specific. Earnings made on Foundation assets were to be used for three purposes.

First, "restoration." "We propoz," Dewey said, "to make it posibl to restore to helth and eficiensi meni of our best education workers at a cost no greater than ther home living expenses, or perhaps les." He was particularly interested in professionals like librarians, home economists, social workers, and elementary and secondary teachers whose "zeal has led them to cripl themselvs by *overwork*," but who were not paid well enough to afford lengthy vacations. Second, the "millionth man quest." Here Dewey hypothesized that the world was "chiefli shaped by a veri fu" who came "oftenest from the humblest home." He wanted the Foundation to "fynd wherever hiden, the boy or girl who givs promis of being a great leader & bring him to Placid in the fynest clymat with the best skools & develop his abiliti as near as posibl to 100%." Finally, "seedsowing." By this Dewey meant providing the environment in which recognized leaders could base and sustain educational campaigns requiring the "long laborius proceses that reqyr much tym." Here he was referring to his own pet projects of metric conversion, simplified spelling, and Decimal Classification.

On January 26, 1922, the University of the State of New York issued a provisional charter to the Lake Placid Club Education Foundation. Officers listed on the charter included Melvil, Annie and Godfrey Dewey, Emily Beal, Arthur Bestor, Harry W. Hicks, Charles B. Hobbs, Hamilton Holt, Henry LaFontaine, William Slocum, John A. Wyeth, and the Reverend C. H. Pankhurst.[26]

On August 25, 1922, Annie Dewey died; upon her death Dewey lost not only a spouse, but also a fellow crusader and business partner. Since 1878, his reforms had been her reforms. Neither had consciously admitted to feelings of selfishness because both justified joint goals in terms of the greatest possible usefulness to others. They reinforced these feelings by publicly

---

26. See Dewey to LPCEF Trustees, 7/28/30, LPEF Mss. Regents changed the charter from provisional to permanent in 1926.

and repeatedly rejecting manifestations of self-serving glory. To Melvil and Annie Dewey, the "cause" was always paramount. Both had convinced themselves that because reforms they advocated were bigger than they were, their lifetime of sacrifice had been justified and ought to continue after their deaths. They considered themselves merely conscientious tools by which these reforms would be effected. While at Lake Placid, the Deweys had also expanded their causes to include cremation, eugenics, birth control, prohibition, women's suffrage, and the League of Nations. All fit their sociocultural goals; all served to reinforce the purposes for which they established the Club, and because of their advocacy, the Club itself became variously identified with them all.[27]

Melvil and Annie's ambitions for the Club and the new Foundation seemed little effected by Annie's absence, however. For example, Annie died in the middle of an expansion project she had been planning for ten years. Already under way was construction not only on additions to existing facilities, but also new buildings like the Agora Theater and a granite Chapel with an oak-timbered Tudor roof and tracery windows. Before she died Annie had ordered a new Austin organ to serve both buildings. Annie's death did, however, improve the financial status of the Company and the Foundation. Within a month the Company paid off loans totalling $400,000, and for more than a year borrowed no new funds. Annie's will also left $85,000 in bonds to the Foundation. To this Dewey said he would add stock if the Foundation allowed him to spend interest generated by it while he lived. He pointed out that the combination of contributions would hike Foundation assets to over $1,000,000, "which is a dignifyd start and wil encuraj gifts from welthy Club members who ar getting more and more interested in the hyer things of the Club."[28]

Although Annie was gone, 1923 proved a banner year for the Club. Cost of expansion and additions to the physical plant totalled $750,000, much of which was raised by members investing in Club securities. Dewey's plans were, as usual, ambitious. A new stable would be erected at the southern end of Club grounds, the old one converted to a printing shop and an

---

27. See Gunther, "Annie Godfrey Dewey," pp. 359; 362–64; *Lake Placid News*, 8/4/22, for an obituary; and 9/8/22 for an account of a memorial concert held in her honor on 8/31/22.

28. Dewey to Foundation Trustees and LP Company Directors, 12/23/22; Dewey to Dun and Bradstreet, 2/6/23, FPA.

employees' club primarily for summer help. A new cafeteria would serve Club employees and connect to two separate dining rooms, one for waitresses, chambermaids, and bellmen, the other for chauffeurs, mechanics, and laborers. A "children's club" would provide nursery services for children of all guests, and a new centrally located golf house would connect the Club's three nine-hole and three eighteen-hole courses.

By that time the newly built Kobl Club had become Placid's eighth clubhouse, linking cottages on 65 acres at the periphery of Club property overlooking the lake, and Cascade Club—several miles away but recently "bo't by a member and given outryt to the Club"—was scheduled to be rebuilt and refurnished as the ninth clubhouse. Westwood, a group of sixteen apartments of three to six rooms located at the foot of the lake, had been completed in spring and was already booked for the summer. And all guests who arrived by car would pass through a renovated ramp, part of which was covered and served as a terrace overlooking the lake. New fireplaces brought the total on Club grounds to 250.

The recently completed Agora Theater could seat twelve hundred on the main floor and balconies, and when partitions were removed could be expanded into adjoining rooms so that three thousand could be seated for large concerts. East of the Agora's stage was the Chapel, which "made adequate provision for the first time for the distinctively religious life of the Club, always a Christian cultural center." The Sunday evening singing of favorite hymns that had been a regular Club feature from its inception moved into the Chapel shortly after it opened. Participants entering walked past a bronze tablet memorializing Annie Dewey. North of the Chapel were the new Agora Suites, consisting of 130 rooms with bath and shower. A 44-x-120-foot library on the west side of the suites overlooked Mirror Lake and opened out to a piazza large enough to accommodate 100 guests.

By this time the Club boasted a membership and guest list from every state in the union and twenty-six countries. In the 1920s wealthy people joined in increased numbers, adding prestige and financial stability and altering the Club's social profile. Because several members were employees of prominent national newspapers and magazines, the Club also received good coverage in the press, especially for its winter activities. In January 1923, for example, Dewey reported to Foundation directors that the *New York Times* had given most of the front page of its Sunday

By 1926, Dewey's Lake Placid Club had achieved world-class fashionability, as evidenced by this Woodbury soap ad (*Chicago Tribune*, February 14).

edition to Club pictures, and that on New Year's Day the Club hosted journalists from the *Chicago Tribune, Harper's,* and the *New York Times, Sun,* and *Herald.* On February 14, 1926, the *Chicago Tribune* ran an ad announcing that two-thirds of the 208 women spending the winter at Lake Placid regularly used Woodbury soap.[29]

---

29. The 1928 *Yearbook* lists Club membership on pp. 69–168. See also *LPC Notes,* no. 144 (10/23): 119–26; Dewey to Directors, 1/3/23, LPEF Mss.

Despite his age Dewey was still heavily involved in daily management of the Club. He regularly referred to his entire Lake Placid staff as "my famili," and treated most like his children. He expected obedience. In March 1923, for example, he circulated a document entitled "Editing Rules." Included were directions to use "NY" for "New York," "US" for "United States," "Co" for both "company" and "county," "buyer" instead of "purchasing agent," "many" instead of "a large number," and "invite" instead of "extend an invitation." "Much of this commercial English is affected by peopl with litl education or nolej of the languaj," he concluded, "who like most negros delyt in uzing a big word when a short one is vastly betr." Dewey's racism surfaced in other ways. When Booker T. Washington accepted Dewey's invitation to dine with him at the Lake Placid Club, Dewey ordered meals served privately at White Birches rather than use Club dining rooms. "Our big Southern clientele" would not permit it, he later told an associate. That same month Dewey purchased property in the Cascade Pass leading to Lake Placid because he was worried the owner might either sell "shanty sites all along the 2 miles of hyway" for $100 each, "or wd sell to Jews."[30]

He continued to walk the grounds daily with his six-foot tapered rule, especially early in the morning when he did his planning, and—to save time—began using a self-designed ever-sharp pencil with different colored leads in two workable ends. Switching from one end to another was faster than switching from one pencil to another, he argued. Dewey's workplace, like always, remained a picture of compactness and efficiency. He had transferred his specially made desk from Albany to Lake Placid in 1906. Work habits mirrored practices he had improved over the decades. He continued to write instructions (always in shorthand or simplified spelling) on previously used P-slips that he then placed in separate pigeonholes. Deo Colburn later recalled regularly going into Dewey's office while he worked there, getting instructions from the pigeonhole assigned him, and leaving without exchanging a word. Oftentimes Dewey did not look up.[31]

---

30. "Editing Rules," 3/12/23, Box 31A; Dewey to Ellis & Farmer, 3/1/23, Box 31, Dewey Mss; Dewey to "Directors," 3/2/23 and 3/19/23, LPEF Mss. Dewey recounted the incident with Washington in Dewey to E. R. Baldwin, 12/24/30, Box 54, Dewey Mss.

31. Colburn Interview, 5/13/1985.

By 1925 the Club was enjoying unprecedented success, and the Deweys' priorities for the Foundation were beginning to take more concrete shape. Temporarily, spelling reform seemed promising. Godfrey Dewey, who had recently completed a thesis on the subject at Harvard (his father had been cultivating Godfrey's interest in it since 1905), had returned to the Club with his family to assume some responsibility for management and to spearhead the simplified spelling movement. By this time Godfrey had become secretary to the Simplified Spelling Board, which in 1918 had lost Carnegie support. His father was still secretary of the nearly defunct SRA, and together, they formed a working relationship with the Simplified Spelling Society of London in March 1925, to begin publication of *Spelling,* proposed as a quarterly organ for all three organizations. Impetus for the movement proved shortlived, however. *Spelling* issued two numbers in 1925, one more in 1931, then died quietly.[32]

Other ventures, however, did not languish. After May Seymour died in 1921, responsibility for editing new editions of the *Decimal Classification* shifted to Dorkas Fellows. By 1927 Fellows had moved with the Decimal Classification Office to the Library of Congress, and three years later Dewey numbers began appearing on catalog cards LC was selling to thousands of libraries. Publication of new editions remained the responsibility of Forest Press, whose offices were owned by the Foundation and located on Club grounds. In 1925 the Foundation hired Maude Graff at Dewey's request to circulate among Adirondack schools and churches and encourage them to improve the quality and quantity of their music program. Graff set up spring school and fall church music festivals on Club grounds and in the Agora Theater, and issued awards for best performance.[33] By 1930 the festivals had outgrown the Club's ability to house them and quickly evolved into district festivals.

In 1925 the Foundation acquired a college preparatory boarding school for boys. The school had been founded in 1905 by John M. Hopkins, a member of the Club. In early 1922 Hopkins

---

32. *LPC Notes,* no. 159 (2/25): 1253; *Spelling,* 1 (3/25): 1; and (6/25): 25; 31; 2 (3/31): 1–5. See also Minutes, SRA meeting, 4/8/25, copy found in Box 86; Dewey to Metric Association, 9/30/25, Box 66, Dewey Mss; and Dewey "To the Directors," 7/15/25, LPEF Mss.

33. Grace Hewitt to Godfrey Dewey, -/-/32, Box 26, Dewey Mss; Dawe, *Dewey,* pp. 86; 241.

sold its twenty-one acres of property and buildings to Anna Ryan (who started Montmare School for Girls) and gave up control of the boys' school to its headmaster H. L. Malcolm (who initially moved it to Whiteface Inn, then relocated it on Club grounds in 1924 in anticipation of takeover by the Foundation several months later). Then, in 1926, the Company bought Montmare from Ryan, merged it with Malcolm's boys school and named the new institution Northwood. For Dewey Northwood represented a place "where mind, body and soul" of children with leadership potential "wil be brought to highest efficiency." At Northwood, Dewey also hoped he could find and develop the "millionth man."[34]

Melvil Dewey did not remain a widower long. On May 28, 1924—one year and nine months after Annie died—he married Emily Beal in the Lake Placid Club Chapel. Beal had come to Club employment in 1916 after a successful career in Boston's social welfare system following her first husband's death. At the time of his second marriage Dewey was just over six feet tall, weighed 186 pounds, and although he had flat feet, continued to walk briskly and erect. For a seventy-four-year-old man, he was very healthy, although he had complained to his doctor several years earlier he had been constipated much of his adult life and had regular bouts of hemorrhoids. He had shaved his beard years earlier, but continued to sport a mustache and by that time had developed such poor vision he was forced to wear glasses.[35] During their courtship Dewey had been careful always to have several other women around for appearances, and he had made certain he and Emily were never alone at White Birches.

There was a compelling reason Dewey was so cautious; in the spring of 1924, he was rebounding from another recent brush with sexual scandal, fed in part by his still-tarnished reputation with women.[36] The controversy stemmed from two incidents

---

34. *Yearbook,* 1928, p. 60; Dewey to LPCEF Trustees, 7/28/30, LPEF Mss; *LPC Notes,* no. 181 (12/26): 1584; *Northwood Mirror* 6 (12/31): 1–2.

35. Historians versed in psychohistory may find value in knowing about Dewey's persistent constipation, which was revealed in a 1922 insurance policy health report found in Box 37.

36. The chronology presented in the next few pages has been pieced together from the following: Tessa Kelso to Godfrey Dewey, 3/15/24, Box 72; Dewey to Frank Hill, 3/22/23[sic]; 3/27/24; 5/10/24, Box 31A; Dewey to C. W. Andrews, 4/4/24, Box 9; Godfrey Dewey to John Lowe, 4/29/24; T. H.

during "Library Week" at Lake Placid in 1920. In the first Adeline B. Zachert, Pennsylvania's Director of School Libraries, was pacing Club grounds late at night to walk off some indigestion when Ruth S. Wilcox, a New York City high-school librarian who was staying with the Deweys at White Birches, invited her in for conversation. While resting on a couch in Wilcox's room, Zachert fell asleep. Existing correspondence suggests that when Zachert left White Birches the next morning, other guests witnessed Dewey bidding her goodbye, and because her bed had not been slept in the previous evening news spread quickly. "I am sorry to have unwittingly caused an awkward situation," Zachert later wrote Dewey. The second incident involved Godfrey Dewey's wife, Marjorie. Until just before "Library Week" in 1920, the Melvil and Godfrey Dewey families occupied the Cedars, a multi-family building on Club grounds with five bedrooms. Melvil and Annie told Godfrey and Marjorie when they moved there in 1914 they were free to enter the senior Deweys' living quarters without knocking; they assumed Godfrey and Marjorie felt the same way. For a time the younger Deweys accepted the arrangement, but as Melvil began to behave towards Marjorie the same way he behaved towards May Seymour, Florence Woodworth, and Katharine Sharp, Marjorie became uncomfortable and complained to her husband. Melvil and Annie moved to White Birches shortly thereafter.

Tessa Kelso, who had known about the 1905 ALA post-conference trip and the scandal it occasioned at the 1906 conference and who had heard about Zachert's evening at White Birches, suspected Dewey's unacceptable behavior with Marjorie was the reason the senior Deweys moved out of Cedars.[37] At the

---

Ferris to Godfrey Dewey, 4/30/24; Adeline Zachert to Emily Beal, 5/10/24; Adeline Zachert to Dewey, 9/27/20; 5/31/24; Lowe to NYLA ExCom, 5/10/24, Box 72; Frederick Faxon to Dewey, 5/14/24, Box 7, Dewey Mss. See also Dewey to Godfrey Dewey, 9/11/31, Box 23, Dewey Mss.

37. It is possible Kelso was one of a group of female librarians still so angry with the way Dewey treated certain women at library conferences before 1906 that they vowed either to oppose any invitation to have him speak or participate at library gatherings or to boycott conferences he attended. In 1915, for example, ALA President Mary W. Plummer rejected a suggestion that ALA meet at Lake Placid for its 1916 conference. "It seems [a] shame to me," she wrote James Wyer, "that those who knew the man's character as well as we do can wish him to figure again as a representative of the profession." She also worried about the painful learning experience

conclusion of "Library Week" in 1920, Kelso spoke to Emily Beal about the necessity for Dewey to control his behavior around women. Instead of going to Melvil, however, Beal spoke to Godfrey who, in turn, reminded his father about the problems he was causing, but to no avail. Dewey's behavior toward women at "Library Week" did not change in subsequent years.

By 1924 Kelso had had enough; she decided to protest NYLA plans to hold its 1924 conference at Lake Placid simultaneously with "Library Week." In mid-March she told Godfrey that if the Club hosted the conference she would file a statement with its executive board proving his father was morally irresponsible and circulate copies to the NYLA membership. "For many years women librarians have been the special prey of Mr. Dewey in a series of outrages against decency," she argued, "having serious and far reaching effects upon his victims while the association has echoed with the scandal." She wanted to give Godfrey an opportunity to withdraw the Club's invitation "before taking steps." Godfrey responded that he was certainly aware of his father's "long-standing and well-known disregard of conventions and indifference to appearances," and he welcomed any sincere criticism "which might help me to impress upon him the importance of regarding not merely facts but also appearances." He then turned Kelso's letter over to his father.

After reading it Dewey feigned righteous indignation. With Kelso he was aggressive, unapologetic. He said her accusations were unfounded and indicated he hoped the matter would be brought before the NYLA Executive Board and President John Lowe for a fair hearing. With NYLA board member Frank Hill—who was Lowe's superior at the Brooklyn Public Library and one of Dewey's oldest friends,[38] he was more circumspect. He told Hill that Lowe might soon be speaking to him about Kelso's accusations, and reminded him about rumors generated at the 1906 ALA conference by "several old maids of both sexes." He said

---

new female members of the profession would have to undergo until "they too would finally come to know his essential falsity. I shall never, as long as I am a member of the profession, consent to meet him." Plummer to Wyer, 8/3/15, Wyer Mss. ALA met in Asbury Park, New Jersey, for its 1916 conference.

38. In 1915 Mary Plummer was convinced Hill was "at the bottom" of the suggestion to locate the 1916 ALA conference at Lake Placid. See Plummer to Wyer, 8/3/15, Wyer Mss.

Kelso intended to paint him "a hopeless scamp that no self re-
specting librarian wd dare be in the same county with." Over the
years, he admitted, "I have been very unconventional . . . as men
ar always who frankly show and speak of their liking for women,"
but he would admit no fault. Kelso certainly could be sued if she
issued such a circular, he argued, but he had also been informed
by his lawyer that bringing the suit might prove more trouble
than it was worth and delay progress on the Foundation's work.
For that reason, he told Hill, if NYLA decided not to hold its 1924
conference at the Club he would not object.

But Lowe wanted to be fair, and to resolve the dilemma he
decided to gather a group of New York-based officers from NYLA,
ALA, and ALI (the latter two organizations had also scheduled
meetings at Lake Placid during "Library Week") to interview
both sides in executive session. He and Carl Cannon, the NYPL
reference department's chief of acquisition, would represent
NYLA, Ernest Reece, the NYPL Library School principal, would
represent ALA, and reference book publisher Frederick Faxon
would represent ALI.

Interviews took place in Manhattan May 10, 1924; Lowe
scheduled Dewey's interview first. Instead of coming himself,
however, Dewey had sent Emily Beal (who would marry him
later that month) and Godfrey to speak in his behalf. Both focused their remarks on Kelso's accusations. Beal began by telling
the group Adeline Zachert had not considered the incident to
which Kelso referred in her statement an objectionable situation,
and that Marjorie would deny every accusation Kelso made. Godfrey added that Kelso's suggestions the junior Deweys "had been
obliged" to separate their residences from the senior Deweys in
1920 because of his father's "attentions" to Marjorie "were absolutely false." They then exited the room. When Kelso arrived, she
reiterated at some length what she had earlier told Godfrey, repeated her accusations about Dewey's behavior at "Library Week"
in 1920, and concluded by saying that over the years Dewey's
treatment of women was "of a vicious type of sexual depravity
and criminal in the eyes of the law." After she left officials discussed the problem, but adjourned without coming to a decision.
They promised to inform each other of their votes after each
took some time to consider the issue.

Lowe did not wait long, however. Shortly after he returned
to his office that afternoon he wrote other members of the group

that because Kelso could offer *"no proof"* of her accusations he doubted their accuracy, and because he thought she would not go any farther with her "threatened circularization," he was "not willing to cast any slur upon the Lake Placid Club by canceling the engagement for Library Week." He stood alone, however. Other members of the group cast their vote against Dewey. Reece, Cannon, and Faxon obviously decided it was better to avoid controversy than confront it openly.[39]

As a result, all three organizations instead spent "Library Week" at Lake George, sixty miles south of Lake Placid. Their decision to move the conference had a lasting effect on Dewey's reputation. Because his conduct had not been discussed in an open forum and Kelso's charges had not been subject to cross-examination, the 1924 NYLA conference became one more occasion when rumors surrounding Dewey's behavior towards women that had some foundation in fact were allowed to go unchecked and feed the myths time was already embellishing. With hindsight, it is also telling to note that none of the men involved in the interview seemed much concerned about the anguish Dewey's conduct had been causing library women over the decades. Instead, all seemed to focus on Kelso and the potential embarrassment she could cause the library associations they represented.

But Dewey was too self-righteous to be affected for very long by the controversy, and forged on with his life.[40] On October 31, 1924, he formally gave copyright of the Decimal Classification and all his Lake Placid common and preferred stock (valued at $868,000) to the Foundation. He retained the right to direct the expenditure of income on $240,000 worth of preferred stock "for the benefit or the purposes of the Foundation." Throughout the documentation detailing conditions of gifts he also laced phrases like "We aim to make sure that those to whom the administration

---

39. Frank Hill later told Dewey he suspected both Reece and Cannon were "under the thumb" of E. H. Anderson, one of Dewey's archenemies who had been NYPL's Director since 1913. See Hill to Dewey, 5/13/24, Box 7, Dewey Mss. See also Dewey to C. C. Williamson, 8/26/26, Box 34, Dewey Mss, in which Dewey complains that Anderson had "joind hartily with my critics and enemies" in 1905 and 1906.

40. He did, however, let Eleanor Duncan, *LJ's* Managing Editor, know about Kelso's "unfounded" accusations. "I think yu shd no that this half crazy woman may explode." See Dewey to Duncan, 5/5/24, Box 13, Dewey Mss.

is entrusted wil do their best to make a success of *our* plan and *in the place selected,*" "the purpose of my gift is to secure a permanent institution . . . and leave no right to *abandon* the plan or to move it elsewhere," and "I wish my *endowment to remove* by its conditions any temptation for *timorous trustees* in the future to let down these [Club] standards . . . [banning the use of] *likor, tobacco, gambling, profanity or vulgarity.*"[41]

By that time the Club had grown to 10,600 acres, including most of Moose Island on Lake Placid and the Adirondak Loj on the shores of Hart Lake, twelve miles to the south. During the summer the Club provided daily worship services in the Chapel, dancing three times a week, eight weekly concerts (one of which was exclusively for children) by a fourteen-member ensemble from the "Boston Simfony Orkestra," and hosted an annual Adirondack Music Festival the third week in September. Forest Lodge housed a number of shops, including a gift shop, a hair salon, "Stedman's Fotografi Stand," and a "farmaci." In addition to its five golf courses the Club maintained twenty-one tennis courts and annually hosted four U.S. Lawn Tennis Association–sanctioned tournaments. Its library subscribed to 100 periodicals and contained 8,000 books, all of which were on "best reading" lists available free of charge to Club members.[42] By mid-decade, Dewey had reason to be satisfied with the results of his work.

---

41. Copies of all of these documents can be found in the LPEF Mss. On September 3, 1928, Dewey wrote a supplemental letter specifying that one area in which Foundation Trustees had to spend income was simplified spelling. He did not say how much, nor how often. See Dewey "To Foundation Trustees," 9/3/28, LPEF Mss.

42. *LPC Notes,* no. 193 (4/28): 1798–1843.

15

Trouble in Paradise

1926–1931

In the fall of 1925, Dewey became very ill with the flu and from November 9 through December 21, he told Foundation trustees, he was "in bed with a traind nurse."[1] Upon the advice of his doctors, he and Emily went south for the winter to Thomasville, Georgia. Although Dewey spent some time recuperating in Thomasville, he and Emily found the winter climate so attractive it was not long before they began traveling into Florida. Emily Dewey had been living in Annie's shadow since her marriage to Melvil, and even though she appeared to show no jealousy, she was an ambitious woman who seemed to be looking for an opportunity to leave her own mark on Dewey's legacy. While traveling through Florida, she got the idea that if extended winters in the South would lengthen her husband's life, perhaps the same pitch could be made to other Club members who were not enamored of upstate New York winters. Together, she and Melvil decided to start a Lake Placid Club South [2] on one of the inland lakes in the southern part of the state.

---

1. Given his well-deserved reputation for unacceptable behavior toward women, it is tempting to speculate how trustees read this phrase. See Melvil Dewey, "How I happen to be in South Georgia," n.d.; Dewey "To the Directors," 1/2/26, LEPF Mss.

2. For clarity, I will refer to "Lake Placid North" and "Lake Placid South" (or some shorthand form of either) for the rest of the chapter to distinguish between the New York and Florida enterprises, even though neither term constitutes an official title.

Lake Placid Club North v. South
1926–1929

In spring they returned to Lake Placid excited by the possibilities, and over the summer developed a plan of action. On September 25 Dewey informed Club trustees he intended to open a Florida branch that he and Emily would manage during winter months. The branch would mirror rules and regulations of the original Club, but would not draw on Club or Company resources. In fact, all profits would be turned over to the Foundation. Finally, he also announced that in mid-October he and Emily would travel to Florida with Godfrey and C. W. Holt to study appropriate locations. Although Club trustees gave Dewey their blessing, they recognized they were bowing to a *fait accompli*. T. Harvey Ferris, Club trustee and legal counsel, expressed the sentiments of most when he wrote Godfrey, "I think it is a very foolish thing for him [Melvil Dewey] at his time of life to start in on this venture." Charles B. Rogers, president of the First Bank and Trust Company of Utica, warned Dewey: "Do not let your enthusiasm get the start of you as far as financial matters go. Keep the Lake Placid Company of New York as strong as you can and let the Florida proposition stand on its own feet."[3]

Before returning to Florida in late October, Dewey took advantage of two invitations to act the part of senior statesman and pioneer in the library world. First, he gave a talk at the fiftieth anniversary ALA conference at Atlantic City on October 6 entitled "Our Next Half-Century." Second, he traveled to Manhattan to watch the New York State Library School return to Columbia University where it merged with the New York Public Library School to become the School of Library Service. By that time the school could boast that a dozen state university libraries, 40 percent of the public libraries in the United States with collections exceeding 100,000 volumes, and six of the fourteen American library schools were being run by Albany graduates. Nicholas Murray Butler, still president of Columbia, presided at the ceremony.[4]

---

3. Minutes, LPC Trustees, 9/25/26, LPEF Mss; "Resolution adopted by Lake Placid Club Board of Directors at Annual Meeting," 9/25/26; Ferris to Godfrey Dewey, 11/22/26; Rogers to Dewey, 12/17/26, FPA.

4. For an account of the merger of the schools, see *LJ* 51 (5/15/26): 476–77; 53 (1928): 665. See also Dawe, *Dewey*, p. 196; and Dewey, "Our Next Half-Century," *ALAB* 20 (11/26): 309–13.

Several months after returning to Florida, Melvil and Emily Dewey settled on the area around Sebring as the site for Lake Placid South. Sebring was located in a section called the "Scenic Highlands," a rectangle of twenty by one hundred miles in the central southern third of the state one hundred to three hundred feet above sea level that was known for its clearwater lakes, its abundant citrus groves, and, of course, its warm winter climate. The Deweys had arranged with H. O. Sebring, Jr., a member of Placid North, to have Placid South temporarily set up quarters in the Hotel Sebring until April 15. Dewey then invited all Adirondack Club members to Florida to enjoy the hotel's hospitality.[5]

Here Dewey also met Walter Coachman, president of Consolidated Naval Stores, who was eager to have Dewey help develop the area. Consolidated had purchased much of the land around Sebring in 1901, and by 1919 had branched into citrus groves. When Coachman heard of Dewey's interest, he offered Dewey an option on 3,300 acres around the Lake Stearns area that developers called the "Roof Garden of Florida." Coachman even had three viewing towers erected from which Dewey could survey the land. Dewey liked what he saw, and, together with Emily, agreed to take Consolidated's option. The Deweys were especially pleased with the size of property, which they thought would allow them to develop a Club at the core and control the development of the periphery to keep out "undesirable" people.

They began work immediately. Initially, they had the Florida legislature change the name of the town of Lake Stearns to Lake Placid. They also had local lakes renamed; Lake Stearns became Lake June-in-Winter, Lake Childs became Lake Placid. Naturally, local residents became excited about a plan that promised jobs and quiet and clean economic development, and Dewey never tired of recounting the successes of Placid North to his new Florida friends. At the same time, however, he never discussed the tenuous financial base upon which he had built the original Club. If Dewey was successful in developing Placid South, they believed, his enterprise would not disturb the local social fabric.

They immediately began sprucing up Main Street by creating a boulevard, planting flowers in vacant lots, and erecting a fountain and sunken garden in the center of the town circle. By

---

5. *LPC Notes,* no. 181 (12/26): 1584.

means of these activities townspeople developed a sense of participation with the Dewey enterprise. Crucial to their success, however, was a $100,000 bond issue that the town agreed to take on and that the Deweys supported. From the beginning, Dewey pushed the concept of developing Lake Placid as a joint venture between the town (with its bonding power), the Lake Placid Land Company (a subsidiary of Consolidated Naval Stores with capital to develop real estate), and the Club (with its northern membership upon whom Dewey counted for investment capital).[6]

Although the economic climate of South Florida was not as inviting as its physical climate, Melvil and Emily Dewey pushed ahead without hesitation. On May 6, 1927, the Deweys closed a contract to start a Lake Placid Club in Florida. The Lake Placid Land Company had given them formal contract for a clear warranty deed within ninety days on three thousand acres the Deweys had chosen for the Club site, and on May 12 the town of Lake Placid promised the Deweys free taxes and water and $2,400 per year for publicity if the Deweys would plan, operate, and take 20 percent interest in the Hotel Stearns. The Land Company then bought fifty Club life memberships at $1,000 each, and when local developer E. C. Stuart pledged $25,000 more, the Deweys believed they had enough money to remodel the Hotel Stearns.

With the money they bought the hotel, immediately changed its name to "Club Loj," and announced plans to expand the building by adding two wings and sixteen rooms, eight of which would have private balconies and open fireplaces. The entire complex would be heated by steam during Lake Placid's infrequent brief cold snaps. The east end was to be a dining room glassed in on three sides with two open fireplaces, the west end a spacious living room glassed in on three sides and capable of seating three hundred. Stuart announced in the *Highland County News* on July 7 that "residents of the new town of Lake Placid will have the privilege of entertaining at the Inn." But he also noted that "Adirondack club standards will be strictly adhered to and dining

6. Information on the history of Lake Placid, Florida, and Dewey's involvement with it, was taken from the following: Albert De Vane, *De Vane's Early Florida History* (Sebring, 1978); Sebring Historical Society, *Bulletin*, no. 3 (10/1969): n.p.; interview with W. O. Ebrite (former Mayor of Lake Placid) in *Tampa Tribune*, 12/10/1979; and Miriam Beck, "Dr. Melvil Dewey—A Genius Organizer," *Lake Placid Journal*, 8/30/1979.

room menus will retain the simplicity and quality for which the club is noted."[7]

From Dewey's perspective, the primary obstacle to developing Placid South was lack of investment capital. Although Emily had some money to invest, Melvil's own options were severely limited. He had already pledged all of his estate to the Foundation, but he still felt he could exercise control of the interest on $240,000 worth of Company preferred stock and use Company Stores to order and bill materials to develop Placid South. Since he reasoned the end result of both would be for the benefit of the Foundation, Dewey anticipated no problem pursuing these options. As usual, he pushed ahead optimistically; as usual, he badly miscalculated. Problems arose almost immediately.

First, the Deweys unnecessarily complicated their situation by trying to mime Placid North's structure. They set up two separate corporations, the Lake Placid Club Company and a subsidiary, the Lake Placid Inn Company. The latter was to function like Placid North Stores and supply Placid South with materials it needed. But the Lake Placid Inn Company began with only a $500 capital investment. Second, while the Deweys were in Placid North in the summer of 1927, Florida state inspectors told Dewey they would not let the renovated "Club Loj" open in November unless he rebuilt the stairways and chimney.

In addition, Dewey had to install refrigeration to store large amounts of food, a sprinkler system to improve fire protection, and a new steam heating system if he expected to keep his guests comfortable during the Highlands' brief cold spells. To do all this he hired the Grinnell Refrigerating Company, which began to extend him considerable credit. Dewey gambled on Placid South's potential to generate a good winter season to pay Grinnell back.[8] Third and most serious, during the summer a local taxpayer filed suit against the Lake Placid Land Company and obtained injunctions against the town to stop all improvements until his case was settled.

Primarily as a result of the injunctions, when the Deweys returned to Placid South November 1 to kick off their first full

---

7. *LPC Notes*, no. 187 (5/27): 1669; Rider, *Dewey,* pp. 144–45; *Highland County News,* 7/7/27; *LPC News* 1 (8/26/27): 7.

8. For an example of his pitch to Placid North members, see *LPC News* 1 (12/30/27): 8; and *LPC Notes*, no. 191 (12/27): 1776–77.

season, none of the improvements the town had promised had been made. Especially troublesome was an inadequate water system. Guests were often without water for several hours a day, and once were unable to flush toilets for a day and a half. Equally important, the town had not been able to deliver on the golf and water sports it pledged. Naturally, Club Loj lost money as guests cut short their stays. Placid South's first season had been a miserable failure, and because revenue fell far short of expectations, Dewey was unable to meet his obligations to Grinnell. To accommodate the latter, he offered to issue notes to Grinnell at 6 percent interest; Grinnell agreed to the arrangement on condition that the Club Company, which the Deweys said they owned and which in turn claimed to own 3,000 acres with no debts, would endorse the notes. The Deweys concurred, in large part because the Lake Placid Land Company promised to loan them $30,000 in short term notes.

Six weeks later, however, Land Company directors wired Dewey while he was back in New York they would be unable to give notes unless the notes could run for twenty months. That put Dewey in a bind. On the one hand he could not turn twenty-month notes into cash by selling them to friends in the North because of Florida's weak economy. On the other hand he was committed to develop Placid South. Together, he and Emily decided to push forward without the notes, and borrowed all the money they could ($41,500) to purchase the materials and furniture needed to reopen Club Loj in the fall of 1927.[9] But the 1927 winter season at Placid South had been a harbinger; matters never improved, and Melvil and Emily Dewey immediately looked to Placid North for help.

By this time, however, New York's Lake Placid Club, Company, and Club Stores had developed a loyalty independent of Melvil Dewey. In the course of developing Placid North, Dewey had called upon friends and family to sacrifice for a set of dreams he had persuaded them all to share. May Seymour, Florence Woodworth, and Katharine Sharp had come to Lake Placid for those reasons. So had Godfrey, who by 1927 had invested his own career, professional reputation, and the future of his family

---

9. Much of this history Dewey recounted in a resolution he wrote two years later that was read into the minutes of a July 28, 1930, Foundation meeting. Copies of these minutes can be found in LPEF Mss and FPA.

in the Club. Following his father's example, he developed an expertise in simplified spelling that promised to advance Melvil Dewey's dream of a movement centered in Lake Placid and funded by Foundation grants. He had also accepted his father's invitation to participate in Club management, and in 1927 was already a director and one of six vice presidents of the Company, president of Club Stores and Northwood Estates, executive vice president and a trustee of the Foundation, stockholder in the Company and Company Stores, and a Lake Placid Club delegate to several international bodies whose work touched on Foundation purposes.

Many other Foundation trustees and Club members and officers shared Godfrey's goals and loyalties. In 1927 they were inclined to resist any threat to these goals, no matter the source. Most made no secret they thought the effort to establish Placid South ill advised. Some thought an aging Melvil Dewey (who had convinced himself Florida winters would prolong his life) was being heavily influenced by a second wife in competition with the memory of the first and eager to leave her own mark on the Dewey legacy. Godfrey Dewey appeared to be among the latter. Willingly or unwillingly, he became spokesperson for that fraction of the Placid North community that decided to resist Melvil and Emily Dewey's unwise plans to harness Placid North assets to improve Placid South's financial situation.

Opening salvo to the inevitable battle between Placid North and South came in late 1927. On December 3, Dewey told Foundation directors he intended to claim income on preferred stock he had pledged to the Foundation, to use Club stores to order and bill materials for Placid South, and to pledge Club properties (including Club grounds) as collateral for loans from Florida banks. When Godfrey received a copy of his father's letter, he immediately went to Foundation trustees Charles Rogers and T. H. Ferris. Together they agreed to question not only the wisdom but also the legality of Dewey's demands. Godfrey assumed responsibility for putting their concerns in a carefully worded response.

When Dewey received it, however, he immediately concluded a conspiracy led by Godfrey had formed against him at Placid North and turned on his son with a vengeance. His first response was to Rogers on January 3, 1928. He told Rogers that the documentation was very clear about his right to use the income on preferred stock "for the Fn future as I thot wisest." If some legal technicality called that right into question, he said, "common honesty requires that it be corrected." On January 4 he wrote trustee I. H. Griswold, "I hope and pray that GD will come to his senses." He criticized Godfrey's "peculiarity" for always wanting his own way, and warned that if Godfrey "kept attacking my plans here" and "creating an anti-MD element that it wud result in his dropping out [of the Club]." Dewey then criticized Ferris, who had suggested that what Dewey proposed was not legal. He forwarded multiple copies of this letter to Godfrey, and attached a note directing him to distribute the copies to Hicks, Holt and Colburn.[10]

Griswold had not yet received Dewey's letter when Foundation directors met January 7 at Placid North. Placid South consumed most of their attention. They agreed to extend guest (but not member) privileges to Florida members, and voted to allow Dewey to draw for his Florida project up to $23,500 from LPC Stores—$13,500 of which would come from Dewey's preferred stock income, the remainder from the sale of bonds. Further, however, they would not go. They refused to approve the loan against Foundation funds owned by the Lake Placid Company Dewey had requested because the Foundation charter "gave them no right or power in the matter."[11]

During the meeting, however, copies of Dewey's January 4 letter to Griswold were delivered to Godfrey. He glanced at one copy, and handed it to Griswold without interrupting the meeting. Toward the end of the meeting both agreed to distribute other copies to Directors as "the quickest and fairest way" to place Dewey's "views and attitude before them." Dewey's letter, however, did not affect the outcome of their deliberations, and when Godfrey relayed the directors' formal decision to his father, he added a personal note. "I am more deeply hurt by your attitude there reveald then by anything yu hav ever done." He was acting in the best interests of the Club, he said, and no one at Placid North doubted his loyalty. He also refused to get into a family altercation. "If yu should later on your own initiativ feel like apologizing, it would make a very difficult situation somewhat more bearable, but so far as I am concerned I shal try to

---

10. Information pieced together from Dewey to Rogers, 1/3/28; and Dewey to Griswold, 1/4/28, LPEF Mss; *LPC News* 1 (8/12/27): 6.

11. Minutes, 1/7/28, LPEF Mss.

ignore all personal aspects . . . and simply carry on to the best of my ability."[12]

Dewey responded January 18. "My warmest appreciation to the directors maild yesterday tels yu how much I was pleased with the outcome of the meeting," he began, then noted that "we agree more fully than yu realize." That was as close to an apology as Godfrey would get. First, Dewey scolded his son for distributing copies of a "private letr" to Foundation directors. He then delivered a series of instructions intermixed with advice and discussion of his future plans, into which he wove at irregular intervals what he saw as Godfrey's obligations to the Dewey legacy. He hoped Godfrey would eventually succeed him as Foundation president, he said, and take responsibility for its "3 great activities of restoration, skools and seed sowing." Godfrey did not reply.[13]

Throughout the winter Dewey sent Placid North rosy reports of winter guest activity at Placid South. He laced his prose with superlatives, even though he acknowledged the depressed economy in which he and Emily were trying to develop the Florida venture. To make it successful he needed to reduce expenses wherever possible, and he counted on the cost savings effected by volume discount buying through Placid Club North Stores to help him along. Here he continued to meet resistance, however. On April 5 Ferris reminded Dewey that Placid North had authorized him to use the name "Lake Placid Club" for his Florida venture only on condition he not involve the New York Club or its subsidiaries in any liabilities. But "when you and your agents charged $35,000 of goods to the Lake Placid Club stores you violated that one condition." Ferris noted that although Dewey had promised repayment "within ten days," five months later bills were still unpaid.[14]

While Placid South languished, 1928 proved a banner year for Placid North. By that time it had become the largest residential club in the world. In part because it enjoyed the greatest increase in life memberships in Club history, in part because so

---

12. Godfrey Dewey to Dewey, 1/9/28, LPEF Mss.

13. Dewey to Godfrey, 1/18/28, Box 23, Dewey Mss. See also I. H. Griswold to Dewey, 1/10/28; and Godfrey to Griswold, 1/12/28, FPA.

14. For an example of Dewey's rosy reports, see Dewey to Directors, 2/8/28, FPA; and *LPC News* 2 (9/7/28): 7. See also Ferris to Dewey, 4/5/28, Box 45, Dewey Mss.

many Club members were new Company bondholders and stockholders, Club trustees decided to change the governance structure Dewey had implemented in 1900 and create a Council to
represent the Club to the Company, to monitor obedience to
house rules and Club customs, and to govern Club membership.
Serving as ex-officio members of the Council were presidents of
the Club Golf Association, which organized in 1908 and was a
member of the U.S. Golf Association, the Camp and Trail Club,
which organized in 1910 to supervise seventy-five miles of trails
in state-owned land regularly used by Club members, and the
"Sno Birds," which incorporated in 1920 to promote winter
sports and maintained ties to the U.S. Figure Skating Association, the National Ski Association, and the U.S. Amateur Ski
Association. Unrepresented on the Council were the Placid Club
Players, founded in 1924 as a voluntary group wanting to promote drama at the Agora, and the Tennis Association, which did
not formally organize until 1929.

House rules and club customs had not changed much over
the years. No disturbing noise was allowed between 10:30 P.M.
and 8:00 A.M. Women were not permitted to smoke in public, but
men were extended that privilege out-of-doors or in designated
smoking rooms inside each of the clubhouses. Alcoholic bever-
ages, gambling of any kind and all "forms of dancing declared
offensiv of good taste or morals," however, were still forbidden.
So were "conduct, dres, or manners which might justly offend
the refined family life which is a chief Club feature."[15]

Dewey spent a quiet summer in Placid North, but in November he was back in Florida preparing for another season. In
contrast to Placid North, his troubles not only continued, they
multiplied. During the summer Mediterranean fruit flies had
wiped out profits on the citrus groves, and a hurricane had done
considerable damage to the Lake Placid area. Although he managed to combine loans against his life insurance policies with
money Emily borrowed from friends in order to pay for Placid
South furniture the Deweys had charged to North Stores, the
Deweys were still cash poor and without adequate collateral to
borrow for their Florida venture. Nonetheless, they pushed forward, patching things together as best they could and putting on

---

15. LPC *Yearbook 1928*, pp. 4, 24, 40–41. See also Rider, *Dewey*, p.
113.

a positive front to a town eager for some success in the depressed Florida economy. In a Placid South circular Dewey listed several Club rules imported from Placid North. Among them he noted: "We have no colord help in the Adirondack club and all our staff is brot down from there. He also reminded prospective members he was trying to recruit from the North that "Florida has fewer negros" than most southern states.[16] But reassurances of racial segregation at Placid South did not help. The Florida Club continued to do poorly; Melvil and Emily Dewey just barely held it together for the remainder of the season.

When they returned to New York in May, they were immediately greeted with a petition signed by several prominent Club women asking the Club Council's newly constituted Board of Directors to reconsider the rule banning women from smoking on Club grounds. Their petition gives some glimpse into how closely members adhered to the "high ideals" Dewey repeatedly touted for the Club. It acknowledged Dewey as originator and moving force behind Club growth, but disagreed with reasons he usually gave for its success. The "marvelous setting which nature has provided" for member activities was the major reason people were attracted to the Club, the petition said, and the Club grew "not by virtue of high ideals but in spite of them." As evidence the petition noted a gradual relaxation of rules over previous years. "Compare the scant coverings of the bathers today with the fully covered limbs and bodies of yesterday," or "the riding astride of the equestriennes," and the decision to allow boating, golfing, swimming, and riding on Sunday. Petitioners also quoted from early Club handbooks citing rules regarding "no tipping" ("Very few observe this today") and "no public cigar stand" (the "farmaci" in Forest Lodge was well stocked with tobacco products). They asked the directors to vote a change in the rules and allow women to smoke anywhere on Club grounds that men did.[17]

---

16. Dewey to LPC Directors, 11/16/28, LPEF Mss. See also *LPC News* 3 (2/1/29):8; (7/26/29): 326; and *LPC Notes,* no. 201 (5/29):2017; and undated circular entitled "What Makes Newcomers Pronounce Club Loj So Satisfying," Box 44, Dewey Mss. See also De Vane, n.p.; and Beck, "Dr. Melvil Dewey," 8/30/1979.

17. Copy of undated petition is in Box 59, Dewey Mss. Westbrook Pegler, a *New York Evening Post* columnist who on occasion frequented the Club, also noted in a column dated 12/31/31: ". . . every year, when the soft snowdrifts vanish from beneath the windows of the guests' or members'

Dewey, who referred to petitioners as the "smoking women radicals," rejected their argument. He cited decades of experience with the Club and a "full knowledge" of the principles upon which it was based. As usual, however, he lapsed into exaggeration when he felt his control challenged. "This Club was founded not as one more candidate for vacation patronage," he wrote, "but *solely* [emphasis mine] to make a home for a reputable minority who greatly disliked and wished to escape from smoking women." Club Directors tried to walk a fine line between Dewey's intransigence and their own sense that rigid enforcement of the rule might cost them members. Ultimately, on May 21 they decided to allow women to smoke only in specific areas on Club grounds, thereby allowing the Club to stay within the letter of its rule banning smoking by women in public. Dewey was disappointed at their decision. He recommended that in the future the Club admit to membership only people "who never smoke under eni circumstances."[18] That he did not protest further, however, reflected the fact that he had other more pressing problems commanding his attention.

One emanated from his old nemesis—a persistent inability to control himself around women. Sight unseen and upon the recommendation of New York City Episcopal Bishop Howard Chandler Robbins, Dewey hired Robbins's former secretary to be his stenographer at Placid South in November 1927. When Dewey met her at the train station, he described her as a "dainty litl flapper" who "was betr looking than I expected."[19] Over time, both Emily and Melvil became fond of her, and when the Deweys returned to Placid North in late May, she went with them. The inevitable happened early in the summer when Dewey kissed and caressed her in public. Emily immediately recognized a potential problem, and told the stenographer "that if she had eni objektion whatever she had onli to say so & it wdn't be repeated."

---

rooms, numbers of bottles of various distinctive shapes, pinched, dimpled and all such, are disclosed upon the ground."

18. Dewey discusses the May 21 meeting and his interpretation of Directors' decision in Dewey to Godfrey Dewey, 12/21/29, FPA. In a note to H. W. Hicks of 11/23/31, Dewey argued that no "heritics or radicals" should be placed on the ballot for Club officer, and protested the nomination of "eni liberals on standards. . . . Unles w keep radicals from boring from within w r doomd." Dewey to Hicks, 11/23/31, Box 54, Dewey Mss.

19. Dewey to Anne Colony, 11/25/27, Box 44, Dewey Mss.

When Dewey agreed to exercise more self-restraint in the future, the stenographer "promist faithfulli . . . she wd tel Mrs. Dewey if she was trubld by enithing unconventional on my part."

Because she wanted to show empathy for Dewey's weakness, however, she shortly thereafter confessed "in an hour of foolish frankness" to a life during the war, when, Dewey reported, "she smokt, drank & swore & had the devil's own temper." Dewey scolded her forcefully that of course such conduct would never be tolerated at the Club (he apparently saw no contradiction in his own behavior towards her). The stenographer then flushed, left Dewey's office without saying a word, and returned to her room, where she penned a resignation note to Emily and indicated she would leave the Club the following morning. Again Emily sensed trouble. She sent for the stenographer and asked why she was resigning. The young woman tearfully insinuated that Dewey's unwelcome familiarity in previous weeks was the reason. Then Emily became anxious. She immediately called a Club employee into the room to record their subsequent conversation, during which, Dewey later reported, the stenographer "confest she had been lying." After the stenographer left Lake Placid, both Emily and Dewey forgot "her existens."

On October 2, 1929, however, two weeks before Dewey was scheduled to leave for Florida, he received a summons from a New York lawyer representing the stenographer that called for $50,000 in damages for the embarrassing way in which Dewey had treated her in public, and especially for a kissing incident in a taxi. Dewey immediately wrote Ferris. "It looks like a blakmail nuisans suit," he said. He suspected the New York lawyer was a "shyster" who smelled quick money. But Ferris warned Dewey not to take the threat lightly; a jury, he noted, almost always sympathizes with a young woman who makes a claim against a well-known and wealthy older man. Dewey was undeterred; he wanted to fight back. Such behavior ought not be rewarded, he argued. Again Ferris counseled caution; he convinced Dewey to place the matter in his hands, and promised to keep Dewey informed while Dewey was in Florida.[20]

By early January 1930, however, the stenographer had enlisted the support of her old boss, Howard Robbins, who scolded Dewey for his improper behavior. Dewey was irritated with Rob-

---

20. Details put together from information in Dewey to Ferris, 10/2/29; 11/6/29; 1/2/30; and 2/1/30, Box 44, Dewey Mss.

bins's letter. Robbins may be "a Mid-Victorian or strong Puritan & honestli sumwhat shokt that a man of hy ideals shd kis a sekretari," he wrote Ferris February 1," but he sureli knows it has been dun in 1000's of cases & is too big a man to distort this into a criminal intent." Dewey expected lenient and understanding treatment for himself because his motives were pure; he was never ready to extend the same courtesy to others. From Florida he told Ferris to work with Godfrey, contest the suit, but quickly settle the problem. "It ot to be withdrawn quietli at the erliest day."[21]

Ferris was not as eager to contest the suit. "This is no Sunday school party," he argued. It would be very difficult to validate Dewey's description of the woman's character in court if Robbins testified in her behalf. Ferris spent most of February 10 and 11 in conference with the young woman's lawyer, shuttling between him and Godfrey with settlement offers. On the 11th he wrote Dewey that all sides had finally agreed to a settlement of $2,147.66, payable immediately. Ferris urged Dewey to take it. Three days later Dewey agreed. He asked if the stenographer's acceptance of the check would render it impossible for her to make any other demands against him, and worried about similar suits from other women, not because they might suggest Dewey had questionable morals, but because someone had found a way to get money from him for services not rendered. "Supoz she spreds rumors that she got $2000 for no work!"[22] That, in Dewey's eyes, was a much greater transgression than the harassing treatment of which he was accused. Dewey's decision to settle, however, ended the incident; it never again resurfaced.

"Fyt to the Limit": The Battle between North and South Continues 1929–1931

The other problem preoccupying Dewey's attention at the turn of the decade was his running battle with Placid North. Directors

---

21. Dewey to Ferris, 2/1/30, Box 44, Dewey Mss.

22. Dewey to Ferris, 2/1/30; Ferris to Dewey, 2/4/30; 2/5/30; 2/11/30; Dewey to Ferris, 2/14/30, Box 44, Dewey Mss. Unfortunately, I was not able to locate a copy of the subpoena filed by the stenographer's lawyers, which would have allowed me to present a better picture of her side of the controversy. I would, however, like to thank David Orenstein and Ellen Sleeter for their research assistance.

of the New York enterprise continued to resist financial connections to Placid South, and strengthened their resolve as the nation's economic depression deepened. Dewey continued to insist Placid South was automatically connected to Placid North through him and his interests; he argued it was part of his vision for the Lake Placid Club and the Foundation. Both parties sparred constantly, usually debating Dewey's contention he controlled interest on $300,000 worth of preferred stock he had donated to the Foundation several years earlier.

Sometimes, however, they squabbled over minor points. In February 1930, for example, Dewey complained bitterly about Placid North's decision to charge the Florida Club for printing all lines referring to it in *Club Notes* and the *Weekly,* and to give it only five lines in Club circulars designed to raise funds. He was especially irritated with the latter because the circular itself had enough blank space remaining in which he could have made a stronger pitch for Placid South. Unless Placid North reversed this decision, he said, he would "fyt to the limit."[23]

On March 4 Godfrey asked a selected group of officers Dewey called his "Cabinet" (Harry Hicks, Deo Colburn, Charles Hobbs, and himself) to discuss his father's letter. All agreed any changes in the circulars would disrupt Placid North's "cultivation campaign."[24] Officers recommended instead that the Club issue a separate mailing for Placid South, and Godfrey appealed to his father "in strong terms to trust our judgment, based on full understanding of all factors involved." Dewey shot a cable back to his son immediately that included the exact language he wanted placed in the next circular, and followed it with a long vituperative letter that concluded: "Thoz not wiling to work *with* me shd resyn."

The Cabinet met again March 6, this time with Ferris present as legal counsel. Ferris said Company Directors could not legally expend Company funds for the benefit of another corpo-

---

23. Dewey to Cabinet, 2/26/30, LPEF Mss.

24. The campaign itself had been authorized by Company Directors on behalf of Placid North to stimulate membership and business. They had given "very careful consideration" to the amount of copy devoted to the Florida branch, but based on their own judgment and the counsel of an advertising firm hired to advise on the campaign, they unanimously decided it would be more effective for Placid South to issue publicity "separateli." See Dewey to Ferris, 3/17/30, LPEF Mss.

ration unless it owned 95 percent of the stock. But in "deferens to D's insistens on his position & to preserv harmony & cordial relations pending more detaild & accurate definition of the relations of the 2 Clubs by LPCo Directors at their next meeting," Godfrey later explained to his father, Ferris recommended that officers include in the second and third circular the exact information Dewey had stipulated in his March 5 cable.[25]

A week later Ferris submitted a lengthy opinion further defining the legal relationship between Placid North and South, and on March 14 Company officers summarized Ferris's opinion for Dewey. The various Florida companies Dewey had set up were separate entities and legally independent of Placid North, they argued, with separate incomes and expenditures. In addition, the $14,400 Dewey's preferred stock generated could not be used for the Florida project until and unless the Florida corporations were given to the Foundation. Because Ferris advised against accepting such a gift at that time, however, the Cabinet would not relinquish control of the funds.

Officers then implored Dewey to defer further consideration of the matter to the next directors' meeting, and although they offered to resign ("as 3 times suggested in your 6 Mr 30 letter") any time Dewey wished, they would not reverse their decision. "We cannot conscientiously disregard legal restrictions as interpreted by Co counsel, directors' votes, reinforst by power of banks to call their loans, or our obvious responsibility to the corporation which we ar trying to serv to the best of our abilities." Temporarily, Dewey chose not to contest their opinion. Officers' willingness to compromise on advertising may have tempered his readiness to fight. Godfrey told Ferris he believed his father would wait until the summer Company directors' meeting to make his case, "tho he will undoubtedly write more than a few statements between now and then to which he wil assume that silence gives assent."[26] Godfrey knew his father well.

As usual, the Deweys returned to New York in May, and everyone at Placid North braced for Dewey's counterattack. By

---

25. Godfrey to Dewey, 3/4/30; Dewey to Godfrey 3/5/30, LPEF Mss; Dewey to Cabinet, 3/6/30, FPA; Minutes, Special "Cabinet Meeting," 3/4/30, LPEF Mss. See also Godfrey to Ferris, 3/17/30, LPEF Mss.

26. Company officers to Dewey, 3/14/30, LPEF Mss; Godfrey to Ferris, 3/22/30, FPA.

this time age was increasingly taking its toll; Dewey was having considerable difficulty walking without assistance, and people around him noticed he was becoming even more intolerant of dissent. The battle took place at the July 28 Foundation trustees' annual meeting. The atmosphere was contentious; even Dewey described it as "sumthing of a strain." Both sides held their ground, neither showed willingness to compromise, although Placid North officers were considerably more diplomatic than Dewey, who continued to believe their resistance to his plans for Placid South was the result of a conspiracy spearheaded by Godfrey. After hours of debate, Dewey won two points he thought would strengthen links between the New York and Florida Clubs.

First, he forced acceptance of a resolution in which Foundation trustees declared their belief in Placid South, and their "willingness and intention to accept control thru acceptance of all L.P. Club Co stock when tenderd." That, in Dewey's mind, would cement the Foundation's commitment to the Florida Club beyond his death. Second, because he believed that Godfrey "intended to unload Fla branch if he had power," he forced a change in the bylaws. From henceforth, a four-fifths vote would be required from the Executive Committee to place any proposal before the Foundation, and the number of Foundation directors would increase from seven to ten, with four-fifths needed to carry a vote on any cause seeking support from the Foundation. (Dewey was convinced Godfrey could never muster a four-fifths majority under such a setup.) Officers were glad when the meeting ended, but everyone realized Dewey's irrepressibility on the issue would inevitably lead to future battles equally as ugly.[27]

But while Dewey fought with Placid North officials over support of Placid South, he met full cooperation from the latter in upholding Club admission standards. Jews continued to be barred from membership, and Dewey continued to show different faces to different people on the issue. In the summer of 1930, for example, a Club member who had recently married a Russian

---

27. Copies of the minutes of this 7/28/30 meeting and the resolutions presented and approved can be found in LPEF Mss and FPA. Dewey's comment on the nature of the meeting is in Dewey to LPCEF Trustees, 8/4/30, LPEF Mss. Dewey's comment on Godfrey can be found in a document headed "Questions to discuss with Fentress 23 March '31," Box 44, Dewey Mss. See also Keyes D. Metcalf, "Reminiscences of Melvil Dewey," in Stevenson and Kramer-Greene, *Dewey,* p. 7.

whose "blood" was one-fourth Jew asked Club officers if she could become a member. He noted she had converted to Christian Science sixteen years before. Dewey expressed sympathy, then feigned a reluctant acceptance of the will of a Club majority. "It galls me to the limit," he wrote a Club officer, that the Club's "no-Jew rule" barred such people, and even though he disliked "exceedingli to hav people accuse us of being Jewbaiters & naro or bigoted," he reminded the officer the Club had ten similar discussions in the previous twenty years and always voted "unanimously" to maintain the rule.

Several months later New York Governor Franklin D. Roosevelt visited the Club to give state endorsement for Lake Placid's bid to host the 1932 Winter Olympics. (Godfrey was spearheading the effort.) Roosevelt's visit drew protests from Jewish Americans, who publicly objected to use of state funds to erect a bobsled

When a Jewish group protested use of state funds for Olympic Games at the exclusionary Lake Placid Club, Dewey called it a "nu Jew attak" which "helps to sho *why* our members have always declined to admit them."

run on Club grounds.[28] In this case Dewey showed aggressiveness and a desire to turn the episode to the Club's advantage. "This nu Jew attak wil giv us much valuabl publisiti," he wrote his Cabinet. "It will *help* the Club & their atak helps to sho *why* our members hav always declyned to admit them." In March, however, he reverted to affected sympathy. In a letter to George Peabody, he reiterated the "moral contrakt" the Club had with its members, and noted that even when Louis Brandeis, Oscar Straus, and "sum of the fynest Jews" in America wanted to become members, the Club refused to bend its rule. "Personali, it hurts me veri much to seem to hav a relijius or racial prejudice."[29]

By the spring of 1931 the nation's economy had deteriorated into its worst depression ever. Although occupancy was down 15 percent in 1931, Placid North seemed strong enough to weather the crisis, but Placid South was not pulling in enough money to cover expenses, and had no means to begin repayment of debts already incurred. Dewey did not see how he could come up with the money necessary to open in the fall or repay any of the loans due January 1, 1932. All of this was complicated by the fact that his Florida company still had not obtained title to the land, and the town of Lake Placid, which owned it, had significant arrears it could not cover.[30]

He needed to borrow money, and looked to Placid North member Calvin Fentress, president of Naval Stores Investment Company of Chicago, for help. Fentress was holding $43,000 in notes he had purchased from the town of Lake Placid, which it had issued to raise money for Dewey's plan. When Florida's economy turned sour, however, Fentress canceled the notes but retained claims to the land that the town had purchased with the

---

28. *NYT,* 11/7/30; 11/8/30; 11/21/30; and 12/4/30.

29. Dewey to Frank Daly, 7/30/30; Dewey to LPCo. Directors, 11/29/30, Box 50, Dewey Mss. See also Dewey to LPCEF Trustees, 12/20/30, LPEF Mss; Dewey to Peabody, Box 54, Dewey Mss; Dewey to Fentress, 8/17/31, Box 44, Dewey Mss; *LPC News* 3 (9/13/29): 397. For other examples of Dewey's habit of hiding his anti-Semitism by playing to the audience, see Dewey to S. D. Matthews of the Ampersand Realty Company in Saranac Lake, 7/28/24, Box 46; and Dewey to Roger Holden, Secretary of the Lake Placid Chamber of Commerce, 1/28/28, Box 68, Dewey Mss.

30. See document entitled "Questions to Discuss with Fentress 23 March '31"; Dewey to J. E. Sims, 12/8/30; Dewey to Calvin Fentress, 3/30/31, Box 44, Dewey Mss.

money. Thus, because the town did not own the land free of liens it could not transfer title to Dewey for the acreage on which he wanted to develop Placid South. And without title to the land, Dewey could not issue and sell certified bonds to Placid North members to improve the Florida Club. At Dewey's invitation, Fentress visited Placid South in late March. He asked Fentress directly if he would authorize the town of Lake Placid to pass title on the three thousand acres to the Lake Placid Company. Fentress declined.[31]

Matters looked even bleaker for keeping Club Loj open. By this time Dewey claimed to have invested $70,000 worth of membership fees in the building and $80,000 of "muni givn to our Foundation but standing in Mrs. D's name." Still the Club owned no deed on the property in which it had invested the $150,000. On April 16 Dewey asked one friend for a loan of "at least" $2,000 to cover wages and supplies for the remainder of the season. On April 21 he asked E. C. Stuart, who had already invested $160,000, to send any possible buyers to him. But serious problems persisted. Dewey had to do something, or face certain bankruptcy.

On April 23 he and Emily met with two Placid North Directors who were traveling through Florida. They urged the Deweys to close down Club Loj and move to the Seven Lakes site. Because the main building on that site had only twenty-five guest rooms, they argued, it could be run at much less cost and still allow the Deweys to save face by keeping Placid South open. The move, they said, would also allow the Deweys to sell Loj furniture, which Emily owned, and use the cash to make immediate improvements at Seven Lakes. Dewey hesitated. "Club Loj stript wil discredit all of us & be much slower for sale or leas," he argued, but ultimately he had no choice. Placid North indicated a willingness to "buy" the furniture and apply that sum to the debt Dewey owed Placid North Stores. A week later the Deweys announced they were going to close Club Loj and move their operation for the next season to the Seven Lakes site. Dewey penned a note to the local newspaper in which he "explained" that Club Loj had been "a syd issue while we were waiting to get the main plant started," and that by confining themselves to

---

31. Dewey summarized this meeting in Dewey to Fentress, 3/30/31, Box 44, Dewey Mss.

Seven Lakes the Deweys were placing themselves in a "safer position to gro as fast as demand warrants."[32]

Emily and Melvil Dewey left Florida in late May in a considerably weaker financial position. Since 1928 they had lost $40,000 at the Florida Club. After Club Loj closed May 1, the mortgage holder assumed ownership because the property could not be sold for even half the $155,000 mortgage. And Dewey still owed the Grinnell Refrigeration Company $13,000. On May 20 he asked Ferris how he could repay his debts; he feared his endorsement of notes taken out against property to which he did not hold title was illegal, and he worried about the embarrassment it would cause him and the Club if it became public knowledge.[33] Despite these problems, however, Dewey was still determined that Placid South would survive.

But he also seemed to sense he would not live much longer, and sought to guarantee the future of his "causes" against potential enemies. When he returned to New York, Dewey immediately began efforts to isolate Godfrey from the Lake Placid Company power structure and insert Emily instead. He continued to view his son as unalterably opposed to Placid South, and anticipated that if Godfrey assumed control of the Foundation upon his death, the Florida Club would lose its "rivet" to Placid North and wither. Dewey was sure Emily would not allow that to happen. On August 31 he memoed Company directors that he soon intended to step down as Company president, and he wanted Emily to succeed him. Although he argued "this chanj is mereli nominal as it wil continu the present administration without a ripl," everyone recognized what he was trying to do.[34] Understandably, Godfrey was incensed, and made no secret of his feelings. Five days later Dewey invited him to a private lunch.

The lunch turned into a five-hour "frank" discussion in which both men exchanged opinions on the reasons for their poor relationship. Dewey later summarized his position in a

---

32. See Dewey to J. E. Sims, 4/16/31; Dewey to "Kelly & Gardner LP Co Directors," 5/7/31, Box 44; Dewey memo entitled "Fla Branch Subsidi," dated 5/16/31; Dewey to LC Directors, 5/18/31; Dewey to Ferris, 5/20/31, Box 45; Dewey to Lake Placid [Fla.] Town Commissioners, Clerk & Attorney, 5/22/31, Box 44, Dewey Mss.

33. Dewey to Ferris, 5/20/31, Box 44, Dewey Mss.

34. Document entitled "Not a Change but to Avoid Change," by Dewey, dated 8/31/31; Dewey to Godfrey Dewey, 9/4/31, FPA.

thirty-five-page letter dictated the following day. First, however, he sent copies to the entire Lake Placid Company Board of Directors, and only thereafter did he release the original to his son. The perspective was paranoid, the tone intimidating, the substance an attempt to discredit Godfrey before Company officers. Over the years, Dewey said, Godfrey had developed "antagonism & hostiliti" towards him reflected in an attitude that "whatever was wrong past or present was entyrli due to father's wrong ideas & manajment." This was especially evident in Godfrey's treatment of Placid South, to which he had been "stedili antagonistic" and even had organized an opposition at Placid North "of which yu wer recognyzed leader."

This attitude was a radical departure from the altruistic spirit in which the Lake Placid idea had been conceived, Dewey argued. "Yur mother, Katharin & May enterd fuli into this altruistic spirit" and "left all they had to the Foundation." That Godfrey wished to take a different direction "hurts me . . . for I hav always despyzd peopl who work simpli for dolars." He then reminded Godfrey of the dangerous position in which he had placed the Club in 1911 when Godfrey refused to return the 10 percent Company common stock he controlled unless Dewey gave him $40,000 preferred stock "outryt."

Since it appeared Godfrey placed a higher value on acquiring money for personal use rather than working in the Foundation's best interests, Dewey said, and since it was obvious "yu ar by nature & experience a *spender* & not a provyder," the people around him had developed "a firm conviktion that the continuiti & safeti of the present Club wd be badli jeopardyzed if yu became *dominant* in LP Co." One of the main reasons for the recent reorganization of the Company's administrative structure, he pointed out, was to remove Godfrey from a position in which he could damage Company assets. The very best thing, Dewey believed, was for Godfrey to succeed him as head of the Foundation without salary, where he could direct "seedsowing"; there he would not be taxed with administrative responsibilities for which by temperament he was ill suited. "Mak me hapi by realyzing this & working with us & not agenst us," Dewey concluded.[35]

Although the letter did not have the effect of completely discrediting Godfrey, it did reflect his reduced role in the Lake

---

35. Dewey to Godfrey, 9/11/31, Box 23, Dewey Mss.

Placid milieu since 1928. Most of the Company directors and Foundation trustees agreed with Godfrey that his father's Florida venture was an ill-conceived and a potentially disastrous effort in which Melvil, whose normally questionable business judgment they thought had been made even worse by his age, was being manipulated by his much younger wife Emily. They were right about the former, wrong about the latter, but in their interpretation of the situation they nonetheless had used Godfrey to front their resistance to the elder Dewey. For his willingness to carry out this role, Godfrey paid a price in further antagonizing his father. Most of the Company directors and Foundation trustees also agreed that Godfrey was not his father's equal, and would never make a good Company president,[36] but no one wanted to press the point; no one wanted to confront Melvil Dewey directly. After all, the old man was nearly eighty, and increasingly talking about not living through another winter. The situation stagnated.

With the Placid North brouhaha temporarily silenced, Dewey returned his attention to Placid South and again publicly bubbled with optimism. He and Emily opened the Club November 1 in "permanent quarters" on three thousand acres three miles south of Lake Placid on the shores of Lakes June-in-Winter and Placid. No longer was Placid South tied to Club Loj, Dewey said; instead, Club activities centered in two main buildings, "Litlloj" and "Lyvok," both of which had unlimited electric service, steam heat, and long-distance phones in each room. Grounds around the buildings sported two thousand new trees and shrubs and twelve hundred rose bushes imported from Texas. In promotional literature sent to Placid North members, the Deweys also informed readers they had returned the same chef and hairdresser, had opened a new nine-hole golf course (the first tee and ninth green were only twenty yards from "Litlloj"), and provided daily free trips around the Seven Lakes area in a fourteen-passenger "new Dodge watercar."

Of course Placid South adhered to the "same ideals, standards, methods and manajment" as Placid North, and because members of the latter were automatically eligible for membership in the Florida Club they would not have to weather a screening process. Even better, initiation fees and annual and life dues

36. Colburn interview, 5/13/1985. See also Dewey to Dorkas Fellows, 8/20/31, Box 13, Dewey Mss.

were only half those of the parent club.[37] And the weather was beautiful. Dewey noted he would breakfast daily surrounded by "brilliant flowers" on "Litlloj" patio, after which he would move to a sunporch covered with flame vine and draped with rosa catalina where he spent most of his working hours while not at his desk.

The public optimism, however, contrasted sharply with private financial anxiety. In a December 19 letter to Ferris he complained that the Club had only two guests instead of the two hundred capacity, and that he and Emily were having a very difficult time meeting current bills. They had just convinced the Swift Company to let their $700 bill for meats carry into the next year, and he indicated they were forced to pay spot cash for wages and foods. As a result, he told Ferris, Placid South would again be unable to meet its obligations to Placid North's Company Stores.[38]

The end of 1931 did not seem any better than the beginning. Placid North was weathering the effects of the Great Depression, but only barely. Placid South was failing badly, and the new year did not promise to improve prospects. On December 10, however, Dewey celebrated his eightieth birthday. He used the occasion to pen a lengthy letter to "a fu frends from our Florida branch." In most of it he reminisced about his "world work," but in a postscript gave thanks to a variety of people who had surprised him that day, including his Adirondack staff for the thirty-year-old palm tree it had planted in his honor on Placid South grounds, the library school alumni association for a bound volume of 100 birthday letters (in "ful toold turki"), and a delegation of the Florida Library Association that came to Placid South to commemorate the event. He also thanked friends and well-wishers for the 300 letters and 100 cables from forty states and several foreign countries that had arrived that day. He would go to bed that evening, he said, feeling fulfilled and grateful for being granted a long life of usefulness in the reforms to which he had dedicated himself for over six decades.[39]

---

37. Pamphlet describing Placid South, dated 9/30/31, can be found in FPA. See also *Bulletin 1,* dated 12/1/31, for "Lake Placid Club in Florida: Sub-tropic branch of Adirondack Lake Placid Club," copy found in FPA, and Beck, "Lake Placid Club," 8/30/1979.

38. Dewey to Ferris, 12/19/31, Box 45, Dewey Mss.

39. "80th birthday letr 10 Dec 31 to a fu personal frends from our Florida branch, 7 Lakes, Lake Placid, Hylands Co, Fla.", Wyer Mss. See also Wyer to Butler, 10/15/31, Butler Mss.

Melvil Dewey, President
Emily Dewey, Vice-president & Tres
Emma C Roche, Vice-president
Douglas Slater, Sub-manajer
Robert Hood, Secretary

Lake Placid Club in Florida
open Nov 1 to May 1

Founded 1927

Subtropic branch of Adirondak Lake Placid Club
founded 1895 – open all year

First unit of Lake Placid Club
in Florida's Scenic Hylands
on Lakes Placid and June-in-winter

Address May 1 to Nov 1 Lake Placid Club, N Y
Nov 1 to May 1 L P Club, Lake Placid, Fla

Lake Placid, Hylands Co, Fla

80th birthday letr 10 Dec 31, to a fu personal frends
from our Florida branch,
7 Lakes, Lake Placid, Hylands Co, Fla

Today starts my 9th decade. When my Albany staf celebrated my 5th decade I felt fairli mature.

At 80 owing to the 5 winters I hav spent in this
best clymat on erth I don't feel as old. My jeneral
helth (& Emily's) is betr than for years. I can't
(& don't) run as fast or as far, don't work 3 ½-days
a.m., p.m. & eve, can't stand as long hours, take a
nap except when I forget it, having lernd that mor can
be dun by not crowding the 80 year old machine too fast.
My purpose all thru thez 80 years has been to shape
my personal habits so to get qualiti & quantiti results. 2 shorter ½ days at my big desk made for me
40 years ago ar reducing arears of mani things I
thot important to clean up whyl I stil hav my apetyt
for work. So whyl the world has mor to wori about
than ever befor in human histori I am bizi & hapi,
not becauz I am indiferent to thez present problems
but becauz my mind is skoold not to wori. I profit
by De Stael's dictum:

'The sumit of human hapines is to feel each nyt yu

World Olympic Winter Games, Feb 4-13, 1932, Lake Placid, N Y

Dewey outlined his life of achievement and self-discipline in a long letter to friends on his eightieth birthday, December 10, 1931. He called himself "a sun dial where no wheels get rusti or slip a cog." He died of a brain hemorrhage sixteen days later.

Epilogue

Legacy of a Hero
and a Villain

Melvil and Emily Dewey spent a quiet Christmas Day 1931, enjoying the mild weather and entertaining friends. They retired early that evening, anxious to resume their efforts to make Placid South successful when they returned to their desks the following day. In the morning, however, Dewey arose earlier than usual and met Emily to discuss Club matters. Suddenly, in mid-sentence his speech thickened, and as Emily moved to his side he lost consciousness. Emily quickly summoned a doctor, who just as quickly diagnosed a brain hemorrhage. Dewey never fully regained consciousness. When he aroused slightly at 8:30, it became apparent his left side was completely paralyzed. He died peacefully at 10:15 A.M.[1] That night the Times Building in New York City flashed news of his death in an electronic message that circled the building.

Several days later the people of Lake Placid, Florida, held a funeral for Dewey; newspaper reporters took special note that Emily dressed completely in white. That same day Placid North held a memorial service in the Agora; it was attended by 387 friends, relatives, and employees. As Dewey wished, his body was cremated after his funeral, and his ashes transported back to the Adirondack Club where Godfrey deposited them in a small crypt beneath the Chapel altar next to those of his mother. In the weeks following Dewey's death numerous cards, letters, and cables poured in to both Emily and Godfrey, all expressing sympathy

---

1. Details of Dewey's last moments are recorded in the *Highland County Pilot,* 12/31/31; 1/1/32. See also Emily Dewey's recollections, as quoted in Dawe, *Dewey,* p. 151.

and acknowledging the vast contributions Melvil Dewey had made over a long and fruitful life. Many added recollections that pointed to character strengths and identified particular kindnesses Dewey had showed in the past.[2] Some reassured his widow and son that the future would certainly validate the accuracy of Melvil Dewey's vision; others predicted the significant and lasting impact of his legacy through the institutions he had created to push his reforms beyond his death.

Once the funeral and memorial services were over, however, his survivors began contesting for vacant positions he left behind. Emily and Godfrey Dewey both wanted control of the Lake Placid Club Education Foundation.[3] When trustees met January 24, 1932, to name Dewey's successor, Arthur Bestor first presented a memorial resolution honoring Dewey's contributions, and after it was approved Emily Dewey outlined plans for a Dewey biography to be published by December 10, 1932, Dewey's eighty-first birthday. She said she hoped for a 350-page book, and projected costs at $3,000.[4] Godfrey Dewey, who served as chair for the meeting, called attention to vacancies in the office of president and on the Executive Committee and Board of Trustees. Bylaws pertaining to the selection of successors to each of these vacancies were read by the secretary, after which trustees Henry Holmes and Arthur Bestor moved to defer election of a president until the July annual meeting. Because Godfrey was a candidate for the presidency, he left the room for the duration of the informal discussion that followed and Holmes took the chair. Holmes then called for an expression of opinion on whether Godfrey should be elected to succeed his father; one trustee voted yes, twelve no. Records indicate no consideration was given to the possibility of Emily Dewey's candidacy. Instead,

2. Obituaries in *Lake Placid News*, 12/26/31. Box 35, Dewey Mss, contains hundreds of letters of condolences, some of which include descriptions of Dewey's death and the memorial services held for him in Florida and New York. In the early 1960s Dewey's ashes were removed to a family vault in the North Elba Cemetery near Lake Placid.

3. On the day Dewey died, Foundation Trustee Henry W. Holmes advised Godfrey to "stick now to your candidacy for your father's post, and all that goes with it except his autocratic powers." See Holmes to Godfrey, 12/31/31, FPA.

4. Deo Colburn contends that part of Emily's motive for Foundation funding of an authorized biography was to pump Lake Placid South. The biography that resulted was Dawe, *Dewey*. Colburn Interview, 5/13/1985.

trustees elected Arthur Bestor acting president to fill Dewey's unexpired term.[5] As a result, neither Godfrey nor Emily inherited Melvil Dewey's mantle of leadership.

But without Melvil Dewey's energetic leadership and irrepressible reform spirit, Placid North and the Lake Placid Club Education Foundation floundered. The 1932 Winter Olympics for which Godfrey had worked so hard temporarily brought Lake Placid and the Club national and international attention, but the Great Depression substantially limited the Olympics' residual effect on Lake Placid, and soon thereafter the Club began to languish. By the late 1930s it passed into friendly receivership and was reorganized; after World War II the Army took over Club grounds as a reconditioning center and spent substantial amounts of money to improve the physical plant. Despite this infusion of new funds, however, the Club never recovered from the Depression and by the 1950s its exclusionary practices had become anathema to most of the middle-class professionals from whom the Club had drawn the bulk of its membership and revenue. Although Club buildings helped house athletes and guests when the Winter Olympics returned to Lake Placid in 1980, the Club itself was by then almost defunct.[6] At decade's end the Club ceased to exist and its physical plant and grounds had been sold to a Boston developer, who a short time later himself went bankrupt. As of this writing, Club grounds are owned and for sale by the Lake Placid Land Corporation, a subsidiary of the USF&G Insurance Company. When I last visited it in November 1992, most of the larger buildings had badly deteriorated for lack of maintenance over the years. Many were irreparable; the previous month half of Forest Towers had been destroyed by fire.

Placid South had an even shorter life after Dewey's death. Emily tried to carry on, but the Depression forced her to declare bankruptcy by the end of the decade. On October 17, 1942, Club grounds were sold at public auction to pay the mortgage. Eventually it was purchased by the Florida Synod of the Presbyterian Church as an educational camp and retreat.[7] Like Lake Placid

---

5. A copy of these minutes can be found in FPA.

6. William C. White, *Adirondack Country* (Syracuse, 1985), p. 138.

7. "Now and Then Bulletin, no. 2: Lake Placid Club in Florida," copy found in FPA; Miriam Beck, "Dr. Melvil Dewey—A Genius Organizer," *Lake Placid Journal*, 8/30/1979; Satoru Tekeuchi, "Dewey in Florida," *Journal of Library History* 1 (1966): 127–32.

North it still stands; unlike Placid North, however, it is in good repair.

Other components of Dewey's Adirondack empire survived by separating from Foundation control. For example, in 1934 Northwood School obtained a separate charter from the Regents, and although it remained part of the Foundation for a while, by the 1950s it was beginning to prosper under an independent leadership that shunned Dewey's exclusionary practices. Also, in 1988 the Foundation sold Forest Press, for eight decades the Decimal Classification publishers, to OCLC, the world's largest bibliographic utility, for a rumored $3,800,000. Under OCLC supervision the Classification has prospered in recent years, and in 1993 celebrated its 120th anniversary. And because of the money realized from the sale of Forest Press, the Foundation has been able to embark on a modest program of philanthropy favoring upstate New York education activities.

For the most part the Spelling Reform Association and the Metric Bureau died with Dewey. Yet efforts to reform in both areas continued beyond his death in various ways; some successes are evident. New Yorkers now travel north from Albany on the New York "Thruway," and "catalog" is now commonplace in American library circles. Students at Northwood, however, are no longer encouraged to use "tho," "altho," and "thruout" in their compositions. Widespread adoption of metric enjoyed slightly more success. After decades of steady agitation from scientific professions, in 1975 Congress passed the Metric Conversion Act, creating a Metrification Board which exhorted the nation to conform voluntarily to the metric system. In 1988 the federal goverment issued a mandate requiring all federally funded construction projects exceeding $10 million to use metric. After September 30, 1996, all federally assisted highway construction must also comply.

Dewey's legacy to librarianship, however, has been most enduring. For the most part the library organizations he started or helped start have survived and prospered. The American Library Association has grown to become the national voice for the library profession Dewey hoped for, with a membership near 57,000 in 1995. The New York Library Association is the second largest state library association in the country; in November 1992, it hosted its 102d annual conference at Lake Placid. *Library Journal* has also survived and prospered. During the first decade of the twentieth century ALA began publishing its own periodical (now called *American Libraries*); once cut loose from ALA, *Library Journal* easily settled into the role of independent commentator on national and international library matters.

The Library Bureau grew substantially in the 1910s and 1920s. In 1926 it was purchased by the Rand Kardex Company which, in future years, merged with other companies to become Sperry Rand in 1955. When Sperry Rand announced it was going to phase out the Library Bureau division in 1976, however, employees bought the assets of the division and returned the Bureau to independent status. As of this writing the Bureau is located in Herkimer, New York, where it does a brisk but modest business in library furniture and automation equipment.

For a while, Dewey's library school did equally as well. In 1938 the Carnegie Corporation donated funds to Columbia University to establish the Melvil Dewey Chair in the School of Library Service. After World War II the School maintained its leadership role in library education as its doctoral program fed scores of graduates into high positions in the library profession. In the 1970s, however, the institution began curtailing support, and after choking it in the 1980s by failing to recruit and tenure promising young faculty, formally closed it a second time in 1992. On this occasion, however, financial conditions defeated efforts to move the library school to a university elsewhere in the metropolitan area. R. Kathleen Molz, latest incumbent of the Dewey Chair, did not choose to use the title upon her transfer to the School of International and Public Affairs. It is uncertain what will happen to the chair when Professor Molz retires.

But the institutions Dewey left form only a part of his legacy. Other influences are equally enduring but more invisible, and some are especially powerful because they have come to be accepted as "natural." For example, the perspectives Dewey cemented into his hierarchical classification system have helped create in the minds of millions of people throughout the world who have used DDC-arranged collections a perception of knowledge organization that had by the beginning of the twentieth century evolved a powerful momentum. In addition, library education, professional classification practices, and the tools that have evolved to facilitate that practice (e.g., MARC records sold to bibliographic utilities like OCLC and RLIN) have tended to perpetuate DDC's advantages. But despite its flaws (which more recent editions of DDC have struggled to correct) one still has to admit that over the decades the DDC has saved librarians and library users millions of dollars and countless hours of confusion because it has served as a widely used and nationally and internationally familiar way to organize collections. For good and ill, Dewey's influence lives on in his classification scheme.

Dewey's influence on the structure of the library profession has been equally enduring, equally as powerful. In large part because of his efforts the library profession came of age in the late nineteenth century. He established a highly efficient organizational scheme for the library which, when combined with local community pride, Andrew Carnegie's philanthropy, and a middle- and upper-class desire to control mass reading interests, created a public library movement (the number of public libraries increased from 188 in 1876 to 3,562 in 1913) that spread first throughout the nation, then throughout the world. Yet Dewey had also created a structure for the library profession that relinquished authority to determine the "best reading" to other professionals. Others more knowledgeable in literary and scholarly matters, he believed, should judge the value (and the rules to determine that value) of the objects librarians acquired, organized, and made accessible; others should separate the "bad" from the "good."[8]

The library science Dewey designed to support this structure and fit this niche was a combination of library management and library expertise (especially reference and classification) built on a service imperative and energized by a "library faith." And because by design the institution served and supported the reading canons of a white middle- and upper-class patriarchy, Dewey found it easy to recruit women into the profession in order to fulfill cheaply and efficiently the supporting role he had assigned it. As he viewed the situation, women did not constitute a threat to the canons of the dominant culture. In fact, the curricula through which many of them came at institutions like the Seven Sister colleges reassured him they would become loyal soldiers in his army of new professionals who were unlikely to question decisions of literary and scholarly experts. Like mid-nineteenth-century Baptist women, turn-of-the-century female

---

8. The only exception to this practice Dewey allowed was in the area of children's literature where, he believed, cultured and refined women had a "natural" ability to distinguish between "good" and "bad" reading.

library professionals could be counted on to deliver uplifting messages others had already prescribed as valuable for the masses.

And the structure of the profession—as Dewey designed it—had a profound impact on the history of librarianship in the last one hundred years. For the most part, it is the structure of the profession and not primarily its gender composition that accounts for librarianship's peripheral position in the panoply of professions. Throughout the twentieth century, western capitalist democracies have allocated the power to determine value in information products to their producers and to their consumers. As long this situation persists (and I am not here suggesting it *ought* to change), librarianship will likely remain a marginal profession, no matter its gender composition, no matter its name in this new "information age." Although Dewey deserves much credit for facilitating the entry of thousands of women into the profession, its feminization is much more an effect than a cause of librarianship's low status.[9]

Dewey also profoundly influenced the history of education in New York and by the example he set there the history of higher education throughout the country. In the area of higher education, between 1889 and 1899 he strengthened the system and security of higher education examinations, significantly pared bogus diploma mills, upgraded the quality of professional and secondary education by insisting that standards be met before distributing state funds, and created a network of officials among New York's established schools through which they exercised significant influence over 1890s legislation that affected the state's educational interests. More important, however, he raised the profile and increased the powers of the Regents so that when political circumstances forced unification of New York's dual system of education in 1904, Regents were strong enough to claim a large share of the outcome. At the same time, however, he strengthened a group of institutions dedicated to homogenizing curricula and culture to reflect a WASP image of the world, and weakened and/or eliminated a group of institutions more culturally diverse in curriculum and student populations. Dewey's efforts as Regents' Secretary in the last decade of the nineteenth

---

9. For opposite points of view, see Garrison, *Apostles of Culture*, pp. 186–95; and Roma Harris, *Librarianship: The Erosion of a Woman's Profession* (Norwood, N.J., 1992).

century helped refine a culturally uniform system more inclined to resist than embrace change.

In the area of university extension and adult education Dewey was way ahead of his time. Although his efforts to establish a university extension suffered in New York for lack of funding, he had anticipated by three decades ALA efforts to link adult education to public library services and by four decades the adult education movement that eventually took root in New York in the 1930s. In fact, Dewey's 1890s agenda for university extension looks very much like the blueprints for adult education and libraries outlined in such standard texts as Alvin Johnson's *The Public Library: A People's University* (1938) and Helen Lyman Smith's *Adult Education Activities in Public Libraries* (1954).[10]

Dewey's endeavors at the Lake Placid Club also deeply influenced the twentieth-century history of New York's Adirondack Mountain region, and especially the town of Lake Placid. Although community residents rarely stepped on Club grounds except as service employees or to deliver merchandise, revenue generated by guests and members fed the local economy for decades. The Club developed a reputation for leadership and for cultivating the finest in American family traditions, and for several decades in the early twentieth century helped set a national standard for style and fashion. In addition, publicity generated by Club activities in the 1920s brought the Lake Placid community much national and international attention. Without the Club and the reputation for winter sports it developed between 1905 and 1930, it is unlikely the 1932 Winter Olympics would have located in Lake Placid; and without the 1932 Winter Olympics as a precedent, it is unlikely they would have returned in 1980. Dewey deserves some credit for both.

At the same time, however, he also deserves blame for giving license to exclusionary practices that fed a well-deserved

---

10. Alvin Johnson, *The Public Library: A People's University* (N.Y., 1938); Helen Lyman Smith, *Adult Education Activities in Public Libraries* (Chicago, 1954). See also C. Harley Grattan, *In Quest of Knowledge: A Historical Perspective on Adult Education* (N.Y., 1955), Chap. 18. Dewey's 1890s initiatives have also been overlooked by historians of continuing and adult education in American library history. See, for example, Margaret E. Monroe, *Library Adult Education: The Biography of an Idea* (N.Y., 1963); and Robert Ellis Lee, *Continuing Education for Adults through the American Public Library* (Chicago, 1966).

reputation in the Adirondacks for racism and anti-Semitism that in recent decades the region has been trying to live down. Dewey intended the Lake Placid Club to be a nest of WASP middle- and upper-class culture to which the nation's underpaid social service educators could repair for rest and healthy outdoor recreation. Ultimately, however, the Club failed because WASP middle-class America grew to dislike the image of itself reflected in the mirror of Club prejudices.

None of Dewey's reforms threatened the dominant political, social, or cultural hegemony; all served capitalism's need for a literate but passive workforce; all were designed, to use the words of historian Thomas Schlereth, to assist WASP efforts "to hold power without property and to maintain hegemony with education and expertise."[11] All his life Dewey espoused "Anglo-Saxonism," a doctrine that touted the unique virtues, mission and destiny of the Anglo-Saxon "race." He assimilated it at Adams Center and Amherst, and stitched it into the fabric of the institutions he crafted. Its threads can be traced through the history of the DDC, American public library collections, formal library education, the *ALA Catalog* (and its offspring and successors), the structure and curricula of education in the State of New York, and most obviously in the Lake Placid Club. So convinced was he of the rightness of "Anglo-Saxonism" that he based his definition of "objectivity" on it. "Objectivity" would emerge from the intellectual pursuits of other middle-class professionals who were in charge of other middle-class institutions.

Dewey's education reforms and institutions (especially his library institutions) were designed to build upon "truths" determined by others, and then make them easily available to a world in need of exposure to their benefits. Like many other pioneers of emerging professions, Dewey had a deep faith in communities of the competent who founded disciplines in the late nineteenth century.[12] And for all the educational reforms he espoused, his

---

11. See Thomas J. Schlereth, *Victorian America: Transformations in Everyday Life, 1876–1915* (N.Y., 1989), p. xv.

12. For good discussions of the 19th-century evolution of communities of the competent and the concept of objectivity as defined by a WASP culture, see Thomas L. Haskell, *The Emergence of Professional Social Science: The American Social Science Association and the Nineteenth Century Crisis of Authority* (Urbana, 1977); Mary O. Furner, *Advocacy and Objectivity: A Crisis in the Professionalization of American Social Science,*

immediate response was always framed in institutional terms. Identify a problem, then create an institution to address and resolve it. The response was certainly not unique to Dewey, but the institutions he created and fostered and the legacy he gave them were. He clearly saw connections between all his reform efforts; for Dewey they formed a coherent whole. All were to exercise a socially benevolent trust; all were to be administered by a group of middle-class professionals trained to follow the cues of communities of the competent. All formed a tightly knit unicultural fabric that resisted the introduction of threads spun by other cultures.

In each of the areas that drew his irrepressible reform interests, Melvil Dewey left a legacy as both hero and villain. Superimposed upon this legacy was Dewey's fascinating and formidable personality. He was driven, tense, often arrogant. He had an obsessive need to control, a preoccupation with time, and an exaggerated moralism. He demanded conformity to the order and rules he defined, overemphasized details, and self-righteously denied his own racism and class prejudices. Dewey's psyche reflects a combination of curious contradictions that mirror the characteristics historians Charles Cole and Hugh Davis found in mid-nineteenth-century northern evangelical revivalists. Like evangelistic ministers Jacob Knapp, Lyman Beecher, Charles Grandison Finney, and Joshua Leavitt, Dewey possessed a huge ego he hid from himself by wrapping it in an intense devotion to the causes he preselected and then claiming to be a mere voice for these greater causes. Like most of them, he had a tendency to greatly exaggerate his point, was strongly emotional, highly energetic, noticeably eccentric, and, once he had made up his mind, decidedly set in his own ways. Like most of them he seemed to cherish a fight involving the defense of his convictions. Like most of them he cared little for the small amenities of life, loved to work, and had trouble handling money. Like most of them, he also felt entitled because of his self-assumed purity to a special relationship with women in which he presupposed a right to take liberties denied "lesser" men. And like most of them, he laced his rhetoric with words such as "causes," "sacrifice," and "faith," all of which he regularly and frequently attached to his reform

---

1865–1905 (Lexington, 1975); and Dorothy Ross, *The Origins of American Social Science* (Cambridge, Mass., 1991), especially Chaps. 2–4.

interests throughout his life, all of which had been prominent in the lexicon of the nineteenth-century Burned-Over-District evangelical revivalist. "I am always profoundly grateful about these library matters," Dewey wrote James Wyer in 1916, "that the Lord let me be that particular Moses that led that particular children of Israel into the promist land."[13]

To accomplish his goals, Dewey was regularly manipulative and duplicitous, repeatedly exceeded his authority, and often even lied to gain his ends. Always he pushed his broader agenda on the institutions that employed him, despite sometimes active, often public, resistance. His goals may have been well-intentioned, but means to those goals frequently alienated others and showed Dewey's worst side. And always, Dewey thought, it was "their" fault; usually he deemed opposition to his "causes" a result of some sinister conspiracy. Dewey's irrepressibility only augmented his tendency to alienate most of his peers. Several intensely loyal subordinates, however, stayed with him throughout their lives, and to amplify the impact of his goals, Dewey harnessed their sometimes blind willingness to follow his dictates. "It is not enough for you to do your duty," Asa Gallup once told him, "but you must make others, as far as possible, see your duty in the same light."[14] Over time, Dewey got much credit for their work. Often his image was embellished and augmented at the expense of their efforts. May Seymour, Walter Stanley Biscoe, Florence Woodworth, Katharine Sharp, Dorkas Fellows, and of course Annie and Emily Dewey—all fed the Dewey aura, all contributed to what has become his legacy, for good and ill.

That there is so much to dislike about Melvil Dewey's character may explain why his legacy has been under-studied in recent decades. Because he crafted into the normal practices of institutions he created the striking character flaws and social prejudices he himself embodied, he reinforced and accelerated the momentum of a relatively unicultural and exclusionary perspective for which dominant groups have justifiably been criticized in recent years. To cite but one example, by late-twentieth-century

---

13. Dewey to Wyer, 12/18/16, Box 23, Dewey Mss. Dee Garrison does a good job of describing Dewey's personality traits in her *Apostles of Culture*, pp. 105–8. Whereas I use the 19th century evangelical revivalist to model Dewey's behavioral characteristics, she uses the "obsessive-compulsive personality" model articulated by modern-day psychologists.

14. Gallup to Dewey, 3/4/98, Box 31, Dewey Mss.

standards Dewey was, like most of his Anglo-Saxon contemporaries, a racist and an anti-Semite. Unlike most of them, however, he was not unwilling to parade his bigotry in public and "sacrifice" himself for the greater good of WASP culture. To cite another example, by late-twentieth-century standards Dewey was, like most of his male middle-class professional contemporaries, also a sexist. Unlike most of them, however, he pushed his harassing behavior with women to such lengths and with such frequency in his polite and genteel society that he was banished from the very profession he helped structure, and then blamed the victims of his behavior for not understanding the purity of his motives.

The role model Dewey projected between 1876 and 1931 is hardly one to be emulated in the late twentieth century, and certainly not one librarians, educators, and members of upstate New York and Florida Highlands communities eager to recount their heritage wish to embrace. Yet for good and ill one has to conclude that Melvil Dewey profoundly influenced the heritage of each group. For good and ill one also has to conclude his powerful influence has extended down to the present in the practices of the institutions he crafted and created. And finally, for good and ill one has to conclude that as an irrepressible reformer Melvil Dewey indelibly stamped his legacy on American history by sheer force of character, flawed though that character was.

Abbreviations

Journals, Documents, and Manuscript Collections Cited in the Footnotes

In order to condense the footnotes as much as possible, citations of these sources have been extensively abbreviated. "Dewey to Godfrey Dewey, 11/25/31, Box 23, Dewey Mss" should be read as "Letter, Melvil Dewey to Godfrey Dewey, November 25, 1931, Box 23, Melvil Dewey Papers, Rare Books and Manuscripts Reading Room, Butler Library, Columbia University, New York, New York." The last two digits in the date sequence refer to years between 1851 and 1932. For dates beyond 1932, the full year is given. Hyphens inserted between slashes in the date sequence indicate that the exact month, day, or year was not given on the original document. Because all of Dewey's diaries are located in Box 35A of the Dewey Papers, the box number is not cited in the footnotes.

ACA	Amherst College Archives Amherst College, Amherst, Massachusetts
Adams Mss	Herbert Baxter Adams Papers, Special Collections, Milton S. Eisenhower Library, The Johns Hopkins University, Baltimore, Maryland
ALA Archives	American Library Association Archives, University of Illinois Library, Archives, Urbana, Illinois
ALJ	*American Library Journal*

Bancroft Mss	Frederick Bancroft Papers, Rare Books and Manuscripts Reading Room, Columbia University, New York, New York
Barnard Mss	Frederick Augustus Porter Barnard Papers, Rare Books and Manuscripts Reading Room, Columbia University, New York, New York
Billings Mss	John Shaw Billings Papers, Special Collections, New York Public Library, New York, New York
Blatchford Mss	Eliphalet W. Blatchford Papers, Archives, Newberry Library, Chicago, Illinois
Bowker Mss	R. R. Bowker Papers, Special Collections, New York Public Library, New York, New York
BR Minutes	University of the State of New York. *Official Minutes of the Regents of the University during the Secretaryship of Melvil Dewey, 1889–1899.* (Albany: University of the State of New York, 1900).
Brett Mss	William Howard Brett Papers, Archives, Cleveland Public Library, Cleveland, Ohio
BSRA	*Bulletin of the Spelling Reform Association*
Burgess Mss	John W. Burgess Papers, Rare Books and Manuscripts Reading Room, Columbia University, New York, New York
Butler Mss	Nicholas Murray Butler Papers, Rare Books and Manuscripts Reading Room, Columbia University, New York, New York
Carnegie Mss	Andrew Carnegie Papers, Manuscripts Reading Room, Library of Congress, Washington, D.C.
Carr Mss	Henry J. Carr Papers, American Library Association Archives, University of Illinois Library, Archives, Urbana, Illinois

CCTM	Columbia College Trustees Minutes, Secretary's Office, Low Library, Columbia University, New York, New York
Cheney Mss	John Vance Cheney Papers, Manuscripts Reading Room, Library of Congress, Washington, D.C.
CLC	Carnegie Library Correspondence, Rare Books and Manuscripts Reading Room, Columbia University, New York, New York
Colburn Interview	Interview with Deo Buffon Colburn, 5/13/1985, Lake Placid, New York
Cole Mss, AAS	George Watson Cole Papers, American Antiquarian Society, Worcester, Massachusetts
Cole Mss, ALA	George Watson Cole Papers, American Library Association Archives, University of Illinois Library, Archives, Urbana, Illinois
Columbiana	Columbiana, Rare Books and Manuscripts Reading Room, Columbia University, New York, New York
Dana Mss	John Cotton Dana Papers, City Library Association of Springfield, Springfield, Massachusetts
Davis Mss	Raymond C. Davis Papers, Bentley Historical Library, University of Michigan, Ann Arbor, Michigan
Day Mss	James R. Day Papers, Syracuse University Archives, George Arents Research Library, Syracuse University, Syracuse, New York
Dewey Mss	Melvil Dewey Papers, Rare Books and Manuscripts Reading Room, Columbia University, New York, New York
Draper Mss	Andrew Sloan Draper Papers, Archives, University of Illinois Library, Urbana, Illinois

Dun Mss	R. G. Dun and Co. Collection, Special Collections Department, Baker Library, Graduate School of Business Adminstration, Soldiers Field, Harvard University, Boston, Massachusetts
Eagle	*Brooklyn Eagle*
Eggleston Mss	Edward Eggleston Papers, Department of Manuscripts and Archives, John M. Olin Library, Cornell University, Ithaca, New York
Fellows Mss	Dorkas Fellows Papers, Forest Press Archives, Forest Press, Albany, New York
Fish Mss	Hamilton Fish Papers, Rare Books and Manuscripts Reading Room, Columbia University, New York, New York
FPA	Forest Press Archives, Forest Press, Albany, New York
Gilman Mss	Daniel Coit Gilman Papers, Special Collections, Milton S. Eisenhower Library, The Johns Hopkins University, Baltimore, Maryland
Godfrey Dewey Mss	Godfrey Dewey Papers, Rare Books and Manuscripts Reading Room, Columbia University, New York, New York
Hall Mss	James Hall Papers, Manuscripts and Special Collections, New York State Library, Cultural Education Center, Empire State Plaza, Albany, New York
Hayes Mss	Rutherford P. Hayes Papers, Rutherford B. Hayes Library, Fremont, Ohio
Holls Mss	Frederick W. Holls Papers, Rare Books and Manuscripts Reading Room, Columbia University, New York, New York
Jay Family Mss	Jay Family Papers, Rare Books and Manuscripts Reading Room, Columbia University, New York, New York

Johnston Mss	W. Dawson Johnston Papers, Manuscripts Reading Room, Library of Congress, Washington, D.C.
Jones Mss	Ada Alice Jones Papers, Special Collections, New York Public Library, New York, New York
Koopman Mss	H. L. Koopman Papers, Special Collections, John Hay Library, Brown University, Providence, Rhode Island
Lane Mss	William Coolidge Lane Papers, Harvard University Archives, Cambridge, Massachusetts
LC Archives	Library of Congress Archives, Central Services Division, Library of Congress, Washington, D.C.
LCE-NA	Letters Sent by the Commissioner of Education, 1870–1909. Records of the Bureau of Education. Department of Interior. Microcopy No. 635. National Archives, Washington, D.C.
Librarians' File	Newark Librarians -Letters (1888–1902), NPL New Jersey Room, Newark Public Library, Newark, New Jersey
Librarian's Office	Librarian's Office Files, Correspondence, Files 1900–1930, Rare Books and Manuscripts Reading Room, Columbia University, New York, New York
LJ	*Library Journal*
LN	*Library Notes*
Low Mss	Seth Low Papers, Rare Books and Manuscripts Reading Room, Columbia University, New York, New York
LPC *Handbook* [*year*]	Lake Placid Club *Handbook*
LPC News	*Lake Placid Club News*

LPC Notes	*Lake Placid Club Notes*
LPEF Mss	Lake Placid Education Foundation Records, Lake Placid, New York
LQ	*Library Quarterly*
MA	*Metric Advocate*
MB	*Metric Bulletin*
McKelway Mss	St. Clair McKelway Papers, Rare Books and Manuscripts Room, New York Public Library, New York, New York
Marshall Mss	Louis N. Marshall Papers, American Jewish Archives, Hebrew Union College, Cincinnati, Ohio
Misc. Docs., NYSL	Miscellaneous Documents, Folder 11343, Manuscripts and Special Collections, Cultural Education Center, New York State Library, Empire State Plaza, Albany, New York
NYSL *AR, [year]*	New York State. State Library, Albany. . . . *Annual Report* (Albany: University of the State of New York, 1887–1906)
NYSLS *AR, [year]*	New York State. State Library School, Albany. . . . *Annual Report* (Albany: University of the State of New York, 1899–1907)
NYSLSAA	New York State Library School Alumni Association Scrapbook, School of Library Service Library, Butler Library, Columbia University, New York, New York
NYT	*New York Times*
NYTr	*New York Tribune*
PL	*Public Libraries*
Plimpton Mss	George A. Plimpton Papers, Rare Books and Manuscripts Reading Room, Columbia University, New York, New York

Poole Mss	William Frederick Poole Papers, Archives, Newberry Library, Chicago, Illinois
Proceedings [year]	Proceedings of the annual American Library Association conferences, 1876–1907, bound into volumes of *Library Journal*
Proceedings, AMS [year]	*Proceedings of the American Metrological Society*
Putnam Mss	Herbert Putnam Papers, Library of Congress Archives, Central Services Division, Library of Congress, Washington, D.C.
PW	*Publishers Weekly*
Regents AR, [year]	New York [State] University. *Annual Report of the Regents* (Albany: University of the State of New York, 1888–1907)
Reid Mss	Whitelaw Reid Papers, Manuscripts Reading Room, Library of Congress, Washington, D.C.
RG/L-8, OSA	Record Group L-8, Oregon State Archives, Salem, Oregon
Roden Mss	Carl S. Roden Papers, Archives, Newberry Library, Chicago, Illinois
Roosevelt Mss	Theodore Roosevelt Papers, Manuscripts Reading Room, Library of Congress, Washington, D.C.
Schurman Mss	Jacob Gould Schurman Papers, Department of Manuscripts and University Archives, James M. Olin Library, Cornell University, Ithaca, New York
Seligman Mss	Edwin R. A. Seligman Papers, Rare Books and Manuscripts Reading Room, Columbia University, New York, New York
SPL Archives	Springfield (Massachusetts) Public Library Archives, Director's Office, City Library Association of Springfield, Springfield, Massachusetts

Thwaites Mss	Reuben Gold Thwaites Papers, Manuscripts Division, State Historical Society of Wisconsin, Madison, Wisconsin
TLCM	Trustees Library Committee Minutes, Columbiana, Rare Books and Manuscripts Reading Room, Columbia University, New York, New York
Utley Mss	Henry M. Utley Papers, Burton Historical Collection, Detroit Public Library, Detroit, Michigan
Walter Mss	Frank K. Walter Papers, University Archives, James M. Olin Library, Cornell University, Ithaca, New York
Wellman Mss	Hiller C. Wellman Papers, Archives, City Library Association of Springfield, Springfield, Massachusetts
White Mss	Andrew Dickson White Papers, Department of Manuscripts and University Archives, James M. Olin Library, Cornell University, Ithaca, New York
Winsor Letters, LJ/RC	Justin Winsor Letters, bound into 1881 volume of *Library Journal*, Rosary College Library, River Forest, Illinois
Winsor Mss	Justin Winsor Papers, Harvard University Archives, Harvard University, Cambridge, Massachusetts
Wyer Mss	James I. Wyer Autograph Collection, American Library Association Archives, University of Illinois Archives, Urbana, Illinois

Index

The following abbreviations are used in the index.

ALA American Library Association
AMB American Metric Bureau
AMS American Metrological Society
DPI Department of Public Instruction
LPC Lake Placid Club
MD Melvil Dewey
RWEC Readers and Writers Economy Company
SRA Spelling Reform Association
USNY University of the State of New York

State names are abbreviated according to United States Postal Service standards; e.g., MA for Massachusetts.

Wayne A. Wiegand, a distinguished historian and library educator, is professor at the University of Wisconsin–Madison School of Library and Information Studies and codirector of the Center for the History of Print Culture in Modern America. He holds a Ph.D. in history in addition to master's degrees in history and librarianship. His publications include *Politics of an Emerging Profession: The American Library Association, 1876–1917*, four other histories, more than fifty scholarly articles, and such edited works as *The Encyclopedia of Library History*.

Among numerous honors he has received are two annual G. K. Hall Awards for Library Literature, the American Library Association's Herbert Putnam and Justin Winsor Awards, and three Research Paper Awards from the Association of Library and Information Science Education. He has held leadership positions in ALA library history and library research organizations and serves on the Advisory Board of the Program in the History of the Book in American Culture at the American Antiquarian Society.

Prior to publication of *Irrepressible Reformer*, researched over a period of fifteen years, numerous shorter publications have established Dr. Wiegand as the world's foremost biographer of Melvil Dewey and his influence on library service, education, and the organization of knowledge.